알고 보면 정답이 보이는

TOEFL 기출필수 배경지식 120

TOEFL 배경지식 120

초판 1쇄 인쇄 2014년 10월 27일
초판 1쇄 발행 2014년 10월 31일
초판 20쇄 발행 2025년 9월 5일

지 은 이	최은실, 유희정
펴 낸 이	박서진
펴 낸 곳	**PAGODA Books** 파고다북스
출판등록	2005년 5월 27일 제 300-2005-90호
주 소	06614 서울특별시 서초구 강남대로 419, 19층(서초동, 파고다타워)
전 화	(02) 6940-4070
팩 스	(02) 536-0660
홈페이지	www.pagodabook.com

저작권자 | ⓒ 2014 최은실, 유희정

이 책의 저작권은 저자에게 있습니다. 서면에 의한 저작권자의 허락 없이
내용의 일부 혹은 전부를 인용 및 복제하거나 발췌하는 것을 금합니다.

Copyright ⓒ 2014 by Eun Sil Choi, Heejung Jennifer You

All rights reserved. No part of this publication may be reproduced, stored
in a retrieval system, or transmitted, in any form, or by any means, electronic,
mechanical, photocopying, recording or otherwise, without the prior written
permission of the copyright holders and the publisher.

ISBN 978-89-6281-589-4 (13740)

파고다북스	www.pagodabook.com
파고다 어학원	www.pagoda21.com
파고다 인강	www.pagodastar.com
테스트 클리닉	www.testclinic.com

| 낙장 및 파본은 구매처에서 교환해 드립니다.

Preface

최은실

강의 시간 외에 토플 수험생들과 지면으로 만나 뵙게 되어 매우 기쁘고 설렌다. 토플 준비로 분주한 여러분들을 위해 본 교재는 토플 리딩의 최근 출제된 주제들을 완벽하게 분석하였다. 이 교재가 수험생들이 목표 점수를 달성하는데 도움이 되는 디딤돌이 되길 바란다.

강의를 하면서 많은 수험생들이 Writing, Speaking, Listening에 비해 Reading을 상대적으로 쉽고 편하게 생각하다 낭패를 보는 경우를 자주 보게 된다. 많은 수험생들이 독해 위주로 영어 교육을 받아왔기 때문에 타 과목에 비해 자신감을 가지고 가벼운 마음으로 Reading 공부를 시작했다가 생소한 주제의 지문과 어휘에 당황하고 예상치 못한 낮은 점수를 받아 뒤늦은 후회를 하는 경우를 많이 보아왔다.

저자는 여러분의 Reading의 고충과 어려움들을 해소하고 Reading 점수를 향상하는데 실질적인 도움이 되고자 본 교재를 저술하였다. 최근 실전 시험에 출제되었던 다양한 분야의 내용들을 철저히 분석하였고, 이를 토대로 주제별로 한글 배경 지식과 영어 지문을 함께 구성하여 학습 효과를 극대화 하도록 하였다. 이 책을 통해 여러분은 Reading부분에 필수인 영문 독해 능력 향상과 최근 출제되는 주제들에 관한 배경 지식의 확장이라는 일석이조를 경험하게 될 것이다. 또한 본 교재에 수록된 Reading 문제 유형 연습과 분야별 필수 어휘는 실제 시험에 출제되는 지문에 완벽하게 준비할 수 있도록 구성하였다.

모든 주제에 전문가가 될 필요는 없다. 특히 시험 준비 기간이 짧은 수험생들에게는 시간은 생명이다. 불필요하게 수많은 주제를 모두 공부하면서 아까운 시간을 낭비말자. 현명하게 이 교재를 통해 엄선된 핵심 주제들만 신속하게 마스터하여 목표 점수로 가는 지름길을 선택하기 바란다. 이 교재가 그 지름길로 안내하는 길잡이 역할을 할 것이다. 이 교재를 통해 티플 공부가 고통이 아닌 즐거움이 되길 기대한다. Reading 고득점, 그날을 위해 모든 토플 수험생들을 응원한다.

끝으로 파고다 출판사와 나의 사랑하는 가족, 친구들과 믿음의 동역자들께 그리고 주님께 깊은 감사의 말씀을 드린다.

최은실

유희정

해를 거듭할수록 지속적으로 상승하는 토플 리스닝의 난이도는 토플을 시작하는 학생들의 사기를 단번에 꺾어 놓으며 고득점으로 가는 길목을 가로막는 역할을 톡톡히 하고 있다. 덕분에 많은 학생들은 스피킹, 라이팅에도 등장하는 예상치도 못한 리스닝 때문에 토플 학습에 있어 고전을 면치 못하고 있다. 각 학문 분야에서 입문수준을 뛰어넘어 여지는 전공과목 수준의 내용이 등장하는 리스닝 섹션을 위해서 모든 분야에 대한 해박한 지식이 아니더라도 빈출 주제에 대한 배경지식을 학습하는 것은 어려운 분야별 어휘를 암기하는 것 보다 훨씬 더 효과적이며 필수적인 학습방법이라 할 수 있다. 그럼에도 불구하고 최신 토플경향에 대한 분석을 바탕으로 시험에 빈출되는 배경지식만을 깊이 있게 다루는 교재를 찾아보기가 힘들어 많은 학생들에게 관련 서적을 추천해줄 수가 없었다. 이러한 문제점을 보완하고자 여러 분들의 도움 및 연구 끝에 실제 후기를 철저히 분석하여 최신경향을 가장 잘 반영한 배경지식 전문 교재를 집필하게 되었으며 따라서 이 교재는 많은 학습자들의 필수 배경지식에 대한 목마름을 해소해 줄 수 있는 가장 심층적이며 체계적인 교재가 될 것이다.

본 교재는 토플 초보자부터 고득점자까지 모든 학습자들에게 필요한 내용으로 구성되었으며 토플뿐만이 아니라 SAT, AP, IELTS 등의 각종 어학시험 및 추후 유학생활에도 도움이 되는 핵심 배경지식을 제공하는 백과사전과 같은 교재이다. 따라서 본 교재에서 강조된 내용을 잘 숙지하여 철저히 준비된 자세와 자신감으로 토플 시험에 임하도록 하자.

이 책을 집필하기까지 도와주신 많은 분들 중에서도 특히 처음부터 끝까지 신뢰해 주시고 지원을 아끼지 않아주신 영원한 멘토 박경실 회장님, 기획부터 제작까지 총괄해주신 파고다 출판사의 박미경 부장님, 김수경 팀장님, 거친 원석을 보석으로 닦아주신 궁정문 주임님께 진심으로 감사의 말씀을 전하며 또한 이 모든 것을 가능케 해준 사랑하는 가족들과 친구들에게 고맙다는 말을 전하고 싶다.

전국의 모든 토플러 힘내자 파이팅!

유희정

:구성 및 특징:

About the Book

본서

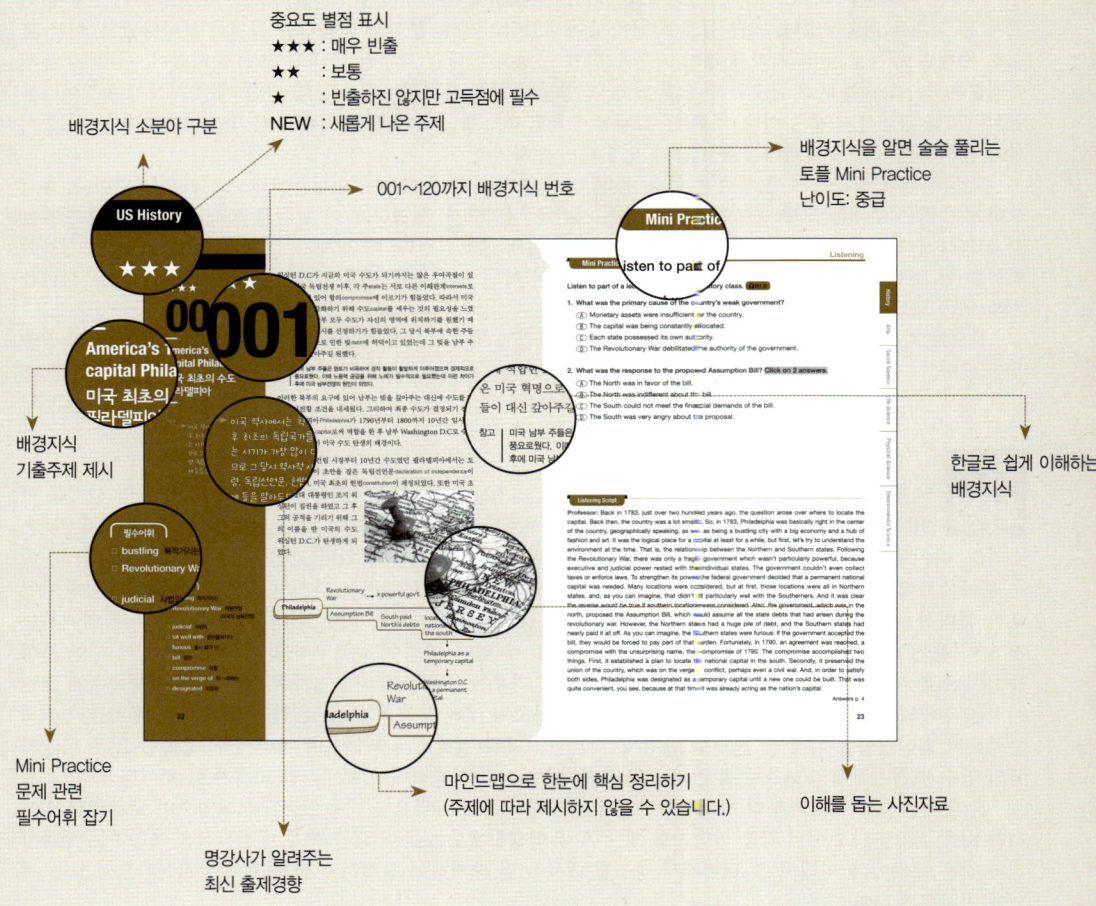

- 배경지식 소분야 구분
- 중요도 별점 표시
  - ★★★ : 매우 빈출
  - ★★ : 보통
  - ★ : 빈출하진 않지만 고득점에 필수
  - NEW : 새롭게 나온 주제
- 001~120까지 배경지식 번호
- 배경지식을 알면 술술 풀리는 토플 Mini Practice 난이도: 중급
- 배경지식 기출주제 제시
- Mini Practice 문제 관련 필수어휘 잡기
- 명강사가 알려주는 최신 출제경향
- 마인드맵으로 한눈에 핵심 정리하기 (주제에 따라 제시하지 않을 수 있습니다.)
- 한글로 쉽게 이해하는 배경지식
- 이해를 돕는 사진자료

TOEFL Vocabulary

주제별 필수어휘 25개 정리

영단어, 발음기호, 품사, 한글 뜻, 동의어/반의어 수록

정답 및 해석

온라인 무료 다운로드
www.pagodabook.com

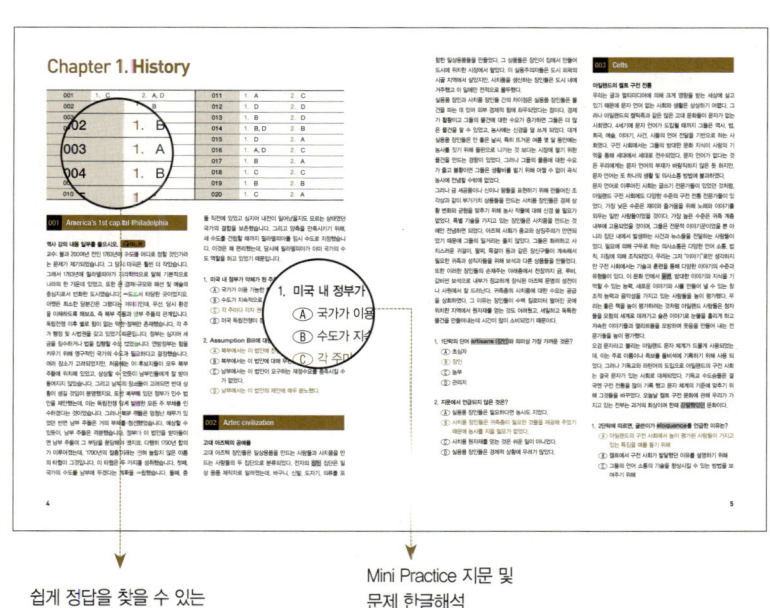

쉽게 정답을 찾을 수 있는
배경지식별 정답 제시

Mini Practice 지문 및
문제 한글해석

Contents

Chapter 1
History 20

001 America's 1st capital Philadelphia
002 Aztec civilization
003 Celts
004 Early history in US
005 Guild
006 Hellenism
007 History of road paving
008 Incan civilization - Khipu
009 Indus civilization
010 Japan
011 Life of peasants in medieval Europe
012 Mayan civilization
013 Ottoman Empire
014 Post WWII housing development
015 Roman aqueducts
016 The Columbian exchange
017 The discovery of Mayan ruins
018 The statue of George Washington
019 Underwater archaeology
020 Works Progress Administration

미국의 역사

Chapter 2
Arts 64

021 Archimedes palimpsest
022 Baroque art
023 Camera obscura
024 Commedia Dell'arte
025 Dadaism
026 Definition of art
027 Design of public spaces in 19C
028 Dynamic range
029 Egypt art
030 Etching
031 Film
032 Gertrude Stein
033 Houses in Renaissance era
034 Linear and aerial perspective
035 Navajo
036 Quilt
037 Roman art
038 Synthesizer
039 The root of rap
040 Travel lecture

서양 미술 사조
서양 문예 사조

Chapter 3
Social Science 110

041	Agriculture
042	Babies' behaviors
043	Competitors in a business sector
044	Digital economy
045	Emotional intelligence
046	Green marketing
047	Hippocampus and spatial memory
048	Industrial revolution
049	Industrialization in US
050	Internet Addiction Disorder
051	Placebo effect
052	Printing
053	Psychology
054	S curve in business
055	Scientific management
056	Thomas Kuhn
057	Transportation revolution in US
058	Urban planning
059	USA Today
060	Variables in decision making

Chapter 4
Life Science 152

061	Altruistic animals
062	Bird
063	Deterioration of coral reefs
064	Flying animals
065	Herbivores
066	Homing instinct
067	Marine trophic relationships
068	Meerkat
069	Natural selection
070	Plant
071	Predator
072	Rattlebox moth
073	Red chlorophyll in leaves
074	Seagrass
075	Seeds and nuts
076	Snake
077	Super-hydrophobic insects
078	The effect of diet on immune system
079	The effect of music on brain organs
080	Thermoregulation

: 목차 :

Chapter 5
Physical Science 194

081	Biofuel
082	Cell discovery
083	Celestial bodies
084	Composting
085	Cosmic rays
086	Distance from a star
087	Erosion
088	Fuel
089	Helium-3
090	Hooker Telescope
091	Jupiter
092	Mars
093	Mercury
094	Periodic table
095	Planets
096	Properties of water
097	Stars
098	The orbits of comets
099	Origins of life
100	Trace metals

Chapter 6
Environmental Science 236

101	Allopatric speciation in Amazon
102	Channeled scabland
103	Cold environment
104	Competitive Exclusion Principle
105	Environmental problems
106	Extinction
107	Fossilization
108	Geothermal energy
109	Global warming and ocean acidification
110	Groundwater
111	Little ice age
112	Magma
113	Northern Lights
114	Ocean energy
115	Predicting volcanoes
116	Seismic Waves & the interior of the Earth
117	Soil
118	Stalagmite
119	Uranium-Lead Dating
120	Wildfire

TOEFL Vocabulary 278

History	280
Arts	286
Social Science	294
Life Science	301
Physical Science	309
Environmental Science	315

전체정답　　　　　　　　326

정답 및 해석 무료 온라인 다운로드
www.pagodabook.com

: iBT TOEFL® 개요 :

About iBT TOEFL®

1. iBT TOEFL® 이란?

TOEFL®은 영어 사용 국가로 유학을 가고자 하는 외국인들의 영어 능력을 평가하기 위해 개발된 시험이다. TOEFL® 시험 출제 기관인 ETS는 이러한 TOEFL® 본연의 목적에 맞게 문제의 변별력을 더욱 높이고자 PBT(Paper-Based Test), CBT(Computer-Based Test)에 이어 차세대 시험인 인터넷 기반의 iBT(Internet-Based Test)를 2005년 9월부터 시행하게 되었다. ETS에서 연간 30~40회 정도로 지정한 날짜에 등록함으로써 치르게 되는 이 시험은 Reading, Listening, Speaking, Writing 총 4개 영역으로 구성되며 총 시험 시간은 4시간이다. 각 영역별 점수는 30점으로 총점 120점을 만점으로 하며 성적은 시험 시행 약 15일 후에 온라인에서 확인할 수 있다.

2. iBT TOEFL®의 특징

1 영어 사용 국가로의 유학 시 필요한 언어 능력을 평가한다.
각 시험 영역은 실제 학업이나 캠퍼스 생활에 반드시 필요한 언어 능력을 측정한다. 평가되는 언어 능력에는 자신의 의견 및 선호도 전달하기, 강의 요약하기, 에세이 작성하기, 학술적인 주제의 글을 읽고 내용 이해하기 등이 포함되며, 각 영역에 걸쳐 고르게 평가된다.

2 Reading, Listening, Speaking, Writing 전 영역의 통합적인 영어 능력(Integrated Skill)을 평가한다.
시험이 4개 영역으로 분류되어 있기는 하지만 Speaking과 Writing 영역에서는 Listening + Speaking, Reading + Listening + Speaking, Reading + Listening + Writing과 같은 형태로 학습자가 둘 또는 세 개의 언어 영역을 통합해서 사용할 수 있는지를 평가한다.

3 Reading 지문 및 Listening 스크립트가 길다.
Reading 지문은 700단어 내외로 A4용지 약 1.5장 분량이며, Listening은 3~4분 가량의 대화와 6~8분 가량의 강의로 구성된다.

4 전 영역에서 노트 필기(Note-Taking)를 할 수 있다.
긴 지문을 읽거나 강의를 들으면서 핵심 사항을 간략하게 적어두었다가 문제를 풀 때 참고할 수 있다. 노트 필기한 종이는 시험 후 수거 및 폐기된다.

5 Linear 방식의 평가
응시자가 시험을 보는 과정에서 실력에 따라 문제의 난이도가 조정되어 출제되는 CAT(Computer Adaptive Test)방식이 아니라, 정해진 문제가 모든 응시자에게 동일하게 제시되는 Linear 방식으로 평가된다.

6 시험 응시일이 제한된다.
시험은 주로 토요일과 일요일에만 시행되며, 시험에 재응시할 경우, 시험 응시일로부터 12일 이내에는 재응시 할 수 없다.

7 Performance Feedback이 주어진다.
온라인 및 우편으로 발송된 성적표에는 수치화된 점수뿐 아니라 각 section별로 수험자의 과제 수행 정도를 나타내는 표도 제공된다.

3. iBT TOEFL®의 구성

시험 영역	Reading, Listening, Speaking, Writing
시험 시간	4시간
시험 횟수	연 30~40회 (날짜는 ETS에서 지정)
총점	0~120점
영역별 점수	각 영역별 30점
성적 확인	응시일로부터 15일 후 온라인에서 성적 확인 가능

Test Section	문제구성	시간
Reading	• 독해지문 3~4개, 총 36~56개 문제가 출제된다. • 각 지문 길이 700단어 내외, 지문당 12~14개 문항 • 지문 3개가 출제될 경우 60분, 4개가 출제될 경우 80분이 주어진다.	60~80분

Listening	• 2개 또는 3개의 Set이 출제된다.
	  Set : 대화(Conversation) 1개 – 5문항
	       강의(Lecture) 2개 – 각 6문항씩 총 12문항
	• 2개 Set만 출제될 경우 60분, 3개 Set가 출제될 경우 90분이 주어진다.
		60~90분

Break		10분
Speaking	• 6개 문제가 출제된다. 독립형 과제(Independent Task) 2개, 통합형 과제(Integrated Task) 4개	20분

Writing	• 2개 문제가 출제된다.
	  통합형 과제(Integrated Task) 1개(20분),
	  독립형 과제(Independent Task) 1개(30분)
		50분

4. iBT TOEFL®의 점수

1 Section별 점수

Reading	0~30	Listening	0~30
Speaking	0~30	Writing	0~30

2 iBT, CBT, PBT 간 점수 비교

iBT	CBT	PBT	iBT	CBT	PBT
120	300	677	81~82	217	553
120	297	673	79~80	213	550
119	293	670	77~78	210	547
118	290	667	76	207	540~543
117	287	660~663	74~75	203	537
116	283	657	72~73	200	533
114~115	280	650~653	71	197	527~530
113	277	647	69~70	193	523
111~112	273	640~643	68	190	520
110	270	637	66~67	187	517
109	267	630~033	65	183	513
106~108	263	623~627	64	180	507~510
105	260	617~620	62~63	177	503
103~104	257	613	61	173	500
101~102	253	607~610	59~60	170	497
100	250	600~603	58	167	493
98~99	247	597	57	163	487~490
96~97	243	590~593	56	160	483
94~95	240	587	54~55	157	480
92~93	237	580~583	53	153	477
90~91	233	577	52	150	470~473
88~89	230	570~573	51	147	467
86~87	227	567	49~50	143	463
84~85	223	563	-	-	-
83	220	557~560	0	0	310

5. 시험 등록 및 응시 절차

1 시험 등록
온라인과 전화로 시험 응시일과 각 지역의 Test Center를 확인하여 시험 희망 응시일 7일 전까지 접수한다.

① 온라인 등록
ETS 토플 등록 사이트(https://toefl-registration.ets.org/TOEFLWeb)에 들어가 화면 지시에 따라 등록한다. 비용은 신용카드로 지불하게 되므로 American Express, Master Card, VISA 등 국제적으로 통용되는 신용카드를 미리 준비해둔다. 시험을 등록하기 위해서는 회원 가입이 선행되어야 한다.

② 전화 등록
한국 프로메트릭(1566-0990)에 09:00~17:00 사이에 전화를 걸어 등록한다.

2 추가 등록
시험을 보고자 하는 날의 3일 (공휴일을 제외한 Business Day 기준) 전까지 US $35의 추가 비용으로 등록 가능하다.

3 등록 비용
2014년 현재 US $170 (가격 변동이 있을 수 있음).

4 시험 취소와 변경
ETS 토플 시험 등록 사이트나 한국 프로메트릭(1566-0990)으로 전화해서 시험을 취소하거나 날짜를 변경할 수 있다. 등록 취소와 날짜 변경은 시험 날짜 3일 전까지 해야 한다(시험이 토요일에 있는 경우, 화요일까지 날짜 변경이나 취소 가능). 날짜를 변경하려면 등록 번호와 등록 시 사용했던 성명이 필요하며 비용은 US $60이다. 단, 시험을 취소할 경우 본래 응시료의 반액인 US $85만 등록 시 사용했던 카드로 환불된다.

5 시험 당일 소지품
① 사진이 포함된 신분증(주민등록증, 운전면허증, 여권 중 하나)
② 등록 번호(Registration Number)
③ 그 외의 소지품은 가능한 한 가져가지 말 것

6 시험 절차

① 사무실에서 신분증과 등록 번호를 통해 등록 확인
② 기밀 서약서(Confidentiality Statement)에 적혀 있는 글을 직접 손으로 써서 작성
③ 소지품 검사(거의 모든 소지품을 사물함에 보관함)
④ 사진 촬영 및 최종 신분 확인을 하고 연필과 연습장(Scratch Paper)을 제공 받음
⑤ 감독관의 지시에 따라 시험실에 입실하여 지정된 개인 Booth로 이동하여 시험 시작
⑥ Reading과 Listening Section이 끝난 후 10분간의 휴식(시험실 밖으로 나갈 수 있음)
⑦ 시험 진행에 문제가 있을 경우 손을 들어 감독관의 지시에 따를 것
⑧ Writing Section의 답안 작성까지 모두 마치면 화면 종료 메시지를 확인한 후에 신분증을 챙겨 퇴실

7 성적 확인

응시일로부터 15일 후 온라인으로 점수 확인이 가능하며 별도로 우편 통지서도 발송된다.

6. 실제 시험 화면 구성

전체 Direction
시험 전체에 대한 구성 설명

Reading Section 화면
지문은 오른쪽에, 문제는 왼쪽에 제시

Listening Section 화면
수험자가 대화나 강의를 듣는 동안 사진이 제시됨

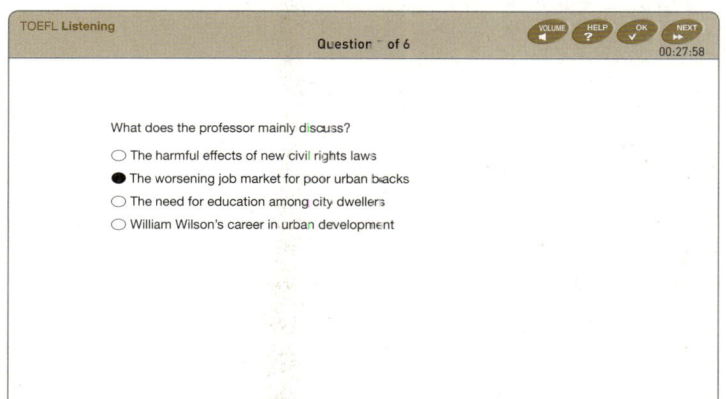

Listening Section 화면
듣기가 끝난 후 문제 화면이 등장

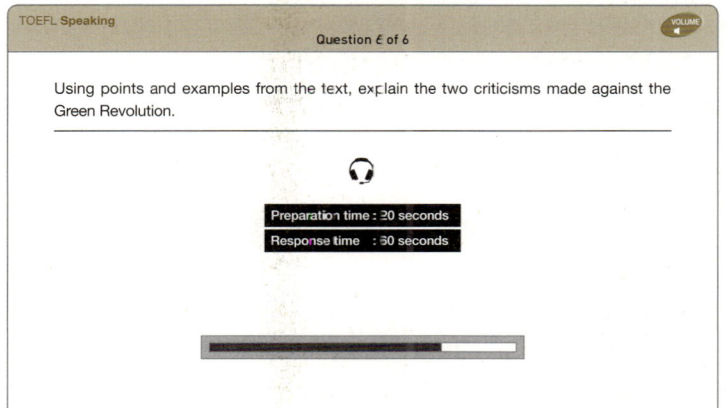

Speaking Section 화면
문제가 주어진 후, 답변을 준비하는 시간과 말하는 시간을 알려줌

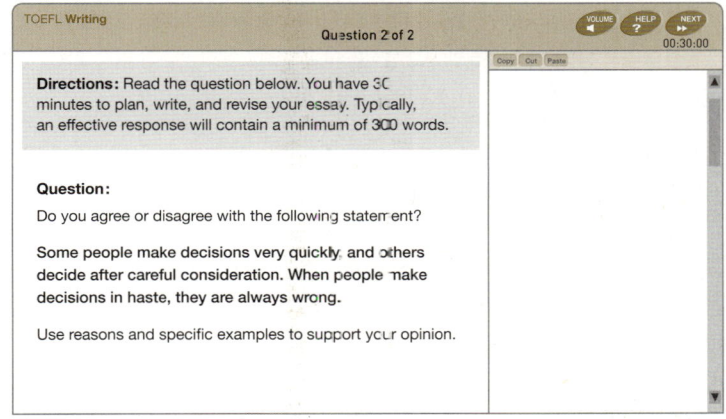

Writing Section 화면
왼쪽에 문제가 주어지고 오른쪽에 답을 직접 타이핑할 수 있는 공간이 주어짐
복사(Copy), 자르기(Cut), 붙여넣기(Paste) 버튼이 위쪽에 위치함

: 왜 배경지식인가? :

Background Knowledge

01 TOEFL Reading 배경지식의 중요성

적을 알면 백전백승이다. 토플 출제 지문을 미리 습득하면 자신감으로 무장하여 시험장으로 갈 수 있다. 리딩 시험 대비의 기본 중 하나가 실전 시험에 출제되었던 분야의 배경지식과 어휘 습득이다. 시험장에서 수험자가 알고있는 친숙한 분야들이 출제된다면야 천만 다행이지만 자신에게 생소한 주제가 출제되면 시험장 모니터 앞에서 머리가 백지가 되어버려 첫 시험 시간인 리딩 시간부터 이미 다음 시험을 계획해야 할지 모른다. 하지만 내가 토플 배경 지식을 공부해 갔다면, 비록 내게 낯선 분야라 할 지라도 효율적으로 빠른 시간 내에 문제를 해결할 수 있다. 긴 지문을 읽고 단순 기초 이해도를 측정하는 문제들뿐만 아니라 논리와 추리력까지 물어보는 문제들을 시간 내에 풀어내어 고득점을 얻기 위해서는 배경 지식을 따로 공부할 필요가 있다. 배경지식을 가지고 있다면 확실히 문제 해결 역량을 배가 시킬뿐 아니라 문제를 풀어내는 시간까지 단축시키는데 도움이 된다. 리딩의 배경지식이 "로또"라는 말은 아니다. 최소한 수험자가 읽어보지 못했고 알지 못하는 최신 리딩 지문들의 주제들을 공부하며 배경지식을 쌓고 독해 실력과 어휘로 내공을 쌓으라는 것이다. 기본 실력이 있다면 비슷한 주제가 나올 때 시험을 대처하는 자신의 실력이 한층 업그레이드 될 것이다. 두려워 말라. 실력을 쌓게될 때 내 손 안에 리딩 지문이 있게 된다!

02 TOEFL Reading 출제경향

여러분들이 생각하는 리딩 과목은 생각처럼 만만치 않다. 토플 시험 자체가 학술적 능력을 평가하는 시험이기 때문에, 단순 독해 능력뿐만 아니라 지문의 이해를 위해 대학의 개론 수업 수준의 전문 지식을 요하기 때문이다. 뿐만 아니라 그 분야까지 광범위하여 자연 과학 (화학, 물리, 생물, 천문, 지질학 등), 인문 (역사, 문화, 예술, 건축 등), 사회 과학 (사회, 심리, 경제 등), 사실상 학문의 전 영역을 다루고 있어 그 어려움을 더하고 있다. 뿐만 아니라 기존에는 하나의 주제에 대해 단편적 수박 겉핥기식의 내용이 지문에 출제 되었으나, 최근 리딩 지문 수준이 질적으로 높아져 심도있는 내용들을 다루고 있기 때문에 학생들이 더욱 고전을 면치 못하고 있다. 지문의 기술 방식 역시, 설명, 논증, 서술의 방법으로 서구권의 사고 방식을 따르고 있어, 문학 위주의 읽기 교육을 받은 한국 학생들에게 상대적으로 생소하게 다가올 수 있다.

03 배경지식 공부방법

리딩, 리스닝 과목별로 60개의 주제를 다루고 있다. 본격적인 영문 지문은 최근 출제되고 있는 주제들로 엄선되었을 뿐 아니라, 이에 앞서 해당 분야를 쉽게 이해할 수 있도록 한글 배경 지식과 핵심 어휘를 공부할 수 있도록 구성되었다. 영문 지문 당 2개의 유형 문제들을 풀어 봄으로써 독자 스스로 지문에 대한 이해를 확인할 수 있을뿐 아니라 리딩 문제 유형 연습도 할 수 있어 여러 수험서를 공부하는 효과를 경험할 수 있을 것이다. 지문 정독 연습을 하다 보면 독해 능력이 크게 향상됨을 스스로 느낄 수 있다. 또한 지문을 읽지 못하고 정확하게 문제를 풀어내지 못하게 하는 이유 중 하나가 어휘일 것이다. 특히 분야별 전문 어휘들은 우리에게 상당히 낯설다. 교재 후반에 정리된 각 분야별 필수 어휘 암기도 잊지 말도록 하자.

01 TOEFL Listening 배경지식의 중요성

토플 리스닝을 수년간 가르치다 보면 학생들 대부분이 학문적이고 딱딱한 리스닝 지문의 내용에 지쳐하는 모습을 많이 보게 된다. 그러나 그런 학생들도 본인이 전공하거나 관심이 있는 분야에 대한 내용이 나오면 눈을 반짝이며 기존에는 보지 못했던 자신감을 보이며 한 단어라도 놓치지 않으려는 적극적인 자세를 취하곤 한다. 실제로 시험장에서 운이 좋게도 자신에게 익숙한 분야에서 지문이 출제되어 예상치 못하게 고득점을 받게 되었다며 기뻐하는 학생들을 종종 보게 된다. 본인이 알고 있는 내용과 지문의 내용이 일치하지 않음에도 불구하고 고득점을 하는 경우를 보면 이는 꼭 그 주제에 관한 지식 때문이라기 보다는 자신이 알고 있는 것이 시험에 나왔다는 데에서 오는 안도감과 그것이 이끌어 낸 자신감 및 강한 집중력이 좀더 적극적인 청취를 가능하게 하지 않았나 생각한다. 이것이 바로 배경지식의 힘이다. 배경지식이 있으면 영어의 기초가 없는 학생이라도 마치 마법처럼 모든 것이 다 들리는 느낌이 든다. 비록 문장은 들리지 않는다 하더라도 익숙한 단어들 만이라도 귀에 쏙쏙 잘 들리기 때문이다. 반면에 전혀 익숙하지도 관심이 있지도 않던 생소한 분야에서 지문이 나오면 듣기도 전에 망했다며 펜을 내려놓는 학생들도 있다. 결국 '아는 만큼 들린다'라는 말이 사실임을 증명하는 것이다. 하루에 몇 백 개씩 생소한 분야별 어휘를 외우는 것 보다 빈출 주제에 대한 배경지식을 쌓는 것이 훨씬 더 효과적이며 효율적인 학습방법임을 기억하고 배경지식이 가져다 주는 자신감을 이번 기회를 통해 꼭 경험해 보도록 하자.

02 TOEFL Listening 출제경향

iBT 토플이 처음 나왔을 때만 해도 리스닝 섹션은 대학강의 중에서도 가장 수준이 낮은 입문단계의 내용을 많이 다루었다. 그러나 지금은 전공강의 수준의 내용이 다뤄질 정도로 리스닝 섹션은 해가 거듭할수록 가장 많은 난이도의 변화를 보여주고 있으며 많은 학습자들의 발목을 잡는 가장 어려운 과목으로 자리잡고 있다. 실제로 iBT 토플이 처음 나온 십여 년 전의 리스닝 교재를 풀어보면 현재 시중 교재들의 난이도와는 대단한 차이가 있음을 알 수 있다. 결국 스피킹, 라이팅 섹션 통합과제에서도 요해지는 리스닝 스킬은 토플을 정복하기 위해 뛰어 넘어야 할 가장 높은 장벽인 셈인 것이다.

03 배경지식 공부방법

이 교재는 리스닝 섹션에 관련된 핵심적인 배경지식을 6개 분야에 걸쳐 각 분야당 배경지식을 10개씩 엄선하여 포함시켰으며 각 지문은 한글해설, 마인드맵, 핵심어휘, 문제풀이를 제공하여 그 지문에 대한 지식을 완벽히 습득할 수 있도록 제작되었다. 특히 한글해설에는 해당 분야에 대한 전반적인 설명은 물론 최근 토플의 출제 경향 및 실제 강의에서 경험한 강사의 코멘터리 commentary를 추가하여 좀더 흥미있게 학습에 몰입할 수 있는 환경을 제공하고 있다. 따라서 한글해설과 마인드맵을 통해 어떠한 내용인지 숙지하고 핵심어휘만큼은 꼭 암기하여 해당 분야와 관련된 지문이 출제될 때 본인이 본 교재에서 배운 개념과 어떠한 차이가 있는지 정도는 비교할 수 있을 정도로 공부하도록 한다.

Chapter 1.
History

US History

001-L

America's 1st capital Philadelphia

World History

002-R

Aztec civilization

World History

003-R

Celts

US History

004-R

Early history in US

World History

005-R

Guild

World History

006-R

Hellenism

US History

007-L

History of road paving

Archaeology

008-L

Incan civilization - Khipu

World History

009-ᴿ

Indus civilization

World History

010-ᴿ

Japan

World History

011-ᴿ

Life of peasants in medieval Europe

World History

012-ᴿ

Mayan civilization

World History

013-ᴿ

Ottoman Empire

US History

014-ᴸ

Post WWII housing development

World History

015-ᴸ

Roman aqueducts

US History

016-ᴸ

The Columbian exchange

Archaeology

017-ᴸ

The discovery of Mayan ruins

US History

018-ᴸ

The statue of George Washington

Archaeology

019-ᴸ

Underwater archaeology

US History

020-ᴸ

Works Progress Administration

US History

★★★

001

America's 1st capital Philadelphia
미국 최초의 수도 필라델피아

➔ 미국 역사에서는 혁명전쟁 이후 최초의 독립국가를 건설하는 시기가 가장 많이 다루어지므로 그 당시 역사적 사건, 대통령, 독립선언문, 헌법, 수도, 경제 등을 알아두도록 하자!

필수어휘
- bustling 북적거리는
- Revolutionary War 혁명전쟁 (미국의 독립전쟁)
- judicial 사법의
- sit well with 받아들여지다
- furious 몹시 화가 난
- bill 법안
- compromise 타협
- on the verge of 막 ~하려는
- designated 지정된

워싱턴 D.C가 지금의 미국 수도가 되기까지는 많은 우여곡절이 있었다. 미국 독립전쟁 이후, 각 주state는 서로 다른 이해관계interests로 정책 결정에 있어 합의compromise에 이르기가 힘들었다. 따라서 미국은 통치력을 강화하기 위해 수도capital를 세우는 것의 필요성을 느꼈으나 북부와 남부 모두 수도가 자신의 영역에 위치하기를 원했기 때문에 적합한 도시를 선정하기가 힘들었다. 그 당시 북부에 속한 주들은 미국 혁명으로 인한 빚debt에 허덕이고 있었는데 그 빚을 남부 주들이 대신 갚아주길 원했다.

> 참고 │ 미국 남부 주들은 영토가 비옥하여 경작 활동이 활발하게 이루어졌으며 경제적으로 풍요로웠다. 이때 노동력 공급을 위해 노예가 필수적으로 필요했는데 이런 차이가 후에 미국 남북전쟁의 원인이 되었다.

이러한 북부의 요구에 있어 남부는 빚을 갚아주는 대신에 수도를 남부로 이전할 조건을 내세웠다. 그리하여 최종 수도가 결정되기 전까지 필라델피아Philadelphia가 1790년부터 1800까지 10년간 임시 수도a temporary capital로써 역할을 한 후 남부 Washington D.C로 수도가 이전된 것이 미국 수도 탄생의 배경이다.

참고로 미국 건립 시점부터 10년간 수도였던 필라델피아에서는 토마스 제퍼슨이 초안을 잡은 독립선언문declaration of independence이 탄생했으며, 미국 최초의 헌법constitution이 제정되었다. 또한 미국 초대 및 2대 대통령인 조지 워싱턴이 집권을 하였고 그 후 그의 공적을 기리기 위해 그의 이름을 딴 미국의 수도 워싱턴 D.C.가 탄생하게 되었다.

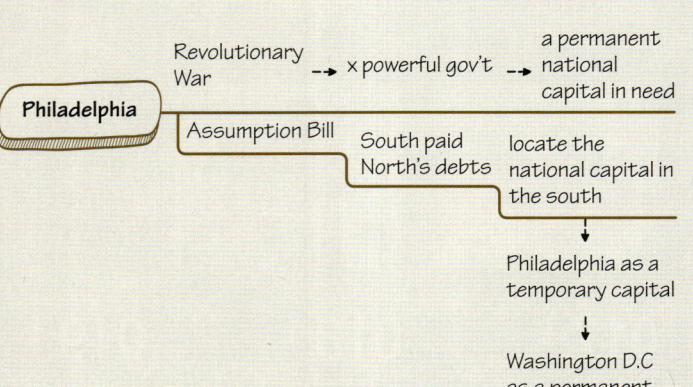

Mini Practice

Listen to part of a lecture in an American history class. 🎧 Ch1_01

1. What was the primary cause of the country's weak government?
   - Ⓐ Monetary assets were insufficient for the country.
   - Ⓑ The capital was being constantly relocated.
   - Ⓒ Each state possessed its own authority.
   - Ⓓ The Revolutionary War debilitated the authority of the government.

2. What was the response to the proposed Assumption Bill? Click on 2 answers.
   - Ⓐ The North was in favor of the bill.
   - Ⓑ The North was indifferent about the bill.
   - Ⓒ The South could not meet the financial demands of the bill.
   - Ⓓ The South was very angry about the proposal.

Listening Script

Professor: Back in 1783, just over two hundred years ago, the question arose over where to locate the capital. Back then, the country was a lot smaller. So, in 1783, Philadelphia was basically right in the center of the country, geographically speaking, as well as being a bustling city with a big economy and a hub of fashion and art. It was the logical place for a capital at least for a while, but first, let's try to understand the environment at the time. That is, the relationship between the Northern and Southern states. Following the Revolutionary War, there was only a fragile government which wasn't particularly powerful, because executive and judicial power rested with the individual states. The government couldn't even collect taxes or enforce laws. To strengthen its power, the federal government decided that a permanent national capital was needed. Many locations were considered, but at first, those locations were all in Northern states, and, as you can imagine, that didn't sit particularly well with the Southerners. And it was clear the reverse would be true if southern locations were considered. Also, the government, which was in the north, proposed the Assumption Bill, which would assume all the state debts that had arisen during the revolutionary war. However, the Northern states had a huge pile of debt, and the Southern states had nearly paid it all off. As you can imagine, the Southern states were furious: if the government accepted the bill, they would be forced to pay part of that burden. Fortunately, in 1790, an agreement was reached, a compromise with the unsurprising name, the Compromise of 1790. The compromise accomplished two things. First, it established a plan to locate the national capital in the south. Secondly, it preserved the union of the country, which was on the verge of conflict, perhaps even a civil war. And, in order to satisfy both sides, Philadelphia was designated as a temporary capital until a new one could be built. That was quite convenient, you see, because at that time it was already acting as the nation's capital.

Answers p. 4

World History

★★
002

Aztec civilization
아즈텍 문명

아즈텍 사람들은 멕시코 서부에서 온 유목민nomad으로, 14세기 초 멕시코 분지basin 중앙에 자리잡았다. 그들은 강력한 군사력을 앞세워 기존의 왕권을 흡수하였고, 테노치티틀란Tenochtitlan을 중심으로 마야 문명을 계승하는 아즈텍 문명을 탄생시켰다.

아즈텍 문명은 엄격한 계급사회였다. 가장 높은 층에는 사제priest, 전사warrior, 귀족nobles이 있었고, 그 다음 계층에는 장인artisans, 농부, 노동자가, 가장 낮은 계층에는 노예slave가 있었다. 노예들은 늪지대marsh의 물을 빼는drain 기술로 농경지를 개간했을 뿐 아니라, 테노치티틀란 주변의 염기가saline 있는 물과 텍스코코Texcoco호수의 민물을 분리하여, 식수를 끌어오는 수로aqueduct도 건설하였다. 그들은 주식staple food으로 옥수수maize, 콩, 호박 등을 먹었는데, 옥수수는 주로 맷돌에 갈아 만든 반죽으로 토르티야tortilla와 비슷한 빵을 만들어 먹었고, 호수에서 잡은 생선과 작은 포유류들로 단백질을 보충했다.

네 구역으로 나눠진 도시의 각 중앙에는 신전과 궁전이 있었으며 사람들은 혈연이나 같은 직종 종사자들끼리 모여 살았다. 그들은 나무껍질을 재료로 한 종이에 다양한 색의 잉크를 사용하여 상형문자hieroglyph로 역사를 기록했는데 이는 통치자와 귀족의 권력을 강화하기 위한 정치적 목적으로 쓰여진 것으로 보인다.

그러나 이 강력했던 제국은 1521년 스페인의 침략invasion으로 멸망했다. 그 원인으로는 스페인 군인들의 총, 대포와 같은 뛰어난 군사기술로 인해 전쟁에 패하면서 멸망했다는 학설이 있고, 스페인 사람들과 접촉하면서 홍역이나 천연두와 같은 전염병epidemic에 걸리면서 침략에 맞서 싸울 수 있는 남자를 포함해 많은 아즈텍 인구가 줄면서 그들의 문명이 쇠퇴의 길로 빠져들었다는 학설도 있다.

필수어휘
- craft 수공예
- craftman 공예가
- flourish 번영하다
  - [syn] prosper, thrive
- utilitarian 실용적인
- expertise 기술, 기교
- dedicate to ~에 전념하다
- jewels 보석
- priest 성직자
- lavish 사치스러운
- adornment 꾸미기, 장식
  - [syn] decoration
- aristocratic 귀족(적)인
- craftsmanship 손재주, 솜씨
- outstrip 앞지르다, 능가하다
  - [syn] surpass

Crafts from Ancient Aztecs

Ancient Aztec craftsmen could be divided into two groups: those producing items for daily use and those making luxury items. The former group of artisans, known as utilitarian artisans, created products for common people to use in their homes, including weaved baskets, sandals, pottery, and clothes. These goods were made in the artisans' homes and sold in the markets located in the cities. The utilitarian artisans lived outside the city in rural areas while the craftsmen producing luxury goods lived in the city and worked full time.

The difference between utilitarian artisans and luxury craftsmen was that the former depended on outside economic forces in selling their products. While the economy was flourishing and the demand for their products increased, utilitarian artisans were able to sell more products and focus less on farming crops. Due to the harsh climate, the utilitarian artisans were more likely to make products to sell in the markets than they were to go to the fields, especially during the hot summer months. However, when the economic situation was unfavorable and their products were not in high demand, they were left with no choice but to resort to the cultivation of crops to make their living.

On the contrary, the luxury craftsmen, who made value-added products such as gold jewelry and statues representing gods and kings, did not need to be concerned with farming crops to balance changes in the economic condition. These artisans with special expertise dedicated their lives exclusively to their lavish crafts. Because Aztec society was permeated with religion and symbolism, they had no shortage of work to do. They usually made jewels and other products primarily for nobles and priests, who constantly demanded fancy and lavish adornments such as earrings, bracelets, and necklaces. Also, the works of these artisans were displayed in Aztec palaces and temples in which their interiors were elaborately decorated with gold, rubies and other expensive stones from the lowest floor to the highest ceiling. The demand from aristocratic classes for luxurious goods outstripped their supply for two reasons: the artisans had difficulty obtaining raw materials from regions located far away, and the production of detailed and exclusively unique products was very time-consuming.

1. The word artisans in paragraph 1 is closest in meaning to
    - (A) beginners
    - (B) craftspeople
    - (C) farmers
    - (D) managers

2. All of the following are mentioned in the passage EXCEPT
    - (A) Utilitarian artisans cultivated if necessary.
    - (B) Artisans for making luxury items did not need to farm because noble classes provided necessities.
    - (C) Getting raw materials for luxurious products was not easy for artisans.
    - (D) Utilitarian artisans were concerned about economic situations.

Answers p. 4

World History

003

Celts
켈트족

초기 문명 발생지의 라이팅 시스템의 발생과 특징에 관한 내용이 출제되고있다. 라이팅이 있기 이전의 상황은 어땠을까? 켈트 문화를 통해 라이팅 체계 이전 구전 사회의 특징을 살펴 보도록 하자.

켈트족은 로마가 영국을 정복하기 직전인 '철기 시대Iron Age(B.C. 750~B.C. 1200)'에 독일 남동부 지역을 시작으로, 아일랜드, 웨일스, 스코틀랜드, 콘월 등의 영국의 작은 섬과 우크라이나 지역에까지 진출했던 서양 고대 종족이다. 수많은 부족으로 이루어져 있었으며, 완전한 통합이 이루어진 적은 없었다. 특히 북서 유럽에서 지금의 프랑스 지역은 갈리아Gauls, 영국은 브리톤Britons, 아일랜드는 게일Gaels이라는 세 개의 주요 켈틱 집단이 지배했다. 로마 침략 이후, 이들의 일부 부족들은 로마 제국에 흡수되었다.

켈트 부족들의 문화를 기록한 문서는 존재하지 않지만, 고고학적 증거와 다른 문화의 역사적 기록을 통해 추정해 볼 수 있다. 몇 가지를 살펴보자면, 먼저 그들은 유럽 최초로 바지를 입었으며 날개 달린 투구를 착용한 것으로 잘 알려져 있다. 로마에서 와인문화가 유행할 당시, 그들은 이미 맥주를 즐겨 마시고 있었다. 또한 오스트리아와 잘츠부르크 주변에서 발견된 켈트족 초창기 유물을 통해 그리스와 교역했던 증거와 철기 문화의 특징을 볼 수 있다. 그들은 기본적으로 작은 마을 단위를 중심으로 농경 문화를 유지했지만, 지역에 따라 목축ranching을 더 중시 여기는 경우도 있었다. 족장제를 기반으로 작은 집단들이 모여 더 큰 종족을 이루었던 이들의 사회체제는 왕, 귀족, 자유농민의 세 계층으로 구성되어 있었다. 켈트 종족은 호전적 집단이었으며, 전쟁의 목표가 경제적 이득이었기 때문에 종족들간의 전면전의 양상으로 개별적 전투가 빈번했다. 그렇기 때문에 그리스와 로마에서는 켈트 민족을 야만스럽다고 여겼지만 켈트 문화는 꽤 발달해서, 게르만족에게까지 큰 영향력을 끼쳤던 것으로 알려져 있다.

필수어휘

- □ verbal 언어의
- □ transmittance 전송, 전달
- □ sophistication 교양, 세련
- □ retain 유지하다
- □ eloquence 웅변
- □ retain 함유하다
- □ vulgar 저속한, 통속적인
- □ monk 수도승

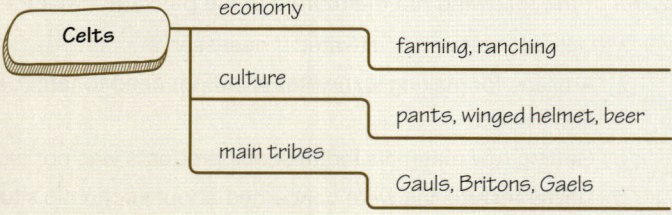

The Celtic Oral Tradition of Ireland

We live in a world heavily influenced by writing and multimedia, so it is hard to imagine a society and lifestyle without a written language. However, many ancient cultures were oral societies, like the Celtic peoples of Ireland. Up until the introduction of a written language in the 4th century CE, they were a society based on oral or verbal transmittance of history, law, comedy, art, stories, events and poems. Within an oral society, this vast collection of cultural knowledge was memorized and passed down from generation to generation. The absence of a written language may seem undesirable to us but it was just a different way of living and communicating.

As societies with written languages had elites who were skilled in the art of writing, the Irish oral societies also had various levels of people who were skilled in oral traditions. The lowest level would be ordinary people who would memorize songs and stories for fun and pleasure. The highest level might be employed within the aristocracy and were professional storytellers as well as communicators of events and news within the country. Oral communication by necessity was structured and organized with many types of oral communication, rules, and guidelines. We might see just a "story" but within an oral society there were levels and types of stories that varied with sophistication and training. This culture valued people who possessed eloquence, the capacity to retain a vast amount of stories and knowledge, the creativity to develop new stories and poems and musicality. Just as we might appreciate a good book, the people of Ireland appreciated skilled artisans who could whisk their listeners away on an adventure, move them to tears with tales of sorrow, and make them laugh with vulgar tales and mockery of the elite.

There was a rarely used Irish form of writing called the Script of Ogham, which was primarily used to record names and genealogies on stone monuments. However, with the introduction of Christianity and a Latin alphabet, the oral society of Ireland was eventually replaced by a written society. The Christian monks ultimately recorded many of the oral traditions but changed them to fit the standards of written mediums. All we have left of the Celtic Oral Tradition is a reflection of the past and a culture that was once vibrant.

1. According to paragraph 2, why does the author mention about eloquence?
   - (A) to exemplify a quality of people valued in the Irish oral based society
   - (B) to explain the reason why the oral communication developed in Celt
   - (C) to show the way people improved their verbal communication skill
   - (D) to argue that keeping a written record in Celt was difficult

2. The word vibrant in paragraph 3 is closest in meaning to
   - (A) vast
   - (B) active
   - (C) virtual
   - (D) widespread

US History

004

Early history in US
미국의 초기역사

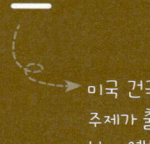

미국 건국 초기에 관한 다양한 주제가 출제되었다. 그 중 주 정부와 연방정부의 역할, 영국 정치와의 차이점, 법 제정에 관해 공부하자. 정치 지문을 많이 어려워하므로 정치 관련 어휘를 숙지하도록 하자.

필수어휘

- New World 신세계 (아메리카 대륙)
- Old World 구세계 (유럽, 아시아, 아프리카)
- mother land 모국, 조국
- colony 식민지
- constitution 헌법
- impoverished 빈곤한
- bicameral 상하 양원제의
- house of Lords 상원
- house of Commons 하원
- property 재산
- vote 투표하다
- governor 총독, 주지사
- council 지방 의회
- assembly 의회
- contract 협약

미국 초기의 식민지colony 시기는 동부 해안으로 영국인들이 이주하면서 시작되었고 뒤이어 독일, 프랑스 이주민들도 그곳 식민지에 정착했다. 영국인들은 1607년 지금의 버지니아 지역에 최초의 영구 정착지permanent settlement인 제임스 타운Jamestown을 건립했다. 신대륙 New World의 금을 채굴하기 위해 이주했던 초기 정착민들은 그 지역의 혹독한 겨울을 이겨내기가 힘들었다. 1620년 2차 정착 집단인 '필그림the Pilgrims'이 메이플라워Mayflower호를 타고 오늘날의 메사추세츠Massachusetts 주 플리머스Plymouth에 정착하면서, 메인Maine 주에서 조지아Georgia 주에 이르기까지 여러 식민지가 대서양 연안에 생겨났다. 18세기에는 더 많은 이주민들이 신대륙에 자리잡으면서 영토 분쟁이 일어나기도 했다. 1750년에는 북미 대륙에 13개의 주가 아래 3개의 집단으로 분류되었다.

이주민의 초기 정착지

1. **The New England Colonies:** Rhode Island, Connecticut, Massachusetts, New Hampshire
2. **The Middle Colonies:** Delaware, Pennsylvania, New York, New Jersey
3. **The Southern Colonies:** Maryland, Virginia, North and South Carolina, Georgia

유럽인들은 전쟁, 폭동rebellion 등의 사회적 혼란을 피해 평화로운 삶을 추구하고 더 넓은 농경지farming area에서 담배tobacco와 같은 상품 작물cash crop을 재배하여 돈을 벌기 위해 미국으로 이주하기도 했지만, 대부분은 종교적 탄압을 피해 자유를 누리기 위한 목적으로 이주하였다. 이주민들은 토착 세력인 원주민Native American과의 교류를 통해 곡식 재배와 혹독한 겨울을 이겨내는 생존 방법을 전수받았지만, 과도한 토지 개간과 재배로 인해 원주민들과 마찰이 발생하기도 했다. 초기 정착민들의 경제 활동은 옥수수와 밀에 기반을 둔 농업이었으며, 남부 지역을 중심으로 담배 등의 대규모 농장이 운영되면서 노예들이 그 지역에 유입되었다. 농업 외에도 철과 섬유 공장이 그들의 경제 기반으로 등장하기 시작했다. 모든 정착지에는 영국 왕이 선발한 주지사governor가 있었으며 영국 의회parliament와 동일한 모습의 의회assembly가 있었다. 그들은 법안을 통과시키고, 세금을 징수하는 역할 등을 했다.

Mini Practice

England & North American Colonies

Early English colonists of North America in the eighteenth century did not see themselves as being different from their motherland England and brought their political values and ideas with them to the New World. However, their societies sometimes actually did differ significantly from those of England. While colonists respected the English constitution as the basis of all liberties, they were alarmed by the actual workings of English politics.

[A ■] England's destitute classes were larger and more impoverished than those in the colonies. [B ■] While less than a third of England's inhabitants belonged to the middle class, the colonial middle class accounted for nearly three quarters of the white population. [C ■] Because of cheap land, labor scarcity and wages for both urban and rural workers being 100 percent higher in North America than in England, it was much easier for colonials to accumulate savings and buy a farm of their own. [D ■]

Early colonialists liked to think that their governments mirrored the English constitution and system in England, which they saw as ideal. In England, while the king or queen represented the ruling family in the House of Lords, which in turn represented the aristocracy, the House of Commons was supposed to represent the common people. The colonies had their own socially or politically prominent families but no titled ruling class holding political privilege by hereditary right. Most English colonies had a governor, a leader who represented the interest of the monarchy. They also had a bicameral (two house) legislature made up of a lower house (the assembly) and an upper house (the council). The democratically elected assembly, like the House of Commons, stood for popular interests, while the councils, which were elected in some colonies and appointed in others, more roughly approximated the House of Lords. However, these formal similarities masked real differences between England and its colonies. For example, if governors tried to wield their full powers, they were quickly met with opposition from their assemblies. In any dispute with their assemblies, most royal governors had to give way, for they lacked the government offices and contracts that bought loyalty.

1. The word accumulate in paragraph 2 is closest in meaning to
   - Ⓐ afford
   - Ⓑ build up
   - Ⓒ capture
   - Ⓓ assume

2. Look at the four squares [■] that indicate where the following sentence could be added to the sentence.

   Consequently, compared to Englishmen many more colonials were able to vote, since in both England and North America, only property owners had the right to vote.

   Where would the sentence best fit?

   Answers p. 6

World History

005
Guild
길드

유럽 중세시대에 도시사람들은 지방농노peasant와 달리 상업에 종사하며 자유롭게 경제 활동을 했다. 특히 11~16세기 번창했던 길드guild 조직은 특정 도시 안에 동일한 직종이나 기술craft을 지닌 수공업자artisan 혹은 상인merchant들의 연합 조직association으로 경제적, 사회적 영향력이 상당히 컸다. 길드 조직은 배타적이면서도 매우 조직적이었으며, 길드 조직 내 구성원들의 권리와 특권은 보호받았다.

길드의 종류
길드에는 상인 길드merchant guild와 동직 길드craft guild 두 가지 형태가 있었다. 상인 길드는 10세기에 등장했으며, 거의 모든 상인들의 연합 형태였다. 이 길드는 거래를 하는 상인들이 이동을 할 때 말, 마차, 물품들을 보호하려는 목적으로 만들어졌다. 이와 달리 동직 길드는 특정 직종의 전문성을 향상시키기 위해 화가, 대장장이, 제빵사, 목수, 석수mason 등의 동일 업종에 종사하는 사람들이 서로를 돕고 공동의 이익을 보호하기 위해 조직되었다.

길드 조직 내 위계 질서는 매우 중요했는데 공인된 실력으로 공장을 운영하는 장인master, 상품을 생산하며 견습공을 교육시키는 직인journeyman, 직업을 교육받는 견습공apprentice으로 조직이 구성되었다. 한편, 길드 조직의 입지가 커지면서 도시의 중요한 특권층으로 성장한 그들은 막강한 영향력을 이용하여 영업 독점을 요구하였다. 그들은 길드에 가입하지 않은 기술자들의 도시 내 수공업 경영을 금지하는 반면, 길드 규제 및 보호정책을 통해 조직 내 멤버들 간 경쟁이 없도록 관리하였다.

필수어휘
- association 연합
- secure 확보하다, 지키다
- stifle 억누르다
- letters patent 특허증
- apprentice 견습공
- apprenticeships 견습 기간
- journeyman 직공
- wage 임금
- capital 자본
- fixed price 정가
- exclusiveness 배타성, 독점성
- petition 청원하다, 탄원하다

Guilds

In many medieval European cities, merchants and artisans formed guilds or formal commercial associations. By banding together, they sought to protect themselves and secure their profits from outside competition. Some have argued that guilds created unfair market advantages that stifled technological advancement, fought against free trade, and limited the passing down of knowledge. However, some have pointed out that guilds played a crucial role in the economy because they tried to guarantee standards for products and regulations for sale.

There were two main kinds of guilds: merchant guilds and craft guilds. Merchant guilds regulated the way that trade was conducted in a town or region through an official charter. [A ■] Once the guild received *letters patent*, a grant of monopoly by the monarch or local ruler, they created rules and regulations for their members. [B ■] Craft guilds were formed by artisans skilled in the same craft such as shoemaking, carpentry, painting or baking. [C ■] New members, known as apprentices, were given training by the guild without pay. [D ■] After a successful apprenticeship, the member would become a craftsman and then a journeyman. Journeymen were paid a small wage and once they passed the examination and acquired enough capital, they could become a master artisan and start their own shop. Some people argued that apprenticeships were unnecessarily long depending on the skills they were learning and, because of their exclusiveness, hindered innovation.

Guilds controlled almost every aspect of the economy in cities and affected societies in both positive and negative ways. They enforced a fixed-price system and banned price cuts to prevent excessive competition between artisans and merchants. Simultaneously, they worked for appropriate protection of consumers by ensuring fair prices and were responsible for ascertaining the quality of goods and items offered to consumers. In addition, the guilds improved the welfare of their members. They looked after sick members and offered property protection while members were traveling. Medieval guilds petitioned for improvement of working conditions and working hours like the modern worker unions. However, artisans and merchants were not allowed to trade products with people who were not members or establish a business, so membership in this association was obligatory.

1. Look at the four squares [■] that indicate where the following sentence could be added to the sentence.

   Another type of guild, the *craft guild* worked in a similar way to the merchant guilds.

   Where would the sentence best fit?

2. The word obligatory in paragraph 3 is closest in meaning to
   - Ⓐ modest
   - Ⓑ requisite
   - Ⓒ rigid
   - Ⓓ manifest

World History

★★ 006

Hellenism
헬레니즘

알렉산더 대왕Alexander the Great(356-323 BC)은 20세의 나이로 즉위한 후 전례 없는 군사 활동으로 무패행진을 기록하며, 30세에 그리스와 이집트에서 파키스탄까지 세계에서 가장 큰 영토를 정복하였다. 그는 정복활동military campaign뿐만 아니라 문화에서도 뛰어난 업적을 달성했다. 군사 원정military expedition 때도 독서를 즐겼던 그는 학자들에게 정복 지역들을 탐험하고 측량하는 일들을 지시했다. 그가 그리스 문화를 중시했던 이유는 어려서부터 그의 개인교사였던 그리스 철학자 아리스토텔레스Aristotles에게 철학, 문학, 정치학 등의 가르침을 받았기 때문이다. 따라서 정복지에는 범 그리스주의Pan-Hellenism를 통해 그리스 문화가 퍼지게 되었고, 그 지역의 토착 문화와 융화되기도 하였다. 그리스 문화는 로마 문화의 토대가 되었으며, 로마가 멸망한 이후 유럽의 암흑 시대(5-10세기)까지 이어졌다.

이 시기의 뛰어난 과학자들로는 기하학의 아버지인 유클리드Euclid와 지렛대lever를 밝혀낸 아르키메데스Archimedes가 있다. 에라토스테네스Eratosthenes는 지구의 지름을 거의 정확하게 밝혀냈으며, 지구와 태양과의 거리도 알아냈다. 그는 지구가 둥글다고 믿었고, 지도에 경도longitude와 위도latitude를 사용했던 지리학자geographer이기도 하다. 또한 지구가 태양 주변을 돈다고 주장했던 사모스의 아리스타르쿠스Aristarchus of Samos와 달과 태양의 식eclipse 현상을 예측했던 히파르쿠스Hipparchus 등이 유명하다.

철학 분야에서는 제논Ho Elea Zénón이 스토아학파Stoics를 창시하여 모든 사물에는 '신, 이성, 로고스' 등으로 불리는 우주를 지배하는 필연적인 질서와 힘이 있다고 보는 범신론을 주장했다.

예술에서는 신체의 이상적인 표현을 중시했던 과거와 달리, 역동적이며 때로는 격렬한 동작을 취하는 인체를 살아있는 듯 묘사하는 데에 초점을 맞췄다. 헬레니즘 미술의 유명한 조각품으로는 라오콘 군상Laocoon and His Sons이 있다. 건축 분야에서는 코린트 양식이 도입되어 공공 건물, 목욕탕, 도서관, 극장 등에 화려한 장식을 더했다.

필수어휘

- **layout** 배열, 배치 [syn] **arrangement**
- **patronage** 후원
- **dynasty** 왕조
- **scholarly** 학자의, 학문의 [n] **scholar**
- **papyrus** 파피루스
- **transcribe** 베끼다
- **equivalent** 동등한

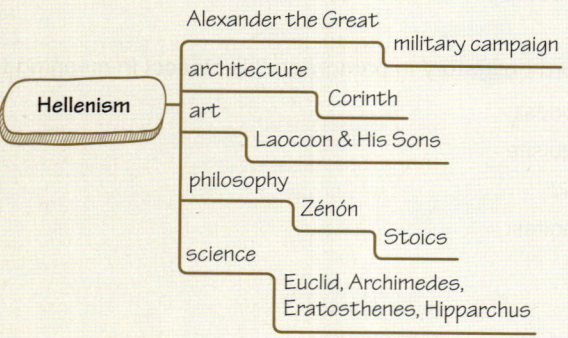

Library of Alexandria

Alexander the Great founded the city of Alexandria on the coast of Egypt and desired that it rivaled the richest cities of the Mediterranean. He had shown great interest in building a library, and he even picked the site and planned the layout of the building but did not live to see its construction. The ancient Library of Alexandria was built under the orders of Ptolemy I Soter, one of Alexander's generals. It was completed in the third century BC and flourished underneath the patronage of the Ptolemaic dynasty for 275 years, becoming a symbol of power and wealth for the dynasty. The Library of Alexandria was famous for being the first public government-operated library, in contrast to the many exclusive private libraries of the time, which existed in the palaces of royal families or in temples. This library was open to anyone who could prove they were a worthy scholar, and became the most remarkable center for intellectual achievements and research of the ancient world.

Having a myriad of documents on various academic topics, the ancient Library of Alexandria was the largest and the most well known library at the time. The Library of Alexandria is considered by many historians to have been a major center for scholarship as a research institution, not much different from our modern-day universities. The Library of Alexandria had at least three buildings: the original museum which served as a research institute, a building for book storage, and the "daughter library." There are no extant records of the library's layout so most researchers can only guess at the dimensions and capacity of the library. As the government strived to entice the best intellectuals to study, learn and discuss philosophy, sociology, politics, religion and most importantly, medicine, state salaries were provided to academics in exchange for transcribing existing works and conducting research. They were even given papyrus, which was expensive at the time, as a gift for writing and copying documents. As a result, the library attracted a variety of scholars including mathematicians, philosophers, and scientists from all over the Mediterranean and Middle East. The scholars included Archimedes, Hipparchus, Hypatia, Aristarchus of Samos, and Euclid. In return for the support of the state, any scholar who studied in the library was required to produce a copy of their writings for the library. This is why as many as 700,000 scrolls, which is the equivalent of more than 100,000 modern printed books, may have filled the shelves.

1. The word extant in paragraph 2 is closest in meaning to
   - Ⓐ great
   - Ⓑ existing
   - Ⓒ important
   - Ⓓ erratic

2. According to the passage, what does the author mention about Library of Alexandria?
   - Ⓐ The library was not open to the public.
   - Ⓑ Salaries and papyrus were given to scholars.
   - Ⓒ Alexander the Great ordered the building of the library.
   - Ⓓ There was only one building in the library.

Answers p. 7

US History

007

History of road paving
포장 도로의 역사

가끔 등장하는 뉴스 표현 "Air Force One has landed, and the president and first lady are now walking across the tarmac."에서 tarmac은 무엇일까? 19세기 최초로 포장도로의 발달을 가능케 한 이 용어에 대해 살펴보자.

19세기 최초의 포장도로paved roads는 그것을 발명한 사람의 이름인 McAdam을 따서 'Macadam roads'라 불렸다. 그 도로는 빗물이 빠르게 배수drain되도록 모난 자갈angular gravel로 만들어졌으나 자동차가 지나갈 때마다 자갈 사이사이에 낀 먼지dust가 심하게 날리는 문제가 있었다. 이 단점을 보완한 도로가 바로 타맥tarmac이다. 이는 Macadam roads에 콜타르coal tar와 모래sand, 그리고 광석에서 금속을 빼고 남은 찌꺼기slag를 더하여 기존 도로보다 더욱 안전하며 견고하게resistant 만들어졌다. Tarmac은 Tar-penetration macadam의 줄인 말로 말 그대로 타르가 통과된(합쳐진) macadam roads를 의미한다.

이후, Tarmac은 2차 세계대전 당시 비행기 활주로runways 건설에 대량 사용되며 오늘날 포장도로를 뜻하는 대표적인 동의어로 사용되어 왔다. 최근에 미국에서는 석유 찌꺼기인 아스팔트asphalt or Hot Mixed Asphald(HMA) 도로가 더 인기를 얻게 되면서 현재 도로의 전형이 되었다.

필수어휘

- □ **airport apron** (공항의) 에이프런 (항공기가 방향을 돌리거나 짐을 싣거나 하는 구역)
- □ **tarmac** 타맥 (타르와 슬래그를 석쇄도로 위에 바른 도로)
- □ **macadam** 쇄석 도로 (잘게 부순 돌로 포장한 도로)
- □ **tar** (석탄을 건류할 때 생기는) 타르
- □ **paved** 포장된
- □ **drainage** 배수로
- □ **sloped** 경사진
- □ **angular** 각이 진, 모난
- □ **aggregate** 집합체
- □ **gravel** 자갈
- □ **furnace** 용광로
- □ **compressed** 압축된
- □ **sturdier** (sturdy의 비교급) 더 견고한
- □ **swirling debris** 소용돌이 치는 잔해
- □ **slag** 광재, 용재

Macadam Road → sloped roadway with layers of compressed gravel → dust problem

macadam roads + tar + sand + slag → dust-resistant tar-penetration macadam

Mini Practice

Listen to part of a lecture in an American history class. 🎧 Ch1_02

1. What best describes tarmac?
   - Ⓐ The name of a famous Scotsman
   - Ⓑ The paved area around an airport
   - Ⓒ A type of pavement with an improved surface
   - Ⓓ Another word for concrete

2. What could be inferred about macadam roads?
   - Ⓐ They caused respiratory disease.
   - Ⓑ They resulted in too much dirt in the air.
   - Ⓒ People discarded waste along them.
   - Ⓓ They were created from fossil fuel.

Listening Script

Professor: Has anyone heard the term "tarmac" before? I guess you're thinking of the pavement at airports, but actually, that material is concrete, not really tarmac, and the correct term is "airport apron." So, what is tarmac, then? Well, tarmac is actually short for a longer word. It means "tar-penetration macadam." And we don't really use it much anymore, generally preferring asphalt instead. If macadam sounds like someone's name, that's because it is. It comes from the name of a Scotsman, John McAdam, who invented a technique for strengthening paved roads and improving water drainage. And no, macadamia nuts are not named after him; that was a different John Macadam born a generation later (laughs). Anyway, macadam roads featured a sloped roadway surface, on which were spread three layers of angular aggregate gravel, which were then compressed using a heavy roller.

Clearly, these roads were sturdier than their predecessors, but with them, a new problem arose. This problem was dust. You see, when automobiles started using those roads, they would kick up clouds of swirling debris and dust. So, in the 1830s, people starting experimenting with ways to solve this problem by covering macadam roads with tar and sand. But it wasn't until 1901 that things really improved. A civil engineer and businessman named Edgar Purnell Hooley, inspired after observing a spilled barrel of tar at a tarworks, invented a mixture of tar and slag, the latter being a furnace waste material, and came up with tar-penetration macadam. That is, of course, tarmac. It really improved the dust resistance on roads to which it was applied.

Very quickly, roads throughout England were being resurfaced with tarmac. During World War II, it was used by the British to build airstrips for jet fighters, and that's why we still use the term as a synonym for the airport apron and runways, even though they are made with other materials these days.

Answers p. 7

Archaeology

★★

008

Incan civilization - Khipu
잉카문명의 언어 Khipu

세계문명의 배꼽, 마추픽추, 태양신 등으로 더 잘 알려진 잉카문명은 서기 12세기경 지금의 페루와 볼리비아 사이에 있는 티티카카Titicaca 호수에서 기원했다. 이 문명은 페루 지역을 중심으로 수세기 동안 발달했던 여러 문명들을 정복하여 정치, 경제, 문화, 언어 및 종교적인 통일을 이루었다. 남아메리카 전역에 걸쳐 있던 잉카제국은 그들의 위대함을 보여주는 많은 유물artifacts들을 남겼는데, 그 중 하나가 바로 잉카 최초의 언어인 '키푸khipu'이다.

다양한 색깔과 방법으로 염색된 매듭knots이 묶인 실 뭉치braided cords로 뜻을 전달하는 '결승 문자'인 키푸는 스페인 정복자에 의해 처음으로 그 존재가 알려진 이래 500년간 학자들의 골치를 썩여 온 미스터리였다. 대부분의 학자들은 키푸가 세금 정보를 담은 회계 장부account book라는 데 동의했으나 그 내용이 최근에서야 해독된 것은 키푸가 4,500년간 복잡한 문자 언어로 사용됐음을 보여준다. 키푸의 해독을 담당한 학자들은 "키푸 해독 작업은 잉카의 계급 사회class society에 대한 정보를 제공한다."고 말하며 "높은 계급 관리들이 키푸를 통해 낮은 계급에게 명령을 전달했다."고 주장한다. 또 반대로 지역의 회계담당자들은 키푸를 사용하여 인구, 자원 등의 지역 정보를 상위 계급에게 제출했다고 설명한다. 현재 박물관에 있는 700여 개의 키푸 중 2/3는 십진법decimal system에 의한 회계 정보를, 나머지는 문자 정보를 기록한 것으로 분석된다. 역사학자들은 키푸가 담고 있는 이야기가 사라진 잉카 문명에 대한 역사적 정보를 풀어내는 열쇠가 될 것으로 기대하고 있다.

필수어휘
- suspension bridge 현수교
- reeds 갈대
- braided cords 땋은 끈
- knots 매듭
- trinkets 장신구
- archaeologist 고고학자
- census 인구조사

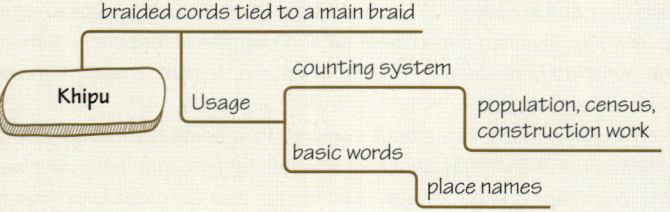

Khipu
- Usage
  - braided cords tied to a main braid
  - counting system — population, census, construction work
  - basic words
  - place names

Mini Practice

Listen to part of a lecture in an archaeology class. 🎧 Ch1_03

1. What function did Lock propose that Incans used the Khipu for?
   - Ⓐ keeping track of a city's construction projects
   - Ⓑ tabulating a city's census
   - Ⓒ calculating measurements needed to build large buildings
   - Ⓓ as a numerical foundation for a writing system

2. Why was it essential to distinguish between city names on a Khipu?
   - Ⓐ to avoid confusion about which city the records applied to
   - Ⓑ to prevent disasters in Incan towns
   - Ⓒ to help establish an identity for each town
   - Ⓓ to form the basis for a logical system of writing

Listening Script

Professor: Up through the 16th century, the Incans had an advanced society spanning thousands of kilometers of land in South America. Their civilization was the first to invent suspension bridge. They made huge, magnificent buildings from stone. They made boats using local plants such as reeds. And they did all this without a writing system. How? Well, they had something else, called Khipu (that's K-H-I-P-U). [show a picture of KHIPU] Just look at this picture! It looks like spaghetti, doesn't it? Well, this series of braided cords, right, are all tied to a main braid. And, you can see, they all have these little knots, which were originally different colors, though that's a bit hard to tell from this photo. So, these Khipu were all over the place! Archaeologists found them all throughout Incan ruins, and, well, for hundreds of years just assumed they were decorative objects, just trinkets. But then, along came Leeland Lock. He was the first to suggest that maybe these Khipu might serve some practical purpose. By examining the knots, he realized that the number of knots could be used as a counting system. Wouldn't that be useful? Just imagine! City officials could keep count of the population, a kind of census. So, from Lock we start with this assumption that Incans had numbers, which would be useful in constructing those big stone buildings. But numbers aren't really enough for the kind of civilization they had, and it wasn't until 60 years later when a mathematician and archaeologist suggested that the knots on Khipu might also represent basic words such as place names. See, the Incans must've needed a way to tell which town a census counted, and how could you tell, unless the Khipu somehow named the town. So, from this necessity, we can say the Khipu could convey basic information about places, as well as recording numbers. Pretty amazing, don't you think?

Answers p. 8

World History

009

Indus civilization
인더스 문명

메소포타미아 문명, 이집트 문명, 황하 문명과 함께 세계 4대 문명으로 꼽히는 인더스 문명은 기원전 2600년경 가가르-하크라 강 Ghaggar-Hakra River 지역에서 발생했으며, 두 대표 도시인 하라파 Harappa와 모헨조다로 Mohenjo Daro 및 작은 도시들로 이루어졌던 것으로 보인다.

사람들은 강 주변에만 국한되지 않고 광범위한 지역에 거주했으며, 세밀하게 설계된 도시마다 공중 목욕탕과 곡물을 저장하는 창고도 있었다. 이집트와 메소포타미아의 도시와는 달리 대규모 신전이나 호화로운 궁전이 보이지 않는다는 점에서 이 문명은 철저한 위계 질서 hierarchy를 가지고 있지 않았다는 학설도 있지만, 방대한 지역에서 지속되었던 문화적 통일성은 강력한 중앙집권화가 아니었다면 불가능했을 것이라는 추측도 있다.

도시의 거의 모든 건물은 규격에 맞춰 제작한 불에 구운 벽돌로 건축했다. 각 가정과 건물에는 배수시설 drainage facilities과 하수도 sewerage가 설치되어 있어 폐수를 효율적으로 처리했으며, 대규모 관개시설 irrigation system을 지어 우기 rainy period의 많은 양의 물을 처리하고 저수지 reservoir와 운하 canal, 우물 well을 만들어 건기 dry period에 대비한 것으로 추정된다. 그들은 이런 효율적인 관개시설과 함께 비옥한 땅에서 나는 농산물과 다양한 동물을 사육 domesticate하여 경제를 이끌었다. 또한 농업에서는 나무 쟁기 plow를 만들어 풍부한 식량을 얻을 수 있었다. 인더스 사람들은 농업 외에도 생산 및 무역 활동도 활발했으며, 도기 pottery, 테라코타 인형, 장신구 등을 제작한 흔적도 남아 있다.

인더스 문명에서 가장 유명한 유물은 상형 문자와 동물 형상이 조각된 도장 seal이다. 문자 도장은 무역활동의 수단으로써 화폐로 쓰였고, 코끼리 같은 동물 도장은 종교적 의미로 사용된 것으로 보인다.

인더스 문명은 기원전 1900년경 쇠퇴하기 시작했는데, 그 주된 원인으로 기후변화를 꼽는다. 인더스 문명의 습한 기후가 기원전 2000년경 건조해지면서 가가르-하크라 강이 말라버렸다는 학설이 있고, 그 외에 지진으로 바뀐 강의 흐름, 외부의 침략, 대홍수 등의 여러 요인들이 쇠퇴의 원인으로 지목되고 있으나 아직까지 명확하게 밝혀진 것은 없다.

필수어휘
- brick 벽돌
- platform 단, 플랫폼
- ceiling 천장
- sewage 하수, 오물
- granary 곡물 저장소
- deluge 홍수 syn inundation
- agrarian 농업의
- fertile 비옥한 ant futile
- inscription 비문
- terracotta 테라코타 (적갈색 점토를 구운 것)
- seal 도장, 인장
- motif 디자인, 주제
- deity 신

Indus Civilization

The Indus Valley civilization flourished around 2500 B.C. and 1900 B.C. in the western part of South Asia, in what today is Pakistan and western India. It was larger than either the Mesopotamian or Egyptian society, and is often referred to as the Harappan Civilization after its first discovered city, Harappa.

Both Harappa and Mohenjo-Daro, two of the largest among the civilization's 500 cities, featured marketplaces, temples, public buildings, extensive residential districts, and broad streets arranged in a grid; but they had no pyramids, palaces, or magnificent tombs. Structures were constructed primarily from fire-baked bricks that were uniform in size and shape, with an impressively organized and regular layout. The function of the brick walls, especially in the construction of the citadel, was to defend the city against invasion, and mud brick platforms might have protected the city against flood waters. For example, in Mohenjo-Daro, the citadel was built on an architectural platform about 45 feet above the plain, and in Harappa, fortified walls in the southeast corner may have protected the city. Both cities were characterized by brick houses two stories high, with thick walls and high ceilings to keep the rooms cool in the hot summer. Each home had its own well and private bathroom, with showers and toilets draining into the city sewage system. In addition, the city had a large public bathing platform which may also have been used for washing clothes as is common in many traditional cities in Pakistan and India today, and the cities had a huge open space, as well as a granary in which food such as grain was stored to prepare for possible deluge.

The civilization was a fairly successful agrarian and commercial society. People employed irrigation systems to take advantage of the fertile ground along the Indus River and controlled the river's annual flooding through walls they built, so they could cultivate several kinds of crops such as wheat, barley, peas and even cotton in large quantities. Also, inhabitants of the Indus valley traded copper, ivory and pearls with Mesopotamia, southern India, Afghanistan, and Persia, in exchange for wool, leather and olive oil.

The Indus people also developed a writing system. Their inscriptions have survived in seals, fragments of pottery and molded terra-cotta, revealing about 600 Indus symbols. In addition to the symbolic signs, the seals contain motifs; mostly pictures of animals, including cows, bears and monkeys, probably representing animal ancestors or deities.

1. The word layout in paragraph 2 is closest in meaning to
   - (A) state
   - (B) configuration
   - (C) construction
   - (D) areas

2. According to the passage, which of the following is true?
   - (A) Homes did not have any private toilet.
   - (B) The cities in Indus civilization had the planned layout.
   - (C) The two biggest cities always competed with each other for water.
   - (D) Indus had a limited agricultural technology and suffered from famine.

Answers p. 9

World History

010

Japan
일본

아시아 국가들 중 중국과 일본이 종종 출제된다. 중국 인구 성장의 원인, 실크 로드, 도자기, 일본과 중국과의 국제 교역 등이 출제되었으며 여기서는 일본의 토지와 농사 기법에 관한 내용을 공부해 보자.

필수어휘

- barren 척박한 [syn] sterile, futile
- waterwheel 물레바퀴
- hone (기술을) 연마하다
- terrace 계단식 논(밭)
- rice paddy 논
- dry crop 밭 곡식
- tuber 덩이 줄기 식물
- rainy season 우기
- double-crop 이모작 하다 (같은 토지에 두 종류의 농작물을 1년 중 서로 다른 시기에 재배하는 농업 기술)
- harvest 거두다, 수확하다 [syn] reap
- ditch 배수로
- canal 운하
- drainage 배수(시설)
- run off 땅 위로 흐르는 빗물, 유출액체

710년 일본 수도capital를 나라Nara에 세운 후, 불교 수도원들이 그 지역에 건축되었다. 그 이후 강한 정치적 영향력을 바탕으로 황제와 중앙 정부의 지위를 보호하고자 나라 지역의 수도를 784년 나가오카로 옮겼으며, 794년 다시 한 번 헤이안Heian(지금의 교토지역)으로 옮기고 나서 1천년 간 수도로서 자리잡았다.

나라 시대와 헤이안 시대의 특징은 기존에 많은 영향력을 받았던 중국 문화로부터 약간이나마 독립했다는 점이다. 한국을 통해서 들어온 중국의 정치제도에는, 일본의 실정에 맞게 정부 기관들이 추가로 생겨났다. 예술적 측면에서도 토착 일본 문화가 점점 더 인기를 끌기 시작했고, 헤이안 시대에 들어온 불교 문화도 일본화 되는 경향이 있었다. 하지만 타이카 개혁에서 가장 실패했던 부문은 토지와 세금이었다. 높은 세금은 농부들을 빈곤하게 만들어 결국 토지를 팔고 귀족이나 유지들의 소작농이 될 수 밖에 없는 결과를 초래했다. 게다가 다수의 귀족층과 불교 수도승들에게는 이 개혁이 유리하게 작용한 결과, 정부의 수입은 줄어들고 정치 권력이 중앙 정부에서 대토지를 소유한 귀족층으로 넘어가게 되었다.

다이고 천황과 후지와라 도키히라가 정권을 잡았던 이 시기에는 인구가 증가하면서 경작할 수 있는 토지가 감소하자 개간한 토지는 개인 소유지(장원manor)로 인정한다는 법령이 제정되었다. 따라서 귀족층은 사람들을 동원하여 더 많은 토지를 개간하도록 했고, 황무지였던 땅까지 농업 기술력을 동원하여 그들의 소유가 되었다. 가난한 농민들이 세금 징수를 피하기 위해 귀족에게 토지를 주는 경우도 있어서, 지방 유력자들과 귀족들의 장원은 날로 늘어 났다. 하지만 운영 체제와 인력 부족으로 인한 토지 소유의 비효율성과 과도한 세금으로 인해 장원제도는 초기 도입된 지 100년 만에 사라질 위기에 있었으나, 세금을 관리하던 관직인 고쿠시의 세력이 강해지고 헤이안(8-12세기)시대에 등장해서 19세기까지 지방의 대규모 영토를 다스리던 권력 세력인 다이묘 daimyo가 이에 결탁하면서 장원 제도가 부활하게 된다. 따라서 중앙의 지배력은 약화되는 반면, 지방 분권화는 계속해서 유지되었다.

Agriculture in Medieval Japan

During the Japanese Medieval Period, between the fourteenth and seventeenth centuries, Japan experienced many changes in government and society, as well as a growing population, and many improvements in agriculture. Land that had been previously barren and uninhabited was reclaimed, and many new villages sprang up in the early 1300s. Terracing, double cropping, and improved irrigation methods along with improvements in rice seed strains, waterwheels, and farming implements were all crucial to the development and cultivation of previously uninhabited land. These improvements were honed through practice and were passed down from generation to generation and preserved with great care.

Terracing is the practice of altering a slope, like the side of a hill or mountain by creating slices of flat land that often look like steps. Japanese farmers would plant dry land crops, such as various tubers or green vegetables, on the upper steps and would cultivate rice in paddies at the bottom of the steps. This allowed farmers to prevent valuable nutrients from being washed away during the rainy season, while at the same time capturing water for rice farming during the summer.

Improvements in fertilizers allowed Japanese farmers to get two and sometimes three crops a year from the same piece of land, a process also known as double cropping. For example, farmers could sow barley in early spring and harvest the crop by early summer. After the barley harvest they could plant rice which they would reap in fall. The rice may be followed by a planting of buckwheat which could be harvested in winter. This allowed farmers to increase the amount and variety of crops, which they could offer for sale in the markets or save for their own consumption.

Farmers also learned how to make every drop of water count and tended to plant close to sources of water such as rivers, streams, lakes, and ponds in order to increase their harvests. Farmers who worked farther away from large sources of water or during the dry period developed complex systems of irrigation ditches and canals that allowed them to bring water over great distances to water their crops. They also invested in on-site water drainage ditches that could catch rain runoff, which could be utilized during the hot summer months.

1. The word barren in paragraph 1 is closest in meaning to
    - Ⓐ constant
    - Ⓑ reliable
    - Ⓒ sterile
    - Ⓓ nearby

2. Why does the author mention various tubers in paragraph 2?
    - Ⓐ to show which plant cultivated in paddy at the bottom of the steps
    - Ⓑ to explain why Japanese farmers developed the farming method of terracing
    - Ⓒ to exemplify the dry crops Japanese farmers planted on the top steps of the terraces
    - Ⓓ to stress the importance of dry crops in Japan

Answers p. 9

World History

★★
011

Life of peasants in medieval Europe
중세 유럽 소작농의 삶

중세 유럽에 관해서는 농업, 교역, 도시 발달 등 다양한 주제가 출제된다. 여기서는 그 당시 발달했던 농사 기술력과 농부들의 삶을 살펴보도록 하자.

필수어휘
- hierarchy 위계 질서
- peasant 소작농 (토지를 지주에게 빌려 농사를 짓는 사람)
- feudal 봉건적인
- fief 영지 (봉건 시대에 노무를 제공하는 대가로 영주가 빌려 주던 땅)
- serf 농노
- lord 영주
- manor 영주의 저택
- filthy 아주 더러운
- pandemic 유행병
- plague 전염병
- rising 반란 [syn] revolt
- curb 억제하다

중세 유럽은 5세기 게르만 족의 이동과 서로마 제국의 붕괴와 함께 시작되어 16세기 즈음에 종식된 것으로 보고 있다. 중세 북유럽의 여름은 강수량이 풍부하기 때문에 밭을 갈아 경작하기 좋았지만, 해마다 농사를 지으면서 토양의 질이 나빠져 수확량이 줄어들었다. 농사의 이 같은 단점을 보완하기 위해 기술혁신이 이루어졌으며, 그 결과 11-14세기 유럽의 인구는 4천만에서 7천 5백만으로 급격히 증가하게 되었다.

농업 생산량은 기존의 2모작two-field method에서 3모작three-field method으로 바뀌면서 한층 더 증가했다. 2모작의 경우 토지의 절반을 쉬게 하고, 나머지 절반에 겨울철 곡식을 심는 방식이었으나, 3모작에서는 토지를 세 부분으로 나누어 1/3에는 겨울철 곡식을 심고 1/3은 귀리, 콩 등을 심었으며 나머지 1/3은 곡식을 재배하지 않도록 함으로써 토질이 회복되도록 했다. 유럽인들은 이러한 3모작을 통해 더 많은 종류의 작물을 재배할 수 있었을 뿐 아니라, 토양의 질이 개선되는 경험을 할 수 있었다.

기존의 마구는 말의 목에 걸 수 없어 짐을 운반하는데 말을 사용할 수 없었지만, 아시아로부터 말에 사용하는 가슴걸이collar가 도입되면서 소 대신 말을 이용한 경작이 가능해졌다. 말은 소에 비해 힘이 세고, 빠르게 움직이기 때문에 가슴걸이의 사용은 생산량 증가의 한 요인으로 꼽힌다. 하지만, 말은 값비싼 사료를 먹었기 때문에, 상대적으로 싼 가격의 건초 더미를 먹는 소가 경제적으로 더 효율적이었다. 게다가 철제 물건을 제작하는 용광로smelting furnace가 이 시기에 크게 발전하면서, 더욱 단단한 철iron을 공급받아 무거운 쟁기plough를 만들게 되었다. 그 결과 개간이 힘들었던 땅까지 경작cultivate이 가능해지면서 농업 생산량이 크게 늘고 인구가 증가할 수 있었다고 학자들은 주장한다.

Life of Medieval Peasants

In the Middle Ages from the tenth to about the fifteenth century, there was a definite hierarchy, in which the king had the most power, followed by the aristocracy. Next were the knights. The tradesmen were below them. Then came freemen. The serfs or peasants were the lowest in this hierarchical social system, and in some cases no better than slaves. In the medieval feudal system, the king awarded land grants or "fiefs" to his most important nobles in return for their contribution of soldiers for the kings' armies. Most farmers lived on a manor, a self-sufficient agricultural estate owned by a lord, where they worked to pay rent or fees for various services. In exchange for their work, the lord offered protection and safety to serfs from the danger of invasion and thieves. Freemen were able to leave the manor, but most serfs were compelled to stay on the land, unable to leave their lord.

The Black Death made their hard life even more difficult. The Black Death, which swept through Europe from 1347 to 1350, was thought to have come from China or central Asia, and was spread by merchants along the Silk Road. The streets were filthy, as animals and humans lived side by side, and a communicable disease like the Black Death would have spread easily in such conditions. It is estimated that this pandemic killed almost half of the British population. The most immediate consequence people experienced after the Black Death struck England was a change in the economic structure. The drastic decrease in population caused a shortage of labor, which led to a subsequent rise in wages. However, the landowning classes and government tried to curb this development through legislation and punitive measures, leading to deep resentment among the lower classes. In the aftermath of the plague, there were religious and social uprisings. Among these, the Peasants' Revolt in 1381 had the most severe effects on the society. Although the Peasants' revolt as a political rebellion was defeated and peasants failed to achieve their goal of abolishing serfdom, it had symbolic significance and the demand for rights and equality had a long term effect on democracy.

1. The word aftermath in paragraph 2 is closest in meaning to
    - Ⓐ result
    - Ⓑ uprising
    - Ⓒ cause
    - Ⓓ rule

2. Which one is true about the Black Death in paragraph 2?
    - Ⓐ It was spread by the farmers along the Silk Road.
    - Ⓑ Its aftereffects in England were much more serious than in other countries.
    - Ⓒ The population dramatically declined after it struck England.
    - Ⓓ The English government tried to restrain the spread of disease.

Answers p. 10

World History

012

Mayan civilization
마야 문명

마야 문명을 포함한 *메소아메리카 지역의 문명들은 토플의 빈출 주제이다. 마야의 발생부터 그들의 농업, 교역 생활, 기후 등의 다양한 내용들이 출제된다.
*메소아메리카: 멕시코와 중앙아메리카 북서부를 포함하는 지역. 마야, 아즈텍 문명 등이 이 지역에서 번성함

필수어휘
- inexplicably 설명할 수 없게
- degradation 저하, 악화
- endemic 고유의, 토착의
- aristocrat 귀족
- peasant 농부, 소작농
- civil strife 사회적 갈등
- strain 짐, 부담 [syn] burden
- fleeting 순간의
- overthrow 타도, 전복

마야는 기원전 수 세기 전부터 16세기 스페인의 정복 활동 이전까지 1,000년이 넘는 역사를 가진, 멕시코와 남미지역에서 가장 우세했던 토착 세력 중 하나로 지금의 과테말라 지역과 유카탄 반도 the Yucatan Peninsula를 차지했으며, 6세기를 전후해서 최대의 전성기를 구가했다. 마야의 역사는 고전기 이전 pre-classic(1200B.C-300A.D), 고전기 classic period(300A.D-1000A.D), 고전기 이후 post classic period(1000A.D-mid 16C)인 세 시기로 나뉜다. 그들은 뛰어난 농업 기술, 도자기 pottery, 상형 문자 hieroglyph writing, 천문학, 수학, 경제 제도, 건축과 예술 유적 등을 남긴 것으로 잘 알려져 있다.

마야 문명의 흥미로운 사실 중 하나는 방대한 지역에 살던 마야인들이 각 지역에 맞는 농사법을 활용했다는 점이다. 예를 들어 강수량이 많은 남부 저지대 지역은 강과 호수가 적었기 때문에, 마야인들은 빗물을 저장할 수 있는 저수지를 만들었다. 고지대나 산악 지역에서는 좁은 계단식 밭 terrace을 경작했고, 습지 swamp 지형에서는 물을 배수 한 뒤 토지를 경작했다. 이들은 또한 화전 농업 slash-and-burn agriculture으로 농사를 지었던 것으로 추정된다. 이들은 대부분 채식을 했는데 주로 옥수수, 콩, 호박 등을 먹었으며 간혹 고기와 생선 등으로 단백질을 보충하기도 했다.

마야인들은 태양, 달을 포함하여 수많은 자연신을 숭배한 것으로 알려져 있다. 마야 문명의 최고 위치에 군림하는 왕이 신과 사람들의 중개자 mediator 역할을 하며 종교적 제사 ritual나 의식 ceremony을 담당했다. 그들의 계단식 피라미드 형태의 신전과 궁전들은 상형 문자로, 기념비나 신전의 벽은 정교한 돌을 새김(양각)relief 및 비문 inscription 등으로 화려하게 장식되었는데, 이를 통해 고대 마야 문명은 메소 아메리카의 최고 예술이라는 명성을 얻게 되었다. 종교 의식 때문에 그들은 세계 최초로 숫자 0을 사용했고, 365일을 기반으로 고안한 달력과 같이 수학, 천문학적으로도 뛰어났다.

Decline of Mayan Civilization

Archeologists and historians have long pondered the mystery of the collapse of Mayan civilization during the 8th and 9th century in Mesoamerica. During this era parts of the northern Mayan kingdoms survived, but many of the major southern cities were inexplicably abandoned. Although remnants of the Mayans would last until the Spanish colonial era, the Mayans never recovered their former glory. Researchers have suggested that the decline involved a complex combination of external stressors on an already vulnerable Mayan society. By the 8th century, populations in the surrounding the lowlands had reached new peaks of size and density. Overpopulation coupled with an overuse of land, endemic warfare, climatic change and civil strife may have played a part in the decline of Mayan civilization.

Some historians believe that by the 9th century the Mayans had exhausted the environment around them to the point where it could no longer sustain such a large population. It is possible that in their attempts to increase food production they exhausted the nutrients in the soil, leading to decreased harvests. [A ■] At the same time, rising demands for timber for construction and fuel would have intensified the deforestation around their cities. [B ■] The inevitable result was environmental degradation. [C ■] Some have suggested that cycles of extremely long, intense periods of drought coupled with damage to the environment may have affected Maya civilization during the Classic period. [D ■]

Mayan scholars argue that constant endemic warfare among competing city-states led to the breakdown of complicated military, family and trade alliances. Southern cities that experienced environmental degradation would lack resources to export and they would need to import food from other cities. This strategy would have placed a lot of strain on the other cities to support failing economies. The probable side-effect was increased competition and friction among cities and regions. Furthermore, serious food shortages, even fleeting ones, could have widened social and economic gaps, already a source of tension between wealthy aristocrats and peasants. Increased pressure on all segments of society was inevitable as aristocrats faced greater administrative burdens. A lack of food and civil strife could have led to peasants resisting demands to build temples and monuments, and may have even ended in governmental overthrows.

1. Look at the four squares [■] that indicate where the following sentence could be added to the sentence.

   This could have led to a scarcity of water and to the desertification of the regions surrounding the Mayan cities.

   Where would the sentence best fit?

2. The word friction in paragraph 3 is closest in meaning to
   - Ⓐ vigor
   - Ⓑ hazard
   - Ⓒ alliance
   - Ⓓ confliction

World History

013

Ottoman Empire
오스만 제국

오스만 제국은 비잔틴 제국이 경제적, 군사적으로 쇠퇴하고 있을 무렵 오스만 1Osman I세가 14세기 초 소아시아Asia Minor 반도에 건국한 이래 20세기 초반까지 지속된 대제국이다. 이 제국은 시리아, 팔레스타인, 이집트, 이라크 등 중동 대부분의 지역과 알바니아, 불가리아, 그리스, 헝가리, 루마니아, 유고슬라비아를 포함한 유럽 일부 지역, 그리고 북 아프리카 지역의 방대한 영토를 정복했다. 그들의 라이벌이었던 합스부르크가Habsburgs처럼 오스만 제국 역시 왕조 국가였으며, 국가, 인종, 종교와 관계 없이 각 시대별 왕권이 장악했던 군사적, 행정적 권력에 따라 제국의 특징이 결정되었다.

오스만 제국은 이슬람교에 헌신하는 공동체적 원칙과 기사도 정신을 기반으로 더 많은 나라를 이슬람 영역에 들이고자 했고, 수도원의 경제적 착취에 시달리던 농민들은 자발적으로 오스만 제국의 보호를 원하며 피지배자로 흡수되었다. 오스만 1세의 뒤를 이은 오르칸Orkhan은 비잔틴의 니케아(1331)와 니코메디아(1337)를 점령하고 해안 지역으로 그 세력을 넓혀 나갔으며, 영토 확장을 위해 훈련된 군사 조직인 야니샤리janissary를 편성하였다. 뿐만 아니라, 비잔틴과 발칸 반도의 국가가 분열되자 용병으로 반도에 진출하면서 대륙의 침략이 용이해졌다. 이 제국의 전성기는 제10대 술탄Sultan(이슬람의 최고 통치자)이었던 술래이만Suleiman(1520-1566)이 크림반도, 아랍반도, 북아프리카를 포함하여 가장 넓은 영토를 차지했던 시기로, 여러 민족, 종교, 문화를 수용하는 포용성과 관용을 보였다.

오스만 제국은 서유럽을 위협하는 막강한 국가였지만, 16세기 말부터 세력의 변화가 시작되었다. 18세기 중반 이후 서양 근대화에 노력하는 등 여러 개혁에 성과가 있었지만 명확한 경제 정책의 부재와 발칸 반도의 독립 운동, 터키 혁명 등의 이유로 1922년 술탄제가 폐지되었으며 터키 공화국이 수립되었다.

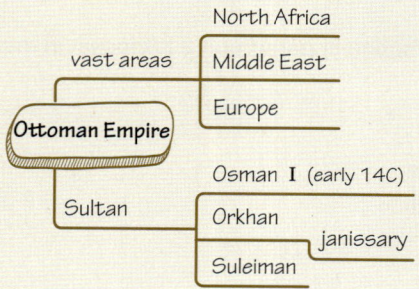

필수어휘
- zenith 정점
- degeneration 악화, 타락, 퇴보
- demise 종말, 죽음, 소멸
- sultanate 술탄의 지위
- reign 통치
- revenue 수익, 세입
- sultan 이슬람의 군주
- junction 교차점
- stagnation (경제의) 침체기
- janissary 터키 병사
- dissolution 파경, 해산

Decline of the Ottoman Empire

At the dawn of the thirteenth century, Osman I established one of the most powerful empires in history, the Ottoman Empire. At the zenith of the Ottoman Empire's power, it controlled a massive area of land, including substantial holdings in the Middle East, North Africa and Europe. During the next 600 years, the empire rose to incredible heights before eventually falling into decline. The demise of the Ottoman Empire was caused by a combination of the internal degeneration and external pressures.

The empire reached its height in power and prestige under the rule of Suleiman the Magnificent (1494-1566). However, this power began to decline when his son, Selim II(1524-1574), allowed the empire to fall into disrepair and abandoned power to his ministers. During his rule, the Empire suffered several military defeats at the hands of the Russians and other European forces. These events finally resulted in the initial weakening of the Sultanate and loss of administrative power.

For a long time the Ottoman Empire served as the gateway to the East, because it was positioned at the junction of Europe, Africa, and Asia. Consequently, revenue from the trade routes formed a large part of the economy. However, as Europeans began to develop new trade routes that bypassed the Ottoman Empire, the Ottoman economy suffered. The Ottomans also failed to keep pace with the industrialization of European countries, and this caused them to lag behind in modernizing their military and industries. Unable to compete with an industrialized Europe, economic stagnation also weakened the empire.

The final major factor in the fall of the Ottomans was a shift in the international balance of power. The shift started internally, with corruption and mutiny among the Janissaries, an Ottoman military division formed hundreds of years before during the reign of Orhan, the second Sultan. Once considered elite corps famed for discipline and order, in their later days the Janissaries hindered military reform. On top of this, numerous wars with land-hungry Russia, including the Crimean War (1853-1856), weakened the empire, as did the many wars fought with the encroaching European nations. The final nail in coffin was the decision of the empire to side with the Central Powers during World War I, which led to the dissolution of the empire when Germany lost the war.

1. What is the function of paragraph 4 in the passage?
   - (A) It relates the fall of Ottoman Empire to natural environments.
   - (B) It presents another cause of the decline of Ottomans.
   - (C) It shows the results of economic situation mentioned in the preceding paragraph.
   - (D) It highlights why the Janissaries were important in the Ottoman Empire.

2. The word encroaching in paragraph 4 is closest in meaning to
   - (A) leading
   - (B) shunning
   - (C) mounting
   - (D) invading

Answers p. 11

US History

014

Post WWII housing development
2차 세계대전 후 주택발달

2차 세계대전 이후, 경제가 어려워지면서 사람들이 합리적이고 저렴한 주거형태housing를 선호하게 됨에 따라 획일적인 모양의 저렴한 조립식 주택cheap assembling house이 탄생했다. 조립라인assembly-line에서 제품을 조립하듯 노동자가 자신이 가진 특정 기술만 담당하는 전문화specialization된 방식을 건축에 사용함으로써 조립식 주택건축은 많은 비용을 절감시킬 수 있었다.

Cape Cod House

미국 북동부 뉴잉글랜드의 케이프 코드Cape Cod 지역의 주택들이 이러한 조립식 주택의 대표적인 예이다. 이 집들은 하나의 주요 배관a major plumbing이 온 집안에 연결되어 있어 추가적인 배관작업 비용을 줄일 수 있었으며 주방과 거실living room이 길 방향으로 향해 있어서 부모가 쉽게 아이들이 노는 모습을 관찰할 수 있었다. 이 주택은 금세 인기를 얻어 전국으로 퍼져나갔지만 사람들은 획일적인ubiquitous 구조에 식상해 하기 시작하면서 랜치하우스Ranch House가 도입되었다. 그러나 랜치하우스는 케이프 코드 하우스와 큰 차이점이 없었으며 차이점이라 할 수 있던 것은 널빤지shingles로 만든 지붕과 거실을 집 뒤쪽에 배치하고 뒷마당 쪽에 큰 창문을 달아 밖을 내다볼 수 있게 함으로서 좀더 가족의 사생활privacy에 큰 중점을 둔 것이었다.

Ranch House

필수어휘

- real estate 부동산
- assembly-line 조립라인
- specialization 세분화
- plumbing 배관
- waste stack 배수 수직관
- sprouting 자라나는
- ubiquitous 어디에나 있는
- offshoot 파생물
- shingles 널빤지 지붕

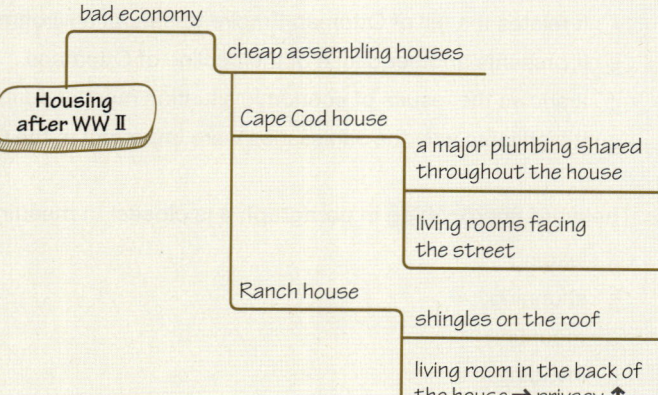

Mini Practice

Listen to part of a lecture in an economics class. 🎧 Ch1_04

1. Which of the following are the characteristics of Cape Cod homes? Click on 2 answers.
   - Ⓐ The living room has a picture window.
   - Ⓑ The bathroom is on the same side of the house as the kitchen.
   - Ⓒ The kitchen and bathroom have independent plumbing.
   - Ⓓ The living room faces the street.

2. According to the professor, why did Levitt and Sons introduce the "Ranch House"?
   - Ⓐ People demanded larger backyards.
   - Ⓑ People found the homogeneity of the houses unsatisfying.
   - Ⓒ Levitt was trying to change the housing trend.
   - Ⓓ Americans were bored with the roof design of the Cape Cod homes.

Listening Script

Professor: Okay, imagine it's the late 1940s, just after World War II. The economy is shrinking and the price of living is rising for ordinary people. Americans start demanding a place to live they could actually afford. So, a popular real estate company, Levitt and Sons, who were famous for building really up-scale, luxury homes, initiated a project to build cheap homes by making all the houses the same. In other words, the houses could be built in an assembly-line fashion; they had workers with specific skills go to each house in order, house to house, doing their particular job. That kind of specialization was one way of reducing cost. In addition, the materials they used in the construction were uniform throughout all of the homes they built. Basically, every house had the same design for both the interior and exterior.

For example, consider the "Cape Cod" home. The name comes from characteristics that the design has in common with homes in New England, in the northeastern United States, characterized by houses in the Cape Cod area. In these homes, the bathroom is right behind the kitchen, on one side of the house, allowing all of the major plumbing including the waste stack to be shared, thus reducing the cost of construction by eliminating extra plumbing. Additionally, it was a very family-oriented design, with the kitchen and living room facing the street, so mothers could watch their children at play while doing housework or just relaxing in the living area.

As you might imagine, these sorts of houses quickly became popular, and soon they were sprouting up all over the country, from one coast to the other. But it wasn't long before people started demanding changes from the ubiquitous structure, and so very soon an offshoot design, the "Ranch House" was introduced. But although the name differs, the other differences are fairly subtle. The only major difference between the two designs, aside from a different choice of shingles, is that the Ranch House placed the living room in the back of the house, proving a view of the backyard area through a large window. This provided the convenience of the Cape Cod, while placing greater emphasis on the family's privacy.

Answers p. 12

World History

015

Roman aqueducts
고대로마의 송수로

> 로마문명은 건축, 예술, 정치 등 많은 분야에서 토플에 출제되었다. 그 중에서도 특히 정원, 빌라, 판테온, 콜로세움 등과 같은 건축에 관련된 주제가 빈번하게 출제되니 배경지식을 꼭 알아두도록 하자.

로마 건축은 이탈리아 반도 내 에트루스칸 전통과 그리스 헬레니즘의 두 갈래의 뿌리가 있다. 에트루스칸 전통으로부터는 실용정신 practicality을, 그리스 헬레니즘으로부터는 고전주의 classicism를 각각 물려받았다.

실용성은 로마건축을 구성하는 한 축이었다. 로마의 주요 건축물 architecture인 시장, 목욕탕, 바실리카 등에는 그 실용정신이 잘 반영되어 있다. 또한 수로와 다리, 십자가로, 군사기지 등과 같은 토목 인프라 또한 로마 문명을 탄생시킨 가장 기본적인 물리적 매개였다. 특히, 로마제국에는 수십, 수백만 명이 거주하는 대도시가 많았다. 그러나 이 도시들은 물의 원천으로부터 멀리 떨어져있었기 때문에 물을 공급하기 위한 수로 aqueducts를 건설해야 했다. 그들은 우선 도시 주변의 샘물 spring과 호수 lake에서 물을 끌어들인 후, 침전지에서 불순물을 제거한 다음, 로마 시 주위에 위치한 각각의 저수조로 물을 모으고, 다시 여러 종류의 파이프를 통해 공중욕장, 주택, 공공건축물 등으로 급수하였다. 이렇게 인공수로를 통해 급수된 물의 양은 오늘날 인구 150만의 도시 급수량에 해당하였다고 한다. 물을 끌어오는 과정에서 수로가 골짜기나 개천을 지나는 부분에는 아치형의 수도교가 건설되었는데 이러한 아치형태의 아케이드 arcade는 고대 로마의 토목공사 civil engineering 중에서도 가장 뛰어난 성과로 평가되고 있다.

필수어휘
- □ functional 기능적인
- □ aqueduct 송수로
- □ channels 수로
- □ slope 경사
- □ lead 납
- □ earthenware 도기
- □ arcade 아케이드 (아치형 모양의 건축물)

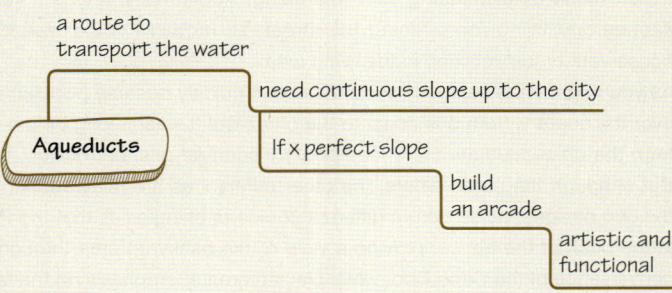

Mini Practice

Listen to part of a lecture in an ancient history class. 🎧 Ch1_05

1. According to the professor, when would an arcade be constructed?
   - Ⓐ when engineers determine that the ground is unsuitable for tunnels
   - Ⓑ if the Romans demand more artistic beauty
   - Ⓒ when the spring is too far from the city
   - Ⓓ if there is a dip or valley between the spring and the city

2. What is one advantage of building tunnels and trenches?
   - Ⓐ The land above can be used for other purposes.
   - Ⓑ More water can be transported compared to other methods.
   - Ⓒ They keep the water fresh.
   - Ⓓ They get the water across dips in the land.

Listening Script

Professor: Many ancient civilizations contributed to the development of important technologies, and the Romans were no exception. Today, I'll focus on one particular development that is both artistic and functional, the aqueduct. Aqueducts were the Romans' water distribution system. They are channels which bring water from sources like underground springs, to locations where it's needed, such as cities. The Roman Empire had many large cities, so without the aqueducts bringing needed water, the empire probably wouldn't have been able to spread so far or support such highly populated cities.

To build aqueducts, Roman engineers would first find a source of fresh water of good quality, typically an underground spring. Then the engineers had to find an ideal route to transport the water. A good route would have a gentle, continuous slope downward to the city. Obviously, therefore, the source had to be higher than the destination, because the system relied solely on gravity to move the water.

The aqueducts consisted mainly of a series of pipes, typically made of lead or earthenware. In order to maintain the slope, tunnels and trenches would need to be dug for the pipes. This had the added advantage that most of the aqueducts were hidden, and land above it could still be used for other purposes. But what if there wasn't a perfect slope available? What if the land included a river valley or a sharp dip? Well, if the aqueduct was built down along that slope, it would be hard to get the water back up again on the other side. So in this case, Romans would build an arcade. That's the iconic series of arches that most people imagine when they think of Roman aqueducts, even though most of the aqueduct is hidden underground. An open channel, usually concrete, runs along the top of the arches, allowing a constant slope to be maintained for the water despite variations in the height of the land. The arcades are where engineering meets art, both artistic and functional.

Answers p. 12

US History

016

The Columbian exchange
콜럼버스의 교환

1492년, 콜럼버스의 신대륙New worlds 발견으로 시작된 유럽세계와 신세계의 만남은, 쌍방에 큰 충격과 변화를 주었다. 황금의 땅을 찾기 위해 유럽에서 온 정복자conqueror들은 산맥을 횡단하고 열대우림rain forest을 파괴하며 미지의 세계를 탐험했고 그 결과 아메리카의 광대한 지역이 스페인과 포르투갈의 식민지colony가 되었다. 그 과정에서 수많은 원주민들이 학살당했으며 정복자들은 인구가 격감한 지역에 쉽게 자신들의 도시를 세울 수 있었다. 그리하여 신대륙에 스페인과 포르투갈의 풍토와 경관을 닮은 라틴아메리카 세계가 출현하게 되었다.

신대륙은 유럽의 문명과 기술로 크게 변화했다. 청동bronze, 철iron, 소, 말, 양, 돼지 등 새로운 금속과 가축livestock들이 등장했고 밀가루flour, 쌀, 설탕, 커피 등이 들어왔다. 농작물 외에 천연두smallpox나 홍역measles과 같은 전염병이 건너오게 되면서 토착민의 수가 급격히 감소하였으며 유럽인들의 가축방목과 무분별한 산림파괴deforestation는 유럽에서 들여온 잡초weeds가 신대륙에 번성할 수 있는 환경을 조성하였다.

이와 반대로 유럽세계도 신대륙으로부터 많은 영향을 받았다. 옥수수, 감자, 고구마, 토마토, 호박, 고추, 파인애플, 파파야, 피넛, 담배tobacco 등의 재배식물이 신세계로부터 들여왔고 나중에 감자는 유럽의 식량위기를 구하는 주요작물로 자리잡게 되었다. 아메리카 대륙에서 유출된 금, 은은 유럽 각국에 유출되어 화폐가격을 하락시켰으며, 신대륙에서의 수요가 유럽의 여러 산업을 성장시키면서 영국의 산업혁명industrial revolution을 일으킨 하나의 자극이 되었다. 콜럼버스의 교환Columbian exchange이라 불리는 이 구대륙과 신대륙과의 교환은 토플에서 자주 출제된 주제 중 하나이니 양쪽이 어떤 물자들을 주고 받았는지 간단하게 알아 두도록 하자.

필수어휘

- mutual 상호적인
- weeds 잡초
- non-cultivated 경작되지 않은
- vice versa 반대로도 마찬가지인
- disruptive 파괴적인
- cattle 소
- deforestation 삼림벌채

The Columbian exchange — Environmental disruption by European settlers by overgrazing, deforestation

weeds ↑ (transplanted from Europe to America)

Listening

Mini Practice

Listen to part of a lecture in an American history class. 🎧 Ch1_06

1. According to the professor, which two factors created favorable conditions for transplantation of weeds from Europe? **Click on 2 answers.**

    Ⓐ European settlement caused environmental damage that was favorable for weeds.
    Ⓑ Temperate regions are favorable environments for weed growth.
    Ⓒ European weeds are more opportunistic.
    Ⓓ It was due to overgrazing by livestock and removal of forests.

2. What is one possible explanation the professor gives for why American weeds did not become established in Europe during the Columbian Exchange?

    Ⓐ The different soil type in Europe was not suitable for weed growth.
    Ⓑ There were fewer livestock roaming freely in Europe.
    Ⓒ Destruction of land and forests was less widespread in Europe compared to the Americas.
    Ⓓ Seeds from American weeds were rarely transported to Europe.

Listening Script

Professor: The exploration and settlement of the Americas, starting with Christopher Columbus and followed by other Europeans, led to mass migration between the eastern and western hemispheres, not only of people, but also of many plant and animal species. Although Christopher Columbus didn't actually do very much in this process, it still came to be associated with his name: the Columbian Exchange. An interesting and somewhat odd aspect of this exchange is that, while in many categories it was clearly mutual, in the case of weeds, it seemed to be entirely one-way.

Okay, so, to start with, we should be specific about what we mean when we say weeds. In this case, we're talking about a kind of non-cultivated plant, usually one that's unwanted, and that can reproduce quite rapidly, even under harsh conditions, thereby easily growing in environments that have been recently disturbed. So, as I said, weeds were transplanted from Europe to temperate areas of North and South America. But not vice versa. Why would they move only in one direction?

Most likely, it's related to the nature of those initial European settlements. Those early settlements were highly disruptive to the environment. There were a lot of cattle, horses and other European livestock just roaming around and grazing the local grasslands, in many cases overgrazing. Further environmental disruption was caused by cutting down or burning forests where the settlers intended to plant crops. This over-grazing by European livestock, combined with rapid deforestation really created ideal conditions for opportunistic plant species, many of which came over with the livestock themselves, since the seeds could be easily stick in the hair of the cattle, horses and other animals. As a result, there were lots of opportunities for these seeds to come to the Americas, and once here, they had a fantastic environment in which to gain a foothold, compared to the land in Europe.

Answers p. 13

Archaeology

★★★
017

The discovery of Mayan ruins
마야 문명의 발굴

스탠포드대 패트릭헌트 교수는 「역사를 다시 쓴 10가지 발견」이라는 저서를 통해 인류 역사에 지대한 영향을 미친 아래와 같은 고고학적 발굴 10가지를 꼽았다.

1. 세 가지의 언어로 쓰여져 이집트 상형문자의 비밀을 밝힌 로제타 스톤the Rosetta Stone
2. 신화로만 알려진 트로이Troy가 실제 존재하는 곳이라는 발견
3. 메소포타미아 문명의 열쇠가 된 아시리아 도서관Nineveh's Assyrian Library
4. 투탕카멘 무덤King Tut's Tomb
5. 잉카문명의 천재적인 증거물이자 역사의 증거인 마추픽추Machu Picchu
6. 폼페이Pompeii
7. 성서 연구의 핵심이 된 사해문서the Dead Sea Scrolls
8. 전설의 아틀란티스라 알려진 티라섬Thera
9. 오스트랄로피테쿠스의 진실을 밝혀준 올두바이 협곡Olduvai Gorge
10. 진시황릉과 병마용the Tomb of 10,000 Warriors

위의 발견들 대부분은 토플시험에도 출제된 적이 있는 주제들이므로 각각 발굴의 흥미로운 점에 대해 알아놓는 것이 좋겠다.

마야문명의 갑작스러운 증발은 언제나 미스터리였다. 고고학자 빌 사투르노Bill Saturno는 마야문명 발굴 지역에 위치한 동굴에서 마야인들이 그려놓은 벽화Mayan murals를 우연히 발견하게 되면서 더 많은 동굴 및 유적ruins을 찾고자 하였다. 그는 미국 NASA로부터 적외선 사진infrared picture을 지원받아 본격적으로 마야 유적을 탐색하던 중 어떤 나무들이 사진에 주변 나무와는 다르게 노란색을 띠고 있음을 발견하게 된다. 조사 결과 나무 색의 차이는 마야 유적지의 부식decay으로 인한 미소서식환경microenvironment 때문인 것으로 밝혀졌다. 즉, 회반죽lime plaster으로 만들어진 유적지가 부식되면서 탄산칼슘calcium carbonate을 배출하는데 이 물질이 나뭇잎 속으로 스며들어 적외선 사진상에서 노란색을 띠었던 것이다. 따라서 빌 사투르노는 이러한 적외선 사진을 통해 마야문명의 위치 및 범위를 파악할 수 있게 되었으며 미스터리로 여겨 온 마야문명 증발의 원인도 곧 밝혀질 것이라 기대되고 있다.

필수어휘
- thrive 번성하다
- baffled 당혹한
- dig site 유적지
- speculate 추측하다
- painstaking 힘든, 공들인
- infrared satellite imagery 적외선 위성 사진
- vegetation 초목
- splotch 얼룩, 반점
- microenvironment 미소서식환경
- ruins 폐허, 유적, 잔해
- lime plaster 회반죽
- calcium carbonate 탄산칼슘

Listening

Mini Practice

Listen to part of a lecture in an archaeology class. Ch1_07

1. How did Bill Saturno find the cave containing Mayan murals?
   - Ⓐ He used a satellite map prepared by NASA.
   - Ⓑ He stumbled upon it by chance while resting.
   - Ⓒ His team determined the area was a different temperature.
   - Ⓓ Plant leaves near the cave were yellow due to uptake of calcium carbonate.

2. What do researchers think might cause the yellow areas in the infrared images?
   - Ⓐ Chemicals from the Mayan ruins
   - Ⓑ Environmental damage in the surrounding area
   - Ⓒ Yellow paint used in the creation of the murals
   - Ⓓ The lime plaster in the buildings retaining heat from the sun

Listening Script

Professor: Mayan civilization once thrived in Central America, boasting a population of 1.5 million at its peak. And then, perplexingly, they all just disappeared, and despite years of searching for clues to the cause, scientists are still baffled by it. Bill Saturno and his team of archeologists lived in the jungles of Guatemala for several years, trying to discover something, anything, related to Mayan civilization. One day in 2001, after a long day surveying a possible dig site deep in the Guatemalan rain forest, Saturno went into a cave to get some rest and escape the hot sun. When he switched on his flashlight, he was surprised to discover numerous Mayan murals on the walls. It turns out that the site had once been a thriving center of Mayan culture for over a century. Incredible, right? Saturno speculated that there must be more temples and caves, but the search was slow and painstaking. Well, it just so happened that NASA heard about the discovery, and offered to provide Saturno with infrared satellite imagery of the area surrounding that site. The images are all in reds, blues and yellows, you know, based on temperature. Interestingly, wherever the trees and other vegetation had grown over the Mayan ruins, a yellow splotch showed up in the picture. And there were a lot of yellow splotches! Using this image as a guide, Saturno was able to walk right up to a Mayan temple. Researchers are still trying to figure out why those specific colors show up in the infrared. Some think maybe it's a microenvironment resulting from the decay of the ruins. The chemicals such as lime plaster and calcium carbonate from the ruins might be taken up into the plant leaves. Well, now, for the first time ever, we can see the big picture, and understand just how far the Maya expanded their cities.

Answers p. 13

US History

018

The statue of George Washington
조지 워싱턴 동상

미국의 초기 역사에서 빠지지 않고 토플에 등장하는 주제는 미국을 건국하고 헌법을 창시한 'founding fathers'에 대한 이야기이다. 이 건국의 아버지들이 누구를 포함하는지, 초기 미국 헌법의 특징과 미국독립전쟁을 촉발시킨 사건은 무엇이었는지 반드시 알아두도록 하자.

필수어휘

- □ hesitant 주저하는, 망설이는
- □ apparent 명백한
- □ plow 쟁기
- □ larger than life 실제보다 과장된
- □ superhuman 초인적인
- □ immortal 불멸의

미국 건국의 아버지들founding fathers은 독립 전쟁과 관련된 미국의 역사 초기의 5명의 대통령들을 포함해, 독립선언에 참여하고 헌법을 창시한 정치인들을 일컫는 표현이다. 1787년 5월 25일부터 3개월 반 동안 필라델피아에서 헌법을 제정하기 위해 제헌회의constitutional convention에 참석한 로드아일랜드를 제외한 주의 대표 55인이 바로 '건국의 아버지들'이라고 일컬어 진다. 역사학자 Richard B. Morris는 이들 중에서도 아래 7명을 미국 건국의 핵심 인물이라 여겼다.

1. 존 애덤스John Adams: 2대 대통령. 1대에는 부통령을 역임했으며 그의 아들 존 퀸시 애덤스는 6대 대통령을 지낸 미국 최초의 부자(父子) 대통령임.
2. 벤자민 프랭클린Benjamin Franklin: 미국의 100달러 지폐에 그려진 인물, 프랑스 군과의 동맹에 있어 중요한 역할을 함.
3. 알렉산더 해밀턴Alexander Hamilton: 외국에서 태어나 대통령이 될 수 없었으며 워싱턴 정부 시절 재무부 장관으로 재직함, 10달러 지폐에 그려진 인물.
4. 존 제이John Jay: 대법원 초대 장관, 뉴욕 주지사 등을 지냄.
5. 토마스 제퍼슨Thomas Jefferson: 3대 대통령. 계몽사상을 역설한 18세기 미국 최고의 르네상스 맨(지성인)으로 여겨지며 가장 존경 받는 대통령 중 한 명으로 추앙 받음. 2달러 지폐에 그려진 인물.
6. 제임스 매디슨James Madison: 4대 대통령. 헌법의 주 저자로 헌법의 아버지라 불림.
7. 조지 워싱턴George Washington: 초대 대통령, 미국 독립 전쟁에서 대륙군 총사령관으로 활동하여 처음에는 국왕과 같은 군주로 인식됨, 처음이자 마지막으로 미국에서 만장일치로 대통령에 선출된 인물. 1달러 지폐에 그려진 주인공.

Mini Practice

Listen to part of a lecture in an American history class. 🎧 Ch1_08

1. Why was the Greenough statue not received well by the public?
   - Ⓐ It too closely resembled the Greek god Zeus.
   - Ⓑ It was located on the east lawn rather than intended placement on the Rotunda.
   - Ⓒ The lack of clothing was considered offensive.
   - Ⓓ It was seen as politically controversial.

2. What was Houdon trying to express through his statue?
   - Ⓐ To show the immortal nature of Washington's legacy
   - Ⓑ To demonstrate Washington's poor health through the depiction of the walking stick
   - Ⓒ To emphasize his role as a father over his roles as a president and general
   - Ⓓ To depict him in the style of the Enlightenment

Listening Script

Professor: It's very interesting to consider the variety of different styles in which a historical figure is depicted by artists. Let's consider George Washington. When you think of him, what image springs to mind? For many people, that image is the father of the nation. That's somewhat ironic, because he was actually quite hesitant about his role and very nearly failed as our nation's leader. This aspect of George Washington is apparent in the statue of him by Jean-Antoine Houdon. Houdon, a sculptor of the Enlightenment, depicted George Washington holding a walking stick, with a plow at his feet. The image is more one of a father than a president or general, which matches the way George Washington himself preferred to be seen. In fact, later in life he actually chose to return to Virginia to live as a farmer.

In contrast, some artists depicted Washington as larger than life, almost superhuman. Among them was Horatio Greenough, who was commissioned in 1832 by Congress to create a marble statue for the Capitol Rotunda to commemorate the centennial of Washington's birth. When the statue arrived in the capital city in 1841, it stirred criticism and controversy. Greenough had attempted to glorify Washington as immortal and super-human, showing him standing above the law. In doing this, he had followed the design of a classical Greek statue of the god Zeus, and some Americans saw this half-naked Washington as offensive or comical. Interestingly, Greenough's statue of Washington bears similarities to Robert Mills' original design for the Washington Monument, which was in the style of Greek revival. In 1843, Greenough's statue was moved to the east lawn of the Capitol, not far from the Patent Office, where Washington's clothes are on display, prompting some to joke that he was urgently reaching for his clothes. Finally, in 1908, Greenough's statue was transferred to the Smithsonian, and there it remained until 1964, when it was moved again to the basement of new Museum of History and Technology, where it has been located ever since.

Answers p. 14

Archaeology

★★ 019

Underwater archaeology
수중고고학

수중고고학underwater archaeology은 해적선 등이 잃어버린 보물뿐만 아니라 해수면 상승으로 인해 물에 잠긴 인간거주지의 발굴excavation에 대해서도 다루는 학문이다. 이러한 발굴 중 1628년 스웨덴 인근 해협에서 침몰한 Vassa라고 불리는 배의 발굴은 많은 대중들의 이목을 끌었다. Vassa는 스웨덴 해안에서 출항한 후 얼마 되지 않아 전복된capsized 배였으며 당시 많은 장식과 유물artifacts, 대포cannon 및 그 당시 선원들의 일상에 대한 상세한 사진이 발굴되었다. 난파의 주된 원인으로는 배에 있던 대포가 풀려 굴러다니면서 배가 균형을 잃고 침몰했다는 주장이 제기되었으나 자세한 연구 끝에 밝혀진 원인은 다음과 같았다. 당시에는 선박의 중심을 낮추고 외력에 의해 배가 기울어졌을 때 복원력을 높이기 위해서 하부에 무거운 돌ballast을 매달아 놓았는데, Vassa는 다른 배보다 선박이 높은 편이어서 더 많이 돌들이 필요했다. 그러나 그 돌이 충분하지 않은 상태에서 강풍을 만난 Vassa는 쉽게 전복되어 버린 것이다. Vassa는 물속에서 300년 이상 있었던 것에 비해 보존상태가 매우 우수했는데 그 이유는 심해의 차가운 온도가 목재를 부식시키는 좀조개shipworm들의 활동을 억제했기 때문이다. 그러나 선박이 인양된 후, 목재 속의 물이 빠른 속도로 증발하면서 선박을 보존하는 것이 힘들어졌고 폴리에틸렌 글리콜(PEG)을 뿌려서 배를 코팅하고 보호하고자 했던 연구원들의 노력에도 불구하고 Vassa는 언제든 무너지기 쉬운 불안정한 상태가 되었다. 따라서 Vassa의 보존은 아직도 진행중이라고 전해진다.

필수어휘

- artifacts 유물, 유적
- shipwreck 난파선
- maiden voyage 첫 항해
- extent 범위
- fitted with ~을 갖춘
- cannon 대포
- capsize 뒤집히다
- ballast 바닥짐 (배나 열기구에 무게를 주고 중심을 잡기 위해 바닥에 놓는 무거운 물건)
- tip over 뒤집히다, 기울다
- shipworm (패류) 좀조개
- burrowing 굴을 파는
- cellulose 섬유소
- rotted away 썩어 없어진
- polyethylene glycol(PEG) 폴리에틸렌 글리콜
- brittle 약한, 깨지기 쉬운

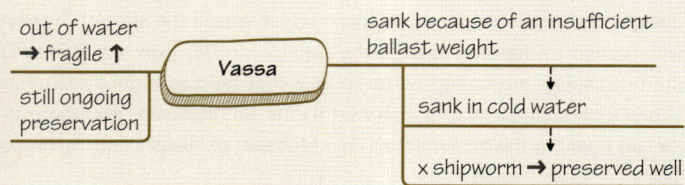

Listening

Mini Practice

Listen to part of lecture in an archaeology class. 🎧 Ch1_09

1. What was significant about the items discovered on board the Vassa?
   - Ⓐ Archaeologists learned about the warship technology of the period.
   - Ⓑ They painted a detailed picture of the daily routine of sailors at that time.
   - Ⓒ Sweden spent a lot of money on the artwork on the ship.
   - Ⓓ The Vassa sank during its very first voyage.

2. According to the professor, what was the actual reason why the Vassa sank?
   - Ⓐ The cannons were not properly tied down, so they rolled around caused the boat to tip over.
   - Ⓑ The ship was very tall, with a high center of gravity and lacking sufficient weight at the bottom.
   - Ⓒ The ballast that was used was made from the wrong material.
   - Ⓓ The sea water was extremely cold, and damaged the wooden structure of the ship.

Listening Script

Professor: As we've discussed before, the equipment needed for underwater archaeology is expensive to buy and maintain, so there's a big focus on making valuable finds, like artifacts and shipwrecks. One find that was important was the Vassa, a Swedish warship that sank off the coast of Sweden during its maiden voyage in 1628. The shipwreck was discovered by an archaeologist in 1956. It took five years to figure out how to raise the ship to the surface. When it finally emerged from the water, many artifacts were found on board, like games, tools, watches, and even cannons (remember, it was a warship!) It really showed the extent of Sweden's power and wealth, while at the same time showing what everyday life was like for the sailors of the era. So why did a ship, setting out in fair weather and fitted with the most modern technology available at that time, sink on its very first trip?

One theory was that the cannons had not been secured properly, and rolled around the deck as the ship moved, caused the ship to capsize suddenly. But the actual reason was that, because the Vassa was very tall and top heavy, it needed a lot of ballast. And unfortunately, the Vassa didn't have sufficient ballast, which meant that its center of gravity was too high, causing it to simply tip over. The ship sank in extremely cold water, which prevented shipworms from burrowing into and destroying the wood, so the ship was well preserved. But it was in water, so the wood became saturated with water and the hard cellulose in it rotted away, with water taking its place. That meant that out of the water, it was very tricky to preserve it. Researchers therefore gradually sprayed the boat with a waxy substance called polyethylene glycol, or PEG, to coat and protect it. They sprayed the Vassa with PEG for seventeen years! And as a result, the wood became quite brittle, and the ship quite fragile. So the preservation of the Vassa is really still an ongoing process.

Answers p. 15

US History

★★★

020

Works Progress Administration
공공사업촉진국

1929년에 불어 닥친 경제대공황Great depression을 극복하기 위해 미국은 뉴딜New Deal 정책을 시행하였다. 이때 만든 국가기관government institute 중 가장 비중이 컸던 단체는 공공산업진흥국Works Progress Administration(이하 WPA)이었다. 이 기관은 국가사업을 통해 많은 실업자들에게 일자리를 제공해 주었으며 특히 후버댐Hoover Dam과 같은 대규모 국가사업과는 맞지 않은 능력을 가진 예술, 문화 종사자에게 직접적인 정부지원을 실현한 최초의 국가기관이라는 점에서 큰 의의를 지닌다.

WPA의 여러 프로젝트들은 대규모 국가예산government funds을 예술공연, 작품전시, 음악회 및 예술관련 교육에 유치하여 예술문화산업을 육성시키고자 하였다. 그 결과 대량의 미국 예술역사와 음악들이 문서화documentation되었으며 다양한 공연활동으로 주요 도시에 있는 극장이 활성화되었다. 또한 국가차원에서 출판사를 설립하여 정기간행물periodicals을 발행함으로써 수천 명의 작가, 기자, 도서관 사서들에게 일자리를 제공해주었으며 오래된 정부문서들과 공공기록들의 보존 또한 가능케 되었다. 그러나 그 후 미국이 2차 세계대전에 참가하면서 많은 수의 일자리가 생기게 되자 WPA는 완전히 해체되었지만 미국 역사상 최초로 예술문화 종사자들에게 국가적 차원의 지원을 아끼지 않았다는 점에서 가장 훌륭한 정부정책사업 중 하나로 평가되고 있다.

필수어휘
- institute 기관, 도입하다
- administer 관리하다
- patronage 후원
- plummet 곤두박질치다
- unprecedent 전례가 없는
- patron 후원자
- theoretically 이론적으로
- humdrum 따분한
- murals 벽화

WPA — part of New Deal program
— support for art → hiring artists
— initiated many art programs & education

Listening

Mini Practice

Listen to part of a lecture in an American history class. 🎧 Ch1_10

1. What was the key difference between WPA-funded art and art produced prior to the Great Depression?
   - (A) The quality of the WPA funded art was considerably higher.
   - (B) Prior to the Great Depression, painting depicted times of satisfaction.
   - (C) Paintings produced during the Great Depression generally showed more realism and focused on social issues.
   - (D) Before the Great Depression, the government disapproved of paintings showing opposition of American life and society.

2. What is the relationship between Diego Rivera and the WPA?
   - (A) Diego Rivera's paintings appealed to a large, diverse group of people, bringing them together.
   - (B) The WPA got the idea for their mural project from seeing Diego Rivera's original murals from Mexico.
   - (C) Diego Rivera used his paintings to communicate his opinions, much like the WPA depicted their feelings about the government.
   - (D) Diego Rivera was representative of the diversity that the WPA was trying to achieve with their projects.

Listening Script

Professor: Okay, as you all know, the New Deal was a series of programs that the government instituted in order to stimulate economic recovery, in particular by providing employment. Among those programs, some of the most important ones were administered by the WPA, or, I should say, the Works Progress Administration. Now, with the collapse of the economy, you can imagine that patronage of the arts pretty much disappeared, and art sales plummeted. So the WPA did something unprecedented. They employed artists, writers, actors, painters, musicians, and so on, essentially stepping in as a patron for artisans where private patrons had disappeared. The government was actually paying writers and actors to write and perform. Can you imagine that? Of course, there was some political opposition to the use of government funds in such a way, but it's hard to argue with the results. Besides, the creation of many important works of art, the programs also gave rise to the creation of hundreds of new community-based art centers and studios, as well as art education centers for training the next generation of artists and writers.

Although the main reason for this patronage was economic, there were still strong cultural and political reasons for it too. The hope was that through the WPA artists, a sense of common culture and national unity could be produced, which, theoretically would restore confidence in democracy nationwide, not just in the system of government, but in the country itself. Leading up to the Great Depression, a lot of American painters had depicted the commonplace scenes, and humdrum realities of everyday life. But the Depression brought with it a greater concern for the impact of economics. Painters of the Depression era had a more realistic outlook and concentrated on social things, like joblessness and poverty. A lot of painters were influenced by the work of these politically aware artists. Among them, Diego Rivera, a Mexican-born painter whose large, bold works and murals clearly expressed strong political views, such as the support of workers' rights. It is said that his works partly inspired the WPA initiative. Roosevelt recognized how people were responding to Rivera's work, that it really brought people together, and so he sought to nourish that kind of attitude.

Answers p. 15

미국의 역사 (15C~21C)

15C

1. Colonial America
식민지 미국 (1492–1763)

- 1607년 영국 이주자들이 Virginia의 Jamestown에 정착하면서 영국 최초의 식민지 건설
- 1620년 청교도인들이 Mayflower호를 타고 지금의 Massachusetts에 상륙하여 Plymouth 식민지 건설
- 1700년대 흑인 노예 유입
- 1770년경 13개 식민지 설립

18C

2. Revolutionary Period
독립 전쟁 시기 (1764–1789)

- 영국정부의 법안을 통한 높은 세금 착취 (Stamp Act: 공문서와 신문 등에 대한 세금, Townshend Act: 영국수입품에 대한 세금, Tea Act: 차에 대한 세금)
- 영국과의 마찰 속에서 1773년 Boston Tea Party 발발, 혁명의 불씨마련
- 1776년 독립 선언 Declaration of Independence으로 미국의 독립 혁명 American Revolution 시작
- 1781년 영국의 항복으로 미국의 식민지는 주state로 명명되고 이들이 연합하여 미합중국United States of America을 이룸

3. The New Nation
새로운 국가 (1790–1828)

- 두 개의 정당, 연방당the Federalists과 공화당the Republicans 출현
- 당시 대통령 Thomas Jefferson의 권한 아래 미국은 서부로 영토확장
- 1812년 2차 독립 전쟁War of 1812 발발 3년간 지속
- 전후 국가주의nationalism가 성장했으나 노예제도를 둘러 싼 갈등 심화

19C

4. Western Expansion & Reform
서부 개척과 개혁 (1829–1859)

- 서부개척지frontier로 많이 이주하여 국내시장을 확대시킴
- 이념적 자유liberty와 평등equality의 의미가 확장되어 노예제도 반대자 및 여성들 사회 참여권에 대한 요구 증가
- 1848년 서부 금광의 발견으로 골드러시가 시작되어 캘리포니아 인구 급증

5. Civil War
남북 전쟁 (1860–1865)

- 유럽 이민자들의 유입으로 혼합 인종을 바탕으로 한 북부와 보수적이며 영국의 전통의 고수하던 남부와의 갈등이 심화됨
- 대규모 농장plantation이 경제의 바탕이 되어 노예 노동력slave labor이 필수적으로 필요한 남부와 척박한 기후와 땅으로 소규모 농장을 운영하여 노예의 필요성이 적은 북부와의 충돌
- 링컨대통령 당선 후 Civil War 발발, 북부의 승리로 노예제도 철폐

20C

21C

6. Reconstruction
재건의 시기 (1866–1889)

- 전후 정치적, 사회적 개혁으로 교통, 도시 및 공업이 발달함
- 철강산업의 발달로 서부를 잇는 철도railway가 탄생하며 Rockefeller와 Andrew Carnegie와 같은 재력가가 생겨남
- 이 시기에 필요한 노동력 보완을 위해 아일랜드, 독일 등에서 이민자 증가

7. Progressive Era
진보의 시기 (1890–1913)

- 1895년 쿠바에서 스페인의 독재에 대한 항쟁이 일어났을 때, 미국은 스페인과의 전쟁에서의 승리로 필리핀, 하와이에 대한 주권을 확보하게 됨
- 비약적인 경제, 사회적 발전으로 세계 중심 국가로 성장

8. Great War & Depression
세계 대전과 공황 (1914–1945)

- 1914년 발발한 1차 세계대전 후 외교적으로 고립주의isolationism 이념 확산
- 전 후 계속된 호경기 속에서 주식 투자가 성행하고 과대 투기가 유행하여 결국 1929년 10월 뉴욕 주식시장의 주가 폭락을 계기로 대공황Great Depression이 일어나고 이는 곧 세계공황으로 번짐
- 1932년 Roosevelt 대통령의 New Deal 정책으로 자본주의의 수정과 정부의 권한이 축소됨
- 1941년 2차 세계 대전 참전으로 대공황 종식
- 1945년 독일의 항복과 Hiroshima와 Nagasaki에 원자 폭탄nuclear weapon 투하 후 미국과 연합군의 승리로 전쟁 종식

9. Modern Era
냉전 시기 이후 (1946–present)

- 베트남과 한국전쟁 등에 가담하면서 냉전시대의 대표적인 영향력을 가진 국가가 됨
- 과학 기술의 발달로 우주 탐사와 여성 인권이 발전함
- 러시아와 동유럽의 공산권의 몰락의 계기로 세계 제 1의 국가로 자리매김

Chapter 2. Arts

Art Conservation
021-L
Archimedes palimpsest

Art History
022-R
Baroque art

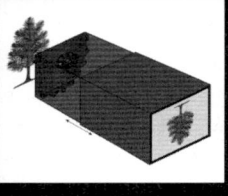

Photography
023-R
Camera obscura

Art
024-R
Commedia Dell'arte

Art History
025-L
Dadaism

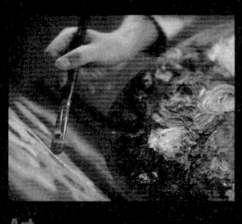

Art
026-R
Definition of art

Landscape Design
027-L
Design of public spaces in 19C

Photography
028-L
Dynamic range

Ancient art
029-R
Egypt art

Art
030-R
Etching

Film
031-R
Film

Literature
032-L
Gertrude Stein

Architecture
033-L
Houses in Renaissance era

Art
034-L
Linear and aerial perspective

Ancient Art
035-R
Navajo

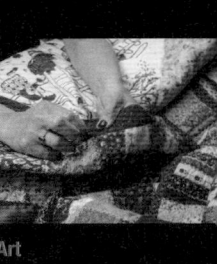

Art
036-R
Quilt

Art
037-R
Roman art

Music
038-L
Synthesizer

Music
039-L
The root of rap

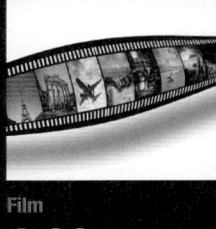

Film
040-L
Travel lecture

Art Conservation

021

Archimedes palimpsest
아르키메데스의 양피지

팰림스세스트palimpsest는 재활용 양피지이다. 아르키메데스Archimedes는 고대 그리스의 과학자 및 르네상스 이전에 태어난 가장 위대한 수학자로 손꼽히는 인물이다(목욕하다가 "유레카"를 외치며 옷도 안 입고 거리를 질주한 바로 그 학자이다). 아르키메데스 생존 당시에는 종이가 없었기 때문에 양피지에 기록을 하였는데 그 중에서도 혁명적인 수학 공식math equations들이 적힌 아르키메데스의 양피지는 수학뿐 아니라, 예술, 문화적으로도 굉장히 중요한 유물artifacts이다. 그러나 1229년 이 문서가 보관되어 있던 도서관의 필경사scribe가 그 당시 부족했던 양피지parchment를 아끼기 위해 아르키메데스의 공식이 적혀있는 양피지의 내용을 전부 지우고 자신의 책을 기록하는 실수를 범하였다. 게다가 14세기의 한 위조범forger은 이 문서를 더 낡아 보이게 하려고 그 위에 고대 문양ancient symbols과 그림paintings을 덧그려 놓고야 말았다. 과학자들은 자외선ultraviolet까지 이용하며 이 문서를 해독decipher하기 위해 노력을 기울였으나 거듭 실패하였고 이후 아르키메데스가 사용한 펜에 철iron이 함유되어 있었던 것이 밝혀지면서 X선x-ray을 이용하여 문서를 복구recover할 수 있었다.

필수어휘
- conservation 보존
- equation 공식
- palimpsest 원래의 글 일부 또는 전체를 지우고 다시 쓴 고대 문서
- parchment 양피지
- forger 위조범
- scratch off 긁혀 내다
- ultraviolet 자외선의
- stumped 어찌할 바를 모르게 된

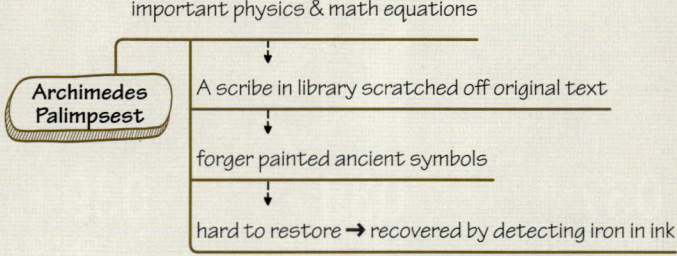

Mini Practice

Listen to part of a lecture in an art conservation class. 🎧 Ch2_01

1. The professor discusses various characteristics of the Archimedes Palimpsest. Indicate to which category each of the following statements belongs.

	True	False
(A) No other artifact is known in which Archimedes' method is recorded.		
(B) It is the first book ever written explaining that physics and mathematics are related disciplines.		
(C) An x-ray was used to detect traces of iron, which helped in restoring the original text.		
(D) The use of ultraviolet light contributed primarily to the ability to restore the text.		

2. According to the professor, why was the original writing scratched off the palimpsest?
   (A) Writing materials were scarce, and a scribe wanted to use the parchment for his own writing project.
   (B) The scientific community at the time disagreed with the conclusions of the original document.
   (C) A scribe decided to replace book's original claims with theories that were more universally accepted.
   (D) Due to a parchment shortage, a law was passed requiring very old books to be reused.

Listening Script

Professor: The restoration of badly damaged and old historical documents by conservationists can be a very long and difficult process. For instance, there was a severely damaged 2,000 year old palimpsest written by the Greek mathematician Archimedes that was re-discovered in Turkey in 1909. A palimpsest is a text, which has had the writings scraped or washed off so that it may be used again for other writing. This palimpsest is significant because it is the only known copy of Archimedes' description of his method and equation for calculating the volume of a sphere. Within this text, he described the relationships between math and physics that he used to create his famous equation.

The original text was stored in the Constantinople library until the year 1229 when a scribe repurposed the manuscript for his own book. Because of a parchment shortage during that period the scribe scraped off Archimedes' original writing and replaced it with his own writing. Later on during the 14th century, a forger found the book and wanted to try to sell it as an ancient text. The forger added additional 'ancient' paintings, symbols, and text over the scribe's writing in order to increase the value of the book.

When researchers had a chance to restore the book, they found it difficult to fully uncover all the previous writings with ultraviolet lights. Because the forger's additions and the scribe's writing were too thick, the ultraviolet light only worked on certain pages. They were stumped until they discovered that Archimedes' ink contained iron and one researcher suggested that they attempt to use an X-ray. By using the X-ray, they were able to read all of Archimedes' text that was previously hidden beneath all the other paintings and writings. With his diagrams and notes, the conservationists were able to translate the text and share with us this amazing discovery.

Answers p. 17

Art History

022

Baroque art
바로크 예술

서양 예술이 본격적으로 시작된 시기는 바로크 시대Baroque Era(1600-1750)이다. 바로크 예술은 정교함과 화려함과 감정 표현의 풍부함을 그대로 담고 있는데, 이러한 예술에 영향을 끼친 요소는 크게 세 가지로 볼 수 있다.

1. 반종교개혁counter-reformation
16-17세기 유럽에서 로마 가톨릭 교회의 쇄신을 요구했던 개혁운동 Reformation 후, 교회는 영국, 독일, 스칸디나비아 등의 신교도와 스페인, 프랑스, 이탈리아 등의 구교도로 분리되었다. 이에 가톨릭 교회는 잃어버린 세력을 되찾고자 예술을 이용해서 구교회에 대한 대중의 신뢰를 회복하여 다시 한 번 세력을 확장시키고자 했다. 그 당시의 예술 작품들은 신앙인들에게 감정적으로 호소할 수 있는 내용들을 다루고 있다.

2. 절대 군주absolute monarchy와의 통합
바로크 궁전과 교회는 중앙 집권화된 정부의 권력과 위엄, 귀족들의 화려함을 과시하기 위해 예술을 표현하였다. 조화와 균형을 강조하고 색감, 역동성을 부각시켜, 조각에는 비상하는 움직임과 다양한 복장을, 회화에서는 격동적이며 두드러진 명암대비를, 건축에는 곡선과 거대함massiveness, 내부의 화려함과 호화스러운 재료 사용을 나타내고 있다. 이러한 건축물의 대표적 사례가 베르사유 궁전이다. 한편, 그 당시 예술 후원자 역할을 했던 중산층은 그들의 사실주의가 예술에 표현되면서 그들만의 문화를 형성할 수 있었다.

3. 학문의 발달
바로크 시대의 과학 발전과 지구 탐사를 통한 자연에 대한 새로운 관심, 그리고 인간의 지적 한계를 확장시키려는 노력이 예술에 영향을 끼쳤다. 물리학과 천문학에 갈릴레오, 코페르니쿠스, 수학에 데카르트, 철학에 스피노자, 중력의 아이작 뉴튼 등의 위대한 학자들이 있어 이 시기에는 지동설과 함께 자연세계의 무궁무진함을 깨닫기 시작했다. 17세기의 풍경화에서 인간이 종종 거대한 자연의 작은 일부로 그려지는 모습에서 그들의 생각을 알 수 있으며, 인간 존재에 대한 시각 변화 등의 시대상을 예술에서 볼 수 있다.

필수어휘
- tonality 조성
- ornamentation 장식, 꾸밈
- instrumental 악기를 위한
- concerto grosso 합주 협주곡
- concertino 소 협주곡
- ripieno 전합주
- concerto 협주곡, 콘체르토

Baroque Music

Baroque music refers to a broad array of music, generally European in origin, which spans almost 200 years from the late 1580s until the early 1730s. Because of the large time span, it has been challenging for the musical world to classify or categorize artists within the Baroque genre. Typically, Baroque music is characterized by elaborate musical ornamentation, drama with heightened emotions, and an increased focus on instrumental music. It also ushered in the use of tonality, and fostered an expansion of musical techniques and forms.

One of the new forms that found its way into mainstream music was the *concerto grosso*, developed by a violinist and composer Arcangelo Corelli (1653-1713). He was extremely influential in the development of musical theory and pedagogy for the violin and diligently worked to pass on his musical forms to his students. He was especially known for the development of the aforementioned *concerto grosso*, where there are two groups of musicians. In the first and smaller group, also known as the *concertino*, the soloists and virtuosos present new ideas that are bolder and entirely thematically different from those presented by the larger group known as the *ripieno*. In contrast, the *ripieno* is a larger group typically made up of the rest of the orchestra, usually comprised of strings and a harpsichord. These groups would alternate between fast and slow tempos during the concerto to further enhance the elaborate nature of the musical piece.

In the latter part of the 16th century at the height of the Baroque period, a group of musicians in Florence, Italy developed a new art form and genre that would come to be known as opera. They drew their inspiration from the Classical Period, looking to ancient Greek and Roman theatre. Opera was a mixture of tragedy, comedy, and dramatic storytelling where the virtuosic voices of the artists were showcased through deeply compelling solos and duets. Opera introduced homophony, where the music and artist were in harmony as opposed to one concealing or overpowering the other. At first, opera was only intended for the nobility but soon its popularity led to the opening of public opera houses that catered to wealthy merchants and the lesser nobility. Opera at this time was extremely exciting and interesting because new and fantastic ideas were being introduced through experimental techniques and new musical forms.

1. The word They in paragraph 3 refers to
   - (A) art form and genre
   - (B) musicians
   - (C) operas
   - (D) theatres

2. In paragraph 3, it can be inferred that
   - (A) baroque music did not differ very much in ideas from those in the previous era
   - (B) baroque music was not completely received and enriched by musicians because it was so experimental
   - (C) in the 15th century opera was not developed by musicians yet
   - (D) baroque music completely abandoned the traditional music

Answers p. 18

Photography

★★★

023

Camera obscura
암상자

> 카메라 발달 역사가 토플에 출제된다. 다게레오타입과 초상화와 사진을 비교하는 내용이 중요하다!

암상자 camera obscura는 라틴어로 '어두운 방 dark chamber'을 의미하며 거울과 렌즈를 사용하여 외부 대상을 관찰하기 위해 작은 구멍을 뚫어 놓은 상자를 말한다. 어두운 암실 한 쪽에 작은 구멍 aperture을 만들어 광선을 통과시키면 구멍의 반대 면에 외부 정경이 뒤집어진 reverse 상태로 보이는 시각적 현상이 나타난다.

암상자의 역사는 암상자의 이 시각적 원리를 이해한 아리스토텔레스(384-322 BC)가 눈을 손상시키지 않으면서 채의 구멍이나 나뭇잎들 사이의 빈 공간을 통해 부분 일식을 관찰했던 것에서 시작되었다. 이렇듯 최초의 암상자는 일식을 조사하기 위한 용도의 큰 방이었다. 16세기에 암상자의 구멍 aperture에 볼록 렌즈 convex lens와 관찰 면에 상이 맺히도록 반사해주는 역할을 하는 거울 angled mirror을 더한 휴대용 작은 상자가 제작되었다. 이것은 17-18세기에 로버트 보일 Robert Boyle과 로버트 후크 Robert Hooke에 의해 좀더 이동이 편리한 상자로 발전되었고, 얀 베르메르 Jan Vermeer, 폴 샌드비 Paul Sandby 등의 여러 예술가들이 여행을 하면서 경치를 스케치하고 캔버스에 좀더 현실적 표현을 하기 위한 보조 기구로 사용되었다. 그 당시의 암상자는 직접 투사된 이미지를 영구적으로 남길 수는 없었지만, 19세기 초반에 발명된 현대적인 카메라의 원조였다. 그 후 사진의 아버지인 니에프스 Joseph Nicephore Niepce(1765-1833)가 감광판 light-sensitive plate(감광제를 바른 금속판을 말하며, 사진이나 사진 인쇄용 제판에 사용되는 판)을 만들었으며, 루이스 다게르 Louis Daguerre(1787-1851)가 은판을 사용하여 최초의 대중적 사진기술인 다게레오타입 Daguerreotype을 완성시켜 사진은 계속해서 발전할 수 있었다.

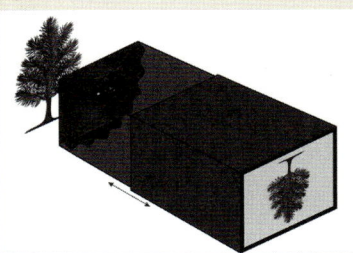

필수어휘

- depict 묘사하다, 그리다
- portrait 초상화
- lifelike 실물과 똑같은
- limner 초상화가
- posterity 후손
- itinerant 떠돌아 다니는
- status 지위, 위상
- portraiture 초상화 기법
- canvas 캔버스 천
- copper 구리
- fumigation 훈증
- saline 소금의
- solution 용액
- likeness 유사성, 닮음
- ambrotype 유리판 사진

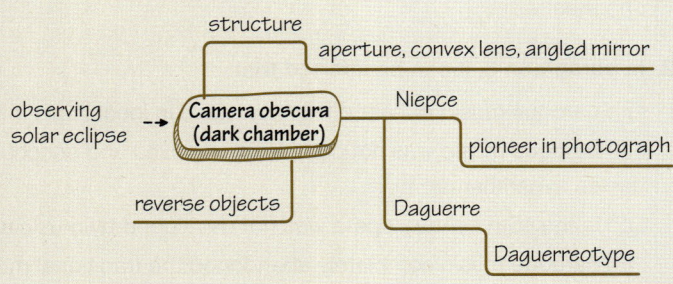

Portrait

A portrait captures the characteristics and even mood of a person's face through painting, photography or sculpture. The earliest surviving painted portraits of people are found in the Egyptian art adorning tombs and holy sites. In the late Middle Ages, artists began to create true portraits depicting their subjects with a more lifelike appearance.

In the early 19th century, wealthy families in colonial America hired limners to paint portraits of their families for the sake of posterity and as a symbol of social status and wealth. The term "limner" refers to a broad group of often nameless itinerant artists with little formal artistic training, who were mostly self-taught. Their painting styles were diverse and, based on their background, followed the Dutch style, the Elizabethan style or the style of the English baroque court. During the Colonial period, limners' portraiture was idealistic and did not truly represent the appearance or personality of the subject. They also focused on presenting the material wealth of the patron or sitter through the detailed representation of clothing and accessories.

After the invention of the daguerreotype by French artist, Louis Daguerre (1787-1851), the age of portrait photographs commenced. Daguerre was interested in capturing visual images and worked with another French scientist, Joseph Niépce on experiments that explored a variety of mechanical processes that could preserve images with a camera. After the death of Niépce, he discovered that a copper plate coated with iodized silver captured an image when exposed in a camera. This image was then developed by fumigation of mercury vapor. He also found out that finishing the process with a strong saline solution created a permanent image. His process spread and became the dominant method of taking photographs in the 1840s. Compared to painted portraiture, photographs were less expensive, were much easier to produce, and accurately captured the likeness of people. Because of these advantages, the daguerreotype spread rapidly and gained popularity across the United States. However, daguerreotypes required long exposure times and could only be taken indoors under soft lighting. As new inventions were made and new processes were discovered, the ambrotype eventually superseded the daguerreotype in the mid-1850s.

1. Why does the author say that daguerreotype could only be taken indoors in paragraph 3?
    - (A) to prove that ambrotypes were inferior
    - (B) to show that daguerreotype had a disadvantage
    - (C) to demonstrate why daguerreotype needed a long exposure time
    - (D) to exemplify how the daguerreotype was effective

2. The word superseded in paragraph 3 is closest in meaning to
    - (A) subsided
    - (B) invoked
    - (C) supplanted
    - (D) sustained

Answers p. 18

Art

024

Commedia dell'arte
코메디아 델라르테

코메디아 델라르테Commedia dell'arte는 기술arte을 가진 사람들이 연기하는 희극commedia이란 의미로 이탈리아에서 16-18세기에 유행했다. 5-10명 정도로 구성된 극단이 지방을 순회하며 공연하는 형태로, 후에 프랑스와 영국 연극 발전에 영향을 끼치게 된다.

이 극의 특징은 뚜렷한 각본script 없이 전체의 흐름을 보여주는 대강의 줄거리plot만 있었다는 것이다. 줄거리를 제외한 나머지는 배우가 임의로 대화를 만들어 가며 진행했기 때문에 자유로운 즉흥극improvisation으로도 알려져 있다. 대부분 비전문가amateur들이 연극 상연을 했던 과거와는 달리 코메디아 델라르테는 전문 연기자professional actor들이 공연했으며, 인간의 질투, 탐욕, 위선, 갈등과 같은 대중적이고 어렵지 않은 주제들을 다뤘다. 연기자들은 극의 캐릭터를 부각시키고자 마스크와 눈에 띄는 의상custom을 착용했으며 오랜 기간 동안 연마hone한 노련한 대사의 유희적 표현이나, 후에 슬랩스틱slapstick의 유래가 되기도 한 곡예 하는 듯한 몸짓으로 극을 주도했다. 무대 위의 흐름은 전적으로 배우의 몫이었으므로 등장 인물의 성격, 갈등 구조는 극에 따라 변화할 수 있었다. 극을 주도했던 대표적 고정인물stock character로는 어린 광대역의 잔니, 욕심 많은 늙은이 역의 판타로네, 허풍쟁이 겁쟁이 군인 역의 카피타노, 박사 역의 독토제, 바람 잡는 하녀 역의 콜롬비나 등이 있었다. 또한, 코메디아 델라르테는 세트와 관객을 구분하는 벽인 프로시니엄proscenium이 만들어져 무대stage와 객석auditorium의 분리가 시작된 시점이기도 하다.

필수어휘

- improvisation 즉흥극
- stock character 고정인물
- lust 욕망
- itinerant 순회하는
- traveling theater 유랑 극단
- adept 능숙한 [syn] competent
- mime 무언극
- costume 의상 [syn] attire
- personage 저명인사
- vivid 생기 있는, 발랄한

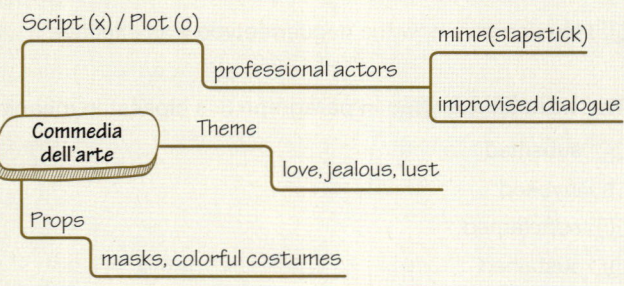

Commedia dell'arte

Commedia dell'arte is a comedy employing the creative talent of improvisation, including characteristics such as improvised dialogue and colorful stock characters. The term refers to the manner of performance rather than the specific subject matter of the play. Commedia dell'arte originated in the fourteenth century during the early Italian Renaissance, although its roots can be traced as far back as ancient Greek and Roman theatre. The form reached the height of its popularity in the sixteenth and seventeenth centuries and influenced theater in Europe, including Spain, England and France. Unlike other classic, stylish and rigorous forms, Commedia dell'arte offered a colorful, loud and humorous presentation, and it was the first time for women to participate in theatrical plays.

Itinerant troupes of at least ten performers played on transitory stages, minimal outdoor structures made from barrels or large pieces of wood. They performed in open places such as streets and marketplaces, and the performances were accessible to diverse social classes. The most renowned teams sometimes performed before kings and nobility. The subjects of Commedia dell'arte did not include any religious or tragic themes, but the scenarios performed usually involved jealousy, love, and lust. The general situation and a basic plot were clearly determined and outlined, but the actors improvised the dialogue and the action. Professional players also needed to be adept at mime, and at a comic acting technique which later became the origin of "slapstick."

Each stock character of the commedia evolved a distinct set of attributes - a characteristic speech, gesture and costume that became the standard to the portrayal of the character. In fact, actors wore leather masks and dressed in certain colors to reflect the emotional state of each character and to help the audience identify to which social class the character belonged. For example, Brighella was a servant or shopkeeper and always wore a costume trimmed in green. The mask of the Dottore (doctor) covered the forehead and nose, signifying his heady thoughts and nosy intrusions, and the character used his hands expressively to clarify his vivid ideas. Captino (Captian) always had the military dress of the day and his attire was generally foppish and overdone, while lovers did not wear masks and dressed the latest fashion at that time.

1. The word adept in paragraph 2 is closest in meaning to
   - (A) competent
   - (B) unique
   - (C) attractive
   - (D) exotic

2. The word attributes in paragraph 3 is closest in meaning to
   - (A) presentations
   - (B) attires
   - (C) traits
   - (D) areas

Art History

★★★
025

Dadaism
다다이즘

토플에 나오는 예술 사조 중 당연 최다 빈출 주제는 인상주의이다. 그러나 인상주의는 예술, 건축, 음악 등 여러 방면에 걸쳐 이미 다년간 출제되어 왔으므로 인상주의는 물론 사실주의, 낭만주의, 르네상스 예술 등 대표적인 예술사조의 특징 및 대표 예술가들은 꼭 알아두도록 하자.

필수어휘

- unconventional 관습에 얽매이지 않는
- formalism 형식주의
- multitude 다수
- simultaneous 동시의
- sacred 신성한
- profane 신성모독적인
- satire 풍자
- defied 반항했다
- mockery 조롱

다다이즘은 제1차 세계대전(1914~1918) 말엽부터 유럽과 미국을 중심으로 일어난 예술운동으로 다다dada 라고도 불리며 조형예술뿐만 아니라 넓게 문학·음악의 영역까지 포함한다. 다다란 본래 프랑스어로 어린이들이 타고 노는 목마를 가리키나, 이것은 다다이즘의 본질에 뿌리를 둔 '무의미함'을 암시한다.

이는 1차 세계대전 후 혼란chaotic속에서 기존 예술이 추구하던 논리logic, 이성reason, 미beauty에서 의미를 찾지 못한 예술가들이 새로운 예술 사조artistic movement를 형성한 것이었다. 다다이스트Dadaist들은 고전예술classical art이 추구하던 모든 개념에 반박하며 논리logic, 순서order 등을 무시한 임의적인 예술randomness을 중시하였다.

다다이즘은 처음 스위스의 취리히에서 시작되었다. 1916년 2월 작가 겸 연출가인 H.발이 카바레 볼테르Cabernet Voltaire를 개점하고, 시인인 T.차라, R.휠젠베크 등과 함께 과거의 모든 예술형식과 가치를 부정하고 비합리·반도덕·비심미적인 것을 찬미하였다. 다다이즘을 보여주는 최초의 행위예술이었던 Cabernet Voltaire Show는 줄거리plot, 순서order 등에 구애 받지 않고 연기자와 관객의 구분이 없는 당시에는 파격적인 형태의 행위예술performance art을 선보였다. 이 밖에 대표적인 다다이즘의 화가인 프랑스의 마르셀 뒤샹Marcel Duchamp은 남성용 소변기a porcelain urinal를 미술작품으로 출품해 세계 예술계를 놀라게 하였다.

```
Dadaism ─┬─ idea ── anti-art, anti-artists, x classical western
         │          art, x conventions, x logic, x beauty, x reason
         └─ e.g. Dadaist's play
                  ├─ x plot, poetry, painting, music,
                  │  dance, all on the same stage
                  └─ x barriers between performers
                     and audience
```

Listening

Mini Practice

Listen to part of a lecture in a modern art class. 🎧 Ch2_02

1. According to the professor, why did some Dadaists pull words out of a hat when writing poetry?
   - Ⓐ It allowed them to convey the randomness of their world.
   - Ⓑ They wanted to articulate the logical, ordered nature of the world around them.
   - Ⓒ The professor was trying to contrast the hat's randomness with the logical nature of a collage.
   - Ⓓ Chance poetry represented ideas popular prior to the Dadaist movement.

2. What does the professor characterize as attributes of a conventional play?
   Click on 2 answers.
   - Ⓐ involvement of the audience
   - Ⓑ plot development
   - Ⓒ barriers separating the actors from the audience
   - Ⓓ multiple acts occurring simultaneously

Listening Script

Professor: During our last class we discussed Dada or Dadaism, the European avant-garde art movement in the early 20th century. After World War I, the artists Hugo Ball and Emmy Hennings created the Cabaret Voltaire as a space for artistic and political purposes and it was here that Dada was born. Dadaists' reaction to the horrors of war was expressed in highly unconventional theatrical performances that rejected the classical formalism in Western art. You wouldn't hear Mozart's Figaro or Beethoven's 5th Symphony. Instead, you would experience art in a multitude of ways! As long as you didn't follow any rules, your work was accepted.

Someone may have begun reading a poem, then they were joined by simultaneous poem reading, spoken word, musical performances, or maybe an anti-war or political address. Anything was fair game as long as it was unconventional and didn't follow normal social rules. You might see a play with no plot, a man dressed as a robot acting in bizarre ways, or spoken word criticizing the sacred with the profane.

It was also quite popular for performers at the Cabaret Voltaire to engage the audience in their performance. The stage was the entire room! The audience could stay in their seats and sing or chant along. If they wanted, they could even join the artists on the main stage! Instead of the artists being distant and removed from the audience as seen in "normal" theatrical settings the artists at the Cabaret chose to tear down those artificial walls.

With no barriers between the audience and artists things could get chaotic and confused. Even the barriers between the types of art were taken down. Imagine this! Poetry, painting, music, dance, spoken word, and comedic satire happened together on the stage and more often than not at the exact same time. In one sense, the goal of Dadaists was to create anti-art and anti-artists to criticize and mock the social movements that they believe led to the terrible destruction of war. Disillusioned, they mocked the sacred, embraced the profane, defied the sensibilities of the people, and delighted in the critical mockery of their world.

Answers p. 19

Art

026

Definition of art
예술의 정의

각 시대별로 생각하는 예술의 의미는 다양하므로 시대별로 정리해보자.

예술은 기본적으로 '미beauty'와 관련된 것을 의미하거나 혹은 그러한 미적aesthetic 결과를 만들어 내는 '기술'을 지칭한다. 그러나 각 시대 또는 사회마다 '미'와 '예술가'를 바라보는 시각이 예나 지금이나 지속적으로 변화하기 때문에, 예술을 보편적으로 정의 내리기는 쉽지 않다.

1500 BC-500 AD 사이 고대 그리스인들은 리버럴 아트liberal art(전반적인 지식과 지식인으로서 능력을 기르는 학문)와 매뉴얼 아트manual art(손기술과 그 기술로 제작된 모든 물건)를 확실히 구분 지었다. 리버럴 아트에는 문법, 변증, 수사학, 산술, 기하학, 천문학, 음악과 신학 과목들이 포함된다. 이와 달리, 매뉴얼 아트는 직업적인 요소가 다소 강해서 장인과 초보자가 그 분야의 기술을 전수하기 위해 작업장에서 교육과 훈련을 주고 받았다. 더구나, 6세기부터 이들이 조직하기 시작했던 길드guild는 비슷한 기술과 직업을 가지고 있는 공예가craftsman 집단이었다. 길드 조직은 전문적 기준으로 물건을 제작하는 장점이 있었지만, 매뉴얼 아트가 리버럴 아트만큼 수준이 높지 않다는 생각을 더욱 고취시켰다는 단점도 있다.

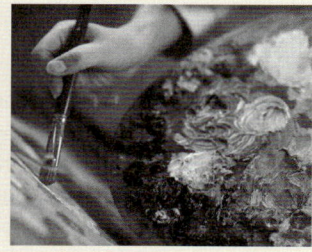

르네상스 시대the Renaissance(14-16세기)가 되어서야 매뉴얼 아트에 대한 시각이 변화하기 시작했다. 이 시기의 예술가들은 리버럴 아트의 기본 이론을 바탕으로 재료와 기술들을 연구하고 그것들을 작품에 가미시켜야 한다고 주장했다. 그래서 화가들은 비율proportion을 위해 산수arithmetic를 배워야 했고, 원근법perspective을 이해하기 위해 기하학을 배워야 할 필요성을 느꼈다. 그래서 예술가들은 예술의 이론과 실제에 있어서 꽤 정통했으며, 지적인 훈련을 지속적으로 받았다. 예술가들의 이러한 관점은 그들의 사회적 위상이 바뀌면서 더욱 구체화되었다. 이들이 왕이나 귀족 계층과 친밀한 관계가 성립되면서 작업장이 예술 학교로 변화했고, 이 곳에서 학생들은 예술뿐 아니라 예술 작품을 완성하는데 필요한 교양 지식까지 충족시킬 수 있었다.

필수어휘
- experimentation 실험
- standing 지위, 위상 syn status
- disegno 소묘, 데상
- composition 예술 작품
- exhibition 전시
- debate 논쟁
- utility 유용(품)
- distinction 차이

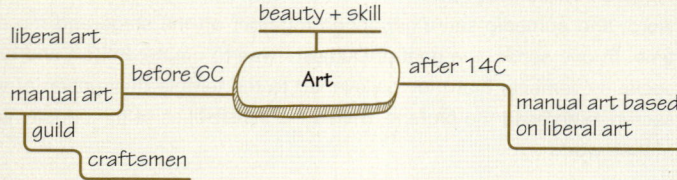

Definition of Art

In the 16th and 17th centuries, the Italians formally developed a highly intellectual form of fine art called *disegno*. *Disegno* was drawing or sketching coupled with creative invention and intellectual experimentation. Famous practitioners included Da Vinci, Botticelli, and Michelangelo, who raised drawing from a mere craft to a fine art. Artists went beyond simply capturing the image in front of them, but instead, manipulated the image in their mind and created complex designs which they expressed through drawing. Whether the final work was a painting, sculpture, or drawing, *disegno* formed the foundation of the finished composition. Eventually, *disegno* became a standard part of art practice and theory, and training in this skill was in high demand.

By the 18th century, students eager to learn the principles of *disegno* and other theories of art would join one of the newly formed art academies that proliferated throughout Europe. One famous academy was the Royal Academy of Art in London, founded in 1768. This academy sought to elevate the status and working conditions of artists in England through formal training and exhibition of their works. The academy also sought to support art by encouraging education, exhibition, and debate of art through its institution.

It was also during this time period that artists began trying to classify various forms of art and make distinctions between "high" and "low" forms of art. For instance in France, "Beaux Art" was a term used to describe and define high forms of art that included dance, painting, sculpture, music and drawings. On the other hand, utilitarian or lower forms of art were less valued because of the lesser skill and detail involved in their production. Architecture was one field that was separately categorized because it involved beauty and utility within the domain of math and science.

The definition of art, and what comprise high and low forms of art, has been constantly changing. Lower forms of art may now be re-defined as high art, and forms of art like *disegno* have lost favor and declined in interest. Art has become broader and more loosely defined as the lines that separate fine art from utility gradually became blurred.

---

1. The author mentions the Royal Academy of Art in London in paragraph 2 in order to
   - (A) show how art developed in history
   - (B) explain why the exhibition was important in 18th century
   - (C) exemplify the art academy that artists could learn disegno and artistic theories
   - (D) emphasize its students were much more eager than those in other academies

2. The word blurred in paragraph 4 is closest in meaning to
   - (A) made unclear
   - (B) clarified
   - (C) refreshed
   - (D) reduced

Answers p. 20

Landscape Design

027 ★★

Design of public spaces in 19th century
19세기 공공장소의 디자인

19세기 공공장소의 건설 계획과 디자인design of public space에는 매우 뚜렷한 두 가지 방법이 있었다. 첫 번째 방법은 유럽에서 기인한 것으로, 자연에 대한 인간의 지배man's mastery over nature를 바탕으로 유럽의 부르주아bourgeois 층을 만족시키기 위해 깔끔하게 정돈된trimmed 꽃과 나무들을 대칭적인symmetrical 형태로 구성하는 것이었다. 그러나 인공적인 아름다움artificial beauty을 강조한 유럽과 달리 자연 그대로의 미를 반영하여 건축하는 방식이 있었으니 그 대표적인 예가 바로 뉴욕의 센트럴 파크Central Park이다. 센트럴 파크를 건설한 건축가 옴스테드Frederick Law Olmsted는 부와 계급에 상관없이 모든 사람들이 즐길 수 있는 공원을 건축하고자 했으며 형식에 얽매인 디자인 보다는 자연 그대로의 언덕, 큰 바위, 식물과 같이 최대한 자연에 가까운look as natural as possible 형태의 정원을 표현하고자 했다. 따라서 자연친화적nature-friendly이며 동시에 친근함과 편안함을 느낄 수 있는 센트럴 파크는 도시 내 모든 사람들이 편히 휴식을 취할 수 있는 미국의 대표적인 공공장소로 자리매김 하였다.

필수어휘

- iconic 상징이 되는
- landscapes 경관
- symmetry 대칭
- ornate 화려하게 장식된
- mastery 지배
- shrubs 수풀
- trimmed 다듬어진
- swamp land 늪지대
- earmarked (특정 목적용으로) 배정된, 예정된
- manicured 깔끔하게 손질된
- mimic 모방하다
- jarring effect 과다한 충격

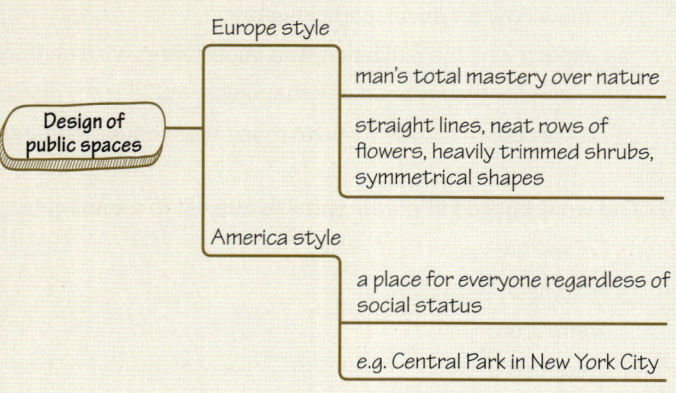

Listening

Mini Practice

Listen to part of a discussion in a landscape design class. 🎧 Ch2_03

1. Which of the following were true about European gardens? Click on 2 answers.
   - Ⓐ They had rows of flowers.
   - Ⓑ They featured many straight lines.
   - Ⓒ They were devoid of any geometric characteristics.
   - Ⓓ Their shapes were in harmony with nature.

2. What goal did Olmsted have when designing Central Park?
   - Ⓐ He was trying to create a place where anyone could visit and feel connected to nature.
   - Ⓑ He wanted to reproduce the natural look of New York's landscape as closely as possible.
   - Ⓒ He tried to avoid much human intervention when creating the park.
   - Ⓓ He desired to strengthen the local economy by creating thousands of new jobs.

Listening Script

Professor: Last week we began discussing urban landscapes and today we will look at Central Park in New York City, probably one of the most iconic urban landscapes in America. But before we do, think about the two most common approaches to planning and design in public spaces. Beginning in the Renaissance the European garden design focused on symmetry and control and until recently was the most popular choice for urban design. Large landscapes were very ornate, organized along lines of symmetry, and were supposed to show man's dominance and mastery over nature. Flowers and shrubs were always planted in neat straight lines and you would see bushes and trees trimmed to match the geometric lines of the garden. These gardens were the exclusive resting places of the elite and bourgeois and were rarely available for the public to enjoy and appreciate.

However, the creation of Central Park sparked a new trend, one that sought harmony with nature as opposed to mastery over nature. In the 1850's the land where Central Park currently sits was totally useless for farming or housing because it was primarily swamp land and unstable. There it sat until the architect Frederick Law Olmstead arrived. In 1857, the local government drained the swamp, cleared the land, and earmarked the site for the development of a public park. Olmstead was not a fan of the traditional method and was against the creation of heavily manicured gardens, the pretentiousness of man's arrogant mastery over nature, and the un-natural symmetry that previously was the norm. Instead, the architect wanted to create a public space that would be easily accessible and enjoyed by all classes of people instead of catering to the elite and bourgeois of New York City. He created a masterpiece that mimicked nature as much as possible. Each part of the park blends with the other and creates a sense of harmony without the jarring effect of symmetry and manicured gardens. It took thousands of laborers to create hills, move boulders and massive rocks, dig streams, and plant the trees and plants that would fill the park. It was an amazing undertaking that took urban landscaping in new directions and provided a public space for all people which is still widely enjoyed to this very day.

Answers p. 21

Photography

028

Dynamic range
다이내믹 래인지

토플에서 사진 관련 주제는 자주 나오지는 않지만 배경지식 없이는 이해하기 힘든 개념과 어휘 때문에 많은 학생들이 어려움을 겪는다. 따라서 사진에 대한 기본개념 및 어휘를 미리 숙지하는 것이 좋다.

사진에 있어서 다이내믹 레인지Dynamic Range는 한마디로 가장 밝은 정도가 흰색과 구별되는 단계가 어디까지 인지, 또 가장 어두운 정도가 검정색과 어디까지 구별되는지 그 범위를 말하는 것이다.

카메라의 센서는 인간의 눈보다 밝은 빛과 어두운 빛을 구별해내는 능력이 현저히 떨어진다. 예를 들어서 사람이 볼 수 있는 가장 어두운 빛은 1, 가장 밝은 빛은 20이라고 가정한다면 사람 눈의 다이내믹 레인지는 20인 반면 카메라의 다이내믹 레인지는 10밖에 되지 않는다. (여기서 이 숫자들은 비교를 위해 만들어낸 수치이다) 다시 말하자면 인간은 어두운 빛과 (1) 밝은 빛을 (20) 모두 선명하게 볼 수 있는 반면 카메라는 1에서 10정도 밖에 보지 못한다. 카메라의 설정을 1~10까지 볼 수 있게 해놓으면 11~20은 매우 밝은 하얀색으로 나와 버리고, 11~20을 볼 수 있게 설정을 해놓으면 0~10까지는 전부 검은색, 5~14를 볼 수 있게 설정을 하면 1~4는 검게, 15~20은 100% 하얗게 나오는 것이다. 이런 경우, 카메라 설정을 어떻게 하던지 눈에 보이는 그대로의 풍경을 담기가 어렵다. 그래서 만들어진 기술이 바로 하이 다이내믹 레인지, 즉 HDR이다. HDR은 일반적으로 허용하는 것보다 훨씬 높은 다이내믹 레인지를 처리할 수 있는 디지털 화상 처리 기법을 가리킨다. 이 기법은 사진 촬영 시 서로 다른 노출multiple exposures로 찍은 여러 장의 사진으로부터 높은 다이내믹 레인지를 갖는 사진을 얻는 방법이다. 즉, 다양한 밝기의 사진들을 여러 장 찍은 후, 후보정을 거쳐 하나로 합쳐서combine photos 적당한 밝기의 사진을 만들어내는 것이다. 이러한 기술의 진보로 좀더 사실에 가까운 선명한 사진들을 완성할 수 있게 되었다.

필수어휘

- complementary 보완적인
- simultaneous contrast 동시 (밝기) 대비
- illusion 환상, 환각
- multiple exposures 다중노출

Mini Practice

Listen to part of a lecture in an art history class. 🎧 Ch2_04

1. What is dynamic range?

Ⓐ The ratio between the largest and smallest luminance values represented in a photograph or painting

Ⓑ The range of detectable light and dark existing in real-world environments, expressed as a mathematical equation

Ⓒ The theory that the much greater contrast visible in reality cannot be reproduced in artificial depictions, such as photographs or paintings

Ⓓ A concept categorizing the shades between pure white and pure black into ten equal sections

2. According to the lecture, why was the Zone System so widely used?

Ⓐ The system produced consistent and effective results.

Ⓑ Ansel Adams and Fred Archer were highly respected photographers.

Ⓒ Before the Zone System, there was no way to measure contrast.

Ⓓ Photographers needed a standardized system to avoid confusion.

Listening Script

Professor: For artists, achieving a sense of detail in their work is one of the harder challenges they face. The human eye is sensitive to very small variations in the level of light and the brightness of colors. The ratio of the brightest color to the darkest color is called the dynamic range. Dynamic range can describe the range of a brightness or darkness in a scene, or the range of brightness or darkness that can be represented by a given medium.

The typical human eye can pick up a dynamic range of about 50,000:1. But paintings are just paints on a canvas. On it's own, a painting doesn't give off any light, making the dynamic range of a painting much smaller; closer to 300:1. Because of this limitation, artists have to employ special techniques to trick the viewer into the feeling of a greater range of contrast.

One way is to use lots of colors. The use of complementary colors in particular can enhance the subjective contrast as perceived by the viewer, an effect known as "simultaneous contrast." There isn't actually more contrast in the painting. It's just an illusion, but it's a useful one.

How about photographs? They're generally more detailed than paintings, so is their dynamic range also greater? Well, due to limitations in technology and technique, traditional photographs typically showed a dynamic range similar to that of paintings. But that was changed in part by the work of Ansel Adams. Together with the photographer Fred Archer, he created the Zone System, which divides the full range from light to dark into ten sections that can be used to judge contrast and adjust exposure in a photograph.

The Zone System was so consistent and effective that it was adopted by most photographers and used well into the 1980s, until technological advances made it possible to use computer software to alter photos. This led to the development of a technique known as HDR or High Dynamic Range photography, where multiple exposures of the same scene can be combined by software to provide a greater range of contrast.

Answers p. 21

Ancient art

029

Egypt art
이집트 예술

이집트는 역사와 예술영역에서 빈출된다. 그들만의 독특한 예술적 특징을 알아보도록 하자.

기원 전 3000년경, 나일강 주변에 발달된 이집트 문명 Egypt civilization은 회화 painting, 조각 sculpture 등의 예술 수준이 높았으며, 작품 안에 부여된 상징적 의미가 컸다. 파라오 pharaoh와 귀족의 무덤 tomb이나 건축물에서 나온 예술품 대부분은 사후 세계 life after death와 망자의 과거의 삶을 그대로 담아 놓았다.

이집트 예술의 특징 중 하나는 권력 확립에 목적을 두고 있다는 점이다. 예를 들어, 무덤 벽에 그려져 있는 인간의 모습은 어깨와 가슴은 정면을 보고, 얼굴은 측면 in profile을 향해 있지만 눈은 다시 정면을 주시하는 비현실적인 '정면성 frontality'을 표현하고 있다. 또한, 조각 작품에서는 그리스나 로마와는 달리 양팔이 몸 측면에 딱 밀착되어 있고, 고개는 뻣뻣하게 들고 있는 모습이 특징이다. 이러한 부자연스러운 모습은 표현기술이 부족해서라기 보다는 그 당시 예술에서 표현하고자 했던 모습을 그대로 반영한 것이라 할 수 있다. 즉, 조각의 경직된 모습은 중앙 집권화된 군주 사회의 획일화된 모습으로, 신성한 왕의 권력 구조를 구축하기 위한 필요 요소였다. 종교적 제사 religious ritual나 의식 ceremony을 거행할 때 정면을 향하고 있는 조각이나 그림들을 바라 보며 그 당시 사람들은 작품에 묘사된 왕이나 신과의 유대감 connection이 형성된다고 생각했는데, 이는 지배층의 힘과 권력을 확립시키려는 의도에서 나온 것으로 추측된다.

이집트 예술의 또 다른 특징은 '원근법 perspective의 무시'이다. 작품 속 사람 크기는 사회적 위계 질서 social hierarchy에 기반하여 위치에 상관없이 절대 왕권 파라오는 지배자의 초월적 힘을 상징하기 위해 가장 크게 표현했고, 정적인 포즈의 고위 정치가 혹은 무덤의 소유자 tomb owner는 그 보다 조금 작게, 하인, 엔터테이너들은 가장 작게 표현했다.

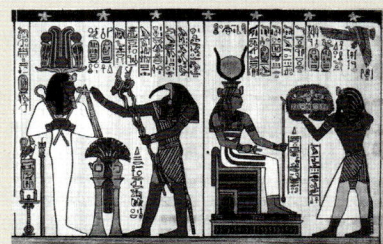

필수어휘
- afterlife 사후 세계
- sculpture 조각
- recreational 오락의
- convention 관례, 관습
- frontality 정면성
- profile 옆모습
- fresco 프레스코화
- longevity 장수, 오래 지속됨
- aesthetics 미학

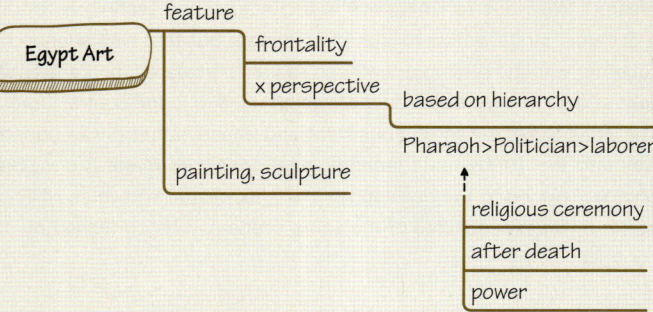

Egyptian Art

The civilization of Ancient Egypt flourished along the Nile about 5,000 years ago. Because the Egyptian culture developed independently, their original art style remained stable and largely unaffected by outside influences. Most of the paintings, sculptures and other works of art created by the Ancient Egyptians were connected to their religion and ideas, and were highly symbolic. In fact, the afterlife of the Pharaoh, the leader of Egypt, was an important theme in Ancient Egyptian art. Many works of art were made with the intention of making the afterlife of the Pharaohs or the deceased more pleasant and enjoyable. For this reason, artisans would ornament the royal tombs of the Pharaohs with paintings and sculptures. The paintings beautifully represented images of slaves, animals, boats and even buildings, using the colors of blue and green to represent the Nile and life, respectively and the color yellow for the sun god, thereby ensuring recreational enjoyment in the afterlife.

Egyptian art had distinctive features. Most Egyptian sculptures, which were made from clay, wood, metal and stone, were created to show the human body from the most visible angle with the left foot pointing forward in a standing pose. Most of all, they followed a very strict convention of "frontality," meaning any figure sitting or standing faced strictly to the front. Also, the paintings had profile views (side views) of the head and legs with frontal views of the eyes and shoulders. Their painting technique was the fresco secco technique, which applied pigments, egg yolk and water on a dry, flat surface of a uniform tone. What is truly amazing is the longevity of their art. These drawings of human figures on walls and pillars survived for thousands of years due to the region's extremely dry climate.

Egyptian architects primarily used sun-baked mud bricks and stones such as limestone, sandstone and granite as building materials because wood was very scarce in Egypt. The columns of buildings were covered with hieroglyphics, pictorial frescoes and carvings painted in brilliant colors. They had shallow grooves running vertically along their surface, designed to evoke harmony and elegance, because the architecture was supposed to be simultaneously both aesthetic and functional.

1. The word ornament in paragraph 1 is closest in meaning to
    - (A) cling
    - (B) adorn
    - (C) obscure
    - (D) manifest

2. The word They in paragraph 3 refers to?
    - (A) columns
    - (B) colors
    - (C) carvings
    - (D) buildings

Answers p. 22

Art

030

Etching
에칭

에칭은 영역을 넘나들며 출제된다. 제작 순서를 기억하도록 하자!

필수어휘

- [ ] metal plate 금속판
- [ ] embellish 꾸미다
- [ ] engraving 음각 인쇄
- [ ] ground 부식방지제
- [ ] armor 갑옷
- [ ] acid-resistant 내 산성의
- [ ] beeswax 밀납
- [ ] coat 덮다
- [ ] etching tool 에칭 도구
- [ ] bath 용기
- [ ] concentration 농도
- [ ] recesses/groove 홈, 파인 곳
- [ ] bitumen 역청
- [ ] varnish 니스
- [ ] squeeze 짜내다

에칭etching은 금속이 산acid에 부식되는 성질을 이용한 음각 인쇄intaglio의 한 기법이다. 구리copper, 강철steel과 같은 금속판metal plate 위에 직접 새기고, 손의 힘에 따라 선의 굵기가 결정되는 인그레이빙engraving과는 달리, 에칭은 판 위에 부드러운 부식방지용액인 그라운드ground를 덮고 그림 작업을 하기 때문에, 선의 표현이 자연스럽고, 산에 부식된 정도에 따라 선의 굵기와 깊이가 다양해진다.

에칭의 역사

처음 에칭은 갑옷armor이나 투구helmet에 그림을 그려 넣는 기술에서 시작되었는데, 이것을 판화 제작자들이 간편한 기법으로 판화에 도입하면서, 16세기부터 예술의 한 표현 수단으로 자리 잡게 되었다. 애칭의 대가인 네덜란드 화가 램브란트Rembrandt(1606-1696)는 그림 안에 빛, 공기, 공간의 느낌을 표현하기 위해 에칭 고유의 자유로움을 적절히 활용한 것으로 유명하다. 19-20세기에도 예술가들은 에칭을 표현의 수단으로 사용했다. 특히, 입체파 화가Cubist의 대표주자인 피카소Pablo Picasso는 입체파Cubism의 기본 사상을 에칭으로 표현해 냈다. 즉, 그는 물체를 다각도에서 바라보며 복합체로 표현하는 수단으로 에칭을 사용했다.

에칭 제작 과정

먼저 금속판을 왁스beeswax와 같은 산에 부식되지 않는acid-resistant 물질인 '에칭 그라운드etching ground'로 완전히 덮고 나서coat 날카로운 에칭 도구etching tool or needle로 그림을 그리면scratch off 선이 그어진 부분은 그라운드가 벗겨져 밑의 금속판이 그대로 드러나게 된다. 완성된 판을 산성의 부식 용액(일반적으로 질산nitric acid)이 담긴 용기bath에 넣으면, 그라운드가 벗겨진 금속판 부분을 산이 부식eat away시켜 그 부분만 우묵하게 파인recessed 선이 남겨지게 되면서 그림이 음각으로 표현된다. 남은 그라운드를 판에서 완전히 제거하고, 금속판에 잉크를 부으면, 그 패인 선 안으로 잉크가 들어가 고이게 되고, 그 위에 종이를 덮어 찍으면 작품이 완성된다.

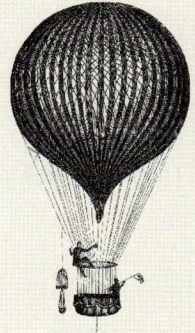

Making of an Etching

Etching is the process of making a print where the lines of an image are created by exposing areas of a metal plate to strong acid. It is believed to go back to medieval times as a means of embellishing armor and metal. Since the 16th century, along with engraving, etching has been an important technique in fine art and commercial printing. Artists can obtain various results by adjusting factors such as the type of plate, the ground, the strength of the acid and the length of the eating time. However, the basic process has changed little over the centuries.

First, a metal plate, usually made of copper, zinc or iron, is polished to remove any scratch and coated with a waxy substance or other coating resistant to acid. This acid-resistant substance, called the etching ground, is typically made of beeswax, bitumen and resin. After the ground dries, an artist scratches the image into the ground with an etching tool or needle, exposing the bare metal. The artist then covers the edges and back of the plate with acid-resistant varnish and submerges it in an acid solution bath. The exposed areas on the plate not covered with the ground or varnish, are eaten away by the strong acid, creating grooves and recessed lines. [A ■] To make lines and dots of different depths and sizes, the artist can place the plate, into baths of different acid concentrations and control the amount of time the metal is exposed to the acid bath. [B ■] After completing the etching process, the remaining ground and varnish are cleaned off, and the plate is covered with a layer of oily ink. [C ■] Then the artist wipes the plate with a stiff cloth until only the sunken lines and grooves hold the ink, removing ink from the unetched areas of the surface. [D ■] Finally, the plate is covered with a sheet of fine paper and placed in a high-pressure printing press. The heavy rollers of the press exert tremendous pressure and the paper is squeezed and imprinted with the ink from the etched lines, making a finished print.

1. The word exert in paragraph 2 is closest in meaning to
   - Ⓐ wield
   - Ⓑ exude
   - Ⓒ expand
   - Ⓓ clear

2. Look at the four squares [■] that indicate where the following sentence could be added to the passage.

   The longer the time is, the deeper and darker the lines are.

   Where would the sentence best fit?

   Answers p. 23

Film

031 — Film 영화

에디슨의 초기 발명품인 키네토스콥에서 필름 영사기로 발전하는 과정, 무성에서 유성 영화로 업그레이드되는 과정 등이 우리가 영화와 관련해 알아야 하는 핵심 내용이다.

'활동 사진motion picture'으로도 불리는 영화film는 스크린에 투사project된 움직이는 영상moving image을 의미한다. 19세기 이전에도 영화 촬영과 상영을 위한 여러 장치들이 발명되긴 했지만, 19세기 말 이후 셀룰로이드 사진 필름celluloid photographic film과 영화 촬영기motion picture camera의 발명으로 렌즈를 통해 영상을 담을 수 있게 되면서 영화는 본격적으로 발전하기 시작했다.

1889년 토마스 에디슨Thomas Edison이 발명한 핍쇼peep show(구멍 안에 여러 가지 그림이 움직이게 보이도록 만든 상자) 장치물의 일종인 키네토스콥kinetoscope은 작은 구멍을 통해 도구 안에 들어 있는 장면들을 볼 수 있는 영화 상영 기구였다. 하지만 한 기계에 한 사람밖에 사용할 수 없었고 상영 시간이 30초 정도로 매우 짧았기 때문에, 지극히 개인적인 영화 관람이라는 한계점이 이 기계의 보편적 사용을 저해했다. 그 외에도 에디슨의 발명품 키네토그래프kinetograph, 축음기phonograph 등은 초창기 영화 발전에 크게 기여했다.

루미에르 형제Auguste and Louis Lumiere의 시네마토그래프cinematograph는 집단 상영을 가능하게 함으로써 영화가 대중적으로 발전하는 계기를 마련했다. 하지만 그때까지도 배우들의 대사dialogue를 영화 장면에 맞춰 상영할 수 있는 기술이 부족했기 때문에 자막subtitle을 통해 내용 전개, 대화 내용 등을 부수적으로 설명하거나 피아노 독주나 오케스트라의 연주가 가미되어 관객에게 흥미를 불어넣기도 했다. 1920년대에 비로소 전자 녹음sound recording 기술이 발전하고 무성영화silent movie의 시대가 종결되면서, 스크린의 움직임과 동시에 대화, 음악, 음향 효과sound effect가 덧입혀진 유성영화taking pictures or talkies의 시대가 열리게 되었다.

필수어휘

- accompany 수반하다, 반주하다
- silent film(movie) 무성 영화
- soundtrack 녹음 부분, 영화 음악
- visual sequence 시각적 연계
- amplitude 진폭, 넓이
- loudness 소리의 세기
- pitch 음의 높이
- timbre 음색

Sound in Film

In the 1920s, the advent of electronic sound recording enabled movie producers to integrate speech, music and sound effects into sound tracks that were synchronized with actions on the screen. One of the most common mistakes that people make about sound and films is thinking that the sound track was recorded simultaneously during the filming process. However, the sound tracks that accompany films are made after the film has been shot, usually in a production studios. The sounds and music are manipulated after filming is finished. This allows for a great deal of control and flexibility as the filmmaker can test several different combinations of sounds, as there are no serious constraints on time.

Even before recorded sound (in this case of music, not spoken dialogue) was first used in the film *Don Juan* in 1926, the importance of music was evident. During silent films, live orchestras, or even just a single piano, played music to enhance the mood of the action happening on screen. Moreover, sound in film directly affects how moviegoers interpret the scenes they are seeing. For example, in *Letters from Siberia*, the same street scene was used three different times during the movie. Each time the sequence of images appeared, a different audio track was played, further emphasizing the repetition of the exact same visual sequence. Audiences interpreted the scene differently each time they saw it because the music affected their understanding of it.

The ability to add recorded sound to a film allowed filmmakers to exercise a new dimension of creativity. Just as a filmmaker can take any two images and connect them to create a relationship, sounds can be strung together for the same effect. With the introduction of sound, the infinite number of possible combinations of images could be paired with a similarly infinite number of possible combinations of sound. Further, a number of different variables can be adjusted, affecting how sound is realized. First, there is loudness—the amplitude of the volume affecting how loud the audience hears the sound. Next, there is pitch—the highness or lowness of the frequency of the sound.

1. According to paragraph 1 and 2, which of the following are true?
   - Ⓐ During the silent films, live orchestra played music to focus on the movie.
   - Ⓑ In *Letters from Siberia*, three-time repetition of music affected audiences' interpretation of each scene.
   - Ⓒ Sound tracks are recorded while the film is being shot.
   - Ⓓ Film producers can have flexibility to manipulate sound after shooting.

2. The word it in paragraph 2 refers to
   - Ⓐ scene
   - Ⓑ repetition
   - Ⓒ soundtrack
   - Ⓓ music

Answers p. 23

Literature

★★★

032

Gertrude Stein
거트루드 스타인

우디알렌 감독의 영화 '미드나잇 인 파리Midnight in Paris'를 보면 주인공이 20세기 초로 시간여행을 하며 당대에 유명한 예술가 및 작가들을 만나게 된다. 영화에서는 베이커, 피카소, 피츠제럴드, 헤밍웨이, 모딜리아니, 달리, T.S 엘리엇 등과 같은 전설적인 인물들의 독특한 개성을 선보이며 그들의 작품에 대한 배경을 시사해주는데 이 예술가들은 모두 한 여성 소설가의 살롱에 모여들어 많은 대화를 나누고 그녀의 평가에 무한의 신뢰를 나타낸다. 많은 예술가에게 영감을 제공했던 그녀가 바로 1차 세계대전 이후 삶에 환멸을 느낀 예술과 청년들에게 '로스트 제네레이션lost generation'이라는 이름을 붙여준 거트루드 스타인이었다.

미국 여류 소설가 거트루드 스타인Gertrude Stein은 소설이나 시에 있어 대담한 언어적 실험linguistic experiment을 통해 문학에 있어 새로운 주류mainstream를 형성한 작가로 평가 받는다. 그녀의 문학작품은 동일어의 반복repetition을 사용한 추상적abstract인 문체로 이루어져있어 대중으로부터 복잡하고confusing 난해한difficult to comprehend 작품이라고 비판 받기도 하였다.

스타인은 피카소Picasso와 같은 입체파cubism의 작품에 많은 영향을 받아 입체파 예술작품이 갖고 있는 추상성을 자신의 문학 작품에도 적용시키고자 하였다. 그리하여 그녀의 작품은 스냅사진의 반복을 연상시키는 독특한 스타일로 '문학적 큐비스트literary cubism'라는 별명을 얻기도 하였다. 이러한 추상적인 특징으로 그녀의 작품들은 처음에는 비난 받았지만 점점 그 독특함을 인정받았고 1차 세계대전 이후 그녀가 명명한 '잃어버린 세대lost generation'에 속하는 많은 작가들(헤밍웨이, 피츠 제럴드 등)에게 지대한 영향을 끼치며 1950년대에는 다다이스트Dadaist들에게서 재평가 받는 등 미국 내 가장 영향력 있는 작가 중 한 명으로 자리매김 하였다.

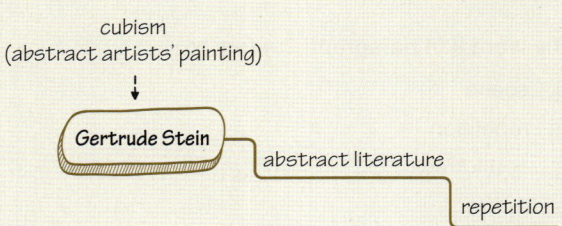

cubism
(abstract artists' painting)
↓
Gertrude Stein — abstract literature
— repetition

필수어휘

- □ **downright** 완전히
- □ **hodgepodge** 뒤범벅
- □ **cobbled** 수선된
- □ **cubism** 입체파, 큐비즘
- □ **geometric** 기하학의
- □ **repetition** (말·행동의) 반복[되풀이]
- □ **notoriety** 악평

Mini Practice

Listen to part of a lecture in a literature class. 🎧 Ch2_05

1. What is Gertrude Stein best known for?

   Ⓐ Writing in a style that is difficult to understand
   Ⓑ Referencing abstract art in her literary work
   Ⓒ Using Cubism in her poems
   Ⓓ Pioneering a new writing style

2. What can be inferred about the latter part of Gertrude Stein's career?

   Ⓐ She gained recognition from the literary community as an influential poet.
   Ⓑ She wrote many stories depicting the fall of humanity.
   Ⓒ Enduring continued criticism, she continued creating confusing and abstract work anyway.
   Ⓓ She switched to painting rather than writing after being heavily influenced by abstract artists such as Picasso and Cezanne.

Listening Script

Professor: Last week we started learning about Gertrude Stein and her unique writings. Now that you have had a chance to read her writings for homework you may have a better understanding of her style. You may have also discovered that her poems and writings seem very confusing, abstract, and downright difficult to comprehend. The abstract nature of her writings is what makes her famous today but during her era it earned her much criticism. People did not understand her writing and looked down on her works because it was not normal or a familiar writing style.

Her style evolved over time and was heavily influenced by famous abstract artists like Picasso and Cezanne. If you remember their paintings, it seems like a hodgepodge of various pieces of paintings, drawings, and random lines cobbled together. Some people have described their artwork as puzzles. These masters of Cubism used abstract and 'unnatural' perspectives along with geometric shapes to create works of art. Stein wanted to mimic Cubism in her writing and created a sense of geometry or completeness by using repetition.

Stein's works began to evolve as she experimented with the creation of a new Cubist influenced writing style. One of her early works, *Three Lives*, is a good example of her testing her ideas. Because of this, we may find it hard to understand what she is trying to convey or what she means. Stein tried to define or flesh out her characters by using repetitive sentences. The repetition of words and phrases build upon each other to reveal the substance of a character or illuminate the plot. Her attempts at utilizing Cubism in her writings met with strong criticism at first. However, as time progressed other generations began to appreciate her work and she gained notoriety and respect. Indeed even Ernest Hemingway was influenced by her work. So although her writings seem hard to understand try to appreciate them as the experimental and bold writings of a woman who attempted something new.

Answers p. 24

Architecture

★★★
033

Houses in Renaissance era
르네상스 시대 주거양식

'부활'이란 뜻의 르네상스renaissance는 신 중심적인 종교적 관점에서 벗어나 그리스와 로마시대의 인본주의humanism 사상으로 돌아가려는 성향의 부활을 의미한다. 따라서 르네상스 시대에는 자연에 대한 인간의 지적 호기심intellectual curiosity을 중심으로 모든 분야에 걸쳐 큰 발전을 이루게 된다. 건축분야에 있어서도 고딕양식gothic에 반발하고 고대 부흥antique revival과 자연 관찰을 위해 고전적인 요소들이 결합된 르네상스 건축양식architectural style이 정립되었다. 르네상스 건축물은 비례감proportion을 중시하고 조화롭고 완성된 느낌을 추구하며 사각형이 많다는 특징이 있다. 또한 건물 중심부엔 둥글고 완만한 돔dome 지붕과 그 아래 넓은 공간이 자리한다. 이러한 양식을 반영하는 대표적인 예가 바로 피렌체의 두오모 성당Duomo이다.

그리스 로마시대를 모방하고자 했던 현상은 공공 건축물뿐만 아니라 거주 공간에도 나타나 그 시대에 지어진 집들은 고대 로마의 거주양식과 흡사하게 축조되었다. 고대 그리스시대의 역사적 사료historical records를 보면 집에 엄청난 크기의 정원garden을 만들고 이국적인 꽃exotic flowers들과 각국에서 수집한 화려한 물품들로 장식하였는데 이는 사회적 지위social status와 부wealth를 나타내는 중요한 상징이었다. 또한 고대 그리스 시대 ancient Greece의 정원과 마찬가지로 정원 내에 분수fountain나 미로maze를 설치하기도 하였다.

예술 분야에서 가장 많이 출제된 르네상스 시대의 과학, 철학, 예술 및 레오나르도 다빈치의 업적 등은 빈출 주제들이므로 그 특징을 간략하게나마 알아두어야 한다.

필수어휘

- □ elaborate 정교한
- □ imitate 모방하다
- □ magnificent 장엄한
- □ statue 조각상
- □ lavishly 사치스럽게
- □ adorned 장식된
- □ symmetrical 대칭적인
- □ functionality 기능성
- □ medieval 중세시대의
- □ maze 미로
- □ dwarf 키가 작은
- □ boxwood 화양목
- □ embrace 포옹하다, 받아들이다
- □ prestige 특권

Houses in Renaissance era
- imitate the style of ancient Rome
- huge fountains, exotic plants, magnificent statues
- fancy villas with extraordinary gardens
- reflect social status

Mini Practice

Listen to part of a lecture in an architecture class. 🎧 Ch2_06

1. According to the professor, what was the main reason for the people in Renaissance-Era to follow the ways of ancient Greeks and Romans?
   - Ⓐ They missed the lavish gardens of the Romans.
   - Ⓑ It was the popular trend.
   - Ⓒ Lives were very dull during the Renaissance.
   - Ⓓ It was a way of showing their social status.

2. The professor mentions mazes as an example of what?
   - Ⓐ An idea that Renaissance people came up with independent of Roman influence
   - Ⓑ A mistake made by the Romans
   - Ⓒ The lengths to which Renaissance people would go in order to live like ancient Romans
   - Ⓓ How the ancient Romans spent leisure time

Listening Script

Professor: The explosion of scientific and artistic advances during the European Renaissance led to improved economy, trade, and wealth. In Italy, those who became wealthy began to sponsor artists and architects who would help them build large houses and elaborate villas to show off their wealth. They tried to imitate Roman and Greek architecture and gardens, which were seen as symbols of high social status. The gardens they built were extraordinary; they contained exotic plants collected from all over the known world, and magnificent statues carved by one of the new masters, and were filled with symbols of wealth. These lavishly adorned gardens were often smaller in the city but in the countryside villas, they sometimes reached over a hundred acres in size.

Gardens became larger, grander, and more symmetrical during the Renaissance period as they tried to imitate and improve up the gardens of ancient Rome. They replaced the functionality of medieval gardens with a focus on beauty and lavish decoration. Sometimes massive fountains were placed in the center of the garden. Large and grandiose fountains highlighted the wealth and social status of the owner. Around these fountains, the gardens would often have a network of mazes. They usually planted low growing evergreen herbs, later replaced by the more popular dwarf boxwood bush. These plants were then trimmed into the desired shape.

Some say that people in Renaissance found a book from ancient Rome, which detailed the construction and use of mazes. However, the book was misinterpreted and had nothing to do with garden mazes. Either way they embraced mazes in their gardens and they became very popular places for displaying wealth, power, and prestige.

Answers p. 24

Art

034

Linear and aerial perspective
선 원근법과 대기 원근법

원근법 perspective은 '투과하여 보다'라는 의미의 그리스어 'perspicere'에서 유래한다. 이것은 대상을 전체 공간과 관련하여 파악하고 그것을 시각적으로 표현하기 위해서 고안된 것으로 크게 선 원근법과 대기 원근법이 있다.

공기(대기)원근법 aerial perspective은 눈과 대상 사이의 공기층이나 빛에 의해 생기는 명도차, 색상차를 포착하는 방법으로 가까운 것은 강하고 선명하게, 중간에 있는 것은 중간 정도로, 멀리 있는 것은 흐리고 엷게 채색하여 나타낸다. 표현에 있어서 원거리의 밀도를 줄이는 방법으로는 다빈치가 모나리자에서 사용했던 경계면을 흐릿하게 만드는 '스푸마토 sfumato' 기법을 예로 들 수 있다. 다빈치는 대기와 흡사한 효과를 나타내면서 색채들의 단계적인 변화를 통해 회화대상 object과의 거리감을 나타내었다. 대기 원근법은 이미 폼페이 벽화 및 10세기 중국의 산수화 landscape painting에서도 많이 사용된 방법이다. 또한 유럽에서는 15세기 초 루벤스 Peter Paul Rubens와 18세기 화가 터너 William Turner의 작품들 속에서도 찾아볼 수 있다.

선(투시)원근법 linear perspective은 르네상스 시대에 체계화된 원근표현법으로 과학적인 방법을 사용하여 대상을 일정한 시점에서 보고 평면에 옮기는 방법이다. 이는 단순히 멀리 있는 것을 위에 또는 작게 그리거나 사선을 사용하여 배경을 표현하는 초보적인 원근 표현방식을 탈피하여 기하학적인 기초 geometric base 위에서 과학적인 방법으로 체계화시킨 일종의 공식 formula이다. 선 원근법은 삼차원의 대상물 three dimensional objects들을 입체적으로 표현하고 대상들이 이루는 공간 내에서의 원근을 표현하기 위해 소실점 vanishing point을 도입하여 물체가 거리에 비례하여 작아지는 것을 표현하였다. 소실점의 기하학적 의미를 명확히 포착한 투시도법의 원리는 이탈리아 르네상스기 피렌체의 건축가 브루넬레스키 Filippo Brunelleschi에 의해 1410년경에 발명되었으며, 후에 많은 화가와 학자들에 의해 발전되었다. 그러나 근현대 미술에서는 서구 원근법의 지배적인 사용에 의문이 제기되면서 새로운 미술을 낳는 계기가 되기도 하였다. 낭만주의 romanticism는 법칙적인 원근법을 표현상의 제약으로 여겼고, 입체주의 cubism는 보다 강력한 방식으로 도전하면서 다시 점을 사용했으며, 데 키리코 Giorgio de Chirico(1888~1978)는 신비감과 불안함을 유도하기 위해 극도의 원근 표현을 이용하기도 하였다.

필수어휘

- aerial perspective 대기 원근법
- linear perspective 선 원근법
- saturated (색이) 진한
- hazy 흐릿한
- blurry 모호한
- embellishment 꾸밈
- converging 수렴하는
- receding 쇠퇴하는
- vanishing point 소실점
- optical 시각적인

Mini Practice

Listen to part of a lecture in a fine art class. 🎧 Ch2_07

1. Turner's painting, "Dido Building Carthage," is mentioned as an example of which technique?
   - Ⓐ Aerial perspective
   - Ⓑ Single vanishing point
   - Ⓒ Linear perspective
   - Ⓓ Multiple vanishing points

2. What reason did the professor give as to why the Renaissance was good for art?
   - Ⓐ It fostered an environment of scientific curiosity.
   - Ⓑ It caused the Classics to be reevaluated from a European point of view
   - Ⓒ It showed how earlier theories of perspective were wrong.
   - Ⓓ It made it possible for Dutch Masters to invent linear perspective.

Listening Script

Professor: Good afternoon students. Today we will discuss the history of visual perspective in Western art. What do we mean by visual perspective? Simply we refer to the ways artists render three-dimensional objects on a two dimensional plane, such as a canvas. Aerial and linear perspective are the two primary types of visual perspectives.

Aerial perspective, also known as atmospheric perspective, refers to the effect that the atmosphere has on the appearance of objects viewed at a distance. For instance, when we view mountains the colors become less saturated as distance increases and they tend to look blue. It makes things in the distance look hazy and blurry. In realist forms of art, the artist took great pains to imitate the scene without embellishments, whereas impressionist artists interpreted the aerial perspective they saw to create their own effects. Examples of aerial perspective in art may be seen in Turner's landscapes, especially the famous *Dido Building Carthage* and in Monet's *Impression Sunrise*.

Linear perspective uses lines converging on a point or horizon to give objects or shapes the illusion of depth and distance in the artwork. For example, if you look at these two paintings of train tracks and a road receding into the distance you can see a point where they gradually vanish. The clever use of intersecting parallel lines creates a vanishing point that helps create a sense of depth. There can even be multiple vanishing points depending on what the artist is trying to create. Examples of linear perspective found in famous paintings include Botticelli's *The Birth of Venus* and de Chirico's *Piazza d' Italia*.

However, these perspectives were poorly understood in Western art until the Renaissance period. Before this era of discovery, the effects of perspective were recognized but artists lacked the ability to represent the perspectives accurately. With an explosion of artistic and scientific discovery from da Vinci, Galileo, Newton, Filippo Brunelleschi, and many others the abilities of artists improved. Indeed, it was Brunelleschi, a fifteenth century Florentine architect, whose optical experiments are credited with the creation of linear perspective.

Answers p. 25

Ancient Art

★★

035

Navajo
나바호족

나바호Navajo 족은 미국 남서부 지역에 사는 원주민 부족tribe으로 미국 전체 부족들 중 가장 규모가 크고 인구가 많다. 과거 유목생활nomadic life을 했으나, 푸에블로Pueblo 인디언과의 교류 이후 농사를 짓기 시작하면서 정착 생활을 하게 되었다settle down, become sedentary. 경제생활의 기반으로 목축과 터키석turquoise 세공을 하였으며, 최근에 부각되고 있는 모래 그림sand painting과 나바호 러그Navajo rug는 예술적 측면에서 가치가 크다.

나바호 종족은 모든 자연에는 생명이 깃들어 있다고 믿으며 신성하게 여긴다. 그들은 거주지를 둘러싸고 있는 산에 신이 있다고 믿으며 그러한 신의 지혜, 공동체의 행복과 평화stability를 얻고자 다양한 종교적 의식ceremony을 행했다conduct. 또한 질병을 치유하고자 행했던 의식은 모래 그림의 기원이기도 하다. 메디신맨medicine man이라 불리는 사람이 노래를 부르면서chant 모래 위에 꽃가루나 여러 가지 색으로 착색된 흙으로 그림을 그렸는데 신화에 등장하는 동식물이나 의식의 춤과 노래를 묘사하는 경우도 있었다. 그들은 모래 그림을 신이 다니는 통로라고 생각했기 때문에, 치료 의식이 끝나면 그림을 바로 없애버렸고, 동일한 그림을 그대로 복사하는 경우도 거의 없었다.

나바호족의 옷감 짜는weaving 기술 역시 큰 예술적 가치를 가진다. 그들은 14-16세기에 푸에블로족으로부터 옷감 짜는 기술을 배워 가운이나 셔츠, 벨트 등의 용도로 처음 사용했고, 17세기에는 스페인에서 들여온 양에서 얻은 울wool로 모포blanket를 만들기 시작했다고 알려져 있다. 그 이후, 제작된 깔개rug나 양탄자carpet는 벽에 걸어놓는 예술작품으로까지 발전했다. 나바호 러그의 바닥 패턴은 조화harmony와 미beauty에 대한 전통적 사상을 구체화한 기하학적인 모양이 네 방향으로 대칭적으로 표현되어 있는 것이 특징이다.

필수어휘
- dwelling 거주지　[syn] habitat
- pole 기둥
- clay pottery 토기
- mockery 모방
- prohibition 금지
- weave (옷감을) 짜다, 엮다
- vertical 수직의
- loom 베틀
- symmetry 대칭
- embody 상징하다, 구현하다

Navajo Art

The Navajo are relatives of the Apache and natives of the Four Corners region, the area where the boundaries of Arizona, New Mexico, Utah and Colorado all come together. They have a unique kind of dwelling called a *hogan*, a traditional building made of a special wooden poles covered in clay, with the main door facing east for good fortune. Hogans come in a variety of shapes, including cone-shapes and multi-sided shapes. The thick earthen walls insulate the inside of hogan, keeping the inhabitants warm and protecting them from strong winds. Navajo art is well-known throughout the world, especially for its variety; Navajo men traditionally made jewelry and sand paintings, and Navajo women wove rugs and sculpted clay pottery.

The Navajos have many different ceremonies involving sand paintings. The Navajo word for sand-painting means "the place where the gods come and go." The sand-painting has been used for centuries in religious rituals, including healing ceremonies performed to cure a patient of sickness. While making the painting, the medicine man would chant, asking yeibicheii (the Holy People) to come into the painting and help cure the patient. Paintings are made on the floor of a hogan by letting soft colored sand and ground minerals flow through the fingers with control and proficiency. When the painting process is going on, which takes a couple of days, the Navajo enforce certain prohibitions, including women's chanting and mockery of the medicine man himself, to protect the honor of the ceremony. The theme of four designs placed around the center is repeated in squares and rectangles. The subjects and patterns of sand paintings are transmitted by memory. After the ceremony, the sand art is considered to be toxic and is destroyed, since it is considered to have absorbed the illness.

The origin of Navajo weaving, predominately created by women, is not known, but is assumed that during 1300 to 1500, Navajo moved into the territory of what is now New Mexico and Arizona and learned weaving skills from the Pueblo people. The traditional way of making Navajo rugs was by kneeling before a vertical wooden-frame loom and using a shuttle to weave colored threads together into large-scale geometric patterns. Originally, Navajo and other Southwest Indian blankets were made of hand-spun cotton thread, but wool was later adopted after the Spanish brought domestic sheep to the region. Many of the rug patterns exhibit a fourfold symmetry which is thought to embody traditional ideas about harmony.

---

1. The word predominately in paragraph 3 is closest in meaning to
   - (A) swiftly
   - (B) mainly
   - (C) subsequently
   - (D) relatively

2. According to the passage, which of the following is true?
   - (A) It was good for the medicine man to reproduce the painting.
   - (B) Men could never weave rugs.
   - (C) Hogan doors opened to the west.
   - (D) The sand art was removed after the ritual, as the completed sand painting was thought to be noxious.

Answers p. 25

Art

036

Quilt
퀼트

퀼트는 3개의 층 - 겉감, 안감과 그 사이에 넣는 솜wadding, batting - 으로 구성되어 바느질stitch로 여러 자수 디자인과 조각들로 장식한 두툼한 패드의 일종이다. 겉감과 안감 사이의 솜은 면화, 울 등의 재질이며, 가볍지만 단열 층insulating layer을 만들어 주는 역할을 한다. 장식과 디자인이 들어가는 부분은 위쪽의 겉감이다. 때론 한 장의 천을 겉감으로 하기도 하지만, 보통은 작은 크기의 여러 천 조각들이 하나의 큰 겉감 천을 만들어 낸다.

퀼트는 기원전 3000년경 이집트 파라오의 모습에서 시작되었다고 한다. 그 이후에는 오랜 기간 동안 여러 나라에서 갑옷armor이나 방한복 등의 실용적 용도로 사용되었다. 특히 미국 초기 정착시기에는 방한을 위한 필수품으로서 퀼트를 애용했다. 그 당시에는 직물의 보유량이 적었고 수입 천의 가격이 비쌌기 때문에, 상업적으로 구매하는 것보다 집에서 수작업을 통해 생산하는 것이 비용적 측면에서 훨씬 더 효율적이었다. 불필요하게 버려지고 조각난 천 조각들을 모아 한 묶음의 큰 조각의 이불, 의복 등을 만들었다. 천 조각들을 이어 붙일 때 더욱 장식적으로 가치를 부여하도록 디자인을 했는데, 주로 사용된 디자인으로는 크게 크레이지 퀼트crazy quilt, 어플리크 퀼트appliqué quilt, 피스트 퀼트pieced quilt가 있다.

퀼트 작업은 주로 여성들이 작게는 가족 단위, 크게는 마을 안에서 이루어지는 공동 작업으로 제작했다. 퀼트를 만드는 여자들의 모임인 퀼팅 비quilting bee가 조직되어 여러 명이 하나의 완성품을 만들었다. 이 모임은 많은 지역 사회 안에서 벌어지는 사교행사social event였고, 결혼 등의 집안의 중요한 행사를 위한 퀼트를 만들 목적으로 여성들이 모여 농번기busy farming season를 피해 바쁘지 않은 시기에 작업했다.

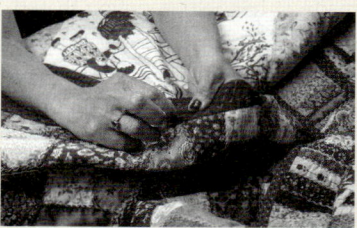

필수어휘

- fabric 직물, 천
- bedding 침구
- batting 이불 솜 [syn] padding
- stitch 꿰매다, 수놓다
- embroider 수놓다 [n] embroidery
- quilter 누비는 사람
- showpiece 전시물
- embellishment 꾸밈, 장식
- scrap 옷감 조각

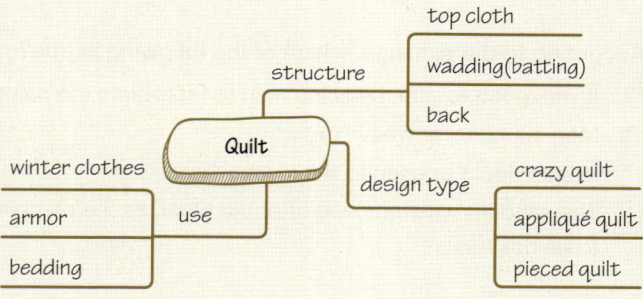

Quilt

Prior to the arrival of European settlers in the New World, quilted fabric was utilized in many parts of the world for clothing, bedding and even armor. In 18th century colonial America, the process of making quilts was extremely expensive and only the wealthy could obtain them. However, beginning in the 1840s, industrialization led to easily obtainable cloth and padding. Quilt making became popular around the Civil War era when it was used by families to earn income and to support the abolition of slavery. It was also employed by soldiers on both sides of the battlefield to keep warm during the frigid winters. A basic quilt has three layers of fabric—a quilt top that is decorated with diverse colors, fabrics, textures and designs; filler as the internal batting layer; and a back. Appliqué and crazy-quilt were very popular styles after the war when quilting became a leisure activity.

Appliqué is a stitching technique where quilters sew smaller pieces of fabric onto a quilt top and then edge them with decorative stitching, either by hand or by machine. Early quilters were able to create designs without having to invest in expensive fabrics and used them as decorations for their homes. Appliqué quilts can involve realistic or geometrical designs drawn from nature, such as plants or animals, or sometimes used local community history as a means of "picture making" in story quilts.

During the late 1890s and into the early 1900s, quilt making changed from being a necessity into a creative art form. The Victorian crazy quilt became popular, and like appliqué quilting, it was a showpiece not intended for functional use. Instead of using geometrical arrangements of fabric like other quilts, crazy quilts featured asymmetrical designs. These designs were scattered across the top layer of the quilt and irregularly shaped scraps were sewed together into larger blocks with highly decorative embroidery. Quilters mostly used exotic luxury fabrics including wool, silk and velvet. For embellishments, they used lace, ribbons and beads. Some families would use pieces of old clothing, or ties or hatbands of family members as a way of preserving family history. Over the years, the practical need for quilts has diminished and instead, quilting has become a popular creative art.

1. The word prior to in paragraph 1 is closest in meaning to
   - Ⓐ since
   - Ⓑ during
   - Ⓒ after
   - Ⓓ before

2. According to the passage, which of the following is true of the quilt?
   - Ⓐ Crazy quilt gained popularity as it was very practical.
   - Ⓑ In the early colonial time, women liked quilt as an art work.
   - Ⓒ Designs of nature in the appliqué quilt were exclusively realistic.
   - Ⓓ Crazy quilt sometimes had additional embroideries.

Answers p. 26

Art

★★★
037

Roman art
로마 예술

로마를 중심으로 형성된 로마 예술(B.C. 8세기~A.D. 4세기)은 로마를 건국했던 로물루스Romulus부터 콘스탄티누스 대제Emperor Constantine까지 거의 천 년 동안 유지되었다. 로마 사람들은 그들의 예술과 건축물이 실용적으로 사용되길 원했으며, 그런 목적으로 도시, 다리, 수로aqueducts, 공중 목욕탕 등을 건축했다. 그들은 광장의 중앙을 장식하는 조각도 로마의 웅장함을 후손에게 알리는 수단이 되길 원했다. 이러한 로마 예술의 많은 특징들은 기원전 600년경, 아시아에서 로마 북쪽으로 이주한 로마의 선조인 에트루리아인the Etruscans과 그리스 헬레니즘 세계의 영향을 받았다.

조각품과 같은 대부분의 로마 장식물은 건축물을 장식하기 위한 용도로 사용되었다. 그리스 형태를 모방한 기둥column들은 실질적인 무게를 지탱하는 역할보다는 장식을 위해 벽면에 세워졌고, 건물 전면facade에 놓여진 경우도 있었다. 신들을 표현 했던 조각품은 그리스의 영향을 받아, 형태와 미beauty를 중시 여겨 이상적으로 묘사되었다. 그러나 로마인들만의 특징은 황제, 장군, 원로 의원senators들의 사실적 묘사에서 찾아 볼 수 있다. 숱이 없는 머리, 이중 턱, 삐뚤어진 코 등의 외모에 대한 사실적 묘사는 로마 초상화에서만 볼 수 있었던 특징이다.

로마의 회화 역시 헬레니즘의 특징을 보여준다. 폼페이 지역에 남아 있는 대부분의 회화는 프레스코fresco 기법을 사용한 벽화wall painting의 형태와 모자이크 방식이다. 벽화는 공간을 더 넓게 보이게 하려는 용도와 창문이 없는 경우, 전원적 경관을 묘사하기 위한 목적으로 그려지기도 했다. 로마인들은 원근법perspective과 명암light and shade을 사용하여 사실적으로 작품을 묘사했고, 자연을 담은 풍경화landscape나 사물을 그린 정물화still life는 그리스 시대에 볼 수 없었던 로마인들의 새로운 영역이었다.

필수어휘

- □ column 기둥
- □ arch 아치
- □ order 양식
- □ capital 기둥머리
- □ scroll 소용돌이 무늬
- □ slender 얇은
- □ flute 세로 홈
- □ shaft 기둥 몸
- □ architect 건축가
- □ infrastructure 기반시설
- □ aqueduct 수로
- □ marble 대리석
- □ dome 돔, 반구형 지붕
- □ vault 둥근 천장

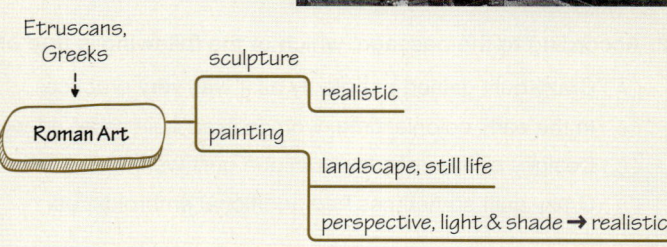

Roman Architecture

The Romans borrowed technology, religion, engineering, and even architecture from the nations that they conquered. They adopted many architectural principles from the Greeks, but also developed several important innovations of their own. These included styles for columns and arches and new recipes for cement and concrete. Romans took what they thought was the best from other cultures and changed it to meet their needs.

Roman architects employed column designs from all three orders of ancient Greek architecture, as well as developing two new uniquely Roman column designs. One kind of the Greek column was that of the Doric order. This was the most basic and common type, sporting a dish-shaped capital with no base, and was used to support heavy structures in buildings. Columns of the Ionic order had scrolls in the capital and carved rings at the base for decorative purposes. The Corinthian order, which was the most decorative and ornate, was characterized by columns with slender fluted shafts and had elaborate capitals that were decorated with acanthus leaves and scrolls. The Romans modified the Doric order by adding a base, which they called the Tuscan order and also combined elements of the Ionic and Corinthian order into a new style known as the Composite order.

Roman architects also improved the arch and used it in civic, religious, and monumental construction. This architectural element could support immense structures, allowing them to build on a greater scale and demonstrate their grandeur and majesty to the rest of the world. They even used arches for public infrastructure such as aqueducts, allowing them to develop cities and maintain the health of their citizens. Their arch technology was eventually rediscovered and employed in the construction of Romanesque and Gothic Cathedrals.

In addition, Romans learned how to use tile-covered concrete as a substitute for marble. This material greatly reduced the weight of their structures and opened up larger spaces in building interiors. The discovery of concrete and cement was a huge advancement in architecture and engineering. Concrete was a mixture of lime mortar, sand, water, and small stones. It could be poured into any shape to make arches, vaults or domes, enabling architects to build immense structures like the Coliseum. Concrete and cement construction proved to be more flexible, easier to transport, and less expensive than working with solid stone.

1. According to paragraph 2, which of the following is true of the Roman architecture?
   - Ⓐ Doric order was not helpful in constructing heavy buildings.
   - Ⓑ Columns of the Ionic order had carved rings at the base for practical use.
   - Ⓒ The Ionic order was modified to create Tuscan order.
   - Ⓓ The Corinthian order was the most ornamental of the orders.

2. The word substitute in paragraph 4 is closest in meaning to
   - Ⓐ subsidy
   - Ⓑ replacement
   - Ⓒ synthesis
   - Ⓓ induction

Music

038

Synthesizer
신디사이저

대중음악 중에 신디사이저synthesizer를 사용하지 않는 음악은 찾기가 힘들다. 신디사이저는 음의 3요소, 즉 음색timber · 음량loudness · 높낮이pitch를 전기적으로 조절하여 원하는 소리를 만들어내는 장치이다. 따라서 신디사이저는 바이올린, 플루트, 기타 등 악기 소리뿐만 아니라 동물, 자동차, 합창단 등 여러 소리를 자유자재로 만들어 낼 수 있는 굉장히 혁신적이며 경제적인 현대악기 중 하나로 손꼽힌다.

신디사이저는 각 음의 사운드 엔벨로프sound evelope를 수집, 분석, 편집함으로써 여러 가지 소리를 낼 수 있다. 사운드 엔벨로프란 특정한 음이 발생한 후 시간이 지남에 따라 그 음량이 변화되는 것을 의미하며 Attack(소리의 발생), Decay(발생한 소리가 낮아짐), Sustain(낮아진 소리가 이어짐), and Release(이어진 소리가 사라짐)의 ADSR의 4단계로 구성되어 있다. Attack은 초기 음이 발생할 때 처음부터 가장 높은 소리의 음량까지 걸리는 시간이고 Decay는 최고 높은 소리의 음량volume으로부터 어느 정도 소리가 유지되는 구간, Sustain은 그 소리가 어느 정도 일직선 상의 상태를 유지하는 구간이며 마지막으로 Release는 완전히 소리가 사라지는 단계이다. 이러한 사운드 앤벨로프의 각 부분을 편집하여 원하는 소리를 만들어 내는 것이 신디사이저의 원리인 것이다.

필수어휘
- **wavelength** 파장
- **alter** 개조하다, 바꾸다
- **sound envelope** 사운드 엔벨로프 (소리의 그래픽 표현)
- **amplitude** 진폭
- **marvels** 경이로운 것들
- **manipulate** 조작하다

Synthesizer → manipulate the sound wave → changing the shape of the sound envelope → attack, decay, sustain, and release

Mini Practice

Listen to part of a lecture in a contemporary music class. 🎧 Ch2_08

1. Based on the lecture, what kind of impact did synthesizers have on composers?
   - Ⓐ Synthesizers made it possible for composers to work with new sounds.
   - Ⓑ Composers can make music using ADSR envelopes.
   - Ⓒ Synthesizers have restricted composers to the kinds of sounds they support.
   - Ⓓ They have helped composers understand and visualize the various stages that are part of a sound.

2. Which of the following is one possible use of a sound envelope?
   - Ⓐ to show the change in volume of a sound over time
   - Ⓑ to graphically indicate the stages of an attack, decay, sustain, and release
   - Ⓒ to demonstrate that some sounds do not contain all four stages
   - Ⓓ to manipulate synthesizer properties

Listening Script

Professor: Technological advancements in the production of synthesizers profoundly influence the way composers create music in this modern era. Previously, music composers had a limited range of instruments and sounds with which to create music. The amazing thing about synthesizers is their ability to change the shape of the sound wavelength and alter its physical characteristics. Synthesizers, which often look like pianos, contain vast libraries of digital sound waves and with the push of a few buttons a composer can reproduce the sounds of many instruments. They can even capture sounds from various environments like birds singing, traffic noise, and children playing at the park. What really makes synthesizers special is their ability to take any sound from the programmed library and change the sound envelope to create new sounds.

Have you heard about sound envelopes? Well, a sound envelope is a graphic representation of a sound that shows how sound gets louder or softer over a period of time. The sound envelope has four parts called attack, decay, sustain, and release which sound engineers refer to as the ADSR envelope. Using a synthesizer we can see the duration of each stage and changes in loudness or wave amplitude. Many sounds, like a single drumbeat, are so short that the human ear has a hard time differentiating the various stages of the sound envelope. That is why we use synthesizers to help us visualize the four stages. These electronic marvels can capture any sound, analyze the sound, and produce a graphic representation of the sound envelope that allows the composer to see each stage. The composer can then manipulate the entire envelope or just a single stage with the push of a few buttons. They can alter the wavelength amplitude, volume, length of time, and even speed up or slow down sounds. With many functions, the synthesizer allows ordinary people and professionals to replicate the sounds of conventional instruments and create many new sounds.

Answers p. 27

Music

039

The root of rap
랩의 유래

랩rap은 14세기 아프리카 부족의 구전 민요와 같이 전승시인Griot을 통해 그 부족의 역사와 전통을 이어온 문화에서 유래되었다는 주장이 유력하다. 그러나 현대 랩의 시작은 자메이카의 '토스팅toasting'이 그 기원이라는 주장도 존재한다. 자메이카의 파티나 클럽에서 DJ들은 음반을 틀어놓고 그 음악 위에 잡담toasting을 더해 청중들과 호흡을 맞추면서 파티 분위기를 고조시켰다. 또한 DJ들은 음반을 틀 때 리듬rhythm과 비트beat가 강한 부분을 집중적으로 틀었으며 그 위에 갖가지 구호catchwards나 은어slangs를 외치면서 최초의 랩을 선보였다. 이는 처음에 음악 사이의 쉬는 시간break에만 적용되다가 인기가 많아짐에 따라 그 분량도 점차 길어졌다. 또한 DJ들은 두 개의 턴테이블turn table에 같은 음반을 한 장씩 올려놓고 오디오 믹서를 사용하여 두 개의 음반 사이를 왔다 갔다 하며 원하는 부분만을 계속 이어서 재생하면서 랩에 맞는 비트를 만들게 되었다. 이렇게 자메이카의 DJ들이 미국에서도 명성을 떨치게 되자 턴테이블을 돌리는 사람과 따로 랩을 담당할 MC들이 영입되었고 이로 인해 전문 랩퍼rapper들이 탄생하게 되었다.

필수어휘
- **wove** 짜다 (weave)의 과거형
- **predecessor** 선조
- **commentary** 해설, 논평
- **turntable** 음반을 돌리는 회전판
- **toasting** 음악을 배경으로 DJ가 멘트를 구사하는 것

Rap
- DJs' toasting in Jamaica → talking to people while playing music
- immigrated to America → the 1st rapper

Mini Practice

Listen to part of a talk in a music history class. 🎧 Ch2_09

1. According to the lecture, why might a DJ have multiple copies of the same song?

    (A) The DJ is able to extend the break and make time for a toast to encourage more dancing.
    (B) Every song has a part where only the instruments are playing.
    (C) The dancers demand that the DJ play good songs multiple times.
    (D) By using two turntables, the DJ can adjust a song's speed and tempo.

2. What happened after Jamaican musicians began immigrating to America?

    (A) DJ styles changed, and DJs could no longer handle so many tasks on their own.
    (B) DJs picked up rap from American musicians.
    (C) They brought Jamaican music to America where it blended with break dancing and rap music.
    (D) Compared to American music, traditional Jamaican music was considerably simpler.

Listening Script

Professor: Some people believe that rap has its roots in the griots of African tribes, a storyteller who wove stories and rhythmic vibrant drum beats together. This form of storytelling was carried over with African slaves to the Caribbean where it survived and over time influenced society and music in a variety of ways. Although modern rap bears little resemblance to its ancient predecessor, rap certainly was influenced by the history of slavery.

In Jamaica during the 1950's one of the most popular social events were dances. Reggae and Blues, also influenced by traditional African music, were very popular. DJ's were hired to bring large collections of music and during the event the DJ's commentary on the people, society, politics, and music became known as "toasting." Sometimes multiple DJ's would gather and use toasting to encourage people to dance, and liven up the mood. The DJ would wait for the break in the song, the part where the vocals ended and instruments played, and would lay down a toast. Sometimes the breaks in the music were too short so the DJ would bring two turntables and two copies of the song. By switching between turntables, they could extend the breaks and do even longer toasts.

Beginning in the 1960's some of the Jamaican DJ's immigrated to New York where they found a place in the African American music community. With the emergence of hip-hop music DJ-ing became complex to the point that the DJ could not manage the music and toasts at the same time. Toasting had changed as it mixed with various cultures in America and break dancing became a part of hip-hop music. This led to a split in jobs with the DJ handling the music, several people would dance and another would toast. Eventually, the toaster was called by a new name and thus the rapper and rap music style was born.

Answers p. 28

Film

040

Travel lecture
기행영화

기행영화는 잘 알려지지는 않은 장르이지만 영화의 탄생 때부터 시작되어 오늘날까지도 근근이 이어지고 있는 장르이다. 이 영화는 영화제작자가 여행을 하면서 여러 풍경을 비디오나 스틸컷video and stills of the landscapes으로 담아 다큐멘터리documentary처럼 제작하여 관객들에게 보여주는 형식으로 오늘날 흔히 접하는 실크로드 기행이나 문화기행과 같은 다큐멘터리들의 모태가 되었다.

기행영화의 특이한 점은 내레이터narrator가 나와서 영화 상영과 동시에 강연lecture을 진행한다는 것이다. 또한 초기 무성영화silence movie만 제작 가능했던 당시 음향효과sound effect를 내기 위해 즉석에서 악기연주live music accompaniment도 함께 곁들여졌다. 줄거리plot가 따로 없는 이 영화는 보통 관객들이 쉽게 접하지 못하는 다른 나라의 축제나 풍경들을 보여주며 강연을 동시에 진행하고 관객들과 질문도 주고받으며 적극적인 참여를 이끄는 영화와 강연이 혼합된 형태이다. 또한 영화관뿐만이 아니라 사람들이 모일 수 있는 곳이라면 어디에서든 기행영화가 상영되었고 이는 텔레비전이 보급되지 않고 세계화globalization라는 말조차 낯설었던 1950년대에 외국 풍물을 접하기 힘든 관객들의 욕구를 충족시켜 주었다.

필수어휘
- wanderlust 방랑벽
- accompanied 동반된
- footage 장면
- snippets 단편들
- leisurely 여유로운

Travel lecture (travelogue)
videos of landscape
+
lecture
+
live music accompaniment

Mini Practice

Listen to part of a lecture in film studies. 🎧 Ch2_10

1. What can be inferred about the goal of travel film?
   - Ⓐ It is to show the audience the endeavor of a filmmaker.
   - Ⓑ It wants the audience to experience new wonders of the world.
   - Ⓒ It is to acquire financial support from the audience.
   - Ⓓ It wants the audience to be educated with different kinds of film.

2. What makes travel films different from normal films?
   - Ⓐ No editing needed
   - Ⓑ A small number of staffs in making the film
   - Ⓒ Various scenes in a film
   - Ⓓ The absence of plot

Listening Script

Professor: There is a little known film genre called travel lecturing. This type of film is very different from the typical Hollywood movie that most of you would expect to see. These films are more educational and appeal to the wanderlust of people. Typically, a filmmaker will travel to exotic locations and capture video and stills of the landscapes, culture, people, food, wildlife, and anything else that might interest audiences back home. When the filmmaker returns they edit all the footage to create a type of documentary that may be accompanied by a narrator or a direct lecture from the filmmaker. With new advances in technology, the types and varieties of travel lectures have increased. Some may be created more like documentaries and some may be more standard lecture and slideshow with video snippets. The main goal is to take the audience on a journey to places that they have never been, engage them in that journey, and teach them something about those special places. Think of travel films as a form of virtual tourism where people can explore other cultures and countries from the safety of their own home.

Historically, travel films were typically shown in any place large enough to hold an audience. This included lecture halls, movie theaters, gymnasiums, private clubs, and community centers. At these events, there could be a mixture of film and lecture that would allow the audience to participate and ask questions about the destinations. What makes these films different from normal films is the lack of plot or absence of a story. Travel lectures are more like a leisurely journey where you can stop and enjoy the scenery. You can make detours and stop wherever you want if you find something interesting. Travel lectures are about bringing a distant world to you and allowing you to experience something new. It can even inspire you to take the risk, travel to those regions, and see the wondrous sites for yourself.

Answers p. 29

서양 미술사조
(15C~19C)

15C — Renaissance Art
르네상스 (15–16C)

르네상스란 프랑스어로 재생, 부흥, 재부활rebirth이라는 뜻으로 인본주의humanism에 바탕을 둔 본격적인 회화양식들이 등장하기 시작한 시기. 원근법perspective을 사용한 회화가 등장.

 Artists

보티첼리 Sandro Botticelli
라파엘로 Raffaello Sanzio
레오나르도 다빈치 Leonardo da Vinci
미켈란젤로 Michelangelo Buonarroti

16C

17C — Baroque Art
바로크 (17–18C)

바로크는 포르투갈의 '비뚤어진 모양을 한 기묘한 진주'에서 온 것으로 르네상스 미술에 대한 실증에서 비롯되어 화가의 개성과 상상력, 풍부한 색채와 경쾌함, 장중한 분위기 속에서 생동감 있는 표현이 특징.

 Artists

카라바지오 Michelangelo da Caravaggio
렘브란트 Rembrandt
루벤스 Peter Paul Rubens

18C — Rococo Art
로코코 (18C)

화려하고 장식성이 강하며 사랑과 연회feast, 신화mythological subject와 같은 프랑스 파리의 귀족 취향의 주제.

 Artists

샤르댕 Jean-Simeon Chardin
장 앙투안 와토 Jean-Antoine Watteau

Enlightenment
계몽주의 (18C)

자연의 이성을 중요시하는 합리주의가 싹트는 시기에 서민들의 생활에 대한 애환과 감성을 주제로 삼음. 로코코와 비슷한 시기에 일어났지만 주제 대상에서 그 차이를 가짐

 Artists

샤르댕 Jean-Simeon Chardin
호가스 William Hogarth

Neo-classicism
신고전주의 (18-19C)

감정표현을 자제하고 내용을 전달하는데 목적을 두어 역사와 신화의 주인공을 실제와 같이 붓자국 없이 매끈하게 표현함. 정확한 형태력이 중요하며 냉철한 표현에 중심을 둠.

Artists
자크 루이 다비드 Jacque-Louise David
벤자민 웨스트 Benjamin West
앵그르 Jean Auguste Dominique Ingres

19C

Romanticism
낭만주의 (19C)

개인의 감정 및 개성의 표현을 바탕으로 서정적이고 낭만적인 심정이나 정취를 담은 풍경화를 통해 인간과 자연과의 친화력을 표현. 자유롭고 다양한 색채 및 화법 사용.

Artists
제리코 Jean-Louis-Andre-Theodore Gericault
터너 William Turner
도미에 Honore Victorin Daumieer

Naturalism
자연주의 (19C) → 농민화가의 등장으로 때론 사실주의에 포함

파리 근교 퐁텐블로 숲 주변의 풍경을 즐겨 그리며, 바르비종 마을에 머물러 때론 '바르비종 파'라고 부르기도 함. 자연 그대로나 실제 사물들의 모습을 있는 그대로 묘사하고 자연 앞에서 인간의 부질 없음을 표현. 특히 밀레의 농부에 대한 존엄한 분위기의 작품이 유명.

Artists
윌리암 베이커 William Bliss Baker
터너 William Turner
밀레 Jean-Francois Millet

Realism
사실주의 (19C)

현실을 변형하거나 왜곡하지 않고 반영함. 주로 농부와 도시의 노동자 계층을 그림.

Artists
쿠르베 Gustave Courbet
밀레 Jean-Francois Millet

Impressionism
인상주의(19C)

일상적인 풍경이나 인물을 대상의 느낌을 살려 밝고 화려한 색감으로 감성적으로 표현

Artists
마네 Edouard Manet
모네 Claude Monet
르누아르 Auguste Renoir
드 가 Edgar De Gas

Neo-impressionism
신인상주의 (19C)

도시의 일상에서 볼 수 있는 풍경과 인물. 화면 전체 구조물들의 질서가 중요함.

Artists
쇠라 Georges Seurat
시냑 Paul Signac

Post-impressionism
후기인상주의 (19C)

누구나의 일상에서 볼 수 있는 풍경과 인물을 화려한 색채를 사용하여 다양한 시각으로 표현. 화가 개인의 다양한 특성을 볼 수 있음.

Artists
세잔 Paul Cezanne
고흐 Vincent van Gogh
고갱 Paul Gauguin

서양 문예사조

Classicism
고전주의

형식적인 조화와 질서를 중시한 미를 추구.

 Artists
단테 〈신곡 La Divina Commedia〉
괴테 〈파우스트 Faust〉

Realism
사실주의

낭만주의의 비현실적 성격에 반발하고 객관적 사물을 있는 그대로 관찰하고 구체적으로 묘사하는 미를 추구.

Artists
찰스 디킨스 〈올리버 트위스트 Oliver Twist〉

Romanticism
낭만주의

형식이나 질서의 구속에 반발하고, 합리적 사고방식이나 이성보다는 인간의 감정과 주관적인 생각을 지향하는 미를 추구. 자연과 현존하지 않는 것에 대한 동경을 기조로 함.

Artists
윌리엄 워즈워드 〈수선화 Daffodils〉
나다니엘 호손 〈주홍 글씨 The Scarlet Letter〉
빅토르 위고 〈레미제라블 Les Miserables〉

Naturalism
자연주의

인간을 자연의 일부로 보며, 인간은 자연 법칙에 의해 운명이 결정되는 나약한 존재라는 사상을 기조로 함.

Artists
에밀 졸라 〈목로 주점 Gervaise〉
토마스 하디 〈테스 Tess of the D'Ubervilles〉
존 스타인백 〈분노의 포도 The Grapes of Wrath〉

Aestheticism
유미주의
탐미주의라고도 하며, 감각과 개성을 목표로 하는 넓은 의미에서의 낭만주의. 단, 퇴폐주의적이고 악마주의적인 경향도 띔.

Modernism
주지주의
시의 음악성과 운율보다는 시각적인 이미지가 강조된 사상을 추구.

Symbolism
상징주의
낭만주의가 감각적 대상에서 쾌감을 느끼는 데 그친 반면, 상징주의는 감각의 대상이 암시하는 이상을 추구하려 함.

Behaviorism
행동주의
인간의 행동을 밖에서 포착하려는 사상을 추구.

Surrealism
초현실주의
프로이드의 정신분석학의 영향으로 무의식의 세계를 표출하는 미를 추구.

Existentialism
실존주의
전쟁 후의 허무의식을 벗어내려 하며 자아 발견과 건설적인 인간다움을 추구.

Chapter 3. Social Science

Sociology
041-R
Agriculture

Psychology
042-R
Babies' behaviors

Business
043-L
Competitors in a business sector

Economics
044-L
Digital economy

Psychology
045-L

Business
046-L

Psychology
047-L

Economics
048-R

Economics
049-R
Industrialization in US

Psychology
050-L
Internet Addiction Disorder

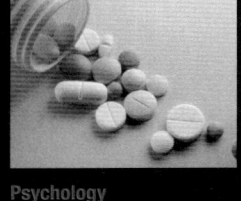
Psychology
051-R
Placebo effect

Sociology
052-R
Printing

Psychology
053-R
Psychology

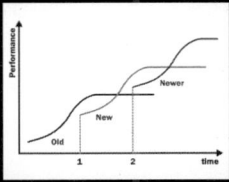
Business
054-L
S curve in business

Business
055-R
Scientific management

Philosophy
056-L
Thomas Kuhn

Sociology
057-R
Transportation revolution in US

Sociology
058-R
Urban planning

Sociology
059-L
USA Today

Psychology
060-L
Variables in decision making

Sociology

041

Agriculture
농업

농사 관련 주제는 신석기 농업 혁명을 시작으로 여러 시대와 지역의 농사의 특징과 농사법이 출제되고 있다.

채집gathering · 수렵hunting 경제에서 생산 경제인 농업 사회로의 전환은 인류 역사상 가장 획기적인 사건 중 하나였다. 신석기 시대 혁명Neolithic Revolution이라 일컬어지는 이때, 처음으로 동물을 사육하고 농사로 풍족한 곡식을 거두어 인구가 증가하는 등 생활 방식에 큰 변화가 있었지만, 정확한 그 발생 시기와 위치를 알아내는 것은 쉽지 않다. 이에 인류학자anthropologist들과 고고학자archaeologist들은 농업 사회의 요건을 충족하는데 필요한 다음 충분 조건 2가지를 조사해야 한다고 말한다. 한 가지는 한 집단이 일년 동안 재배해 얻은 식량이 집단에서 필요로 하는 영양의 절반 이상이 되어야 한다는 점, 다른 한 가지는 식물과 동물이 자연적으로 생장하는 것이 아닌 인간의 손에 의해 재배되고 사육되어야 한다는 점이다.

고고학자들은 농업 생산의 시작 시기를 정확하게 알아 내기 위해, 전 세계 여러 발굴지에서 증거를 조사하면서 이스라엘 지역의 작은 저장소에서 재배용으로 사용되는 종자seed들을 모아놓은 흔적을 찾아냈다. 이것은 적어도 그 당시 사람들이 식물 종의 생물학적 과정을 조작하는 법을 알고 있었다는 분석이 있다. 다른 신석기 유적지에서는 여러 동물 뼈가 발견되었는데, 이 중 작은 영양gazelle의 뼈 수가 다른 동물들에 비해 훨씬 많았다. 학자들은 이 증거를 바탕으로 고대 사람들이 식용을 위해 선택적 사육selective breeding을 했거나, 적어도 그 동물 종을 의도적으로 활용exploit했을 것이라고 주장한다. 그러나 이후에 영양이 아닌 다른 동물 종들이 발견되었는데 이러한 사육 동물 종의 변화는 고대 사람들이 그들에게 더 적합한 동물을 선택한 것이라는 등 다양한 의견이 존재한다.

필수어휘

- □ cultivate 경작하다 syn farm
- □ output 산출량, 생산량
- □ productivity 생산성
- □ irrigate 관개하다
- □ photosynthate 광합성 산물(광합성으로 만들어진 물질)
- □ fertilizer 비료
- □ physiological 생리학적인
- □ genetically 유전적으로

Increasing Productivity of Land Cultivation

From the dawn of agriculture 10,000 years ago until the 1950s, farmers' primary method for increasing productivity was expanding the land on which they farmed. However, in the 1950s the amount of new available farmland in the world has decreased dramatically. This has forced many farmers to find alternative methods to increase productivity on the lands they currently cultivate.

From 1950 to 2000, the productivity of agriculture increased by 160%, which is very impressive considering that the amount of new farmland expanded by only 14%. High-yield crops, genetically modified organisms (GMOs) from Japan and hybrid corn from the United States have been major contributors to increased productivity. However, it has been already more than two decades since bioengineers first introduced genetically enhanced crops into farming and there have yet to be any new significant scientific breakthrough. Part of this may be due to consumers beginning to fight against genetically engineered food.

The amount of irrigated land also greatly increased as a result of newly developed technologies. In 1950, almost 3,000 square miles of land was irrigated, but that number had increased to one million square miles by the year 2000. This increase in irrigated land corresponded with a sharp increase in the amount of fertilizer used by farmers. The amount of fertilizer used in 1950 was about 14 million tons and this number rose to 137 million tons by 2002, almost a tenfold increase. The gains in productivity came largely from geneticists increasing the amount of photosynthate (a byproduct of photosynthesis) used in seed production from 20% to 50%. Any further increase in photosynthate would put the plant under considerable stress. Over time, it slowly became inefficient to increase the amount of fertilizer used, as it did not result in any significant increases in productivity. Since 1980, the productivity of rice in Japan has not increased and productivity of wheat in American leveled out by 1985. Therefore, many countries have reduced the amount of fertilizer. Even China, the world's largest consumer of fertilizer, has begun to slowly level off the amount of fertilizer that it consumes. However, there are still markets in the world, such as Brazil and India, in which using fertilizer is profitable.

1. Why does the author mention about Japan in paragraph 3?

    (A) to prove that the fertilizer boosted the agricultural productivity
    (B) to argue that America tried to improve agricultural productivity more than Japan
    (C) to show that the fertilizer functioned inefficiently as a booster to increase productivity
    (D) to demonstrate how the fertilizer negatively affected the natural world

2. The word profitable in paragraph 3 is closest in meaning to

    (A) reluctant
    (B) proliferating
    (C) lucrative
    (D) reasonable

Psychology

042

Babies' behaviors
유아의 행동

어린 아이의 인지 발달 단계, 기억 능력, 사물 인식, 분리 불안 등 유아 관련 주제가 토플에 출제된다. 심리 관련 어휘도 함께 정리해두자!

필수어휘

- habituation 습관화
- stimulus 자극, 자극제 pl stimuli
- response 반응
- stare 응시하다
- vocalization 발성
- percept 지각
- perceptual 지각의
- pitch 음의 높이
- assess 평가하다 syn evaluate

분리 불안separation anxiety은 아기가 자신을 돌보는 사람, 주로 엄마와의 분리로 경험하게 되는 심한 고통과 불안을 말한다. 이 증상은 대략 8개월에 드러나고 10-18개월에 가장 심하게 나타나며, 이때 아기는 애착 대상의 부재로 불안해하고 흥분하여 울며 불쾌해한다. 아기는 부모나 보모caregiver와 떨어지는 것을 꺼리는데 이것은 아기와 아기를 돌보는 사람 사이에 애착attachment 관계가 형성되었다는 것을 의미한다. 한편, 아이는 시간이 지나면서 각각의 사람과 사물이 별개이며, 영구적이라는 것을 이해한다. 즉, 대상 영속성object permanence(시야에 있던 물체가 무언가에 가려져 보이지 않아도 그것이 사라지지 않고 지속적으로 존재하고 있다는 것을 아는 능력)이 발달한다. 하지만 그들은 아직 시간 개념이 없기 때문에 애착 대상이 언제 돌아올지 또는 자신에게 돌아올 지 여부를 인지하지 못한다. 이 단계에서 아이는 자신이 스스로 자립하려는 욕망과 애착대상에 의존해 안전을 보장받을 필요 사이에서 갈등하기도struggle 한다.

아기는 성장하면서 여러 감정을 경험한다. 8개월 이전 세상은 그들에게 매우 새롭기 때문에 무엇이 안전하고 위험한지 쉽게 인지하지 못한다. 정상적 발달 단계에서 이 어린 시절은 가정환경에 익숙해 지는 시기이며, 부모나 자신을 돌보는 사람이 옆에 함께 할 때 안전하다고 느낀다. 이 시기를 지나게 되면 아기는 낯선 무언가가 발생했다고 인지할 때 두려움을 느낀다. 부모가 자리를 비우게 되면 불안해하는 것이다. 그러나 분리 불안은 아이의 발달에서 정상적 단계이다. 그 단계에서 아이는 주변환경에 익숙해 지는 방법을 배워가는데 10-18개월에 심한 불안감을 보이다가 부모가 지금은 없지만 다시 돌아올 것이라고 인지하는 2세 정도에 대게 그 불안감은 사라진다.

Mini Practice

Perceptual Ability in Infants

It was generally believed that infants could not see as we do, because their visual development was supposedly not complete at birth. However, according to new research findings, we now know that this is incorrect and that infants are able to perceive the world around them. Moreover, it is believed that they see and view things in a way comparable to the way an adult sees things, although not as sensitively. Many clues, such as where and how long a baby stares, indicate that they can distinguish particular objects. Recent research experiments have revealed that infants are able to tell differences between many aspects of an object, such as color, shape and size.

Infants cannot communicate with researchers directly so research methods have been developed to let their behavior speak for them. The habituation theory describes a type of learning in which repeated exposure to a stimulus leads to a decreased response. When infants were presented with stimuli, researchers found that it gained their attention for some period of time before they no longer found it amusing. Once they become bored with it, babies would look away and would no longer be stimulated by the presence of the object.

An experiment was performed to see whether infants showed increased or decreased responses when shown certain objects for a certain amount of time. Two red spheres were shown to a baby and as expected with habituation, the baby eventually lost interest and started looking around the room. After a while, the same baby was shown one red sphere and one red cube. To the surprise of the psychologists, the baby stared longer at the red cube. This indicated that the baby was able to see the difference between the two objects, meaning that they were able to distinguish one shape from another. In addition, researchers also observed infants' vocalization and examined the pitch of their voice for clues about visual perception. For example, if they are stimulated when shown an object they may make a high-pitched noise. Body language and heart rate can also be evaluated to assess an infant's perceptual development.

1. The word comparable in paragraph 1 is closest in meaning to
   - Ⓐ magnificent
   - Ⓑ obvious
   - Ⓒ susceptible
   - Ⓓ similar

2. All of the following are mentioned in the passage EXCEPT
   - Ⓐ Even though researchers communicate directly with infants, they need other research methods.
   - Ⓑ In habituation theory, infants' response decreases, when infants are exposed to the repeated stimulus.
   - Ⓒ After babies become bored with something, they may no longer look at it.
   - Ⓓ Their body language and heart rate allow researchers to evaluate infants' perception.

Answers p. 31

Business

043

Competitors in a business sector
비즈니스에서의 경쟁자

비즈니스를 시작할 때 중요한 점 세가지는 ① 아이템 선정, ② 상권분석, ③ 차별성이다. 이 중에서 세 번째 차별성을 두기 위해서는 우선 경쟁자를 분석하고 경쟁자와 다른 나만의 아이템을 마케팅 해야 한다. 즉, 경쟁자competitors를 파악하고 그에 따른 경영전략 management strategy을 세우고 비즈니스를 진행하는 것은 성공을 위한 매우 중요한 단계이다. 상대회사의 경영전략을 추측하기 위해서는 그 회사의 과거 실적past performance과 지도체제leadership structure를 분석하는 것이 도움이 될 수 있다. 과거 실적을 알게 되면 회사의 미래 전략을 예측할 수 있기 때문이다. 예를 들어 여러 해 동안 끊임없이 성공해온 회사라면 실적이 좋지 않은 사업분야에도 자신 있게 접근할 수 있는 반면, 실적이 부진했던 회사라면 새로운 결정에 지나치게 주저할 수도 있다. 또한 경쟁자 분석에서 자주 간과되는 경영 구조를 통해서는 회사를 이끄는 사람들의 배경을 알 수 있기에 이들이 후에 어떤 결정을 할지 짐작할 수 있다. 즉, 경영진들의 전공이나 과거 경험들이 그들의 미래 행동을 추측하는 데에 도움이 될 수 있다는 것이다. 이러한 분석을 통해 경쟁상대의 향후 전략을 예측한다면 그 기업보다 더 나은 제품을 더 싼 가격에 제공할 수 있고, 결국 경쟁에서 우위를 차지할 수 있는 것이다.

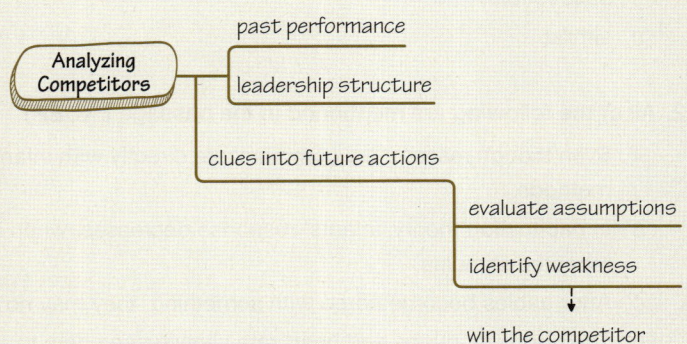

필수어휘
- analysis 분석
- assumption 추측
- clue 실마리
- insight 통찰력
- underperforming 기량발휘를 못하는
- diversity 다양성
- lucrative 수익성이 좋은

Mini Practice

Listen to part of a lecture in a business class. 🎧 Ch3_01

1. What characteristic is implied about a board of directors containing too many similar members?

    Ⓐ Decisions can be made more quickly compared to a board of directors with diverse membership.
    Ⓑ They would exhibit strong unity due to mutual understanding.
    Ⓒ They could encounter problems when hiring employees from a different industry.
    Ⓓ Their assumptions can be too easily predicted, resulting in a competitive disadvantage.

2. According to the lecture, what should be done when an assumption is identified?

    Ⓐ Act swiftly to build a line of advertising aggressively attacking the company
    Ⓑ Compare the assumption with assumptions made by other companies
    Ⓒ Take advantage of the assumption through prompt action
    Ⓓ Begin building a strategy on a course of action to take against the company

Listening Script

Professor: When starting up a business, you'll agree, I think, that it's important to start with a careful analysis of your competitors. But how to go about it? Well, if you understand the kind of assumptions that a competitor is making, you can identify weaknesses within their business model.
When evaluating these assumptions, there are lots of areas to consider, but today I want to talk about two frequently overlooked areas. I'm talking about a company's past performance and leadership structure. A careful analysis of a company's past can give you valuable clues and insight into the firm's future actions. Consider a company with an unbroken chain of success stories over many years. This might lead to a feeling of overconfidence even in business areas that could be underperforming. Similarly, if they'd had a string of failures, they might be overly timid about making similar decisions in the future.
Another useful but often overlooked place to look is the competitor's management structure. Companies are run by people, whether individuals or groups, and their past experience will shape their future actions, and the assumptions they make when running the company. That means you can make guesses about their behavior based on their background. For example, if everyone in the top management of a certain company had extensive background in the financial sector, their behavior might be very predictable based on that shared background. As you might imagine, that means it can be good to have a lot of diversity in top management.
Understanding these assumptions is important because if you can identify the assumptions your competitor is making, you may find a lucrative opportunity through using those assumptions against them. Whether they are overly-arrogant or overly-hesitant, if you can act quickly, their response will be too little, too late.

Answers p. 31

Economics

044

Digital economy
디지털경제

디지털 경제란 인터넷을 비롯한 정보통신산업 information and communication industry을 기반으로 이루어지는 모든 경제 활동을 말한다. 산업 혁명 industrial revolution을 계기로 시작되었던 산업 사회의 경제와는 달리, 인터넷을 주요 기반으로 하는 사업인 전자상거래 e-commerce나 인터넷 쇼핑몰, 검색 서비스 등을 통한 경제 생활을 의미한다.

이러한 사업들은 디지털 기술의 발달로 세계적인 네트워크를 통해 생산 production과 소비 consumption, 유통 distribution의 새로운 질서를 확보함으로써 시공간을 뛰어넘는 새로운 경제 패러다임 paradigm으로 확산된 지 오래되었다. 특히 소비자는 인터넷을 통해 공급자 supplier 및 상품에 대한 정보를 무한정 얻을 수 있어, 아날로그 경제 시대와 달리 판매자 seller와 소비자 buyer 간 힘의 역학관계에서 우위를 차지하게 되었다. 판매자 또한 어느 한 도시나 지역에 상점을 낼 필요가 없어지고 인터넷 상거래만으로 거래를 할 수 있기 때문에 디지털 경제는 여러 커뮤니티의 특성 또한 바꿔놓았다. 예를 들어 미국의 디트로이트 Detroit는 자동차 산업 automobile industry으로 유명한 도시였으나 인터넷으로 작업이 가능한 자동차산업 종사자들이 그곳에 더 이상 머물 필요가 없어지면서 다른 도시로 이주하게 됨으로써 디트로이트는 자동차 산업이 집중된 도시로서의 특징을 잃어버리게 되었다.

필수어휘
- ☐ ubiquitous 어디에나 있는
- ☐ ports 항구
- ☐ manufacturing sector 제조업 부문
- ☐ comprise 구성되다
- ☐ automotive 자동차의

Digital economy
- Internet development
- x importance on location
- community losing its people
  ↓
- disappearance of unique communities

Listening

Mini Practice

Listen to part of a lecture in an economics class. 🎧 Ch3_02

1. What is the main topic of the lecture?
   - Ⓐ How the digital economy has affected local communities
   - Ⓑ A hypothesis about the lack of news coverage on the digital economy
   - Ⓒ Economic risks of outsourcing in the digital economy
   - Ⓓ New research in quantifying how certain regions have been affected by the digital economy

2. According to the researcher, what is one drawback of the digital economy?
   - Ⓐ Traditional communities are unable to compete with workers using newer technologies such as e-mail.
   - Ⓑ The impact on local communities is too unpredictable.
   - Ⓒ Traditional communities may lose their uniqueness.
   - Ⓓ It places homogenous communities at risk.

Listening Script

Professor: Okay, this time I want to discuss a somewhat negative aspect of the digital economy. And by that, I'm not just talking about websites that sell products online, but the whole system, including the consumers, hosting services, and so on. Through that, I want to explore how the digital age has changed our concept of community.

Before the internet became so ubiquitous, one of the most important decisions for a business owner opening a store was location, but these days, it doesn't matter so much. It used to be that factories would need to be located near ports. But these days, only 15% of the American workforce works in the manufacturing sector. The result has been a dramatic shift in where businesses are located. There's nothing to stop a business in Florida selling winter jackets to someone in Alaska in the middle of the summer. This has significantly changed how communities form.

Seems positive so far, right? But consider this: communities generally consist of people that have a lot in common. They share similar basic needs and concerns, and such characteristics comprise a kind of identity. So what happens when some people running an online business choose to move to some random city in the southwest to escape the humidity? The community could start to lose some uniqueness as outsiders' interests are included. One more example. Imagine you're a talented automotive designer. In the past, maybe you had to live near Detroit, the automotive capital of America. But now car designers can live far away from their employer, merely emailing designs they create on their computer.

But losing a highly skilled resident would be bad for Detroit. What could such a city do to keep people from moving away? One reliable way is to lower the tax rate, encouraging people to stay. Anyway, this is what I'm talking about when I say the digital economy has directly contributed to the disappearance of many unique communities.

Answers p. 32

Psychology

★★ 045

Emotional intelligence
정서지능

요즘 각종 서적과 매스컴에서 강조하는 인간 능력은 지적 능력이 아닌 정서적 능력, 바로 정서지능 emotional intelligence이다. 정서지능이 대두하게 된 것은 지능이 높은 사람이 사회적으로 반드시 성공하는 것은 아니라는 인식이 퍼지면서부터였다. IQ가 높더라도 다른 아이들과 잘 어울리지 못한다거나, 대학 생활을 제대로 하지 못하고 중도에 휴학이나 자퇴를 하기도 하고, 직장 생활에서 효과적으로 일을 처리하지 못하여 낙오되는 경우가 자주 일어난다고 한다. 우리는 흔히 지적 능력이 좋으면 사회적으로 성공할 거라고 생각하게 되는데, 오히려 사회에 잘 적응하지 못하고 능력을 발휘하지 못한 채 실패자로 낙인 찍히는 사례가 자꾸 나타나니 지적 능력에 대해 의문을 가질 수밖에 없는 것이다.

그렇다면 인간의 어떤 능력이 사회적 성공을 이끌 수 있을까? 많은 사람들이 여기에 관심을 두고 연구하기 시작하였고 과학자들은 정서지능인 자신의 정서에 대한 이해능력 perceiving emotions, 스스로 감정을 조절할 수 있는 능력 managing emotions, 다른 사람에 대한 감정이입능력 understanding emotions에 주목했다. 그들은 이러한 정서지능을 갖추고 있어야만 중대한 난국에 빠졌을 때, 좌절을 딛고 목표를 향해 나갈 때, 삶의 위기에 직면했을 때 비로소 극복할 수 있게 된다고 말한다. 앞으로 사회가 더 발달할수록 인간의 지적 능력이 더욱 높아질수록 정서지능에 대한 연구와 관심은 계속 지속될 것이다.

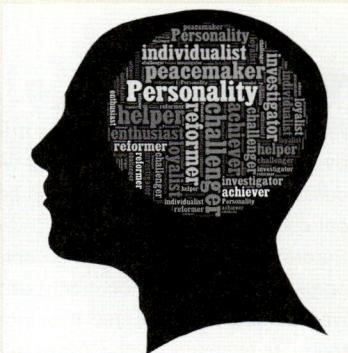

필수어휘
- non-verbal cues 비언어적 신호
- gauge 측정하다
- spectrum 범위
- consistently 일관하여, 지속적으로

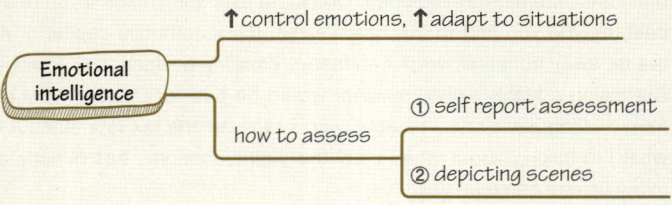

Mini Practice

Listen to part of a lecture in a psychology class. 🎧 Ch3_03

1. According to the lecture, why are Self Report Assessments easy to administer?
   - Ⓐ They are an easiest method for measuring emotional intelligence.
   - Ⓑ People usually want to learn about themselves, so they usually enjoy taking the tests.
   - Ⓒ The test is very simple, making it inexpensive and fast to administer.
   - Ⓓ An online version of the test is available.

2. In the lecture, the professor describes looking at people's faces and reading emotions. What is the significance of this? Click on 2 answers.
   - Ⓐ Test takers that answer correctly can be assumed to be adept at related types of tests.
   - Ⓑ Measuring the proportion of true and false answers makes it possible to evaluate a subject's ability to perceive emotions in others.
   - Ⓒ The subject must be informed that the faces depicted may sometimes have incorrect statements associated with them.
   - Ⓓ The ability to read someone's expressions makes adapting to different people in social contexts easier.

Listening Script

Professor: Emotional intelligence is the ability to understand emotions, both your own emotions, and those of others. Facial gestures, posture, and various non-verbal cues can give you clues about what someone else is feeling. People who can recognize them have high emotional intelligence. Okay, so there are two parts to emotional intelligence. The first is using your own thoughts to understand your own emotions. In other words, you adjust or control your own emotions by thinking about them. The second is the ability to react to various situations by using thoughts to guide your emotions. There are a variety of tests that can be used to gauge a person's emotional intelligence, and I'm going to talk about two of those tests. Okay, so the first one is the Self Report Assessment, and as you might guess from the name, subjects measure their own emotional intelligence by answering a set of simple yes/no questions, like, "Even when I'm having a really bad day, I can control my anger." Each answer has a value associated with it, and after answering, all of the values are added to determine a score, which is checked against a chart. That shows where your emotional intelligence lies within the spectrum of possible scores. One good point about the Self Report Assessment is that participants often enjoy taking the test, because many people like learning more about themselves.

The other type of test I want to talk about involves looking at a series of pictures depicting various scenes. For example, maybe there's a picture of a man smiling. The associated text might read, "I can see anger on the man's face." Typically, there are a range of answers to choose from, such as "Very much," "A little," "Not at all" and so on. If a subject can consistently match up the appropriate answers with the expressions in the photographs, then the test would indicate an ability to accurately read other people's emotions. The neat thing is that this approach of teaching emotional intelligence as a science is really just getting started, so that means it will continue to develop and improve, so we can expect to have better and better tests at our fingertips to use in measuring emotional intelligence.

Answers p. 32

Business

046

Green marketing
친환경 마케팅

외식, 미용, 의류, 건축 등 여러 산업분야에서 기업들이 친환경 마케팅, 즉 그린 마케팅을 하는 이유는 바로 소비자 인식이 중요해졌기 때문이다. 대중의 환경에 대한 인식이 갈수록 높아지면서 소비자들에게 제대로 다가가기 위한 최고의 마케팅 수단이 바로 그린 마케팅이라고 여겨지고 있다.

그린 마케팅Green Marketing에는 세가지 사전적 의미가 있는데 그 첫 번째는 공해 요인causes of pollution을 제거한 상품을 제조·판매하여 인간의 삶의 질을 높이려는 기업활동을 가리킨다. 두 번째는 환경적 역기능adverse effect을 최소화하면서 소비자가 만족할 만한 수준의 성능과 가격으로 제품을 개발하여 환경적으로 우수한 제품 및 기업 이미지를 창출하는 마케팅을 지칭한다. 마지막 세 번째는 자연환경 보전, 생태계 균형 등을 중시하는 시장접근 전략을 뜻한다. 간략하게 **그린 마케팅은 자연환경을 보호하면서 기업의 이익 실현에 기여하는 마케팅**이라고 볼 수 있다. 기업의 친환경적 행동이 기업의 이미지를 향상시키고 제품에 대한 구매까지 이어지게 할 수 있다는 것이다. 예를 들어 친환경 전구eco-light bulb를 광고한 한 미국회사는 친환경적인 제품과 에너지 사용을 줄이는 회사 정책으로 국민들에게 친환경 기업으로 인정받고 이윤 역시 극대화 할 수 있다. 그러나 친환경 기업environmentally-friendly company으로 인정받기 위해서는 환경법을 잘 준수하며 환경 보호를 위해 헌신하는 모습을 보여 소비자의 신뢰를 얻어야 한다.

필수어휘
- rallies 집회
- bulb 전구
- go back to the drawing board 계획을 다시 세우다
- concrete 구체적인
- inflate 부풀리다
- charm 주문, 마법
- lean 군살을 뺀

Green marketing
- environmentally-friendly products
- tangible benefits for consumers
- reducing waste and energy

Mini Practice

Listen to part of a lecture in a marketing class. 🎧 Ch3_04

1. How does the professor organize the information presented in the lecture?

    Ⓐ She provides general background and then discusses a particular cases as an example.
    Ⓑ She defines a concept and shows some ways it can be applied practically.
    Ⓒ She explains how environmental laws affect a company's profitability.
    Ⓓ She shows how a concept was developed and explains its weaknesses.

2. Based on the lecture, why didn't consumers buy eco-lights initially?

    Ⓐ The company's early advertising didn't clearly show why eco-lights are more desirable than conventional light bulbs.
    Ⓑ The number of people who were concerned about the environment was too small.
    Ⓒ Consumers felt the original slogan was vague and did not relate to the product.
    Ⓓ Standard light bulbs cost less and offered more quality and convenience.

Listening Script

Professor: You might imagine that green marketing is a pretty new concept, but it actually goes back a few decades. It really started on the first Earth Day, back in 1970, when rallies all over the country drew attention to the environmental practices of organizations and individuals. Advertisers imagined this new focus on the environment could be used for the benefit of business. Let's take compact fluorescent light bulbs as an example. When they were first introduced, advertisers tried out a green advertising campaign. The problem was, these "eco-bulbs," let's call them, were much more expensive than regular bulbs. But advertisers ignored that and framed the ads as, well, buying the bulbs was a way to save the planet. Well, it flopped. They didn't sell. Consumers still wanted the quality, price, and so on of ordinary bulbs.

So they went back to the drawing board and designed a new campaign. Rather than the abstract goal of saving the planet, they focused on something concrete that consumers wanted. So the next group of ads emphasized the long-lasting and money-saving nature of eco-bulbs. A bulb that you would rarely ever need to change, that wouldn't inflate your electric bill? It worked like a charm. And this eco-bulb company I'm talking about would be considered an extreme green company, because in addition to its environmentally friendly product, it also tries to reduce energy usage in its offices and factories as much as possible. Compare that, for example, to a company that merely recycles its paper trash, and doesn't do anything else particularly environmentally friendly. Such a company would be called a "lean green" company.

Answers p. 33

Psychology

★★★
047

Hippocampus and spatial memory
해마와 공간기억

인체기능을 다루는 주제에서는 신경계에 관한 내용이 자주 나오는데, 이때 빈출되는 용어인 대뇌 변연계 limbic system와 그와 연관된 배경지식을 꼭 알아두도록 하자.

변연계는 대뇌 피질cerebral cortex과 뇌줄기brain stem의 중간에 있는 기억memory과 감정emotion 그리고 호르몬hormone을 조절하는 중앙부midbrain area로, 포유동물mammals에서 가장 잘 발달하여 있기 때문에 '포유류 뇌'라고도 부른다. 포유동물이 꼬리를 흔들며 애정 표시를 하거나, 흥분과 두려움으로 울부짖거나, 으르렁거리며 움츠릴 수 있는 것도 바로 이 변연계가 잘 발달되어 있기 때문이다. 포유동물은 변연계에 해마hippocampus와 편도핵amygdala이 있어서 파충류와는 달리 학습 기능과 기억 기능을 가지고 있다. 그렇기 때문에 변연계가 손상되면, 포유동물의 학습 기능과 기억 기능이 사라져버리면서 파충류와 비슷한 행동을 하게 된다.

해마가 공간기억spatial memory에 중대한 영향을 끼치는 것은 이미 과학적인 사실이며 해마가 클수록 기억력 또한 오래간다는 사실도 많은 실험을 통해 밝혀졌다. 그렇다면 반대로 인간이나 동물의 행동이 해마의 발달에 끼치는 영향은 없을까? 최근 여러 실험을 통해 공간기억과 연관된 인간의 행동이 해마의 활동을 활발하게 하고 해마가 더욱 커지게도 할 수 있다고 밝혀졌다. 그 예로 일반인보다 공간기억을 많이 해야 하는 택시기사들의 해마 크기가 일반인에 비해 더 큰 것으로 밝혀짐으로 인간 및 동물의 행동이 해마의 발달에도 영향을 끼친다는 사실이 입증되었다.

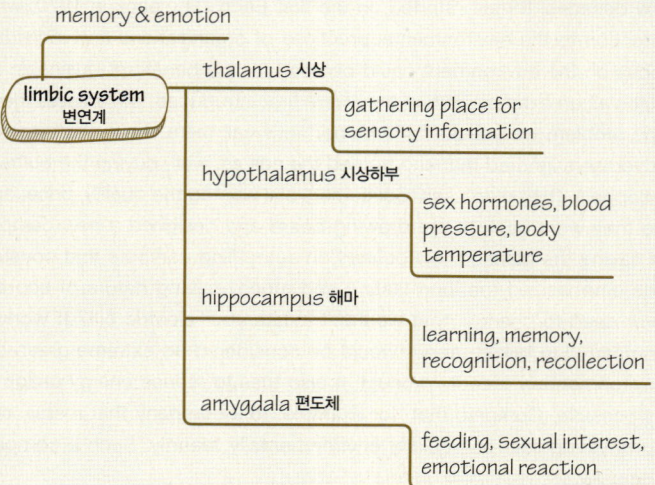

필수어휘

- **hippocampus** 해마
- **spatial memory** 공간기억
- **correlation** 상관관계
- **commonplace** 아주 흔한
- **anatomy** 해부학적 구조
- **evident** 명백한
- **experimental group** 실험군
- **prolonged** 장기적인

Mini Practice

Listen to part of a lecture in a psychology class. 🎧 Ch3_05

1. According to the study discussed by the professor, what was discovered about birds that hide food to use later?

    Ⓐ Compared to other birds, their hippocampus is larger.
    Ⓑ Their chances of survival are higher than birds which do not store food.
    Ⓒ Storing food to use later is a behavior most commonly seen in migratory birds.
    Ⓓ Crows rely principally on spatial memory when locating food they have hidden.

2. What conclusion does the professor draw from the study of taxi drivers?

    Ⓐ Individuals born with a large hippocampus often end up working as taxi drivers.
    Ⓑ Taxi drivers who only recently joined the profession exhibited larger hippocampus than older taxi drivers.
    Ⓒ Brain scans of the taxi drivers indicated structural changes due to the controlled environment.
    Ⓓ The study indicates that the structure of the human brain changes in response to an individual's experience.

Listening Script

Professor: OK. So, last week I talked about the part of the brain called the hippocampus. You'll recall that the hippocampus plays a critical role for memory formation. Let me begin by introducing a study that was related to spatial memory. Spatial memory is uh… is basically remembering where places are, for example not forgetting how to get home from this campus. Some families of wild birds store food and eat it later on, so it is really important that they remember where they have put the food. That's why these food storing birds depend heavily on spatial memory. Researchers found that these birds have a much larger hippocampus in their brain than other kinds of birds that eat whatever they got immediately. Moreover, we can see a correlation between the size of the hippocampus and food storing behavior in other species of birds, which shows that this phenomenon is commonplace regardless of bird species.

Now, let's turn to another interesting finding, which is that brain anatomy can noticeably differ even between individuals of the same species. A case in point is an interesting study on human behavior and the size of hippocampus. A group of researchers examined the brains of sixteen London taxi drivers, and, you know, spatial memory is really important to cab drivers. Oh, and the researchers' first study showed that when taxi drivers had to recall complicated routes around the city, the hippocampus in their brains became highly active. So it was evident that the hippocampus was related to this behavior. So, the next step was to find out if their job has actually contributed to the enlarged hippocampus of these taxi drivers. The experimental group consisted of male taxi drivers, while the control group was a group of men who were not taxi drivers. When the structural brain scans of these two groups were compared, it turned out that the hippocampus region of the taxi drivers was bigger than that of the males in the control group. So this study supports the claim that driving taxi for a prolonged period of time has affected the size of the hippocampus parts that were related to spatial knowledge.

Answers p. 34

Economics

★★★
048

Industrial revolution
산업 혁명

모두가 잘 알고 있는 그 유명한 산업혁명! 영국에서 처음 산업혁명이 발생한 원인과 과정, 그 결과를 다시 한 번 정리하도록 하자.

필수어휘

- **deforestation** 산림 벌채
- **lumber** 목재
- **iron ore** 철광석 (철을 함유한 광석)
- **blast furnace** 용광로 (철광석에서 선철을 만드는데 사용)
- **condenser** 냉각기
- **coke** 코크스 (석탄으로 만들어진 탄소질의 고체 연료)
- **puddling furnace** 연철로 (연철 wrought iron 부식에도 꽤 강한 성질을 띠며, 주철 cast iron보다는 강하며 강철보다는 약한 철를 만드는 용광로)

18-19세기, 영국에서 가장 먼저 시작된 산업혁명 industrial revolution은 농업 사회가 산업 도시로 전환되면서 새로운 기계, 공장, 향상된 생산성, 삶의 질 개선 등 사회 전반에 변화를 가져온 사건이었다. 산업 혁명 이전, 18세기 후반의 영국 제조업은 육체 노동 manual labor을 기반으로 간단한 기구와 기계를 이용한 가내 공업 cottage industry으로 이루어졌다. 하지만 산업 혁명으로 이러한 모습은 기계, 공장, 대량 생산의 모습으로 탈바꿈하게 된다. 증기 엔진 steam engine 개발과 더불어 제철업과 의류 산업 textile industry이 산업 혁명에서 주도적 역할을 했으며, 이와 함께 운송, 통신, 은행 체계가 발달했다. 1800년 이후, 국민 소득이 10배 정도 증가하고 인구는 전례 없는 증가율을 보였다. 그러나 산업화의 이면에는 빈곤층이나 노동 계층의 삶은 혹독했다는 부정적인 측면도 있었다.

영국이 산업 혁명의 발상지가 된 데에는 여러 요인들을 꼽을 수 있다. 우선 영국에는 산업화의 동력인 석탄과 철광석 iron ore이 풍부했고, 다른 나라들과는 달리 정치적으로 안정되어 있었다. 또한 세계 제일의 식민지 강국 colonial power으로 식민지로부터 다양한 원자재 raw material를 제공받았을 뿐 아니라, 가공 물품을 팔 수 있는 시장 역시 확보되어 있었다.

가내 수공업으로 이루어 졌던 영국의 섬유 산업은 1700년대 산업혁명 이후 기계의 도움으로 인간 노동력에 대한 수요가 크게 줄어들었다. 제철 산업 역시 산업 혁명에서 중요한 역할을 했다. 18세기 에이브러햄 다비 Abraham Darby(1678-1717)가 코크스 cokes를 연료로 하는 용광로를 사용하여 무쇠 cast iron를 더 값싸고 손쉽게 만드는 방법을 발견했고, 헨리 베세머 Henry Bessemer(1813-1898)는 강철을 대량으로 생산하는 방법을 고안했다. 이렇듯 철과 강철이 도구, 장비, 기계, 배, 건물, 기반 시설 등을 만드는데 필요한 핵심 재료로 사용되면서 산업화는 더욱 가속화됐다.

Steam Engine in Britain

In the seventeenth century, the growing population in Europe resulted in rapid deforestation. This phenomenon affected many areas in Britain including homes but also industries, where lumber was used as an important source of fuel and for producing pig iron. In 1740, Britain's iron industry stagnated due to the limited supply of wood. In order to mitigate the energy crisis, Britain turned to coal reserves, which could be found abundantly all over the country. Soon this new source of fuel became an alternative to wood fuel and allowed industries to carry on making products.

New mines sprang up all over the country and they dug deeper in order to obtain more coal. The deep mines eventually filled with rainwater and something needed to be done to allow the miners to continue their mining operations. In 1705, Thomas Newcomen (1664-1729) invented the first primitive steam engine, which was used to pump out water from the coal mines. Although the new invention worked much better than the previous method of using animals to remove water, it was very inefficient because it needed to burn coal in order to make steam. Nevertheless, by the 1770s, many of them were operating successfully, although inefficiently, in Britain's coal mines.

By the 1770s, Scottish inventor James Watt (1736-1819) had improved Newcomen's design by adding a separate condenser and the steam engine went on to power machinery, locomotives and ships during the Industrial Revolution. Steam engines also replaced the water-powered cotton-spinning mills, ultimately leading to the rise of industrialization.

Eventually, Britain's iron industry had to find an alternative to charcoal, a byproduct of burning wood, which was becoming rarer and very expensive. They switched over to using readily available and inexpensive *coke*, a byproduct of "cooking" coal, as the fuel source for smelting pig iron. Later in 1780, Henry Cort developed the puddling furnace, which significantly contributed to Britain's rising economy. The puddling furnace is an adaptation of a type already used for casting iron. With the continual rise in iron production throughout the 19th century, the economy naturally grew quickly and more jobs were created, bringing in much wealth for the country and its people.

1. Which of the sentences below best expresses the essential information in the highlighted sentence in the passage? *Incorrect* choices change the meaning in important ways or leave out essential information.

    (A) The steam engine was not very productive since it needed to utilize coal for it to work, but still an improvement from employing animals to pump out water.
    (B) Pumping out water by steam engine was not much more efficient than using horses since coal had to be burned.
    (C) Using steam engines led to an inefficient result because it wasted the resources.
    (D) Using animals to pump out water in some cases could have been more efficient than using steam engines.

2. The word available in paragraph 4 is closest in meaning to

    (A) communicable   (B) transportable   (C) possible   (D) accessible

Answers p. 34

Economics

049
Industrialization in US
미국의 산업화

남북 전쟁 이후, 산업 발전으로 경제가 발달하기 시작한다. 그 전후의 과정들을 살펴보자.

산업 혁명 Industrial Revolution으로 인한 기술혁신은 노동 부문을 포함하여 삶의 다양한 영역에서 획기적 변화를 유발했다. 아직 기계가 공장에서 돌아가기 전에는 큰 자본이나 작업장은 필요 없이 가족 단위로 집cottage에서 수작업으로 물품을 제작했다. 그러나 산업 혁명 이후 기계를 구매하는 데 많은 자본이 필요하긴 했지만, 적은 수의 기계와 적은 양의 노동력으로 대량 생산이 가능해지면서 큰 이윤을 얻게 되었다.

가내 공업cottage industry은 상인으로부터 원자재raw material를 구매하여 그것을 자신의 집으로 가져와 물건을 만드는 작업 형태를 말한다. 물건을 완성하는 과정에서 복잡한 기계 공정 없이 간단한 도구와 장인artisan의 숙련된competent 기술만이 필요했다. 하지만 작업 속도가 전반적으로 느리고 상품을 완성하는데 다소 많은 시간이 소요되었으며, 소규모인데다가 조직적이지organized 못했기 때문에 생산성productivity이 상당히 낮다는 단점이 있었다. 그래서 완제품의 가격은 높을 수 밖에 없었고, 구매객은 주로 부유층에 국한되었다.

반면, 공장제도factory system는 돈 있는 사람이 자본capital을 투자하여 많은 기계를 구매해서 이를 공장에 설비하고 작업할 사람들을 고용하게 한다. 공장 제도는 완제품의 가격이 가내 공업 제품보다 훨씬 낮아지는 장점이 있었으나, 노동자들의 삶의 질과 제품의 질은 떨어질 수 밖에 없었다. 여성과 아이들이 공장 노동력의 상당 부분을 차지했고, 긴 노동 시간과 여러 질병 발생과 같은 노동자 인권 문제가 공장제도의 문제점으로 대두되었다.

필수어휘
- fabric 직물
- artisan 장인
- labor intensive 노동 집약적인
- manufacturing 제조업
- patent 특허권
- water wheel 수차
- exploit 이용하다, 착취하다
- improve 개선하다, 향상시키다
  syn enhance

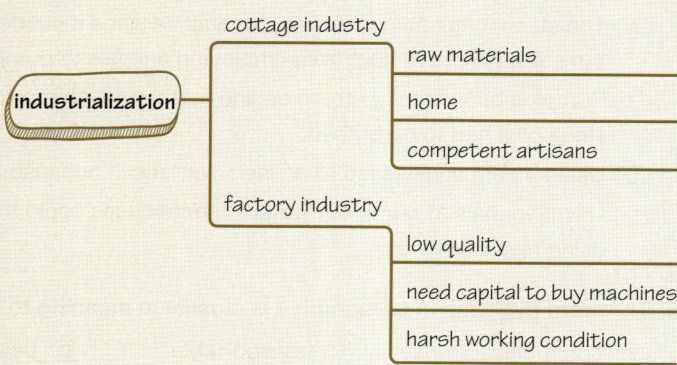

Mini Practice

The American Industrial Revolution

Before the American Industrial Revolution, majority of products and services were provided by cottage industries, where production of goods or services was based in the home. For example, individual families or groups of artisans would create fabrics or clothing by hand. However, this labor-intensive process was eventually replaced by modernized manufacturing processes.

Beginning in the 1760s, American and European inventions were revolutionizing the way products were manufactured. American patent laws that were favorable to inventors fostered creativity and encouraged European experts and inventors to emigrate to America to profit from their inventions. This was later followed by periodic mass immigration from Ireland and other European nations. These immigrants were sources of cheap labor, which further decreased the costs of production and allowed factory owners to mass-produce enormous quantities of goods.

The majority of these factories depended on water wheels for power, so they were naturally concentrated in New England and northern regions of America, where there are many rivers. This played a vital role in the American Civil War (1861-1865). Not only did the presence of so many factories allow the North to produce large quantities of armaments, but the war also sparked a new wave of inventions and improvements in manufacturing processes. These improved processes, combined with the expansion of transcontinental railroads and the introduction of the telegraph and telephone allowed America to become a world industrial powerhouse. With the discovery of massive coal and oil deposits after the war, factories and industries were able to spread across the country. This also spurred the development of new industries and added the types of goods that could be produced. This technology boom and the improvement of manufacturing processes would continue until the early 1900s.

However, this rise in power and wealth came with a very high social cost. To improve efficiency, many factory owners would provide housing for their employees. Workers often lived in squalid and cramped conditions, which often led to poor health and the easy spread of diseases. At that time, children and women were often exploited to work in high-risk jobs in mines and factories. There was a great divide between the wealth earned by the factory owner and their employees. This ultimately led to social reforms that vastly improved the lives of workers.

1. The word massive in paragraph 3 is closest in meaning to
   - (A) recurrent
   - (B) prominent
   - (C) rough
   - (D) huge

2. According to paragraph 4, which of the following is true?
   - (A) Factory workers' problems were completely solved after the social reforms.
   - (B) More children and women worked than men in the factories.
   - (C) Employees were required to live in the houses that factory owners provided.
   - (D) Factory workers often had health problems at work.

Answers p. 35

Psychology

050

Internet Addiction Disorder
인터넷 중독 질환

인터넷 중독Internet addiction, 사이버 중독, 병적 인터넷 사용Pathological Internet Use(PIU), 인터넷 증후군, 웨버홀리즘Webaholism 등으로 다양하게 불리는 인터넷 중독 질환은 '정보 이용자가 지나치게 컴퓨터에 접속하여 일상 생활에 심각한 사회적, 정신적, 육체적 및 금전적「지장」을 받고 있는 상태'라고 정의된다. 즉, 지나친 인터넷 접속으로 인한 의존성과 금단 증상 등으로 일상 생활이 힘든 상태이다. 1980년대 이후 컴퓨터가 보급되면서 컴퓨터 중독이라는 용어가 새로이 등장하게 되었고, 1990년대를 넘어서자 인터넷이 보급되면서 1996년에 들어서면서 인터넷 사용이 증가함에 따라 인터넷 중독이 나타나게 되었다. 인터넷 중독 질환(IAD)이라는 용어를 처음으로 사용한 사람은 1996년 정신과 의사인 이반 골드버그Ivan K.Goldberg였다. 그는 인터넷 중독에 대한 진단 기준을 크게 다음 7가지로 분류하였다.

❶ 인터넷을 사용하면 할수록 더 많은 시간을 인터넷 상에 있기 원하는 경우 (내성 – tolerance)
❷ 인터넷을 사용하지 않으면 불안, 불면 등 금단 증상을 느끼는 것 (withdrawal symptom)
❸ 생각했던 것보다 더 자주, 길게 인터넷을 사용하는 경우
❹ 인터넷 사용을 줄이거나 조절하려는 욕구가 지속적으로 있었거나 혹은 그 시도에 성공하지 못하는 경우
❺ 많은 시간을 인터넷 사용과 관련된 행동에 소비하는 경우
❻ 중요한 사회, 직업, 혹은 여가활동이 인터넷 사용을 위해 포기되거나 감소되는 경우
❼ 인터넷 사용에 의해 유발되거나 악화되고, 지속적이거나 반복적인 신체적, 사회적, 직업적, 심리적 문제를 갖고 있음에도 불구하고 인터넷 사용을 계속하는 경우

골드버그는 적어도 12개월 동안 최소한 3가지 이상의 항목에 해당하는 경우가 인터넷 중독증에 해당한다고 말한다. 인터넷 중독을 치료하기 위해서는 다른 중독치료와 마찬가지로 인터넷 사용량을 기록하고 스스로 문제점을 인식하며 조금씩 사용량을 줄여야 한다. 언제나 중용이 제일 좋다는 것을 기억하고 인터넷의 홍수 속에서 빠져나와 주위를 둘러보고 여유를 느끼는 법을 잊지 말도록 하자.

필수어휘
☐ substitute 대체하다
☐ indicator 지표
☐ disorder 장애
☐ addicts 중독자들

How to cure IAD?
- Examine the pattern of Internet use
- Think about the reason for using the Internet
- Make a plan to reduce Internet use
- Reduce Internet use little by little

Mini Practice

Listen to part of a lecture in a social studies class. 🎧 Ch3_06

1. Based on the lecture, how might Internet Addiction Disorder affect sleep?

    (A) People with Internet Addiction Disorder sleep more soundly because they are tired.
    (B) The onset of the REM stage of sleep is faster in patients suffering from IAD.
    (C) People may have dreams about being online.
    (D) It causes interference in brain wave activity while sleeping.

2. The professor mentions several ways to address IAD. Which of the following is NOT an approach mentioned in the lecture?

    (A) prepare a plan for reducing Internet use
    (B) examine Internet usage patterns
    (C) limit time spent on the Internet to a specific daily allowance
    (D) implement a plan for addressing the problem

Listening Script

Professor: Today I'm going to talk about Internet Addiction Disorder, or IAD. Doctors have identified seven indicators of this disorder. The first is simply wanting to spend more time on the Internet. Second, having dreams about being online, including moving their fingers or sleep-typing. Third, actually thinking that being on the Internet feels physically good. The fourth sign of IAD is spending more time online than intended. And even off-line, people with IAD spent lots of time doing Internet-related things, such as reading books about the Internet, attending related conferences, and so on. That's the fifth sign. And the sixth is beginning to substitute time online for social activities. The final sign is where Internet use becomes more important than even essential things like showering, homework, job loss, child care and even eating. Addicts will lie about the amount of time they spend online and they will keep using the Internet despite threat of punishment.

What can be done for people suffering from IAD? Well, IAD is fairly new, so doctors don't have much experience treating it. Some attempts include programs similar to those for smoking or gambling addicts. The doctor who coined the term IAD, Ivan Goldberk, thinks people who believe they might be addicted should try and help themselves. They should be aware of their pattern of Internet use, keeping track of how much time they spend at their computer. They should also be aware of how often they think about the Internet. They should consider why they spend so much time online. Perhaps they are escaping from some other problem? And they should make a plan to solve the problem, rather than ignoring it, such as planning their Internet use and trying to reduce the time spent online a little each day. That raises another question: How much time should someone spend on the Internet each day? According to one doctor who studied IAD, the important thing is balance. Online time should not distract from other enjoyable things and should not take away from time they want to spend with family and friends.

Answers p. 36

Psychology

051

Placebo effect
위약효과

심리학 지문은 추상적 개념과 용어로 인해 한글 설명 마저 이해하기 어렵다는 학생들이 많다. 빈출 주제들과 심리 관련 어휘를 체크하여 심리적 안정감을 찾자!

위약효과란 의미의 플라시보 효과Placebo Effect는 의학적 효과가 전혀 없는 설탕이나 밀가루, 생리 식염수 성분으로 만들어진 가짜 약을 환자에게 투여하여 치료 효과가 나타나 병세가 호전되는 현상을 말한다. 플라시보 효과에서 환자의 심리적 안정과 믿음, 기대 심리가 중요하게 작용하기 때문에 환자가 기대하는 만큼 결과가 드러난다.

플라시보 효과에 대한 하나의 가설은 엔도르핀endorphin의 분비로 플라시보가 유발된다는 것이다. 이 가설에 따르면, 엔도르핀이 모르핀morphine과는 다른 아편 진통제와 비슷한 구조로 이루어져 뇌가 만들어낸 천연 진통제의 역할을 한다고 한다. 연구자들은 뇌 사진을 통해 플라시보 효과를 입증하기도 했다. 한 조사에서는 실제 약품과 플라시보를 주입한 후, 양전자 단층 사진(PET)을 통해 뇌의 모습을 촬영한 결과 뇌의 전대상회피질anterior cingulate cortex 부분이 플라시보나 실제 치료를 했을 때 모두 활성화 되는 것을 보여주었다.

플라시보 효과의 또 다른 가설은 훈련, 자극, 기대 등의 환자의 심리 상태가 영향을 끼친다는 것이다. 플라시보는 원하는 효과가 유발될 때까지 실제 치료와 함께 병행될 수 있다. 이것을 고전적 조건 부여classical conditioning라고 하는데, 이는 조건 자극과 무조건 자극을 병행하여 나중에는 조건 자극만으로도 반응을 유발할 수 있도록 하는 것을 말한다. 플라시보를 받을 때 치료가 효과적일 것이라고 기대하는 환자들의 기대감과 신뢰가 그 효과를 더욱 효과적으로 만들 가능성이 크다.

한편, 플라시보 효과와는 반대인 노시보 효과nocebo effect가 있다. 이것은 진짜 약을 투여했는데도 환자가 효과가 없다고 생각하거나 오히려 그 약이 해롭다고 생각하면 약효가 전혀 드러나지 않는 현상으로 참고로 알아 두도록 하자.

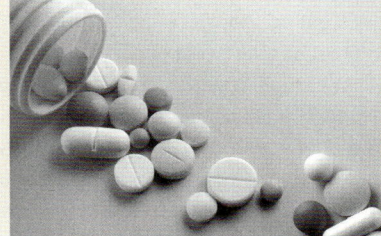

필수어휘

- fake 가짜의
- treatment 치료, 처치
- stimulate 자극하다
- reinforce 강화하다, 보강하다
- deteriorate 악화되다
- inert 화학 작용을 일으키지 못하는, 활발하지 않은
- physiological 생리학적인
- trigger 계기, 자극 ⓥ 유발하다

Placebo

A placebo is a "fake" treatment or medicine that is given to a patient who is deceived into believing it is real. This may sound brutal or inhumane, but it is a part of a long history of research in the field of medicine. Placebos are an important part of medical research that seeks to determine whether the treatment is effective. Often, the only way to determine a treatment's usefulness is to compare the results of patients who receive the placebo with those of patients who receive the real treatment.

Although a placebo is "fake," there is a unique phenomenon known as the "placebo effect" where patients' health actually improves. It is a fairly complicated process that medical researchers still do not understand but somehow a patient's belief that they are receiving the real treatment can actually allow their medical condition to improve. This belief that they are healing is thought to naturally stimulate their immune system and fight against depression and anxiety, both of which negatively impact the body's ability to heal itself. It is also possible that the positive and reinforcing attention given to patients during the placebo treatment improves their mood, supports a positive attitude toward healing, and contributes to an overall happier and healthier condition. However, sometimes patients may come to depend on the placebo treatment and believe that without that treatment, their medical condition will deteriorate.

In some cases, the reverse happens, where a patient's negative beliefs result in further deterioration of their health and they become even more ill, both with the real treatment and with the placebo. Although the placebo is an inert and harmless substance, this "nocebo effect" is thought to be caused by a patient's belief that regardless of receiving the placebo or real treatment they strongly believe that treatment is hopeless. It seems that a real psychological belief has a serious and often negative impact on the biological and physiological systems of the body, all stemming from what the patient thinks about the treatment. Researchers know that psychological beliefs can negatively and positively impact physiological processes within the body but still struggle to understand the mechanisms of these processes.

1. The word phenomenon in paragraph 2 is closest in meaning to
   - (A) occurrence
   - (B) stratum
   - (C) problem
   - (D) chain

2. The word deteriorate in paragraph 2 is closest in meaning to
   - (A) deject
   - (B) deviate
   - (C) worsen
   - (D) menace

Answers p. 36

Sociology

052

Printing
인쇄술

인쇄술이 발명되기 전에는 여러 사람들이 복잡한 공정 과정을 거쳐 책 한 권을 완성했다. 책의 재료인 소, 양, 염소의 가죽으로 만들어진 양피지parchment가 준비되면, 필기사scribe가 직접 책을 베껴 썼다. 각 장의 글, 그림 등을 그대로 베끼는데 시간과 정성이 많이 들기 때문에 책의 가격은 비쌀 뿐 아니라 수요를 충족시킬 수 없는 어려움이 있었다.

6세기 말 중국에서 발명된 인쇄술printing은 13세기가 되어서야 베네치아 상인들에 의해 서아시아를 거쳐 유럽에 전파되었다. 현대 활판인쇄술typography은 독일의 요하네스 구텐베르크Johannes Gutenberg(1398-1468)가 판면에 글자를 볼록하게 조판한 다음, 잉크를 묻히고 압력을 가해 인쇄하는 법을 발명하면서 본격적으로 시작되었다. 그것은 나무틀 안에 활자type를 조판typeset해서 잉크를 묻히고 종이에 대고 눌러 찍는 형태였다. 유럽에서 인쇄술이 발달할 수밖에 없었던 이유는 ① 로마 알파벳의 철자 수가 많지 않았고, ② 활자 재료인 금속의 가격이 비싸지 않았을 뿐 아니라, ③ 활자에 잘 붙고, 종이 재질에 번지지 않는 유성잉크를 사용했으며 ④ 값싼 종이가 14세기에 중국에서 유럽으로 전파되었기 때문이다. 15세기에는 인쇄기가 유럽 전 지역에 보급되면서, 비교적 저렴한 가격에 책을 대량 생산mass produce할 수 있게 되었다. 이러한 책의 보급으로 정보 공유와 지식의 발전이 가속화되었고, 새로운 사상과 학문이 빨리 보급되었다.

그 후 값싼 인쇄술의 보급은 1840-50년대 영국과 미국에 상당한 파급효과를 가져왔다. 특히 인쇄물의 질 보다는 가격을 우선시했던 미국에서 그 효과가 상당히 컸는데, 신문과 소설의 가격이 급격히 떨어지게 되면서 출판사publisher들이 더 많은 독자를 끌어 모으기 위해 많은 책들을 싼 가격으로 찍어냈다. 게다가 기존에는 종교적 주제에 국한되었으나, 다양한 주제들을 다루는 인쇄물들이 대량 출간되면서 더 많은 사람들이 책을 접할 수 있게 되었다.

필수어휘
- movable type 활판
- literate 글을 읽고 쓸 줄 아는
- Linotype 라이노타이프 (자동 주식가 활자를 주조하거나, 원고 내용대로 활자를 골라 뽑고, 뽑은 활자를 원고 내용대로 조판하는 것을 자동적으로 할 수 있는 기계)
- character 글자
- font 폰트 (같은 크기, 서체의 활자 한 벌)
- dime novel 싸구려 소설, 삼류 소설
- publishing market 출판 시장

parchment		paper
scribe by hand	before → Printing → after	typography
costly		mass production

Mini Practice

Printing

    Prior to the printing press, books were copied by hand mainly by scribes or monks, so it could take several months for one person to write out a copy of a book. That all changed in 1450, when the German blacksmith and printer Johannes Gutenberg was credited with the introduction of movable type in Europe. This system made it possible to combine pieces of metal bearing individual letters and produce pages of text that could be printed repeatedly, opening the door for the first time to mass distribution of books. However, at that time, the number of literate people was small and Gutenberg's printing process was slow and costly compared to hand-copying, so people did not adopt his improvement quickly.

    Until the nineteenth century, despite several attempts to improve the printing process, Gutenberg's basic print technology had not changed dramatically, and printers completed each step of the printing process by hand, just as the printers did in Gutenberg's print shop. Then, the Linotype came along. Created in the U.S., it was a significant leap forward in printing technology, automating the process of arranging characters into lines of type. With type set by machine instead of by hand, Linotype led to an improvement in efficiency and allowed typesetters to readily change the font size to fit the copy. The New York Times was the first paper printed by this print technology, and it spurred a huge growth in books, magazines and newspapers.

    In the United States, the effect of advances in printing technology was more dramatic than in Europe. First, the price of printed books and paper dropped and publishers were able to mass-produce printed books at a cheap price. In the late nineteenth century, Americans enjoyed "dime novels": cheap, sensational tales that generally cost less than ten cents. Some criticized the quality of paper and the immoral subject matter, but publishing companies chose not to concentrate on one version and instead offered various printings, so they were able to attract both the readers who could afford only cheap paperback books and those wanting more luxurious leather-bound editions. While the printed books of the past were exclusively religious or political, with advances in printing, the subject-matter of books became more diverse and sensational, which led to a shift in people's values and interests. The U.S citizens of all societal strata were able to read mass-produced, affordable printed books, and the publishing market in the United States abruptly expanded.

1. What can be inferred from paragraph 2?

    Ⓐ Even before the advent of Linotype, printers quickly finished the printing process.
    Ⓑ Because of the improved printing technique, New York Times were expensive.
    Ⓒ During the nineteenth century, Gutenberg's basic technology started to change noticeably.
    Ⓓ Printers were not satisfied with Gutenberg's printing press, as it was inconvenient.

2. The word abruptly in paragraph 3 is closest in meaning to

    Ⓐ appropriately   Ⓑ suddenly   Ⓒ effectively   Ⓓ arduously

Psychology

053
Psychology
심리학

심리학psychology은 인간의 의식 상태와 행동에 대해 과학적인 연구를 하는 학문으로 1차적 목적은 이론을 확립하고 특정 사례들을 조사함으로써 개인과 집단을 이해하는 것이지만, 궁극적으로는 사회 전반에 유익을 주는 것을 목표로 한다. 심리학자psychologist들은 개인 혹은 집단의 지각perception(감각을 통해 인지하는 것), 인지cognition(지각, 문제해결, 사고, 언어 능력 등의 지적인 심리적 기능), 감정emotion, 동기motivation, 성격personality, 대인 관계interpersonal relationship 등을 통해 심리학을 연구한다.

유명 심리학자들

대표적인 심리학자인 오스트리아의 정신의학자 프로이트Sigmund Freud(1856-1939)는 정신분석학psychoanalysis을 창시함으로써 인류학, 교육학, 사회학에 이르기까지 다양한 분야에 영향을 끼쳤으며, 특히 꿈과 무의식unconscious mind의 세계를 연구한 것으로 잘 알려져 있다. 프로이트의 영향을 받은 스위스의 정신의학자이자 심리학자인 융Carl Jung은 심리 발단단계에는 개인적인 것과 집단적인 것이 융합하여 작용한다고 주장하며 집단 무의식collective unconsciousness을 연구했다.

발달 심리학developmental psychology의 대가인 피아제Jean Piaget(1896-1980)는 인간의 인지 발달 단계cognitive developmental stage를 나이에 따라 4단계로 구분하여 교육 심리학에 큰 영향을 끼쳤다. 1단계 감각 동작기Sensorimotor Stage(0-2세)는 언어 없이 감각기관을 통해 세상을 배워가며 간단한 상징체계를 이해하고 2단계 전조작기Preoperational Stage(2-7세)에서는 단어, 그림 등을 통해 표현하기 시작하고, 사물의 이름을 인지하며 언어가 발달한다. 3단계는 구체적 조작기Concrete Operation Stage(7-11세)로 구체적인 사례들을 통한 논리적 사고logical thinking가 가능하며 마지막 4단계 형식적 조작기Formal Operational Stage(11-15세)에서는 추상적 사고abstract thinking와 논리적 판단이 가능하다.

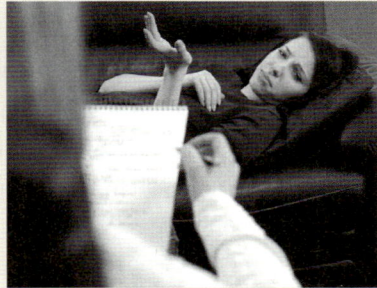

필수어휘
- attribution 귀인
- internal 내부의
  - [ant] external 외부의
- consistency 일관성
- consensus 의견 일치
- distinctiveness 특수성
- bias 편견 [syn] prejudice
- attribute 탓으로 돌리다
- objective 객관적인
  - [ant] subjective 주관적인

Attribution Theory

"Attribution theory" discusses the ways in which people unconsciously come to understand and describe causes of other people's behaviors as well as their own. This theory was introduced by Fritz Heider in 1958 and subsequently developed by Harold Kelley and Bernard Weiner. The theory proposes that people's actions are attributable to internal factors such as personality, mood, ability and effort; and external factors including other people, luck, pressure and weather.

Considering a man's behavior when he is late for a flight provides a good example. Imagine he is rushing through a terminal, running with his bags, bumping into others and does not take time to apologize to those that he disturbed. How would you interpret his behavior? Is he being selfish and aggressive in nature, or is he justified in doing so because of his situation? Kelley argued that people consider three factors when making a personal or situational attribution: 1) Consistency—does this person consistently react this way when faced with this situation? 2) Consensus—would others have the same reaction if they were in the same situation?; and 3) Distinctiveness—does this person exhibit the same behavior in other situations? These questions allow an individual to determine if a behavior is internal or dependent upon situational factors. By answering these questions, the observer can assess the actions of an individual and, in theory, accurately determine their personality type.

However, when people try to find and explain the cause of results or events, they are likely to make frequent errors due to their own biases and prejudices. First, when evaluating others' behavior, people tend to attribute the success of others to the influence of external factors, while attributing failure to the influence of internal factors. This is called "fundamental attribution error." On the other hand, when someone succeeds at a task, they are likely to want to attribute this success to their own abilities, but when they fail, they will want to attribute their failure to factors over which they have no control, such as bad luck or bad weather. This is called "self-serving bias" in which people do not make objective situational or personal attributions in regard to their own behavior.

1. The word attribute in paragraph 3 is closest in meaning to
   - (A) initiate
   - (B) ascribe
   - (C) change
   - (D) apply

2. The word which in paragraph 3 refers to
   - (A) factors
   - (B) failure
   - (C) abilities
   - (D) success

Answers p. 38

Business

054
S curve in business
S 커브이론

S커브 이론이란 글로벌 컨설팅 기업인 액센츄어Accenture가 성공 기업들의 공통요인을 뽑아 만든 개념으로, 기업이 혁신innovation을 채택adopt하는 속도speed를 나타내는 측정값measure이다. 이것은 기업이 새로운 혁신을 얼마나 빨리 받아들이는지가 기업의 성공을 좌우한다고 주장하며 혁신을 받아들이고 성장하는 단계를 「완만한 성장세growth cycle → 가파른 성장세get on top → 성장 정체stay there」 등 3가지로 나누었다.

1단계는 한 기업이 새 상품을 출시하고 얼리어답터early adopter의 주목을 받아 완만한 성장을 시작하는 구간이고 2단계는 그 기업이 경쟁자를 제칠 만큼 대중의 관심을 끌면서 빠르게 성장하는 구간이며, 3단계는 소비자 선호 변화와 다른 경쟁자 출현으로 성장세가 정체되어 퇴조하는 단계이다.

첫 번째 S곡선에서 성공하기 위한 3개의 열쇠는 시장을 찾아내는 통찰력, 사업 확장보다는 실력 쌓기, 그리고 인재 양성이라고 하였다. 특히 높은 성과를 이루는 기업의 경우 S커브에 올라간 후 새로운 S커브로 계속 갈아타는 과정을 반복한다. 이렇게 새로운 S커브로 갈아타며 성공을 거듭하는 기업을 하이 퍼포먼스 기업high performance company이라 지칭했으며 이러한 기업이 되기 위한 비결은 하나의 사업이 가파른 성장을 보일 때 기존의 S곡선에 안주하지 않고 다음에 올라탈 성공을 향한 S곡선을 미리 준비하는 것이다. 하이퍼포먼스 기업의 예로는 애플이나 P&G와 같은 기업들이 있다.

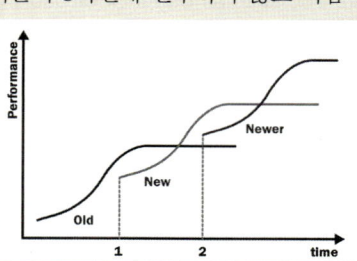

필수어휘
- innovation lifecycle 혁신주기
- accelerating 가속화하는
- steeply 가파르게
- wane 시들해지다
- level off 수평을 유지하다
- marginal 미미한, 주변의
- constitute 구성하다

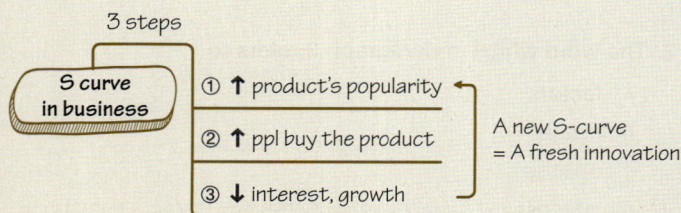

Mini Practice

Listen to part of a lecture in a business class. 🎧 Ch3_07

1. What is the main focus of the lecture?
   - Ⓐ The characteristic success of "Kind of Blue"
   - Ⓑ The traits of a specific kind of graph and how certain music closely follows those traits
   - Ⓒ How Miles Davis succeeded as a jazz musician
   - Ⓓ How music genre relates to innovation

2. What is implied about running a business, based on Miles Davis' approach to recording "Kind of Blue"?
   - Ⓐ Like creating an album, running a business can be very difficult.
   - Ⓑ The kind of risks taken in music industry are not appropriate in other areas of business.
   - Ⓒ What Miles Davis did was very difficult.
   - Ⓓ Sometimes it is necessary to take a big risk in order to make a profitable business.

Listening Script

Professor: Let's continue last week's discussion about innovation in business. Here's the graph we were looking at, this S-curve, which represents the innovation lifecycle. Let's consider a new innovation, starting on the left. At this point, the product is new; few people have heard of it. But then popularity starts increasing, first slowly, and then accelerating quickly. You can see here, in the middle, people are getting excited about this product, so the line is going up quite steeply. And then we move to the right, and you can see interest is starting to wane, so sales growth levels off. So at this point, the market for the product is mature. It can still be sold, and marginal improvements made, but it's not this great, innovative new thing anymore, so there aren't these exciting growth opportunities. At this point, a business person is faced with a choice. Do they stick to this old, proven idea? Or do they take a risk and move on to a new innovation, where the rewards are big, but there's no guarantee of success?

Let's consider a case study of Miles Davis, you know, the famous jazz musician, and his album, "Kind of Blue." Prior to that album, his music was so complex that nobody could really understand it. But then in this new album, his playing style sounded amazingly simple. Of course some people were disappointed that he'd abandoned his traditional style, but most of his fans quickly came to appreciate the new style. And it also appealed to a completely new group of jazz listeners. In the end "Kind of Blue" became the single most commercially successful album ever, in the whole history of jazz. If we consider this in the context of the S-curve, his old style was also a kind of product, one that had been taken as far as it could, essentially a mature form. So he made the choice to risk something completely new. Such a fresh start left lots of room for artistic development. So, a market analyst could say that "Kind of Blue" constituted a jump to a brand new S-curve, with lucrative development potential all in the future.

Answers p. 38

Business

★★★
055

Scientific management
과학적 경영

미국의 프레데릭 테일러 Frederick Winslow Taylor(1856-1915)는 철강 회사에서 기술직으로 일하는 동안 노동자들의 나태한 근무 상태와 발달된 기술력에 비해 비효율적인 inefficient 경영을 목격하면서 새로운 과학적 경영법 scientific management 을 고안한 창시자이다.

그는 시간과 동작을 결합한 '동작 연구'를 통해 인간 노동을 기계화하여 최소한의 노동 시간으로 최대한의 능률적 노동 결과 output 를 이끌어 내도록 했다. 그는 당시 일의 성과대로 노동자들에게 급여 wage 를 제공했던 성과급 제도 piece-rate system 가 근로자의 성과가 많을수록 시간 당 급여를 더 주는 것이 아니라, 오히려 낮추었기 때문에 노동에 대한 동기부여가 떨어져 노동자들이 근무에 태만해질 수 밖에 없다는 것을 깨달았다. 그래서 테일러는 많은 시간과 노력을 투자한 끝에 공장에서 이루어지는 모든 작업 과정을 규격화된 노동 형태로 전환하여 표준화된 노동력 labor force 에 따라 성과급을 지급하는 차별적 성과급제도 differential piece rate system 를 만들어 냈다. 또한 과거 주먹구구식의 rule-of-thumb 관리법을 지양하고, 관리자와 노동자를 엄격히 분리하여 전문화된 관리자는 과학적 관리법에 따라 업무량과 업무를 수행하기 위한 방법, 노동의 시간 배분 등을 계획하는 업무를 담당했고, 노동자는 그의 지시에 따라 작업을 수행했다. 하지만 업무 계획을 세울 때 노동자의 창의성과 의사 결정이 엄격히 무시되었고, 기계적인 노동 생산성만을 강조했기 때문에 20세기 초 발생했던 노사 갈등의 부분적 원인이 되기도 했다.

필수어휘

- □ **economic efficiency** 경제효율
  (희소성의 경제 자원을 가장 효율적으로 사용함으로써 얻을 수 있는 효율)
- □ **scientific management** 과학적 관리법
- □ **defective** 결점이 있는
- □ **superintendent** 관리자
- □ **specialization** 전문화, 특화
- □ **meticulously** 면밀하게
- □ **conduct** (실험, 행동을) 하다
- □ **accomplish** 성취하다 [syn] achieve
- □ **designate** 할당하다
- □ **implement** 시행하다, 실시하다
- □ **performance** 성과

Taylorism

Frederick Winslow Taylor was the founder of scientific management, a business theory and practice that was supposed to improve economic efficiency and labor productivity. Taylor developed this theory after he observed low productivity and inefficiency caused by defective management systems while working at a steel company. He realized that owners and managers of the company were not closely involved with the production of their goods, thus leading to ignorance of production processes. Moreover, supervisors were responsible for planning tasks but did so without recognizing employees' various roles. Furthermore, procedures in the factory were determined by the "rule of thumb" among individual mechanics based on their personal experiences, preferences and what tools were available for the job. However, because employees received the same payment regardless of the work amount, they had little incentive to increase their productivity.

In scientific management, Taylor believed that specialization and division of labor increased productivity and efficiency, resulting in higher income for workers and higher profits for owners. Taylor first started by meticulously conducting various experiments to find and improve efficiency based on time and motion studies. For example, using a stopwatch to measure each production step, Taylor eliminated unnecessary movements, substituted these with faster movements, and designed standardized instruction cards for employees, which resulted in increased output. Furthermore, he realized that wages tied to productivity motivated laborers to work harder and so Taylor advocated for workers to be paid based on their individual performance rather than their position or status. With the slogan, "more effort, higher wages" he maximized output for employers and increased wages for employees. This provided opportunities for workers to achieve greater financial rewards such as bonuses and incentives. Finally, Taylor proposed the equal division of work and responsibility between workers and management, which meant that managers were responsible for designing task instructions and training and evaluating each worker scientifically according to his or her accomplishments. While there were some benefits, this theory also had some drawbacks. Focusing solely on the productivity led to the disregard of workers' welfare. Specialization led to workers becoming bored with routine tasks and being limited to only one type of work, which resulted in a loss of productivity.

1. The word substituted in paragraph 2 is closest in meaning to

    (A) subordinated
    (B) suppressed
    (C) subsidized
    (D) replaced

2. In paragraph 2, the author mentions a stopwatch in order to

    (A) exemplify the meticulousness of his experiment
    (B) show his preference for accuracy
    (C) prove that the remuneration system was effective
    (D) demonstrate the importance of time at work

Answers p. 39

Philosophy

★★
056

Thomas Kuhn
토마스 쿤

철학은 토플에 잘 나오진 않지만 난이도가 높아서 배경지식 없이는 쉽게 이해하기가 힘들다. 철학 주제는 기존 이론에 대한 비판, 새로운 개념의 핵심 및 결과 위주로 내용이 흘러간다는 것을 인지하고 중심 내용을 잘 파악하도록 하자.

필수어휘

- notorious 악명 높은
- controversial 논쟁적인
- absolute truth 절대적 진실
- disregard 무시하다
- explanatory 이유를 밝히는
- alternative 대안적인
- paradigms 패러다임
- hinder ~를 못하게 하다, 방해하다
- geocentric theory 지구 중심설
- counter 반박하다
- variation 변화
- planetary orbits 행성궤도

토마스 쿤Thomas Kuhn은 1922년 미국 오하이오 주에서 태어나 하버드 대학에서 물리학 박사를 취득하였다. 학위 취득 후 과학사 강의를 준비하면서 그는 뉴튼역학의 뿌리를 보여줄 수 있는 역사적 사례를 찾기 위해 아리스토텔레스의 「자연학」을 읽다가 잘못된 점을 발견하고 유명 철학자가 어떤 주제에 대해 그렇게 잘못된 생각을 할 수 있을까라는 심각한 물음을 가지게 된다. 결국 이러한 발견은 쿤으로 하여금 이 세상에 절대적 진실absolute truth이란 없으며 사물의 현상을 설명하는 이론theories들만 있다고 주장하며 과학철학scientific philosophy 분야에는 크게 기여하였지만 기존 과학자들로부터 굉장한 비판을 몰고 온 혁신적인 이론을 창시하도록 한다.

그의 저서 「과학혁명의 구조The structure of Scientific Revolutions」에서 토마스 쿤은 과학의 변화와 발전은 축적되는 것이 아니라 비연속적이거나 '혁명적revolutionary'이라고 주장한다. 과학의 변화가 혁명적이라면, 혁명이 일어나기 전에 비혁명적이고 안정된 기간이 있어야 하는데, 쿤은 이 안정된 기간을 '정상과학normal science'의 기간이라고 정의한다. 여기서 정상과학의 특징을 지어주는 중요한 개념이 바로 '패러다임paradigm'이다. 패러다임은 원래 어떤 한 시대 사람들의 견해나 사고를 지배하고 있는 이론적 틀이나 개념의 집합체를 정의하는 말이지만 쿤은 패러다임을 과학과 사회전체에서 공유된 이론, 법칙, 지식, 방법과 가치관, 습관, 규범을 통틀어서 지칭하는 용어로 적용했다. 이후 정상과학이 기존의 패러다임으로 해결할 수 없는 변칙적인 문제를 만나게 되면, 과학혁명의 조짐이 나타나게 된다. 이렇게 현존하는 패러다임에 반하는 연구가 나오고 새로운 패러다임이 혁명적으로 받아들여지는 것을 패러다임의 전환paradigm shifts이라 일컫지만 이는 상당한 혼란을 초래하기 때문에 자주 발생하지 않는다고 주장하였다. 이와 같이 과학자이면서 동시에 철학을 연구한 토마스 쿤은 기존의 패러다임이 새로운 패러다임으로 대체되는 새로운 이론을 제시하여 과학 철학과 과학사에 새로운 장을 열었다.

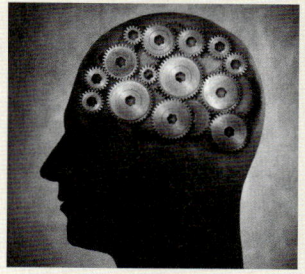

Thomas Kuhn × absolute truth

temporary, replaceable → paradigm

paradigm shift (a new paradigm emerges)

Mini Practice

Listen to part of a lecture in a philosophy class. 🎧 Ch3_08

1. What did Kuhn believe about how paradigms affect scientific thought?

   Ⓐ He believed that paradigms interfered with the ability of a scientist to think for themselves.
   Ⓑ He believed that paradigms only need to be studied while scientists are in school.
   Ⓒ He believed that paradigms give scientists deep understanding that leads to the development of new theories.
   Ⓓ He believed that paradigms are antithetical to scientific thought, motivating scientists to refute existing paradigms.

2. According to the professor, which of the following is true about paradigm shifts?

   Ⓐ They occur infrequently due to the repercussions they might have.
   Ⓑ They radically change scientific knowledge.
   Ⓒ They result in a cascade of changes in other related paradigms.
   Ⓓ They are strongly tied to the creation of new technology.

Listening Script

Professor: Thomas Kuhn is one of the most important philosophers of all time. His notorious theory has become controversial among a lot of scientists and drew attention from many other philosophers. Basically he argued that there was no such thing as absolute truth, but that there existed only theories about how things happened. The reason why certain theories are accepted while others are disregarded is that the accepted theories seem to have more explanatory power than other alternative theories. The theories that are accepted at the present time are termed paradigms. Therefore, paradigms are not referring to the absolute truth about the way things happen in nature; paradigms are widely accepted because they appear to provide quite reasonable explanations.

Now, what he argued was that the paradigms have led scientists' thinking in a negative direction, because the very existence of a paradigm hindered scientists from thinking more creatively. A case in point is the Greek philosopher Ptolemy, who invented and taught the geocentric theory of the universe. This theory became a commonly accepted paradigm at that time. Although a number of scientists had found evidence indicating that the geocentric theory was wrong, they disregarded any claim that could counter the dominant paradigm. However, when Copernicus presented evidence from various observations of the night sky and argued that the earth was not the true center of the universe because the geocentric theory could not explain the variations in planetary orbits, people compared such findings with the existing paradigm and decided that Copernicus's new theory did a better job in explaining how planets moved. Even though it took a long time to accept the new paradigm, they did so in the end. Now, when people disregard the previous paradigm and accept a new one, this is referred to as a paradigm shift. You should keep in mind that such paradigm shifts do not happen very often because, as Kuhn put it, if a new belief is accepted every time one comes up, then people would stop believing anything at all and everything would be just chaotic.

Answers p. 39

Sociology

★★★
057

Transportation revolution in US
미국의 교통혁명

미국 발달 초기의 원동력이었던 교통수단들 중 기차와 운하의 건설 과정과 그 영향에 대한 내용이 종종 출제된다. 지역 개발과 경제 발달에 크게 기여했던 교통 수단들을 알아보도록 하자.

필수어휘
- freight 화물, 화물 수송
- stagecoach 역마차
- muddy 진흙투성이의
- seaboard 해안지방
- ditch 배수로
- tributary 지류
- level 평평하게 하다, 비슷하게 만들다
- quandary 당황, 곤경
- implement 사용하다
- aqueduct 수로
- harbor 항구, 항만

19-20세기 사이 미국인의 이동 수단은 변화하기 시작했다. 1800년 초반에만 해도 방대한 미국땅을 이동할 수 있었던 실질적 교통 수단은 바다와 강 등의 물길waterway뿐이었기 때문에, 사람들은 물에 인접한 지역에 국한적으로 거주했다. 주요 도시로 연결되는 도로road가 있긴 했지만 도로 이동이 쉽지 않았으며, 시간이 많이 걸리는 한계가 있었다.

20세기 초 철도railroad가 미국 전역에 빠른 속도로 퍼지기 시작했다. 또한 대규모 선박vessel이 건조되면서 많은 승객passenger과 화물freight을 이송했고, 크고 작은 배boat는 강, 호수, 운하canal 등에서 볼 수 있었다. 게다가 도로가 많이 건설되면서 자전거, 마차, 전차trolley 등의 수가 나날이 늘어 났고, 과거 물에 가까운 지역에만 국한되었던 거주지도 전국적으로 새롭게 닦인 길route을 따라 확대되었다.

이러한 급성장을 보였던 신생 도시들 중 가장 발달한 도시는 시카고였다. 시카고가 경제 대도시로 급부상할 수 있었던 이유 중 하나는 바로 그곳이 강, 호수, 철도 노선의 교차점이었기 때문이다. 덕분에 시카고의 산업, 제조업, 상업이 눈부시게 빠른 속도로 발전할 수 있었다. 호수 기선Lake steamer(호수의 화물 운반용 기선)이 석탄과 철광석iron ore을 철강 공장으로, 철도가 가축livestock을 가축 사육장으로 운송해주었다. 이러한 교통 시설의 발전으로 1900년대 미국 시민들은 불과 100년 전만 해도 경험할 수 없었던 빠른 속도로 먼 곳에서 그들이 얻고자 하는 생필품들을 손쉽게 얻을 수 있게 되었다.

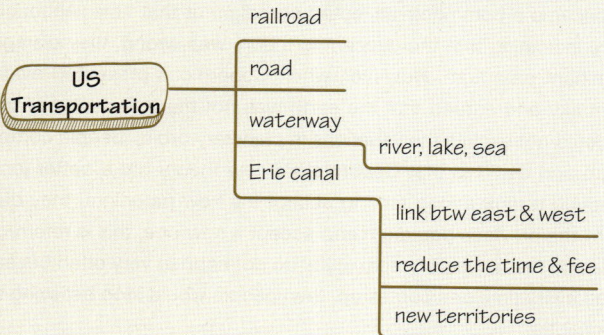

The Erie Canal

In the 18th century, transporting freight and passengers from the eastern part to the western part of the United States was an arduous, expensive and time consuming process. Shipping goods from Buffalo to New York City by a stagecoach, the primary mode of transportation, took two weeks. For this reason, Governor Clinton proposed a canal, a man-made waterway for boats to travel along, as an alternative to the muddy roads of the stagecoach, in order to provide a link between New York and the Great Lakes.

Stretching from New York City on the eastern seaboard via the Hudson River to the Great Lakes in the western interior, the Erie Canal is considered one of the most important civil engineering works in North America. Construction of the canal started in the summer of 1817, a project that would connect the Hudson River to Lake Erie, a length of about 360 miles. However, the land around Lake Erie is 560 feet higher than the Mohawk River, the tributary of the Hudson where the canal was to connect. The task of leveling all 360 miles of the canal presented quite a quandary for the builders. To overcome this problem, it was constructed using 32 aqueducts, a special kind of bridge used to carry a canal over a stream or river; and 83 locks, enclosed sections of the canal with doors on both ends which can be used to raise or lower boats by pumping water in or out while the doors are closed.

The effect of the canal was immediate and dramatic. The canal linked the west with the east, thereby changing the primary transportation axis from north-south to east-west. This waterway enabled farmers to transport their farm products at one-tenth the previous cost, and significantly reduced travel time. In addition, it spurred the development of numerous cities along the canal's route and immigrants flooded into many other western towns and cities in western New York, Ohio, and Michigan, opening up a wide range of economic activities. In particular, the canal fostered a population surge in western New York State and helped New York City become the chief U.S harbor. The Erie Canal ultimately provided a viable model for a successfully financed and operated public works project. Later enlarged and deepened, the canal even survived competition from the railroads in the latter part of the 19th century.

1. The word arduous in paragraph 1 is closest in meaning to

    (A) anxious
    (B) difficult
    (C) akin
    (D) copious

2. All of the following are mentioned in paragraph 3 as the effect of the Erie Canal EXCEPT

    (A) After construction of the canal, more people moved to western cities than before.
    (B) The canal made cheaper and quicker travel possible.
    (C) New York became the primary port in the country.
    (D) In the latter part of 19th century, passengers preferred railroad travel to the canal.

Answers p. 40

Sociology

058

Urban planning
도시 계획

산업화industrialization로 인해 제조 물품이 더욱 효과적이고 저렴하게 생산되면서 보다 다양한 계층의 사람들이 물건을 구매할 수 있게 되었다. 효율적인 농기구와 증기 기관차steam locomotive가 제조되면서 음식 가격은 하락했고, 일반 가정에서도 다양한 가구를 구매할 수 있게 되었다.

삶의 질standard of living 또한 개선되면서 유럽인들과 미국 초기 정착민들의 인구가 급격히 증가하였다. 19세기 초 이러한 인구 급성장은 사람들이 좋은 음식을 섭취하고 체계적인 질병관리로 사망률mortality이 감소하고 출산율birth rate / fertility은 증가한 덕분이었다. 게다가 일자리를 찾아 지방에서 새로운 산업 도시로 사람들이 대거 이동을 하기 시작하면서 이주migration와 도시화urbanization가 급속도로 진행되었다. 영국의 산업화는 도시화를 촉진시켰고, 1800년대 영국 인구의 1/5 가량이 1만여 명으로 이루어진 도시와 마을에 거주했다. 1900년대 초반에는 시골지역이 도시화를 겪으면서 도시에 거주하는 인구가 전체 인구의 75% 가량을 차지하게 되었다. 이러한 패턴은 다른 유럽 지역과 미국에서도 동일하게 나타났다.

그러나 급격한 도시화의 결과로 비위생적인unsanitary 지역들이 생겨나고, 도시의 물과 공기가 심각하게 오염되었다. 도시의 공장에서 화석 연료가 심각한 수준으로 연소되면서, 환경오염과 직업병으로 인한 사망률이 높아졌다. 게다가 오염된 물과 깨끗하지 않은 거주 조건들로 유행병epidemics이 도시 내에 만연하게 되었고, 안전상의 문제로 계층간의 거주 지역이 분리되는 부작용이 나타나기도 했다.

필수어휘
- infrastructure 기반시설
- fraction 일부, 조각
- sanitation 위생
- disposal system 처분 시스템
- conflagration 대형 화재
- enact 시행하다
- fire-prevention policy 방화 대책

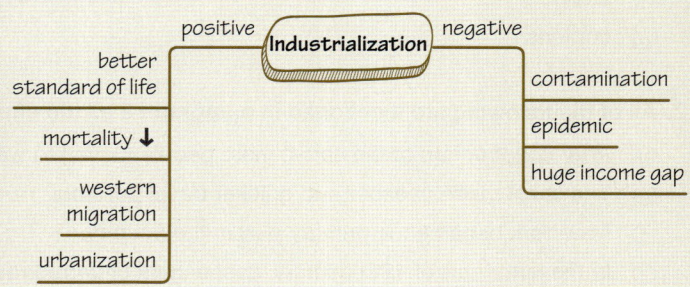

Early cities in America

Today, urban planners optimize the effectiveness of a community's land use, development, and infrastructure to improve the safety and well-being of its citizens. However, in the early 20th century in the United States, the lack of urban planning had an exceptionally negative effect on cities and their residents. The lack of proper urban planning in New York City in the late 1800s and early 1900s led to severe health problems for its rapidly growing population. The problem stemmed from the fact that no one had planned for the massive immigration that took place in New York City and that most buildings were arbitrarily constructed when an individual or a business had a personal need to do so. In 1800, New York City's population was approximately 30,000 and most were confined to crowded living spaces in an area that took up only a fraction of the modern city's total footprint today. The population boom and subsequent overcrowding in the city created perfect conditions for the spread of infectious diseases such as typhoid fever, malaria, and cholera.

The lack of urban planning also posed sanitation problems. In the early years of New York City, transportation was based entirely upon workhorses and it is estimated that as many as 200,000 workhorses were in use by the end of the 19th century. Horses produced massive quantities of waste, and without a proper disposal system, the waste often accumulated throughout the city. In addition, the overworking of horses led many of them to die in the streets, yet there was no system to clean the carcasses up.

One of the worst fires in American history can also be blamed on a lack of urban planning. Known as the Great Fire of Chicago, the disastrous fire began in a small barn on a windy evening on October 10, 1871. Because the majority of buildings and homes were constructed of wood and were tightly packed together, the fire turned into a massive conflagration. As a result, the fire spread incredibly quickly and consumed a large portion of the city. Later city building efforts addressed this problem by standardizing the distances between buildings and enacting many fire-prevention policies.

1. The word arbitrarily in paragraph 1 is closest in meaning to

   Ⓐ intricately
   Ⓑ haphazardly
   Ⓒ integrally
   Ⓓ wholly

2. The author mentions the Great Fire of Chicago so as

   Ⓐ to prove America needed a systematic urban plan
   Ⓑ to describe that lives of early settlers in America were harsh
   Ⓒ to demonstrate that there were disastrous fires before urban planning
   Ⓓ to mention that people suffered from sanitation problems

Sociology

059

USA Today
일간지 USA Today

월스트리트 저널The Wall Street Journal, 뉴욕타임즈The New York Times에 이어 USA Today는 미국에서 가장 많은 판매부수circulation로 3위에 오른 미국을 대표하는 일간지daily newspaper이다. 그러나 25년 전 그 시작은 굉장히 저조했다. USA Today가 출판을 시작할 당시에는 사회 전반적으로 신문에 대한 흥미가 떨어진 상태였다. 이에 따라 기존 일간지와는 차별화를 추구하고 좀 더 많은 독자의 관심을 끌기 위해 기존 신문들이 고수하던 긴 기사를 짧은 기사short stories로 대체하고, 컬러 사진color photos과 도표graphics, 스포츠 경기 결과sports scores, 연예가 소식entertainment stories 등을 추가하는 등 젊은 독자층을 끌어들이기 위한 다양한 방법을 사용하였다. 하지만 짧고 흥미위주로 제작된 기사에 대해 사람들은 너무 단순하다dumb down고 비웃으며, 일간지의 패스트푸드라는 의미로 USA Today를 "Mcpaper"라 부르며 비난하였다. 그러나 USA Today는 이에 흔들리지 않고 인공위성satellite까지 활용하며 대중들에게 발 빠른 최신기사latest news와 신속한 스포츠 경기 결과를 전달함으로써 점차 호응을 얻기 시작하였고 결국 대중의 신뢰와 인기를 차지하는 미국의 대표 일간지로 자리잡게 되었다.

필수어휘
- tremendously 엄청나게
- circulation 유통
- readership 독자 수
- catchy 기억하기 쉬운
- dumb down 지나치게 단순화하다
- surpass 초과하다
- promptness 신속성

USA Today → short stories / color photos / prompt sports scores / entertainment stories → America's #1 selling newspaper

Listening

Mini Practice

Listen to part of a lecture in a social science class. 🎧 Ch3_09

1. In the lecture, what comparison is made between McDonald's and USA Today?
   - (A) The quality of McDonald's hamburgers is compared to the quality of USA Today's stories.
   - (B) The design of McDonald's restaurants is compared with the design of USA Today's pages.
   - (C) The sudden success of McDonald's is compared with the sudden success of USA Today.
   - (D) The early growth of McDonald's is compared with the early growth of USA Today.

2. According to the lecture, which of the following is a key feature of USA Today?
   - (A) Timely international news
   - (B) Colorful charts and photos
   - (C) Stories about murder and malfeasance
   - (D) Stories that are continued on a separate page

Listening Script

Professor: Well, continuing our focus on newspapers since our last class, I'm going to talk about our national newspaper, USA Today. USA Today has been around for more than 25 years now. When it first came out, few people thought it would last this long. Well, it didn't just last; it has succeeded tremendously. USA Today has the largest circulation in America. However, that only shows part of the picture. The true success of USA Today is that it has changed America's newspaper industry. USA Today changed how papers look. It changed how reporters write. And it also changed how newspapers gather and provide news.

USA Today was different from the beginning. At that time, newspaper readership was much smaller in general, and the articles were mostly about crime and murder. They had long stories without any color photos or graphics. Moreover, many papers could not include the latest sports game scores. However, USA Today changed all of these. It made the stories shorter, and unlike other newspapers, most of the stories did not jump from one page to another. It used catchy images such as color photos, colorful charts, and graphics. Instead of delivering a lot of international news, it featured more sports, entertainment and human-interest stories. It was aiming at younger readers, who grew up watching television and naturally had difficulty paying attention to longer stories. What they wanted was entertainment, not information. At first, many people made fun of USA Today. Other newspapers criticized that it was "McPaper" – just like burgers, it looked OK but lacked important contents. People argued that USA Today "dumbed down" the news. But then, an amazing thing happened. More and more people opted for USA Today. In about a year after its first publication, its readership surpassed one million. Today, it sells more than two million copies. When other newspapers realized its growing popularity, they became anxious. So they began to copy USA Today's style. They made shorter stories, and they also started to include a lot of color photos and charts. However, what made USA Today in high demand was not just the appearance. One of the big reasons for its success was the promptness of information. USA Today transmitted news via satellites, so it was possible to include the latest sports score. This, alone, attracted many people to buy this paper.

Answers p. 41

Psychology

★★
060

Variables in decision making
의사결정에서의 변수

미국 속담 중에 "Sleep on it before making a big decision(중대한 결정을 내려야 한다면 하룻밤을 자면서 곰곰이 생각해보라)"라는 말이 있다. 과연 어려운 결정을 앞두고 의식적으로 그것에 대해 계속 생각하는 것이 더 나을까 아니면 무의식적인 상태에서 내리는 결정이 더 나을까.

우선 어려운 결정complex decision은 보통 단순한 결정simple decision보다 더 많은 변수variable를 갖고 있다. 더 고려해야 할 사항들이 많아질 때 그만큼 결정을 내리기가 더 어렵다는 뜻이다. 그럼 사람들은 어떤 상태에서 더 올바른 결정을 할 수 있는 것일까? 한 조사에 따르면 사람들이 의식적인 상태conscious mind에 있을 때보다 무의식적인 상태unconscious mind에 있을 때 어려운 결정을 더 잘 내리는 것으로 나타났다. 즉, 아무 생각이 없을 때 결정을 내리기가 더 쉽다는 것이다. 그 이유는 계속해서 무언가에 대해 의식적으로 사고하는 것은 어느 특정 변수에 집중하면서 다른 여러 변수를 종합적으로 고려하지 못하게 되기 때문이라고 한다. 반대로 무의식적인 생각은 여러 변수들을 객관적으로 비교하여 올바른 결정을 내리는데 더 성공적인 것으로 밝혀졌다. 따라서 변수가 많은 복잡한 결정일수록 그것에 대한 의식적인 생각을 멈추고 잠시 다른 것에 정신을 집중한 다음 무의식적인 상태에서 결정을 내리는 것도 나쁘지 않다는 것이다.

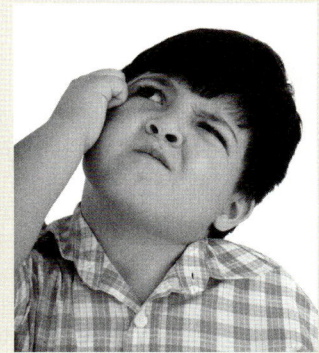

필수어휘
- adage 속담
- variable 변수
- conscious mind 의식적 사고
- unconscious mind 무의식적 사고
- practical implications 실용적 암시

Variables in decision making
— unconscious mind → weighing variables equally → correct decision
— conscious mind → focus on specific variable → incorrect decision

Listening

Mini Practice

Listen to part of a lecture in a psychology class. 🎧 Ch3_10

1. Which two conclusions were made about the unconscious mind?
   - Ⓐ For complex decisions, the conscious mind did not correctly judge the relative importance of factors and made incorrect choices.
   - Ⓑ The unconscious mind showed a superior capacity at combining factors related to a decision.
   - Ⓒ People felt more comfortable about trusting conclusions reached by their unconscious mind.
   - Ⓓ The conscious mind is comprised of simpler mechanisms.

2. Why was one group of participants asked to do word puzzles?
   - Ⓐ to distract them from being able to think consciously about their decision
   - Ⓑ to help them make better decisions
   - Ⓒ to encourage them to make specific, concrete decisions
   - Ⓓ to test a theory that word puzzles can improve decision making

Listening Script

Professor: Have you ever heard an old saying, "when you need to make a big decision, you should sleep on it"? Do you think sleeping can actually help you when you need to make an important decision? Well, why don't we look at a study that proves this old folk adage? In this study, researchers compared two different groups. Participants in Group A were asked a simple question. They had to choose the best car out of eight different cars while considering only 4 variables such as price or gas mileage. After they were introduced to this question, half of the group was asked to keep thinking about what they would choose for 4 minutes, while the other half was asked to work on word puzzles for 4 minutes. As you can see, concentrating on word puzzles prevented these participants from thinking about their decision consciously. Participants in Group B were asked the same question: which of the 8 cars would be the best? But this time, they were asked to consider as many as 12 variables instead of just 4. Again, half of the group was allowed to think about the question for 4 minutes while the other half was asked to solve word puzzles for 4 minutes. What do you think was the result? As you may have guessed, the conscious mind was better at making simple decisions, but interestingly, the unconscious mind was more capable of making a better choice in complex decisions. But the important question is, why? Well, the researchers argued that the unconscious mind was better at incorporating a large number of variables and giving equal weight to them in making a decision. The problem with the conscious mind was that it placed too much value on certain variables when people had to consider a lot of variables. The researchers also pointed out that the findings of this study have practical implications in making real-life complex decisions: people should let the unconscious mind make a decision when there are a large number of variables.

Answers p. 42

Biology

061-L
Altruistic animals

Biology

062-R
Bird

Marine Biology

063-L
Deterioration of coral reefs

Biology

064-R
Flying animals

Biology

065-R
Herbivores

Biology

066-L
Homing instinct

Marine Biology

067-L
Marine trophic relationships

Biology

068-R
Meerkat

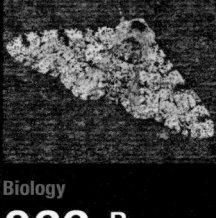
Biology
069-R
Natural selection

Botany
070-R
Plant

Biology
071-R
Predator

Entomology
072-L
Rattlebox moth

Botany
073-L
Red chlorophyll in leaves

Marine Biology
074-R
Seagrass

Botany
075-L
Seeds and nuts

Biology
076-R
Snake

Entomology
077-L
Super-hydrophobic insects

Biology
078-L
The effect of diet on immune system

Biology
079-L
The effect of music on brain organs

Biology
080-R
Thermoregulation

Biology

★★★
061

Altruistic animals
이타주의적 동물

사회생물학sociobiology은 모든 사회 행동의 생물학적 기초에 관해서 체계적으로 연구하는 학문이다. 이것은 인간을 포함한 동물의 사회적 행동social behavior은 자연선택natural selection을 주요인으로 하는 진화과정의 결과로 형성된 것이라 주장한다. 사회생물학의 창시자는 미국의 곤충학자이자 진화이론가였던 E.O. 윌슨Edward O. Wilson이다. 그는 인간을 포함한 동물의 사회적 행동은 설명 가능하다고 하며 결국 사회학sociology은 생물학biology의 일부로 귀속될 것이라고 주장하여 사회학자들로부터 많은 논쟁을 불러일으켰다. 사회생물학으로 인간의 여러 가지 행동에 대한 설명이 가능해졌지만 이타주의altruism는 사회생물학이 풀어야 할 수수께끼로 남아있다. 왜냐하면 사회생물학이 근거를 두는 자연선택의 이론에 따르면 우월한 유전자를 가진 개체가 적자생존 법칙survival of the fittest을 통해 살아남는데 반해, 이타적인 행동은 다른 개체를 위해 스스로의 생존이나 이익을 포기하기 때문이다.

예를 들어 개미와 일벌 등은 여왕과 그 새끼를 보살피고 둥지를 보호하는데 평생을 바친다. 이러한 특이 행동에 대해 윌슨은 곤충의 이타적인 행동을 지배하는 유전자는 그 유전자를 가진 자신이 희생되더라도 전체 개체의 번식을 위해서라면 세대를 거쳐 전이pass on된다고 주장하였으며 이를 혈연도태kin selection라 일컬었다.

이후에 또 다른 사회생물학자인 리차드 도킨스Richard Dawkins이 그의 저서 「이기적 유전자The Selfish Gene」를 통해 '사람을 비롯한 모든 동물은 유전자가 만들어 낸 기계'라 주장하며 인간은 이기적으로 태어났으며, 선택의 기본 단위, 즉 이성의 기본 단위가 종도 집단도 개체도 아닌, 유전자라고 주장하여 많은 종교학자로부터 수많은 논쟁을 낳았다. 현존하는 최고의 지성인이라 알려진 사회생물학자 리차드 도킨스의 이론 및 저서는 토플에서도 빈번히 언급되어온 바가 있으므로 반드시 배경지식으로 알아두도록 하자!

필수어휘
- entomologist 곤충학자
- natural selection 자연도태
- altruistic behavior 이타적인 행동
- altruism 이타주의
- refrain from ~로부터 삼가다
- termites 흰개미
- colony 집단
- specialization 세분화

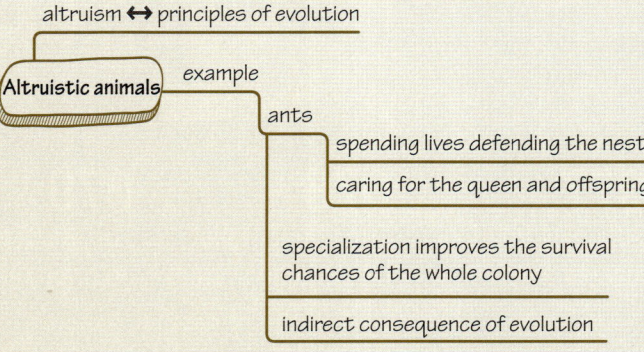

Mini Practice

Listen to part of a discussion in a sociobiology class. 🎧 Ch4_01

1. According to Dr. Wilson, what is the primary factor determining the behavior and the actions of animals?
   - Ⓐ an individual's environment
   - Ⓑ the society one is raised in
   - Ⓒ biological evolution
   - Ⓓ education

2. Based on the lecture, which of these is NOT typical of social insects?
   - Ⓐ combative behavior
   - Ⓑ specialization of labor
   - Ⓒ altruism
   - Ⓓ colony-oriented life

Listening Script

Professor: Good morning, everyone! Welcome to Sociobiology 101. To start with, I want to explain what, in general, sociobiology is all about. The term "sociobiology" first came into use in the 1940s, but it wasn't until 1975 when people started to take notice. That's when the noted entomologist, E. O. Wilson, talked about it in his book, Sociobiology: The New Synthesis. Wilson wanted to explain the development of social behaviors in the context of — and through application of — the theories of natural selection and evolution. Wilson's research focused primarily on the altruistic behavior of ants. Altruism is behavior that benefits another at one's own expense.

Ants and other so-called social insects, such as bees, termites and so on, spend their lives defending the nest and caring for the queen and the queen's offspring. Only the queen gets to pass any genes along to the next generation. In the context of evolution, Wilson wondered how such an altruistic system could evolve. How could any organism evolve to refrain from passing on its own genes, and instead help increase the chances of another individual — the queen, in this case — passing on their genes? He was certain that there had to be some advantage to this sort of behavior, so he worked to discover what kind of advantage might result. He speculated that all the members of an ant colony share such similar genes that a worker ant that defends the colony or cares for the queens offspring is still really indirectly ensuring the survival of its own genes. If specialization of behavior like, you know, where workers work and the queen lays eggs... if this specialization improves the survival chances of the colony as a whole, then the process of evolution may actually favor this altruistic behavior. So as you can see, altruism can develop as an indirect consequence of evolution through natural selection.

Answers p. 43

Biology

★★
062
Bird
새

시조새가 새일까? 파충류일까? 이에 대한 논란이 지속적으로 출제되고 있다. 또한 새의 이동은 토플의 또다른 빈출 주제이기도 하다.

날개wing로 비행하는 조류는 온몸이 깃털feather로 덮여 있는 척추동물vertebrate이다. 그들은 중생대Mesozoic Era 때, 육식 공룡theropod dinosaur에서 진화한 것으로 보인다. 가장 오래된 새로 알려진 시조새archaeopteryx는 깃털, 두개골skull, 소화기관 등이 오늘 날의 새와 유사하지만, 파충류만의 특징인 이빨 달린 부리, 긴 꼬리뼈, 날개에 달린 발톱claw이 있는 발가락, 'S'자로 움직이는 목 때문에 시조새가 조류인지 파충류인지에 대한 학계의 논쟁은 아직까지도 이어지고 있다. 또한 골격 형태와 공중을 활주하는glide 모습은 파충류reptile와 조류의 중간형태로 파충류에서 진화한 최초의 모습으로 여겨지기도 한다.

조류는 몸의 기능과 형태가 비행에 최적화되어 있다. 먼저 씨앗, 과일, 벌레, 곤충, 물고기 등 섭취하는 음식에 따라 진화된 여러 모양의 부리beak는 이빨이 없는 대신 인간의 손톱이나 머리카락과 같은 단백질 케라틴keratin으로 만들어져 머리 쪽의 무게가 적게 나간다. 또한 뼈 안이 비어 있어 가볍지만 강한 골격을 가지고 있다. 날개는 앞발이 진화한 것으로 대부분은 비행이 가능하며, 비행이 불가능한 종으로는 펭귄과 타조류ratite 등이 있다. 그리고 거의 모든 조류는 커다란 비행 근육이 붙는 부분인 흉골sternum 위에 넓고 얇은 용골keel을 지니고 있다. 새의 두 발은 걷거나 수영하거나 나무 가지에 앉을 때perch 사용되고, 부리와 마찬가지로 모양이 다양하다. 유선형streamlined인 몸의 형태와 더불어 소화 기관과 호흡기관 역시 비행에 적합하다. 먼저 소화 기관은 두 개의 방으로 이루어져있는데, 첫 번째 방은 소화액gastric juice을 분비하고 두 번째 방인 일명 모래주머니gizzard는 음식물을 갈아주는 중요한 역할을 한다. 호흡기관은 비행 시 필요한 높은 신진대사 활동에 최적화되었다.

필수어휘

- inhospitable 살기 힘든
- photoperiod 광주기
- breeding grounds 번식지
- latitude 위도
- gonad 생식 샘
- molt 털갈이 하다
- planetarium 천체 투영관 (천문관)
- warbler 울새, 휘파람새
- cage 새장
- compass heading 나침반의 북쪽을 기준으로 한 비행 방향 측정
- axis 축
- ornithologist 조류학자

156

Bird Migration

Many species of birds annually migrate between two locations: their breeding area and a wintering area. Migration is done on a seasonal basis using well-established routes, and it ensures the survival of the migrating species while allowing the environment to restore itself. By leaving for the winter, migrating birds are able to avoid inhospitable cold weather, shortage of food and a shorter photoperiod, and can return to higher latitudes in the summer in order to find suitable uncongested breeding grounds, abundant food and longer days. It is widely known that the stimulus for migration is highly related to hormone levels caused by changes in day length, combined with energy balance and physiological state. For example, around mid-July the gonads of many bird species begin to shrink, they begin to molt or lose old feathers, and they start to accumulate fat, the most essential fuel for migration. Around mid-September, the days become shorter, signaling the start of the migration and causing migratory birds to move southward. However, when the weather becomes warmer again and less energy is utilized in temperature regulation, the change in hormones urges birds to return home for breeding.

Migrating birds use various clues to keep track of their migratory route every year. Some birds recognize the route through visual cues such as the presence of clouds and landmarks including rivers, coastlines and mountain ranges, while others navigate by smell, gravity and sounds like the roar of the ocean. Researchers have conducted a variety of experiments relating to bird migration. For example, Franz and Eleanore Sauer (1957) demonstrated that some bird species orient themselves via the stars. By caging garden warblers in a planetarium, they showed that birds oriented themselves north in the "spring" and south in the "fall" under simulated night skies. They also observed that when they rotated the north-south axis of the planetarium 180° the warblers also reversed their compass headings. Merkel and Wiltschko (1965) proposed that bird migration be related with the magnetic field. They showed that the European Robin could orient itself in a solid steel cage without celestial cues, and they demonstrated that the birds reversed their orientation when the magnetic field imposed on the cage was reversed. The way that birds navigate is still one of science's mysteries, but some ornithologists have concluded that the sun is the primary source of directional information during navigation, and the secondary system is the earth's magnetic field.

1. The word clues in paragraph 2 is closest in meaning to
   - (A) tools
   - (B) signs
   - (C) methods
   - (D) efforts

2. According to paragraph 2, which one is NOT true?
   - (A) Garden warblers changed the direction when the north-south axis of the planetarium was reversed.
   - (B) When in steel cages, the European Robin could not orient itself.
   - (C) Landmarks could be one of the signs used for navigation.
   - (D) Celestial bodies help some birds migrate.

Answers p. 43

Marine Biology

063

Deterioration of coral reefs
산호초의 감소

열대 바닷속 아름다운 산호초는 과연 식물일까 동물일까? 얼마 전 한 다큐멘터리에서 방영하기도 했었던 수백만 개의 알들이 산호에서 산란되어 나오는 과정은 굉장히 신비롭고도 놀라운 광경이다. 이처럼 산호는 산란을 하고 수많은 폴립polyp(산호를 이루는 가장 작은 단위의 세포)으로 이루어진 자포동물cnidarians이다. 야행성인 산호는 낮에는 석회물질lime material로 만들어진 외골격exoskeleton 속에 있다가 밤이 되면 독성이 있는 촉수tentacle를 펼쳐 지나가는 동물성 플랑크톤이나 갑각류, 물고기 등을 기절시켜 잡아먹는다. 하지만 이렇게 얻는 양분은 일부일 뿐이고, 대부분은 산호 속에서 공생하는 식물 플랑크톤의 일종인 조산텔라zooxanthella가 광합성photosynthesis을 통해 만든 영양분으로 살아간다. 때문에 산호는 햇빛이 풍부하고 수온이 높은 열대 바다에서 많이 자라며, 이러한 산호들이 켜켜이 쌓여 만들어진 산호초 지대는 다른 곳보다 산소 함량이 높고 먹이가 풍부해 전 세계 바다 생물의 4분의 1이 살아가고 있다.

그러나 이렇게 생태계에 도움을 주는 산호초가 점점 감소하고 있는데 이에는 크게 세 가지의 원인이 있다. 그 첫째는 해양 속 과도한 미생물infection from microorganism 수의 증가이며, 두 번째로는 어류남획 over-fishing이 있다. 마지막 세 번째로는 해조green algae 량의 증가로 산호초와 공생하는symbiotic 박테리아의 수가 과도하게 증식하여 주변 산소가 부족해지면서 산호가 질식하게suffocated 되는 것이다.

죽기 전에 꼭 한 번 보고 싶을 만큼의 장관을 이루는 대표적인 호주의 산호섬인 Great Barrier Reef와 산호가 번식하는 과정은 토플시험에도 자주 나왔던 주제이니 이 신비로운 해양 생물의 특징을 꼭 알아두도록 하자.

필수어휘
- polyps 폴립(산호를 이루는 가장 작은 단위의 세포)
- extensive 광범위한
- infection 감염
- deterioration 악화, 저하
- symbiotic 공생의
- thriving 번성하는
- breakthrough 대발전
- suffocate 질식시키다

Deterioration of coral reefs (polyps)
↑ symbiotic bacteria due to simple sugars around corals
use up O₂ → suffocate corals

Mini Practice

Listen to part of a discussion in a marine biology class. 🎧 Ch4_02

1. Which of these is a key aspect of coral reefs?
   - Ⓐ All of the algae growing in the ocean are dependent on them.
   - Ⓑ They support a particularly diverse ecosystem.
   - Ⓒ They lend to the natural beauty and color of the ocean.
   - Ⓓ The Caribbean cannot exist without them.

2. What is the main factor in the deterioration of coral reefs?
   - Ⓐ disease caused by a parasitic infection of the coral
   - Ⓑ hazardous material dumped into the ocean by laboratories
   - Ⓒ insufficient resources the coral needs to thrive
   - Ⓓ bacteria exhausting the supply of oxygen in coral reefs

Listening Script

Professor: Can anyone name one of the most important ecosystems on our planet? Okay, it's kind of an easy question. This is an aquatic marine class so I'm clearly talking about the fascinating world of the coral reef. Thousands of species of fish live in and around the corals, in the shelter provided by the coral reef. Also known as polyps, coral reefs are comprised of many tiny living organisms and grow continuously over time. So, as you know, there's a growing concern over coral reefs, which is why I want to talk about them today. You see, it's come to the attention of scientists that coral reefs have been disappearing in a slow and gradual but continuous process. I'm part of a research team that has been doing some really extensive studies on coral reefs for more than six years at this point.

What we've discovered is that there is a serious problem affecting the reefs, I suppose you could call it an infection. Among the many problems contributing to the deterioration of the coral reef, we discovered that the primary issue is related to a symbiotic bacteria growing amongst the corals. So, unlike a healthy symbiotic relationship, in this case the bacteria are benefitting from the coral, but it seems the benefit doesn't go the other way. You could say the bacteria are really thriving. They're growing and spreading all over the place. There are simple sugars that can be found around corals, and the bacteria reproduce by breaking down and consuming the minerals from those sugars. We wanted to know precisely how these bacteria are affecting the coral, so we went back to the lab to conduct some extensive research. And just a few days ago, we made a breakthrough. You see, it's the overwhelming population of the bacteria that causes the problem. They are doing so incredibly well that they are using all of the available oxygen in the coral reef, and in turn causing the coral to suffocate. Interesting and amazing, isn't it? And at the same time, very worrisome.

Answers p. 44

Biology

NEW 064

Flying animals
비행하는 동물들

남아메리카의 열대 우림tropical forest 지역에는 나무와 나무 사이를 활강해서 이동하는 날다람쥐flying squirrel와 날도마뱀flying dragon lizard 과 같은 동물이 많이 서식하고 있다. 날다람쥐는 다람쥐 과에 속하는 동물로서 대략 3천만년 전 다람쥐에서 진화한 것으로 알려졌다. 그것은 몸을 펴지 않을 때는 일반 다람쥐의 모습과 유사하지만 팔, 다리를 쫙 펼쳤을 때 몸 양쪽에 붙어 있는 익막(또는 비막patagium)이 날개 역할을 하면서 나무 사이로 10m 내외를 미끄러지듯 활강gliding 할 수 있다. 날도마뱀 역시 날다람쥐와 비슷한 모습으로 익막을 통해 나무 사이를 이동할 수 있으며, 작은 개미와 같은 곤충을 먹는 파충류과reptile에 속한다. 남아메리카 지역에 사는 비행 동물들의 진화 관련 이론은 효율적 이동economical locomotion, 최적화된 먹이 사냥 foraging optimization 등에 초점을 맞추고 있다.

먼저 학자들이 주장하는 'tall-tree 학설'은 키가 큰 열대 우림 나무들 사이를 동물들이 급 하강하면서 높은 속도를 얻을 수 있고 나무 아래까지 내려가서 다시 다른 나무에 오르는 것 보다 나무 사이를 점프하는 것이 이동하는 데에 에너지가 덜 들 수 있다는, 이동의 효율적 측면을 부각시키며 발단된 이론이다. 두 번째 학설은 남아메리카의 열대 우림이 그 지역에 서식하는 동물들에게 먹이가 부족한 지역이어서 먹이 감을 찾아 이동하는 습성이 활강하는 능력으로 진화했다고 보는 이론이다. 이것은 그들의 서식지가 먹이 부족 지역food-desert이었기 때문에 도출 가능한 이론이다. 즉, 이 지역에서 진화한 동물은 두 종류가 있는데, 그 중 하나는 나뭇잎을 먹는 초식동물herbivore로 유해물질 농도가 짙은 나무들로 인해 먹을 수 있는 잎을 찾아 먼 거리를 이동해야 했기 때문에 나무 사이를 점프하게 되었다고 추정된다. 또 다른 진화된 종은 작은 곤충을 먹이로 삼는 육식 동물carnivore로, 그들의 먹잇감인 작은 곤충이 먹을 나뭇잎이 많지 않았기 때문에 동일한 'food-desert' 현상을 경험하고 먹잇감을 찾아 활강하는 능력이 진화되었을 지도 모른다고 추측된다.

필수어휘

- mimic 모방하다
- maneuver 조작하다
- glide 활강하다, 미끄러지듯 움직이다
- sweep 미끄러지듯 움직이다
- membrane 막
- wrist 팔목
- ankle 발목
- flap 덮개, 날개
- dewlap (도마뱀 등의) 처진 턱살
- abdomen 복부

Mini Practice

Flying animals in Southeast Asia

Flying squirrels and lizards are animal species that use their special bodies to mimic flight and maneuver within their environments. However, their "flying" is not an actual flight like that of birds or bats, but just gliding; they lack the ability to sustain powered flights and are only capable of gliding through the air.

Flying squirrels in Southeast Asia and South America are endothermic mammals that live in moist evergreen broadleaf forests, deciduous forests and coniferous forests. They are commonly active at night, when they forage for food, because flying squirrels like to avoid natural enemies like birds of prey that hunt during the day. Depending on their habitats, they consume diverse kinds of food including seeds, insects, spiders, tree sap and bird eggs. All species of flying squirrels are able to sweep from tree to tree by gliding with the help of a membrane of skin extending from their wrists to their ankles called a *patagium*, like a parachute between their front and back legs, which allows them to fly between trees for long distances and to conserve energy. For example, in regions where the trees are very tall, ground squirrels that climb up and down those trees in search of food waste a lot of energy, especially if the food is scarce. However, because flying squirrels can glide between the trees, they reduce travel time between patches of trees and have more foraging time, while at the same time, being able to escape from predators more easily.

Flying lizards such as Draco volans, colloquially known as *Flying Dragons*, will spread flaps of skin, also known as dewlaps, along their abdomens and glide out of trees or from other high areas. The Flying Dragons will point its head toward the ground when it is about to take off, and can be fussy about gliding in rainy or windy conditions. They seem to have a similar function of "flying" as that of flying squirrels.

1. The word mimic in paragraph 1 is closest in meaning to
    A) form
    B) imitate
    C) manipulate
    D) make

2. What is mentioned in paragraph 2 about flying squirrel?
    A) To save energy, they climb up and down tall trees.
    B) Predators easily catch them during the daytime.
    C) They are nocturnal for safety from their natural enemies.
    D) They exclusively consume insects and birds.

Answers p. 45

Biology

★★
065

Herbivores
초식동물

초식 동물herbivores은 해부학적으로나 생리학적으로 열매, 나뭇잎foliage, 뿌리root, 줄기stem와 같은 섬유질fibrous matter의 녹색 식물을 섭식에 특수화된 동물들로, 대부분은 먹이사슬food chain의 1차 소비자primary consumer에 해당되는 포유류가 이에 속한다. 섭취하는 식물의 종류에 따라 소화기관digestive system, 이빨tooth, 행동 방식 등이 다르게 발달하며, 종류는 크게 되새김질 동물ruminant과 비 되새김질 동물nonruminant로 구분할 수 있다.

되새김질 동물
되새김질 동물의 위는 4개의 방으로 이루어져 있으며, 두 개의 앞니는 크기가 작거나 거의 없는 경우도 있다. 이들은 섬유질 함유량이 높은 줄기나 단단한 뿌리를 먹는 성향이 있다. 음식물은 거의 씹지 않고 빠르게 섭취한 후, 위의 첫 번째 방rumen으로 보내어 그 곳에서 음식물이 부드러워지면 그 물질을 '되새김질 거리cud'의 형태로 게워내어regurgitate 입으로 돌려 보내는데, 이러한 행위를 여러 번 반복하며 소화한다. 되새김질 동물은 대부분 육식 동물의 먹이가 되는 경우가 많기 때문에, 주로 아침이나 저녁에 활동하며 신속하게 먹이를 위의 첫 번째 방에 담아놓고 이 물질들을 천천히 되새김질하며 소화, 흡수하는 것으로 알려져 있다.

비 되새김질 동물
되새김질하지 않는 초식 동물들의 경우, 되새김질 동물과는 달리 이빨이 다양하게 발달되어 씹는 활동을 통해 충분히 으깬 음식을 식도esophagus를 거쳐 위로 내려 보낸다. 위에서는 위산과 소화 효소digestive enzyme로 음식을 분해하여 장기intestine 안에 있는 기관에서 발효 작용fermentation이 일어나 소화를 돕는다. 그러나 그들은 소화 장기의 흡수 능력이 약하기 때문에, 하루의 많은 시간을 풀을 찾아forage 움직이는데 보낸다.

필수어휘
- herbivore 초식동물
- carnivore 육식동물
- omnivore 잡식동물
- antelope 영양 syn wildebeest
- cud 되새김질거리
- forage 먹이를 찾다
- fibrous 섬유로 된
- fiber 섬유, 섬유질
- feed (동물의) 먹이
- gastric 위의, 위장의
- mastication 저작, 씹음

Ruminants vs. Non-Ruminants

Different species of animals each have digestive systems adapted to make the most efficient use of the food that species consumes, so the anatomy and physiology of the digestive systems of herbivores, carnivores, and omnivores all differ. Herbivores are generally mammals, including deer, sheep, antelope, zebra and wildebeest, which depend entirely on vegetation for nourishment. However, they fall into two categories — ruminants and non-ruminants — and according to kinds and parts of the plants they eat, they develop particular digestive process.

Ruminants are herbivores adapted to digesting fibrous plant matter such as grass, tree bark or foliage. They are characterized by their multi-chambered stomach and cud-chewing behavior. For the most part, the digestive systems of ruminants are analogous to those of other mammals, but the stomach is considerably different and allows the ruminants to gain the majority of their nutrition from forages and other fibrous matter. First, they consume rapidly and do not chew their food completely before swallowing. Then solid parts go to the rumen, the first chamber of their stomach, and feed there is mixed and partially broken down by bacteria. When the rumen has been filled, the animal regurgitates the food to the mouth and re-chews the partially digested feed, called the cud. The cud goes down to other chambers of the stomach: the reticulum, omasum, and abomasum. The reticulum breaks feed into smaller particles, then the omasum grinds the feed and may squeeze some water out, and in the abomasum, the true stomach with gastric juices, digestion is carried out just like in non-ruminants, with the aid of various microorganisms that live in the stomach. This is the key to the ruminant digestive system's efficiency, extracting nutrition from low quality food. Finally, the small intestine absorbs most of the food material into the bloodstream and gains protein and energy from the plant source.

Unlike ruminants, the non-ruminants' stomach is limited to temporary storage and preliminary conversion of the food into a liquid mass; little or no absorption of nutrients takes place. Non-ruminant animals cannot obtain much nutritional value from plant sources unless the food has been modified, ground, or mashed. Therefore, when they consume food, they have to break it down through physical and chemical action in the mouth first (that is, mastication or chewing). Their stomach then breaks the food down further through chemical action, and allows some absorption of small particles. Then, the small intestine performs enzymatic digestion and absorption of proteins, and in the large intestine, water is received.

1. The word rapidly in paragraph 2 is closest in meaning to
   - (A) strictly
   - (B) strikingly
   - (C) incidentally
   - (D) swiftly

2. The author begins paragraph 3 with the phrase Unlike ruminants in order to
   - (A) indicate that a thorough discussion of ruminants follows
   - (B) show that ruminants and nonruminants have similar features
   - (C) clarify the ideas of ruminants that were previously presented
   - (D) indicate that the discussion is moving from one type of herbivore to the other

Answers p. 45

Biology

066

Homing instinct
귀소본능

새의 이주 방법이나 패턴은 과거부터 현재까지 리딩 및 리스닝 영역에 자주 출제되었던 주제이므로 내용을 꼭 정리해 두자!

17년 전 고향이었던 진도에서 대전으로 팔려간 백구가 탈출해서 7개월 동안 300km의 고난의 행군 끝에 무사히 집을 찾아간 믿지 않는 이야기가 우리나라를 떠들썩하게 한 적이 있다. 조류 중에서는 비둘기가 돋보이는 귀소본능homing instinct을 가진 대표적인 동물이다. 전쟁이 났을 때 비둘기를 날려 메시지를 주고받았던 것이 바로 이 때문이다. 동물의 대부분 행동은 인간의 수준에는 미치지 못하지만 그들의 귀소본능만큼은 도저히 인간이 따라잡을 수 없다고 한다. 여러 동물의 이주 및 귀소본능 중에서도 특히 조류 (철새migratory birds)의 특징은 토플에 굉장히 자주 나왔으므로 그 특징을 잘 기억해두자.

철새migratory birds들이 장소를 이동하는 이유는 크게 두 가지이다. 첫 번째 이유는 기후 변화climate change이며 또 다른 이유는 그에 따른 먹이의 부족scarcity of food이다. 철새는 봄과 가을에 일정한 곳으로 날아갔다가 다시 집으로 돌아오는데 이주하는 것을 migration이라 하고 다시 돌아오는 것을 homing이라 한다. 연어가 산란하기 위해 태어난 곳으로 돌아오는 행동 또한 귀소본능에 속한다. Homing에 사용되는 방법에는 여러 가지가 있는데 그 중 하나가 인간보다 수십 배나 좋은 시력eye-sight을 사용하여 산이나 건물과 같은 이정표landmarks를 따라가는 것이다. 만약, 특별한 지형 지물이 없다면, 낮에는 태양을 기준으로, 밤에는 별자리celestial body를 보면서 방향을 잡는다. 게다가, 철새의 부리 위에 있는 콧구멍에는 지구의 자력선magnetic field을 감지할 수 있는 나침반compass이 있어 길을 찾는데 유용하게 사용한다.

필수어휘
- homing instinct 귀소본능
- winter 겨울을 나다
- pigeon 비둘기
- olfactory 후각의
- magnetic field 자기장
- landmark 표지물
- conclusive 결정적인
- hatchling 갓 부화한 새끼
- gannet 가넷, 부비새류

164

Mini Practice

Listen to part of a lecture in a zoology class. 🎧 Ch4_03

1. According to the professor, what can be inferred about the homing instinct of animals? Click on 3 answers.

   (A) Homing can occur over shorter distances.
   (B) Homing only occurs in some species of birds.
   (C) Homing is not linked to seasonal change.
   (D) Homing is not affected by the wind.
   (E) Homing is primarily based on the use of landmarks.

2. What are some benefits of using a different route to get home? Click on 2 answers.

   (A) Additional food is obtainable.
   (B) The offspring can get food more quickly.
   (C) Parents spend less time in the open.
   (D) It's harder for predators to find the nest.

Listening Script

Professor: Birds possess amazing homing instincts. Every year birds migrate across vast distances to winter in better climates and then every spring they return home. Even if they are blown off course by a storm birds still manage to find their way back home. Scientists have long studied species like the homing pigeon to try to understand what gives birds this homing instinct. There have been several theories that birds have internal maps and compasses that guide them. Some have proposed that birds have olfactory maps, smell based maps that help them find their way home. Others believe that birds use the Earth's magnetic field and can sense the strength of the field and get a rough idea of where they are located. Some scientists have conducted research and found that the sun, stars, and magnetic fields may act as compasses for birds. They also discovered that some birds use sunset and physical landmarks like rivers and mountains to navigate back home. Although there is no conclusive evidence that can explain birds' homing instinct, it seems that birds may draw from a variety of tools to find their way back home.

Birds also use the homing instinct during their daily life. Birds that are raising young hatchlings often search far and wide for food to bring back to their babies. When they return, they take the shortest path back to the nest instead of the original path. When their babies leave the nest they have to begin their own mapping but still seem to possess a natural homing instinct. Baby gannets, a sea bird that lives on islands in the ocean, begin exploring their world by flying in expanding spirals. They begin with their home and slowly begin to increase their range until they discover coastlines and other islands. Eventually they acquire knowledge of their local region and use that knowledge to find places to nest and find food. Therefore, it seems that birds have to explore their world in order to understand it and utilize their homing instincts to ensure that they return safely.

Answers p. 46

Marine Biology

067

Marine trophic relationships
해양영양관계

생물의 영양관계 또는 먹이사슬을 떠올리면 생산자, 소비자, 분해자의 피라미드가 어렴풋이 기억이 날것이다. 이러한 관계를 이제는 영어로 다시금 정리해보도록 하자.

영양단계trophic levels란 먹이사슬food chain에서 물질에너지가 전달되는 과정, 즉 먹고 먹히는 과정을 단계별로 분류한 것이다. 이 에너지는 각 단계를 거치면서 일부는 소실되고 일부는 다음 단계로 전달되며 각각의 영양단계는 피라미드형으로 구성된다.

피라미드 제일 아래에 있는 생산자producer에는 직접 먹이를 생산하는 자가영양 플랑크톤autotrophic plankton과 종속영양 플랑크톤이 heterotrophic plankton이 있다. 쉽게 설명해서 태양에너지로 스스로 먹이를 만드는 생물과 스스로 먹이를 만들지 못하여 독립영양 플랑크톤에게 의지하는 두 종의 생물이 있는 것이다.

다음으로 소비자consumer에는 쉽게 초식동물herbivore, 육식동물 carnivore, 그리고 이들을 먹는 포식자 잡식동물omnivore이 있다.

마지막 분해자decomposer는 동물의 사체나 배설물을 분해하는 종속영양세균heterotrophic bacteria을 가리키며 분해자의 활동으로 결국 다시 생산자에게 먹이를 공급하게 되면서 해양 영양관계 사이클이 완성되는 것이다.

생태계 내의 먹이 연쇄관계는 복잡하여 한 생물이 두 개 이상의 영양단계에 속해 있는 경우가 많다. 또한 연령이나 조건에 따라 속하는 영양 단계가 변하기도 한다. 따라서 먹이 사슬보다 먹이망food web이 이러한 복잡한 관계를 가리키는 데 더 적합하기도 하다.

필수어휘

- trophic relationships 영양관계
- producer 생산자
- consumer 소비자
- decomposer 분해자
- metabolic 신진대사의
- autotrophic 자가[독립] 영양의
- heterotrophic 타가영양생물의
- herbivores 초식동물
- carnivores 육식동물
- omnivores 잡식성동물
- biomass 생물체에서 얻어지는 에너지원으로 사용할 수 있는 에탄올이나 메탄가스

```
                    producers
                        └── autotrophic planktons, heterotrophs
Tropic          
relationships ──── consumers
                        └── herbivores, carnivores, omnivores
                    decomposers
                        └── heterotrophic bacteria
```

Mini Practice

Listen to part of a discussion in a marine biology class. 🎧 Ch4_04

1. In the lecture, which level contains the highest efficiency of energy transfer in trophic relationships?
   - Ⓐ producers
   - Ⓑ consumers
   - Ⓒ decomposers
   - Ⓓ all levels

2. According to the lecturer, what is a good example of authotrophs that he used in his lecture?
   - Ⓐ herbivores
   - Ⓑ zooplankton
   - Ⓒ phytoplankton
   - Ⓓ omnivores

Listening Script

Professor: This time, we will discuss trophic relationships in marine food webs and food chains. Trophic is a term meaning related to feeding or nutrition, so as you can guess, a tropic relationship is a relationship between food producers and food consumers. Trophic relationships can help us diagram those chains and webs. Okay, so, just like other ecosystems, in marine ecosystems food is necessary for both substance and energy. That is, food is needed for growth, reproduction, and also for metabolic processes. And like any other ecosystem, there are producers, consumers and decomposers in marine ecosystems. Autotrophic planktons, meaning planktons that can manufacture their own food, are the primary producers. Autotrophs are in turn, eaten by other organisms. These consuming organisms are called heterotrophic. As you should know, the prefix "hetero-" means "other." So a heterotrophic organism is an organism that cannot produce its own food, and has to rely on consuming other organisms for food instead. Whether directly or indirectly, heterotrophs eventually rely on autotrophs for their food energy. On the consumer side in marine food chains, the primary consumers are herbivores or plant eaters, and the secondary consumers are meat eaters, which include carnivores that eat meat exclusively, as well as omnivores which eat plants as well as meat. Finally, we come to the decomposers, heterotrophic bacteria which get their energy from bodily waste matters and dead tissues, completing the cycle back to the producers.

This energy transfer in marine food chains is not particularly efficient. One type of autotroph, phytoplankton, get their energy from the sun. But they make use of barely one percent of the available energy. The majority of the energy produced by producers or consumed by heterotrophs, about 70 to 90 percent or so, are used directly inside their bodies or excreted as waste. A mere 10 to 30 percent is retained as biomass in the body, so only that small percentage is available for the consumers of the next higher trophic level. So, the amount of biomass at each trophic level is directly related to how efficiently the energy can be transferred. At the lowest level, organisms typically have high biomass, and you can find a large quantity of small producers. Contrast that to the highest level, where organisms generally have a relatively low biomass, and you can see how there won't be as many large animals.

Answers p. 47

Biology

★★
068

Meerkat
미어캣

다람쥐만한 크기의 미어캣meerkat은 남 아프리카에 서식하는 몽구스mongoose과의 포유류로 집단 서식한다. 건조하고, 탁 트인 장소를 선호하는 그들은 주로 잔디와 낮은 관목이 있는 건조한arid 평야 지대에서 거주한다. 이들은 넓은 평야를 응시하며 뒷다리로 똑바로 서 있는 자세upright posture로 잘 알려져 있는데, 이 자세는 밤 동안 떨어진 체온을 높이기 위해 햇볕을 쬐거나sunbathe 포식자의 접근을 관찰하는 모습이다. 미어캣 눈 주위의 검은색 얼룩은 강한 햇볕의 눈부심을 막아준다. 그들은 뿌리나 과일로 수분을 섭취하고 곤충, 도마뱀 등을 먹으며, 어른 미어캣의 경우 독venom에 면역immunity이 있기 때문에 뱀이나 전갈을 먹기도 한다.

최대 30-40마리로 이루어진 미어캣 집단은 굴burrow을 만들어 아프리카의 뜨거운 태양을 피할 수 있는 서늘한 공간을 마련한다. 땅속 공간에 만들어진 이 영역들은 넓게 펴져있는 터널과 방으로 이루어진 방대한 망network을 형성한다. 미어캣은 자신들의 영역 내에 있는 구멍 위치를 잘 기억하기 때문에, 위험에 처한 순간에도 재빠르게 자신의 현 위치에서 가장 가까이에 있는 구멍을 찾아 신속하게 대피할 수 있다.

암컷은 일년에 두세 마리 정도의 새끼를 낳고, 서 있는 자세로 새끼들을 돌본다. 수컷과 형제자매sibling가 새끼를 기르는 것을 돕고 새끼 미어캣은 어른 미어캣의 행동을 관찰하고 모방하여, 사냥법과 먹이를 먹는 방법 등을 습득한다. 특히 어린 미어캣은 새와 같은 포식자에 대한 두려움이 크며, 위험에 노출되었을 때 그것을 인식하고 피하는 방법에 대해서도 알아간다. 공동체 구성원들은 서로의 털을 다듬어groom주면서 사회적 유대를 강화한다.

필수어휘
- altruistic 이타적인
- altruism 이타주의
- forage 먹이를 찾다
- sentry 보초(병)
- bark 짖다
- burrow 굴 / 굴을 파다
- kin 친척, 친족

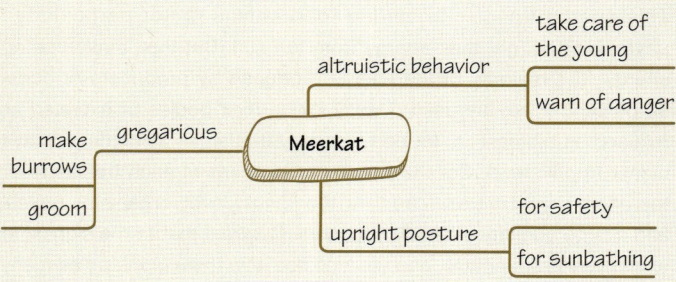

Meerkat

Unlike some other animals, the meerkat displays the altruistic behavior that is thought to offer benefits to the rest of the group while putting an individual meerkat at greater risk. While other meerkats forage or take care of the young, certain meerkats in a group take on the role of sentries or guards, alerting the group of danger by barking, while putting themselves at risk. In recent years, scientists have begun to question whether this behavior really is altruistic, or if it is actually done for the benefit of the individual meerkat.

The altruism theory suggests that sentries assume the role for the sole benefit of the group with no expectation of receiving any personal benefit in return. The presence of a sentry allows the other members of the group, who roam far from their burrows, to focus their attention on foraging, since the sentry's warning calls can alert the group to danger, allowing them to escape harm. By helping the other members of the group find food more efficiently and allowing them to escape danger, the sentry is obviously more concerned with the survival of the group than with its own survival.

However, another theory suggests that the sentry may be somewhat less concerned about the survival of the group. In one study, a group of scientists noticed a curious fact about sentries: the meerkats that typically decided to act as sentries had already found food that day, and upon sensing danger and calling out to the rest of the group, the sentry immediately found a burrow and was often the first one to reach safety. Furthermore, not a single one of the meerkat sentries in the study was killed by a predator. This survival rate led researchers to conclude that acting as a sentry may be, in fact, a selfish behavior intended to allow the meerkat to be the first to find safety in case of danger.

Another possible explanation for this behavior represents a middle ground between the two theories mentioned above. By alerting the group to danger, a meerkat gives its kin a far better chance of surviving an attack, while at the same time, by being the first one to spot danger, the sentry is afforded enough time to find safety itself, allowing it to survive. As a result, the alarm call is simply a way to increase the chances that a meerkat and its kin will survive.

1. The word afforded in paragraph 4 is closest in meaning to
    - (A) diffused
    - (B) provided
    - (C) advocated
    - (D) devised

2. What can be inferred about other animals in paragraph 1?
    - (A) They perform individual activities but don't participate in group work.
    - (B) Some of them do not need to forage.
    - (C) They use sentries to protect other members in a group.
    - (D) Some of them do not display altruistic social behaviors.

Answers p. 47

Biology

069
Natural selection
자연선택

자연선택설은 토플에서 다양하게 출제되고 있다. 리딩에서는 최근 공업 암화와 관련된 나방의 실험을 기억하도록 하자!

찰스 다윈Charles Robert Darwin이 제기한 자연 선택설natural selection은 생물의 과잉번식으로 인한 서식지의 포화로 생존 경쟁struggle for existence이 치열해지면, 주변 환경에 더 적합한 유전 형질gene pool을 가지고 있는 개체가 결국 살아 남게 된다는 이론이다. 이는 같은 종species이라 하더라도 주변 환경 요건에 더 적합한 유전자 형질을 지닌 개체가 그렇지 않은 개체에 비해 생존survival과 번식breeding에 우위를 가지게 되기 때문이다. 그리고 그 개체는 살아남기 위해 환경에 맞춰 변화하는 현상인 '변이variation'를 다음 세대에게 전달할 수 있는 확률이 더 높으며, 결국 적합한 개체의 유익한 변이가 오랜 기간 동안 누적되면서 전혀 다른 종으로 진화evolution하기도 한다.

자연 선택설의 사례

자연선택을 보여주는 과학적 사례로 공업 암화 현상industrial melanism이 있다. 영국에는 예전부터 나무 줄기stem에 앉는 습성이 있는 점박이 나방peppered moth이 있었는데, 이들은 색이 밝았다. 그러나 산업혁명industrial revolution 동안 공업화로 인해 그을음soot으로 나방이 앉는 나무의 색이 어두워지면서 어두운 색을 지닌 나방은 새와 같은 포식자로부터 숨을 수 있는 이점을 지니게 되었다. 그렇게 어두운 색을 지닌 나방의 생존 확률이 더 높아지면서 그들의 어두운 색 유전적 기질genetic trait이 자손에게 전해지게 되었고 맨체스터 지역의 나방은 거의 다 어두운 색의 나방으로 바뀌게 되었다.

필수어휘

- peppered moth 회색가지나방, 얼룩나방, 점박이나방
- industrial melanism 공업암화
- carbonaria 흑화형 (영국 공업도시 주변의 매연으로 오염된 산림에서 흔히 볼 수 있는 고추나방의 흑색변종)
- industrial revolution 산업혁명
- soot 그을음, 검댕
- camouflage 위장, 변장, 변장하다, 가장하다
- bark 나무껍질, (동물 개 여우 등이) 짖다
- stem (식물의) 줄기, 대 syn stalk
- predator 포식자, 포식동물
- surveillance 관찰, 감시
- morphological 형태학상의
- hypothesis 가설

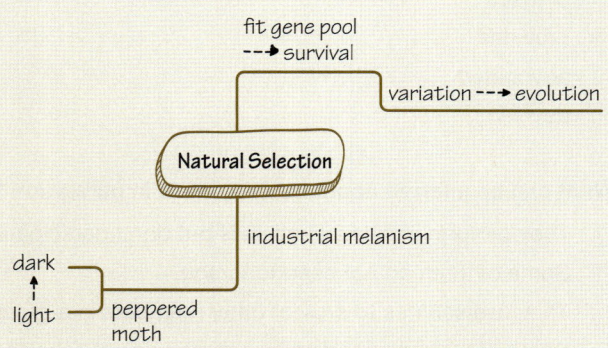

Industrial Melanism in Peppered Moths

The light-colored peppered moth was more common than the darker colored or *melanic* one in England prior to the Industrial Revolution, and the light-colored moth's spotted wings were difficult to pick out against the white bark of trees common in England at that time. However, over the course of 100 years, the population of melanic moths increased dramatically. Naturalists wondered why the white form of these moths was gradually disappearing in the forest near industrialized areas. Through surveillance and a series of thorough experiments, scientists began to figure out the mystery behind the famous peppered moths.

During the late 1950s, H.B.D. Kettlewell, a British geneticist, settled in the woods close to an industrialized area to scrutinize the behavior of predators of the moths, particularly birds. He noticed that the moths that contrasted with their backgrounds were easily picked off by birds, but moths whose color matched their background were more difficult for birds to find. Kettlewell performed experiments using a "mark-and-recapture" method to investigate just how the moths' morphological color affected their survival rate. He captured the same number of both the melanic and light-colored moths and marked them with special collagen drops on the underside of their wings, so he could identify them later. Then he released the marked moths into a polluted forest near an industrialized area and an unpolluted forest in a rural area and after some time recaptured them, and counted the moths to see which populations survived in the separate areas. He discovered that peppered moths whose color was closest to the bark of the trees survived. This was a significant discovery in that it supported the hypothesis that morphological color played an important role in determining survival.

Kettlewell concluded that the increase in the dark-colored moth population in the polluted area could be correlated with pollution from industrialization, which darkened the originally white bark of trees, an effect which was termed *industrial melanism*. Trees in industrial areas became darkened by soot from factories, giving the dark-colored moths resting upon those trees an advantage in hiding from predators, which in turn gave dark-colored moths a better chance of survival. Through natural selection, moths adapted to their changing environment and produced dark-colored offspring. In just fifty years, nearly all of the moths in and about industrialized cities were of the dark, melanic variety.

1. The word significant in paragraph 2 is closest in meaning to

    Ⓐ important   Ⓑ expansive   Ⓒ spectacular   Ⓓ competent

2. According to paragraph 2, what method did Kettlewell use to carry out his experiment?

    Ⓐ He captured moths by placing traps and then marked them between their wings to identify which ones he captured.
    Ⓑ After capturing the moths he placed little drops on them.
    Ⓒ He was able to capture the moths by using pheromones of both genders, then marked and released them back into the forest.
    Ⓓ He placed drops under the wings of the two species and released them, only to recapture them later.

Answers p. 48

Botany

070

Plant
식물

식물은 엽록소chlorophyll로 광합성photosynthesis 하여 영양분을 만들어 내는 생물 종으로 현화 식물[1] flowering plant, 침엽수[2] conifer, 겉씨식물gymnosperm, 양치식물[3] fern, 이끼moss, 녹말green algae등이 있다. 엽록소는 식물을 녹색으로 만들어 주는 엽록체chloroplast 안에 있는데, 바로 이 엽록소가 이산화탄소와 물과 더불어 태양 에너지를 화학 에너지로 전환하는 광합성을 한다. 광합성은 주로 식물의 잎에서 발생하며, 아주 드물게 선인장cactus의 경우 줄기stem에서 일어나기도 한다.

식물의 잎은 상면 표피upper epidermis, 하면 표피lower epidermis, 잎맥[4] vein, 잎살[5] mesophyll, 관다발vascular bundle, 기공stomata으로 구성된다. 표피에는 엽록체가 없기 때문에 광합성이 일어나지 않으며 대신 나뭇잎을 보호하는 기능을 한다. 기공은 주로 하표피에 존재하는 구멍들로 이산화탄소가 들어오고 광합성의 부산물인 산소가 나가는 통로이다. 관다발과 잎맥을 통해 영양분과 물이 이동하고, 엽록체가 있는 잎살 세포에서 광합성이 발생한다. 식물은 주로 무성생식asexual reproduction을 하지만, 때로는 유성생식sexual reproduction, 혹은 세대교번[6] alternation of generations 으로도 번식한다.

필수어휘

- soak up 흡수하다, 빨아들이다
- anchor 고정하다, 정박하다
- opportunistic 기회를 노리는, 기회주의의
- germinate 싹트다
- seedling 묘목
- tap root 곧은 원뿌리
- lateral root 곁뿌리
- root plate 뿌리 판
- fibrous root 수염뿌리
- spruce 가문비 나무
- willow 버드나무
- fir 전나무
- canopy 덮개, 숲의 나무가 지붕모양으로 우거진 것

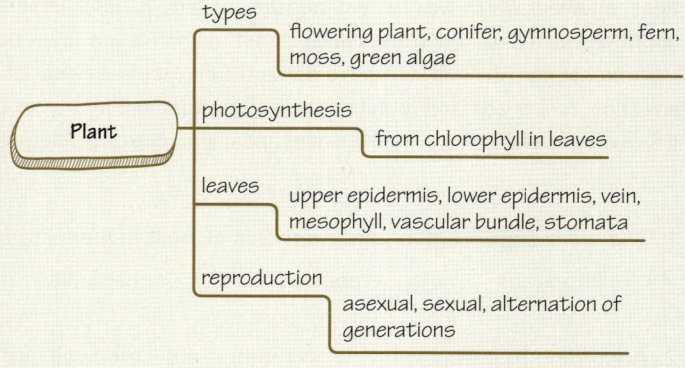

1 현화식물: 꽃으로 생식활동을 하며 밑 씨ovule가 씨방ovary 안에 들어 있는 속씨 식물
2 침엽수: 상록수로 바늘 같은 잎을 지님. 추운 지방에 생장
3 양치식물: 고사리류 등으로 온대의 비옥하고 습기 있는 지역에서 생장
4 잎맥: 잎 속에 있는 물과 양분의 이동통로
5 잎살: 잎의 표피와 잎맥을 제외한 나머지 부분
6 세대교번: 한 종의 생물체가 두 개 이상의 생식법을 지녀, 세대마다 그 생식방법을 바꾸는 것

Roots

The root is the parts of plants that typically lie beneath the surface of the soil, and performs various diverse functions. The most crucial role of this structure is to soak up water and inorganic nutrients from the soil and to anchor the plant or tree to the ground, holding it up. Water and dissolved minerals move slowly through soil, and as a result roots have to go where the water is rather than waiting for it to come to them. Although roots respond in a general way to gravity, they do not grow towards anything or in any particular direction; rather they are opportunistic in following cracks, worm runs, and old root channels and in proliferating where they find water.

Newly germinated seedlings produce a single root, the tap root, which grows downward. In some species with small seeds such as willows and birches, the tap root is small, easily deflected and seldom fills a crucial role. In a few species, such as willows, the tap root is so rudimentary that it becomes nearly indistinguishable from the other roots; these species can be described as having *fibrous root systems*. In other species, including pines and oaks, the tap root grows more vigorously and initially dominates the root system; in oaks it may reach half a meter in the first season. In all but a handful of species the importance of the tap root is diminished over time as a number of major *framework roots* grow out sideways from the top of the tap root.

Lateral roots may stay very close to the surface, as in the spruce and fir, or they may descend obliquely down several tens of centimeters before growing horizontally. As these roots grow out from the tree like the spokes of a wheel, they fork, branch and overlap. Within this criss-crossing framework the large rigid roots cannot move. As they grow bigger and so are inevitably pushed hard against each other, the internal tissues fuse together, creating an actual connection between the roots. This produces a solid root plate, the same width as the canopy or slightly wider, which moves as a unit as the tree sways and provides much of the anchoring and supporting for the tree.

1. The word proliferating in paragraph 1 is closest in meaning to
    - Ⓐ following
    - Ⓑ matching
    - Ⓒ converting
    - Ⓓ multiplying

2. Why does the author mention about willows?
    - Ⓐ to provide an example of a fibrous root system
    - Ⓑ to show the importance of the tap root
    - Ⓒ to argue that willows do not have tap roots
    - Ⓓ to contrast them with trees that have fibrous root systems

Answers p. 48

Biology

★★★
071

Predator
포식자

생태계ecosystem에서 포식자predator는 먹이prey를 포획행위foraging behavior로 얻는다. 그런데 포획 행위는 상당한 에너지를 소모하기 때문에 포식자는 에너지 소비를 최소화하면서 최적의 에너지를 얻을 수 있는 먹이를 사냥해야 한다. 또한 포획 방법은 생물체의 전반적인 삶에 중요하게 작용하여 특정 기간 동안 개체가 지니는 에너지 중에서 번식에 소비되는 비율인 번식 노력reproductive effort, 에너지 수지 energy budget, 이동 방법locomotors mode에 이르기까지 행동적, 생태학적, 생리학적, 그리고 형태학적인 특징에까지 영향을 끼친다.

활동적 사냥과 매복 사냥
사냥법은 전략에 따라 크게 활동적 사냥법active or widely foraging과 매복 사냥법ambush or sit-and-wait foraging 두 가지로 나뉜다. 활동적 포식자의 경우 보통 힘이 세고 행동이 매우 날렵하며, 사냥감을 찾아 자주 서식지 주변을 돌아다닌다. 이에 반해 매복 포식자들은 위장술 camouflage을 이용해 먹이가 그들 앞에 나타날 때까지 오랜 시간 동안 가만히 기다렸다가 포획한다. 흔히 위장술은 포식자로부터 피식자prey 자신을 방어하기 위한 보호 방법defensive strategy으로 알려져 있으나, 매복 포식자들은 사냥감의 눈에 띄지 않음으로써 먹이가 자신에게 최대한 접근했을 때 온 힘을 다하여 공격해 포획한다.

필수어휘
- predation 포획
- physiological 생리학적인
- ambush 매복 (공격)
- camouflage 위장하다
- detection 발견, 발각
- strike 공격하다
- stalk 몰래 접근하다
- expenditure 지출
- wander 배회하다 [syn] roam

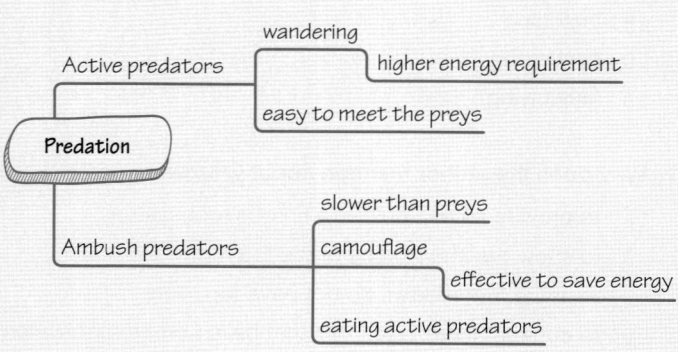

Predation

Predation, a behavior in which a predator captures and consumes prey, plays a critical role in an animal's life because it is closely related with its behavioral, ecological and physiological characteristics, such as its reproductive process and energy balance. Depending on how the predator catches its prey, there are several kinds of interactions between predator and prey, including ambush predation (sit-and-wait) and active predation (foraging).

Ambush predators use a concealed position or camouflage to catch prey that move within their attacking distance. On one hand, camouflage is one of the most common survival adaptations used by prey to hide from predators by blending in with the surroundings while on the other hand, the camouflage of ambush predators helps them to prevent detection by the prey, so they remain motionless for some time while waiting to rapidly strike the prey as it appears before them. These strategies enable ambush predators to capture highly mobile prey that move within their striking distance. Sometimes ambush predators seem to be lazy and helpless, but this strategy allows them to save their energy. Predation also refers to a type of predators that consume other predators; that is, an ambush predator could catch a foraging predator, because a widely foraging predator wanders more frequently and has more of a chance to come within striking distance of an ambush predator. For example, a sit-and-wait snake predominately eats widely foraging lizards. The features of ambush predators are 1) their prey density must be relatively high, 2) they are in less danger because they rarely expose themselves to their predators 3) they are slower than their prey and 4) their energy requirements are not high.

On the other hand, a foraging predator or active predator wanders around its habitat looking for prey, and then a short chase, stalking or an ambush may happen depending on the situation. They usually hunt victims that are moving and therefore, must be faster than their prey. Generally, active predators' energy requirements are higher than those of sit-and-wait predators because of the energy needed to search for prey. For example, the energy expenditure of widely foraging lizards is estimated to be 1.3-1.5 times greater than that of ambush lizards in the feeding ground. Foraging predators have an advantage when their prey is scarce but widely foraging predators may encounter their own predators more frequently since they wander around.

1. The word foraging in paragraph 1 is closest in meaning to

    Ⓐ consuming
    Ⓑ seeking for food
    Ⓒ providing
    Ⓓ mastering

2. The word that in paragraph 3 refers to

    Ⓐ foraging lizard
    Ⓑ feeding ground
    Ⓒ energy expenditure
    Ⓓ searching mode

Entomology

★★★
072

Rattlebox moth
활나물 나방

곤충 변태과정, 특정 곤충의 행동(거미-절지동물, 개미가 집을 짓는 행동 등), 진화 등이 토플에 출제되었다. 무엇이 나온다 하더라도 그 곤충의 특징, 예 등을 잘 파악하면 되니 처음 들어보는 곤충이나 동물이 나와도 당황하지 말자!

나방moth 날개를 만지고 눈을 비비지 말라는 말이 있다. 그 이유를 절실히 보여주는 나방이 바로 **활나물 나방**rattlebox moth이다. 이 나방은 보통 나방과는 달리 날개에 독이poison 있으며 우리가 흔히 보는 탁한 색의 나방과는 달리 아주 밝은 색의 날개를 가지고 있다. 그렇다면 이 나방은 어떻게 해서 독 날개를 가질 수 있게 된 것일까?

활나물 나방은 유충larvae 때부터 독성이 있는 활나물 잎rattlebox plant을 먹고 자라며 고치cocoon를 거쳐 나방이 되면 날개에 활나물 이 파리의 독성분toxic chemical이 저장된다. 이 독성분은 천적들에게predators 불쾌한 맛foul taste이 나기 때문에 활나물 나방에게는 아주 유용한 방어체계defence mechanism의 역할을 해준다.

또한 활나물은 독성잡초toxic weed로써 가축livestock이 이 나물을 섭취했을 때 독성으로 피해를 보기 때문에 사람들에게는 골칫덩어리로 알려져 있다. 그러나 활나물 나방이 독초를 소비해주므로 사람들은 활나물 나방의 존재를 환영한다고 알려졌다. 연구 결과에 의하면 활나물 잎을 먹고 자라지 않은 활나물 나방은 날개에 독성분이 없는 것으로 밝혀졌으며 이는 활나물 나방의 독특한 성질이 활나물 섭취와 밀접한 연관이 있음을 뒷받침해 준다.

필수어휘
- defense 방어
- poisonous 독성분의
- larvae 유충
- cocoon 고치
- eponymous 동일한 이름의

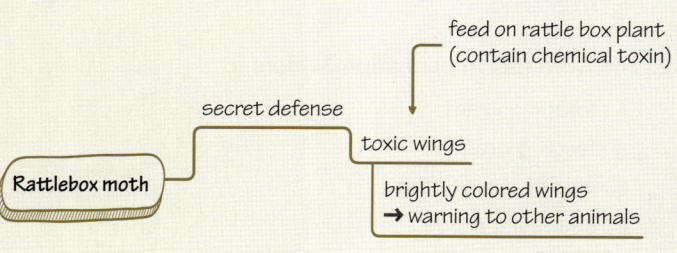

176

Mini Practice

Listen to part of a discussion in an entomology class. 🎧 Ch4_05

1. According to the professor, what are two characteristics that rattlebox moths have and which other moths do not have? Click on 2 answers.

   (A) They are brightly colored.
   (B) Their wings contain a chemical that is unappealing to predators.
   (C) They have a poisonous attack.
   (D) They struggle when caught in a spider's web.

2. What was confirmed by the laboratory experiment mentioned in the lecture?

   (A) The poison in the rattlebox moth's wings depends on the diet of the larvae.
   (B) The rattlebox moth can safely eat the leaves of the rattlebox plant.
   (C) Typical adults do not show any indication of toxin in their wings.
   (D) Larvae prefer the leaves of the rattlebox plant over other food sources.

Listening Script

Professor: We're going to be discussing an unusual kind of moth that's very unlike typical moths. I'm talking about the rattlebox moth. If a rattlebox moth gets caught in a spider web, what would you expect it to do? Surprisingly, it doesn't struggle. In fact, it actually remains really, really still and just waits patiently for the web's owner to come find it. I know, you're thinking it must be crazy, right? But the rattlebox moth has a secret defense: its toxic wings. The wings contain a poisonous chemical that makes a terrible flavor for the spider. So, if a spider tries to eat the moth, all it takes is one tiny drop of that poison and the spider learns that it's not going to make a good meal. The result? The spider actually cuts the moth free from the web and then the moth just flies off. Can you imagine that?

Another point that's uncharacteristic compared to other moths is that the rattlebox moth has very brightly colored wings. Now you're thinking that having bright colors would just serve to attract attention, but in reality the bright colors form a warning to other animals. Those bright colors say "Hey, look! You really don't want to try eating me!" At the larval stage, as scientists studying the rattlebox moth learned, the rattlebox larvae eat the leaves of a plant called the rattlebox plant, which is where the moth's name comes from. It's those rattlebox leaves that contain the chemical toxin that later appears in the adult moth's wings. The larvae have some way of storing the toxin, so that after emerging as an adult from its cocoon, some of that toxin ends up in the moth's wings.

Scientists wanted to determine if the plant was the source of the toxin, so they tested it in the laboratory. In the experiment, some rattlebox larvae were prevented from eating any of the toxic leaves, and were instead given beans containing no toxin. The adult moths that developed from those laboratory larvae showed no toxins in their wings. As you can see, the chemical ecology here is that the rattlebox moth is dependent upon the leaves of the eponymous plant to ensure survival and stay safe from predators.

Answers p. 50

Botany

★★★
073

Red Chlorophyll in leaves
붉은 엽록소의 작용

광합성, 삼투압현상, 신체의 항상성 등 과학분야의 기초지식은 토플에 자주 등장한다. 특히 광합성은 토플 단골 주제이니 내용을 꼭 숙지하도록 하자!

광합성이란 식물이 태양에너지solar energy를 이용해서 이산화탄소carbon dioxide와 물로부터 포도당glucose과 산소oxygen를 얻는 과정을 말한다. 다른 말로 태양에너지를 화학에너지chemical energy로 변환시키는 식물의 대단한 능력을 일컫는 용어인 것이다.

광합성은 엽록소chlorophyll가 있는 식물의 잎에서 일어난다. 햇빛이 풍부한 계절에는 엽록소가 초록색을 띄지만 날씨가 추워지면 초록 엽록소는 분해되어 사라지고 빨간색을 띠는 안토시안anthocyan이 잎에 생성되어 나뭇잎은 결국 빨간색으로 변한다. 이것이 우리가 부르는 단풍 색깔fall colors이 되는 것이다. 빨간 엽록소는red chlorophyll 나무에게 중요한 두 가지 역할을 하는데 하나는 나무가 겨울을 준비하기 전 충분히 햇빛을 받아 더 많은 영양분을 축적하는 것을 돕는 것이며 두 번째로는 잎에 있는 질소nitrogen를 나무 몸 속으로 운반해서 에너지를 공급하는 것이다. 질소는 나무 속에서 물과 영양분을 운반하는 중요한 역할을 하므로 겨울을 맞이하기 전에 충분한 질소를 저장하는 것은 겨울 동안 살아남아야 하는 나무에게는 중요한 과정인 것이다. 겨울을 나기 위해 식물이 거치는 과정은 수없이 토플시험에 출제된 적이 있으므로 반드시 기본 용어 및 기본개념을 기억하도록 하자.

필수어휘
- chlorophyll 엽록소
- photosynthesis 광합성
- dominate 지배하다
- convert 전환하다
- nitrogen 질소
- allocating 할당하는

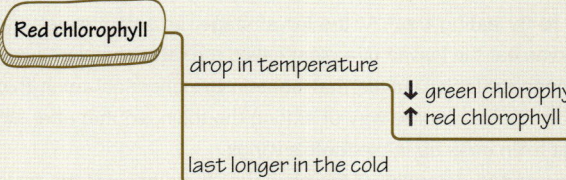

Mini Practice

Listen to part of a discussion about photosynthesis. 🎧 Ch4_06

1. What is the primary focus of the lecture?
   - Ⓐ the importance photosynthesis in trees and how it varies during certain times of the year
   - Ⓑ how red chlorophyll differs from green chlorophyll
   - Ⓒ how carbohydrates and sugar fill an important role in photosynthesis
   - Ⓓ how producers manufacture their food supply

2. How is red chlorophyll important to a tree's survival? Click on 2 answers.
   - Ⓐ It makes it possible for the tree to gather additional energy from the sun before the leaves fall off.
   - Ⓑ The extended period of photosynthesis gives the tree the energy and time needed to move nitrogen from the leaves to the body of the tree.
   - Ⓒ It allows the leaves to absorb the extra nitrogen necessary to detach themselves from the tree and fall to the ground.
   - Ⓓ It can endure the cold winters better than green chlorophyll.

Listening Script

Professor: Okay, so there are all these different colors of chlorophyll, each with its own function. That's what we want to examine today. What are the functions of the different colors? Anyone have a guess? Of course, everyone knows about the green ones. Those make up a large part of what plants and trees use to convert the energy from the sun. But, uh, you know of course that some trees change color depending on the season, and you might be surprised to hear that it's really significant to their survival. In seasons when there is a lot of sun, such as the spring and summer, green chlorophyll dominates. But as the year moves on, the air gets colder and the days get shorter, and little by little we can observe that the green chlorophyll begins to disappear, and in its place emerge yellows, oranges and sometimes quite brilliant reds. That red is also a kind of chlorophyll, and compared to the green one, it can last longer into the winter, so trees can use it to seek out a bit more energy from the sunlight after the green chlorophylls have all died off. Now, sunlight converts to food for the tree, so more sunlight means the tree can produce more food, which means its chances of survival are higher. Trees don't undergo photosynthesis during the winter months, so they need as much energy as they can to make it through winter without food, so the trees store as much energy and sugar as possible.

There's another important role this red chlorophyll plays in improving the survival chances of the trees. See, there's nitrogen in the leaves, and it's important for that nitrogen to be moved to the body of the tree before the leaves fall off. Nitrogen is uh, an important chemical for the tree. Nitrogen serves, um, to support many internal functions in a tree, for example, water movement, distributing and allocating nutrients, and so on. That makes it a really important chemical. So if the tree can store the nitrogen and use it later when the weather gets warm again, that improves the tree's survival chances. But, uh, you can guess that energy is needed to move that nitrogen around. Out of the leaves and into the core. So the red leaves staying on longer provide the tree with not only the time needed to move the nitrogen, but also the extra energy to do it with. Essentially, what the leaves accomplish by turning red is that they can extend their own life longer and collect enough energy to transfer their nitrogen into the tree's body, before eventually falling off.

Answers p. 50

Marine Biology

★★
074

Seagrass
해초

해초의 특징과 해양 생태계에서의 역할을 기억하고 가자!

해초seagrass는 염분이 가득한 얕은 바다에 서식하며 꽃을 맺는 현화식물flowering plant이다. 열대와 아열대 지역의 갯벌이나 하구 지역에서 자라는 육상 식물인 맹그로브mangrove에서부터 진화한 해초는 오늘날 전세계적으로 50여 종이 있는 것으로 알려져 있다. 해저 밑바닥seafloor의 퇴적물sediment에 뿌리를 고정하고anchor, 긴 잎사귀를 가진 모습이 잔디와 매우 비슷하다. 또한 꽃, 뿌리, 영양분을 체내로 운반해 주는 잎맥vein이 있는 것이 육지 식물과 유사한 점이자, 조류algae, 해조류seaweed와는 구분되는 특징이다. 육지 식물들처럼 중력을 버티는 데 필요한 단단한 줄기가 없는 대신, 파도나 해류에 노출될 때 유연하게 움직일 수 있도록 물의 부력에 몸을 지탱한다.

바다식물은 일반적으로 무성생식asexual reproduction을 한다. 포자spore로 무성생식을 하는 조류는 꽃과 열매를 맺지 않지만, 해초는 암술, 수술이 있어 씨앗seed과 열매를 맺는 온대나 열대 해저에서 유일한 유성생식 식물이다. 해초는 썰물이 일어나는 때에 수술의 꽃가루를 만드는 꽃밥anther이 떠오르면서 암꽃과 만나 가늘고 긴 실 모양의 화분pollen이 되어 해저에서 발아된다. 해초는 자라는데 태양빛, 적당한 온도, 영양분을 필요로 하는데 뿌리가 영양분과 광물질을 흡수하므로 이 모든 필요 요소들을 얻을 수 있는 해안 주변의 수심이 얕은 바다에서 서식한다.

필수어휘
- submerge 잠기다, 잠수하다
- aquatic 수중의
- marine 해양의
- alga 조류, 말   pl algae
- anchor 산업혁명
- carbon storage 탄소 저장
- eutrophication 부영양화
- sequester 격리시키다
- phytoplankton 식물성 플랑크톤

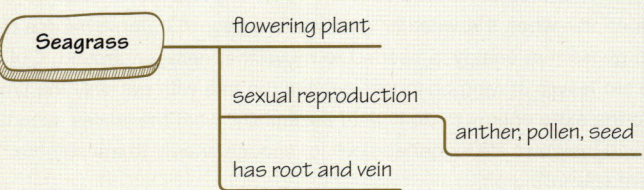

Seagrass

Seagrass is a type of underwater aquatic vegetation which evolved from terrestrial plants and is specialized to live in the salty coastal waters of most continents. Its morphological traits are similar to those of marine algae, but deep analysis reveals that seagrass has more characteristics in common with terrestrial plants, such as specialized tissues which perform specific tasks within each plant and true roots to anchor it to the bottom and absorb mineral nutrients from the sediment. What seagrasses need to grow and thrive are suitable temperature, salinity, light, current and nutrients, so the places where they can be found are usually shallow, soft-bottomed marine coastlines and estuaries.

Seagrass meadow, which looks like a grassland, plays multiple key roles in the marine ecosystem. First, the vast volume of leaves seagrasses produce every year make their habitat a marine nursery ground for numerous other animal species. They support countless herbivores like green turtles, manatees, and even fish which do not directly consume seagrass leaves because of their low nutritional value, but instead feed on dead seagrass material that bacteria have broken down. Further, the habitat of seagrasses functions as a protective shelter where many marine animals, including juvenile animals, can hide from predators. Therefore, many vertebrates and invertebrates such as microalgae migrate to seagrass meadows, thereby promoting biodiversity there. In addition, seagrass can clean water. When ocean current hits seagrass, the water flow is reduced and particles of sediment can settle. Seagrass meadows also prevent fast currents from stirring up existing sediment on the bottom. Finally, they have large carbon storage capacities, capturing and sequestering twice as much as carbon dioxide as rain forests.

However, because they are sensitive to changes in water quality, seagrasses have suffered from a number of stresses like global warming, diseases, excessive grazing by herbivores, decreasing water clarity, pollutants and invasive species, leading to a seagrass decline. Of these stressors, eutrophication, the ecosystem response to the excessive introduction of nutrients such as nitrogen or phosphates to an aquatic system, is toxic to seagrass, but induces the growth of microalgae. The result of the dramatic increase of these sea algae or phytoplankton in the water makes the sunlight weak and reduces photosynthesis in the seagrass, which requires some of the highest light levels of any plant group worldwide.

1. The word anchor in paragraph 1 is closest in meaning to
   - (A) allocate
   - (B) expand
   - (C) hold in a place
   - (D) convert

2. According to the passage, which of the following are true? Click on 2 answers.
   - (A) Even though seagrass leaves have low nutritional value, because of the scarcity of food in ocean waters marine lives directly consume them.
   - (B) Due to their sensitivity to changes in the ambient environment, seagrasses have suffered from various factors.
   - (C) Unlike other marine algae, seagrasses have real roots to anchor them to the bottom.
   - (D) Seagrass meadow can store much less carbon dioxide than rain forests.

Answers p. 51

Botany

075
Seeds and nuts
씨앗과 견과류

도토리acorns, 밤chestnuts, 호두walnuts는 씨앗seeds일까 견과류nuts일까? 답은 씨앗과 동시에 견과류 이다. 왜냐하면 견과류란 씨앗을 포함하는 식물의 열매fruit를 나타내는 말이기 때문이다. 따라서 견과는 식물의 씨앗이 될 수 있으나 모든 씨앗이 견과류가 되는 것은 아니다. 씨앗이 땅에 묻혀서 발아되면germinated 꽃을 피우는 식물flowering plant이나 나무로 성장하게 되며 인간의 난자ovary가 정자sperm에 의해서 수정이 되면fertilized 태아embryo가 되듯이 식물배아embryo가 외피integument에 의해 둘러싸이게 되면 씨앗이 만들어지게 된다. 해바라기 씨sunflower seeds를 얻으려면 검정색의 외피를 벗겨내야 그 속에 하얀 배아(씨앗)를 얻을 수 있다. 그러므로 해바라기 씨는 견과가 아니라 "씨"라고 부르는 것이다.

반면 견과는 한 개의 씨앗을 가지고 있는 열매이며 씨앗 주변에 외피가 있을 수도 없을 수도 있다. 보통 견과는 건조하고 딱딱한 겉껍질outer shell을 가지고 있기 때문에 씨가 떨어지거나 튀어나가지 않고 남아있으며 여물어도 터지지 않는다. 보통 견과류는 복자방compound ovary(씨앗과 열매를 포함하는 방이 여러 개)이므로 씨앗이라고 일컬어진다. 보통 수박에서 씨만 골라서 뱉어내듯 씨앗은 과일에서 분리될 수 있지만, 견과는 단단한 껍질 내부에 씨앗과 과일이 모두 포함되어 있기 때문에 껍질에서 쉽게 분리되지 않는다. 견과의 단단한 껍질 내부에는 알맹이kernel가 있으며 이는 사실 열매이지 견과가 아니다. 그러므로 우리는 밤을 먹을 때 사실은 밤이라는 견과 속에 있는 열매를 먹는 것이다.

필수어휘
- culinary 요리의
- botanical 식물의
- germinate 발아하다
- embryo 배아
- fertilization 수정
- indehiscent (열매가) 열개하지 않는
- integument 외피, 표피
- ovary 난소, 씨방
- kernel (견과류·씨앗의) 알맹이

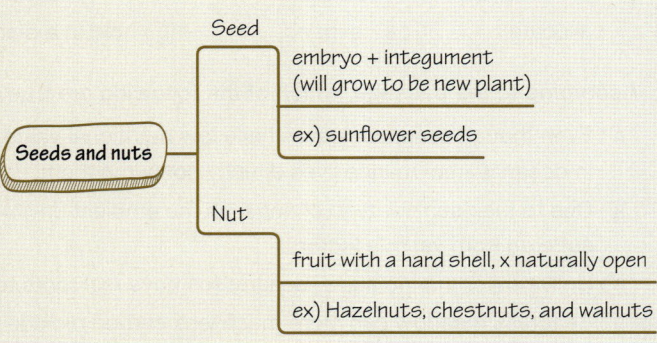

Mini Practice

Listen to part of a discussion in a botany class. 🎧 Ch4_07

1. According to the lecture, how would a botanist define a seed?
   - Ⓐ The part of the plant that can reproduce when germinated
   - Ⓑ Any kernel found within an outer shell
   - Ⓒ A fruit that remains detached from the ovary of a nut
   - Ⓓ The embryo of a plant encased in its integument

2. Why are kernels mentioned?
   - Ⓐ To compare the seeds of chestnuts seeds and sunflowers
   - Ⓑ To demonstrate the confusion between nuts and seeds
   - Ⓒ To show how the botanical definition of a nut is inaccurate
   - Ⓓ To show the importance of compound ovaries

Listening Script

Professor: There's a lot of confusion, stemming from a difference in classification, about the difference between seeds and nuts, even among scientists. All nuts are seeds, but not all seeds are nuts. Isn't that nutty? The distinction between nuts and seeds differs depending on whether you're discussing them in a culinary context or a botanical one. From a botanical standpoint, a seed is part of a flowering plant or tree that, when buried in the ground and germinated, will grow to become new plant or tree. That's kind of similar to a human egg, which becomes an embryo after fertilization. In some species, plant embryos are enclosed in a covering called an integument, and a seed is the embryo and integument. Sunflower seeds are a good example. The integument is the tough black outside part, which you crack open to reveal the white embryo. It's a seed in both botanical and culinary senses, so everyone calls them sunflower seeds, not "sunflower nuts."

What about nuts? Technically speaking, from a botanical standpoint a nut is a fruit with a hard, woody shell. Nuts typically contain a single seed (rarely, two seeds) that is separate from the shell. It doesn't matter if there's an integument. A key distinction is botanical nuts are indehiscent, meaning that they don't naturally crack open, and the seed doesn't naturally free itself from the shell. That's a major difference from the culinary definition. Hazelnuts, chestnuts, and walnuts are all botanical nuts; all of them are indehiscent. Almonds, however, aren't true botanical nuts. And of course, any nut can also be considered a seed from a botanical point of view, because it's a compound ovary, containing both the seed and the fruit. In most plants, the seed and fruit can be separated. For example, seeds are removable from a grape. But nuts are different. Inside the hard shell are both the seed and the fruit, but these cannot be separated. That inside part, the nut excepting the outer shell, is called the kernel. The kernel alone can most certainly not be considered a nut; it is a fruit. Yet, people often say thing like "I like to eat pecans" or "I like to eat hazelnuts." Technically, that's wrong. You should say, "I like to eat pecan meat" or "I like to eat hazelnut kernels."

Answers p. 52

Biology

★★
076

Snake
뱀

뱀은 팔, 다리가 없는 가늘고 긴 몸을 지닌 파충류retile과 동물이다. 청각과 시각이 약한 대신 특수한 구멍 기관pit organ과 갈라진 혀forked tongue가 그 역할을 담당한다. 얼굴 양쪽 콧구멍 아래에 있는 구멍 기관은 적외선 열 감지 기능을 하며 대게 살모사와 같은 독사류에 있다. 구멍 기관 안에 있는 막membrane이 1m 이내에 있는 먹이prey인 쥐나 새와 같은 항온동물endortherm의 몸에서 발산되는 열을 감지해 포획할 수 있게 해준다. 뿐만 아니라 최근 연구에 따르면 이 구멍기관의 역할이 먹이 포획에 그치는 것이 아니라, 체온 조절thermoregulation과 적이나 포식자predator를 알아차리는 등의 다양한 목적으로 쓰인다고 한다.

뱀의 청각과 시각을 보완해 주는 역할을 하는 또 다른 기관은 끝이 두 개로 나눠진 '갈라진 혀'이다. 양쪽으로 갈라진 혀는 표면적이 넓어 지면이나 공중에 떠 있는 냄새 성분volatile chemical에 더 많이 노출된다. 보통 때는 입 속에 있는 혀 주머니에 있지만 주변에서 움직임의 변화를 감지하거나 환경이 변화하면 계속해서 혀를 날름거리며 민감하게 반응한다. 그렇게 얻어낸 냄새 성분은 주머니 모양의 후각 기관olfactory system인 야콥슨 기관Jacobson organ으로 운반되어 먹이를 찾아내고, 교미할 짝mate을 선택하는 등의 다양한 방법으로 사용된다.

필수어휘

- ambient 주위의, 주변의
- scale 비늘
- serpent 큰 뱀
- amniotic 양 막의
- flick 잽싸게 움직이다
- retract 움츠리다
- vomeronasal 서비골의 (서비골: 비강과 서골 지역의 연골의 기관)
- vent 구멍
- nostril 콧구멍
- substrate 기질 (결합조직의 기본 물질)
- bone conduction 골전도

Snake — pit organ, forked tongue
- find prey
- avoid predators
- thermoregulation

Snake's sensing organs

Snakes, like lizards, turtles, crocodiles, and alligators, are reptiles, and their body is long and thin without any limbs. They are ectothermic, which means that their body temperature changes depending on their ambient environment. In fact, they regulate their own body temperature by exposing themselves to the sun to heat up or by going underground or into the shade to cool down. The horny scale covering their whole body is shed once a year. Another characteristic they have in common with reptiles is that they lay amniotic, shelled eggs. However, in majority of serpents, their sense of hearing and olfactory sense do not function properly, so snakes needed evolutionary adaption to cope with the problem.

While moving along the ground, the flicking of a snake's tongue is an important sensory behavior. Even though they have nostrils, snakes can augment their sense of smell by sticking out their tongue to essentially taste the air. [A ■] An even more interesting thing is that the tip of their tongue is widely separated into two distinct parts, which allow the snake to have more surface area in contact with the chemicals in the air. [B ■] After picking up odor particles from the air, the tongue is retracted to the vomeronasal organ (also called Jacobson's organ), a secondary olfactory sensing organ in the roof of the mouth, delivering chemical stimuli gathered and sending the information to the brain, allowing the animal to taste the scent particles, find food and identify potential mates or enemies. [C ■] The deeper the fork in a snake's tongue, the more the snake can use its Jacobson's organ. [D ■]

Some species of snake have heat-sensing pits or vents between the eye and nostril on either side of the head which allow the snake to detect less than 0.003°C differences in temperature. Along with the forked tongue, Jacobson's organ and inner ears that enable them to sense vibrations in the air or substrate using bone conduction, this heat-sensing pit gets snakes precise information about the direction and distance to their target prey.

1. The word distinct in paragraph 2 is closest in meaning to
   - (A) permeable
   - (B) discrete
   - (C) dramatic
   - (D) eerie

2. Look at the four squares [■] that indicate where the following sentence could be added to the sentence.

   Another reason snakes have a forked tongue is so that the tongue can touch the two pits in this organ.

   Where would the sentence best fit?

   Answers p. 52

Entomology

★★★
077

Super-hydrophobic insects
내수성을 가진 곤충

곤충은 작은 털hair들이 아주 많아 물에 뜰float 수 있는 능력이 있으나 물에 뜨는 곤충은 벽을 기어오르지는 못한다. 하지만 모기는 이를 거스르는 예외적인 곤충이다. 모기가 물에 뜨는 원리를 이해하기 전에 물의 성질에 대해 먼저 살펴보도록 하자.

물은 서로 뭉치려는 성질이 매우 강한 여러 분자molecule들이 결합attraction된 물질이다. 표면에 떨어진 물방울을 현미경으로 들여다 보면 동그란 모양으로 이루어짐을 볼 수 있다. 이는 물속의 분자들이 서로 결속하려는 힘 때문에 만들어지는 것이다. 또한 물방울 두 개를 가까이 떨어뜨리면 서로 합쳐져서 하나의 더 큰 물방울이 만들어지는데 이렇게 액체 표면의 분자들이 서로 잡아당겨 생기는 힘을 표면장력surface tension이라 부른다. 이처럼 액체 분자들이 서로 당기는 힘으로 형성되는 액체의 표면은 마치 탄성 막처럼 팽팽해지는데, 이런 물 분자 위에서 모기나 소금쟁이와 같은 작은 곤충들이 다리 털을 이용해서 미세한 진동으로 표면을 통통 튕기며 거닐게 되는 것이다. 특히 모기는mosquitoes 체중을 각 다리에 분산distribute시켜 무게를 가볍게 만듦으로써 물에 뜨며 모기의 다리는 물에 저항력이 크다는 뜻인 super-hydrophobic이라 불린다. 이러한 물의 표면장력을 이용하여 모기는 트램펄린 위에서와 같이 뛰면서 물 위를 이동할 수 있다.

필수어휘

- bristle 짧고 뻣뻣한 털
- setae 강한 털
- adhesive 들러붙는
- secretion 분비
- hydrophobic 소수성 (물과 친화력을 갖지 않는 성질)
- microscopic 미세한
- maneuver 조종하다
- surface tension 표면장력
- proficient 능숙한

Super-hydrophobic insects
- mosquitoes
  - having super-hydrophobic legs (water-resistant)
  - strong surface tension propels them forward over the water

Mini Practice

Listen to part of a discussion in a biology class. 🎧 Ch4_08

1. What features allow an insect to climb walls? Click on 2 answers.

   Ⓐ The sticky substance secreted from their feet
   Ⓑ The tiny scales which cover their legs
   Ⓒ The fact that their legs are super-hydrophobic
   Ⓓ The tiny hairs covering their legs

2. According to the lecture, how can mosquitoes move on water?

   Ⓐ By bouncing on the surface of the water to create ripples which push them forward
   Ⓑ By paddling with their hind legs while using their front legs to steer
   Ⓒ By using their wings to propel themselves along the surface
   Ⓓ By pushing down on water to use the surface tension to move forward

Listening Script

Professor: Most people know that lots of kinds of insects can climb walls or even cling upside down from the ceiling, just like flies. How can they do this? Well, they not only have a lot of fine hairs on their legs, but they also have these very special bristle-like structures on their feet called setae. These structures are covered with a secreted adhesive substance that allows them to stick to just about any kind of surface and prevents them from falling off.

While some insects can stick to walls, other insects such as water striders, spiders and beetles, can actually walk on water. How do they do this? It has nothing to do with secretion. Rather, they are incredibly light and therefore they can just float on the water. But, there's a very interesting thing. Insects can either float on water or can climb walls, but they can't do both, with a single exception: the mosquito. Mosquitoes have a special adaptation that gives them both abilities. They can stick to walls and also walk on water. It's very interesting how they do this. By bending their legs to distribute their weight, they can walk on water. A mosquito's legs are super-hydrophobic, which means they are incredibly water-resistant. But water-resistance alone isn't the whole story. A mosquito's legs are covered with thousands of microscopic scales that can trap air much like the feathers on a duck. To help you picture how incredibly hydrophobic they are, consider that a single leg is so water-resistant that it can support more than twenty times the mosquito's weight! That's amazing, isn't it?

Another interesting thing is how mosquitoes move around when walking on water. It's the surface tension of the water that enables them to maneuver on the surface. It's almost as if the water behaves like a trampoline. See, when a mosquito pushes down with its rear legs, the strong surface tension propels them forward over the water. Have you ever seen one on a pond or a lake? If so, you'll know how proficient they are at this.

Answers p. 53

Biology

078

The effect of diet on immune system
영양분 섭취와 면역체계와의 관계

인체의 특징 중에서도 특정 질병(비만, 당뇨, 불면증 등)이 체내에 끼치는 영향이 자주 출제된다. 이러한 질병의 영향을 직접적으로 받는 곳이 면역체계이므로 기초지식을 알아놓도록 하자!

우리 몸에서 면역을 담당하는 세포인 백혈구white blood-cell는 몇 종류의 면역세포immune cell로 나뉘는데, 그 중 하나가 림프구lymphocyte이다. 림프구는 또 다시 T세포와 B세포로 나뉘며 그들은 특정한 단백질, 다당류 또는 바이러스에 반응하는 항체를 만들어 질병에 대응한다. 이 중 T세포는 주로 흉선(가슴샘thymus)에서 만들어지며 박테리아와 접촉한 적이 없는 미접촉 T세포naïve T cell가 박테리아와 접촉하고 나면 기억 T세포memory T-cell로 변하게 된다. 신체가 나이가 들어감에 따라 미접촉 T세포의 수는 점점 줄어들며 기억 T세포의 수는 자연히 증가하게 되는데 이는 인체 면역력immunity을 떨어뜨리며 노화를 이끌게 된다.

그러나 최근 영양분 섭취와 노화의 관계 연구에서 흥미로운 결과가 밝혀졌다. 그것은 평소보다 영양분을 덜 섭취했을 때underfed 체내에 섭취되는 칼로리가 제한되면서 신체가 자극을 받아 미접촉 T세포의 생산을 증가시킴으로 인체의 면역 기능을 향상시킨다는 것이었다.

따라서 영양분을 덜 섭취할수록 더욱 건강하고 더 오래 살게 된다는 이 흥미로운 연구 결과는 결국 소식할수록 장수한다는 말을 더욱 뒷받침해주고 있다.

필수어휘
- lymphocytes 림프구
- immune system 면역체계
- originate from ~로부터 유래하다
- hematopoietic stem cell 조혈모세포
- bone marrow 골수
- thymus 흉선, 가슴샘
- protein marker 단백질표지
- pathogens 병원균
- gland 샘
- susceptible 민감한, 예민한

Mini Practice

Listen to part of a discussion in a biology class. 🎧 Ch4_09

1. Based on the lecture, why are some cells referred to as naïve?

    Ⓐ They cannot yet recognize protein markers.
    Ⓑ They must be called naïve before they can be referred to as a T cell.
    Ⓒ They recognize and destroy foreign cells that enter the body.
    Ⓓ They don't possess any protein markers from invading cells.

2. In the study that the professor mentioned, what was the main difference between monkeys which have been on a normal diet and those which haven't?

    Ⓐ Monkeys on a normal diet seem to age faster.
    Ⓑ Monkeys on a lower-calorie diet had shorter life spans than the average.
    Ⓒ Monkeys on a normal diet had a lower number of naïve T cells.
    Ⓓ Monkeys receiving fewer calories were less healthy.

Listening Script

Professor: T cells or T lymphocytes are part of the human immune system and are important for good health. T cells originate from hematopoietic stem cells produced in bone marrow. These cells undergo a positive and negative selection process within the thymus, a small organ in our body. Cells that successfully mature into lymphocytes are called T cells because they come from the thymus. When these immune cells encounter a foreign object in the body, like a bacteria or virus, they learn to recognize it as the enemy through protein markers. If the virus or bacteria is encountered again, the T cell remembers the protein marker and helps the white blood cells attack and kill them. That's why it is called a memory T cell. However, there are some T cells that haven't been exposed to a protein marker and they are called naïve T cells. Naïve T cells respond to new pathogens that the body has not been exposed to or yet encountered. As humans and animals age, their immune systems becomes less effective. As naïve T cells meet various pathogens in the body and become memory T cells they get used up. The body can only produce a limited amount of naïve T cells and this ability is greatly decreased as the thymus gland begins to shrink in middle age. With fewer naïve T cells being produced, the body is more susceptible to disease and this results in a weakened immune system. However, one study found that a caloric restriction diet in monkeys had an interesting effect on the number of naïve T cells. Monkeys that were given thirty percent less calories over a long period of time had greater numbers of naïve T cells than monkeys who had a normal caloric intake. It seemed that this reduction in caloric intake slowed down the aging process. Scientists were fascinated by this result and are beginning new research to discover whether a reduced caloric intake can help other areas such as hearing, eyesight, wound healing, and other bodily functions that are typically influenced by aging.

Answers p. 54

Biology

079
The effects of music on brain organs
음악이 뇌에 끼치는 영향

왜 우리는 음악을 듣고 감동할까? 우리 신체는 좋아하는 노래를 들을 때 정서적으로 각성된다. 동공이 확장되고, 맥박과 혈압이 상승하고, 피부의 전기 전도성이 느려지며, 신체 운동과 관련된 소뇌가 활성화된다. 혈액도 다리 근육으로 이동하게 되어 나도 모르는 사이에 발을 구르게 된다. 즉 음악은 우리의 생물학적 뿌리를 자극한다.

이렇게 음악이 우리 신체에 즉 뇌에 끼치는 영향이 어떤 것인지를 밝히기 위한 많은 연구들이 진행되었다. 우선 음악에 감동받은 경험이 있는 사람들을 모아서 음악을 들려주는 동시에 그들의 뇌활동을 PET scan을 통하여 관찰하였다. 관찰 결과 음악은 청각기관뿐만 아니라 시각을 담당하는 기관에도 영향을 미친다는 것이 밝혀졌다. 그 기관은 '뇌의 눈'이라고도 알려져 있는 브로드만 영역 Broadmann areas 18과 19이다. 즉 음악을 들으면 그 소리와 함께 이미지를 떠올리게 되며 이것이 감정에도 영향을 끼친다는 것이다.

또한 음악은 기억과 정서를 담당하는 변연계 limbic system에도 영향을 미친다는 것이 밝혀졌다. 이것은 음악을 들음으로써 과거를 회상하고 그 추억과 정서를 연관시키는 것을 설명한다. 결국 음악은 신체적, 정신적, 정서적인 모든 부분에서 영향을 미치는 것이다.

필수어휘
- frequency 주파
- internal organs 내부 장기
- auditory cortex 청각 피질
- Broadmann areas 브로드만 영역
- limbic system 변연계
- primal area 원초적 영역

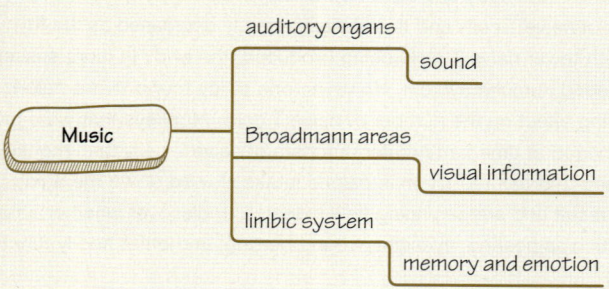

Mini Practice

Listen to part of a lecture in a physiology class. 🎧 Ch4_10

1. Why was activity in Broadmann areas 18 and 19 significant?

    Ⓐ This signified the brain's attempt to visually symbolize the music being heard.
    Ⓑ These areas of the brain are most commonly referred to as a symbol of the mind's eye.
    Ⓒ This led to the conclusion that audio information is processed in these symbolized regions of the brain.
    Ⓓ These parts of the brain are symbolized by an image of a large mental canvas.

2. What two things does the limbic system affect? Click on 2 answers.

    Ⓐ Emotion
    Ⓑ Sound
    Ⓒ Vision
    Ⓓ Memory

Listening Script

Professor: How is it that music affects the way we feel? Well, music stimulates parts of the brain. Say, for example, you hear a low frequency sound followed by a high frequency one? Well, that actually makes something react inside your brain. So, I want to talk about some new research done about this relationship, between music and your brain, which was based on PET scans of participants listening to music. PET or P-E-T stands for Positron Emission Tomography; it's a special kind of scan that shows 3D images of internal organs, and it can even show which areas of the brain are active. So what did researchers find out from these PET scans? Well, there's one really obvious region, of course, near Brodmann areas 41 and 42, the auditory cortex, which processes sound information. Well, duh, it's music. But surprisingly, another area also showed activity! What area was it? Interestingly, it was the area that processes visual information. More specifically, Brodmann areas 18 and 19, part of the outer layer of the visual cortex, an area some refer to as the "mind's eye," something like a mental canvas. When you listen to music, your mind is sort of painting a picture to go with what you hear. But that's not all! Remarkably, researchers found that music also activated the limbic system, a primal area deep within the brain connected with emotion and memory. I mean, don't you find that when you listen to a song, say, from your childhood, you also experience again the feelings you had at that time? Similarly, fast, upbeat music will generally make you feel a bit happier. Really, listening to music is kind of physical, mental, and emotional all at once, affecting one's whole body.

Answers p. 54

Biology

★★
080

Thermoregulation
체온조절

동물의 체온은 외부 환경에 영향을 받는다. 열은 고온부에서 저온부로 이동하기 때문에, 주변 온도가 체온보다 낮은 경우 항온동물 endotherm(warm-blooded animals)은 체온을 외부 환경에 빼앗기게 된다. 따라서 온도 조절 작용 thermoregulation은 많은 에너지가 필요하지만 항온동물에게 꼭 필요하다. 포유류 mammal의 경우 36~38℃, 조류의 경우 39~42℃를 유지하기 위해 동물들은 태양 주변으로 이동하면서 체온을 조절하거나, 뛰거나 몸을 떨어 shivering 근육을 움직여서 체온을 유지하고, 호르몬 작용으로 시작되어 재빨리 정상 상태로 되돌리는데 필요한 체열을 제공하는 갈색지방 brown fat을 활용하기도 한다. 또한 깃털 feather, 털 fur, 지방층 fat layer은 열 손실을 차단해 주는 역할을 한다. 조류의 경우, 깃털이 따뜻한 공기 층을 만들어 온도를 유지해준다.

해양 생물의 경우 열손실의 비율이 육지 생물보다 훨씬 크기 때문에 특별한 열 조절이 필요하다. 따라서 고래는 물에 젖으면 역할을 제대로 하지 못하는 털 대신 두꺼운 지방층 blubber으로 열 손실을 차단한다. 그리고 다른 동물들에 비해 노출 면적이 넓어 열을 많이 빼앗기는 참다랑어 bluefin tuna의 경우, 동맥 arteries(arterial blood)과 정맥 vein(venous blood)의 혈액순환을 통해 심장으로 들어오는 차가운 피를 따뜻하게 유지한다.

반대로 외부 온도가 지나치게 높은 경우에도 열 조절이 필요한데, 여기에는 발한 sweating이 일어나거나 호흡을 헐떡이며 panting 몸의 열을 식히는 동물뿐 아니라, 몸에 자신의 타액 saliva이나 물을 뿌려 온도를 낮추는 코끼리와 같은 동물도 있다.

필수어휘

- ambient 환경의, 주변의
- frigid 매우 추운
- extremity 말단
- forelimb 앞다리, 앞 지느러미
- pad 발바닥
- fur 털
- insulation 단열
- counter current exchange 역류 교환
- arterial 동맥의
- venous 정맥의
- conduction 전도

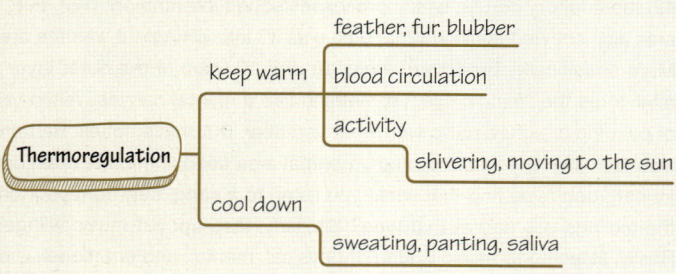

Thermoregulation

Homeotherms (warm-blooded animals) have developed various adaptations to maintain their body temperature at a constant point, independent of the ambient temperature. In extremely frigid climates, one way to maintain an optimal body temperature is to shut down blood circulation to the extremities to prevent further heat loss. For example, the internal temperature of an Alaskan husky dog is about 38°C, but the temperature in its forelimbs is generally 14°C and 0°C in its pads. In addition, its specialized fur insulates the body and reduces heat loss to the environment. Another effective adjustment to increase resistance to cold weather is that of the polar bear. Polar bears have excellent insulation consisting of thick fur covering a layer of blubber that can be up to 11cm thick, as well as black skin which absorbs light energy. The arctic fox, dressed in its winter fur, can survive in temperatures of -50°C without any need to change its metabolic rate to warm up. In the ocean, bluefin tuna, uncommon warm-blooded fish, maintain the temperature of certain parts of their body, such as their muscles, brain and eyes above the temperature of the ambient seawater to help them function better. In particular, Atlantic bluefin tuna regulate body temperature using *countercurrent exchange*, where heat in the arterial blood transfers to the venous blood.

In contrast to these "warming" strategies, animals in very hot climates have had to adapt reverse strategies to keep their bodies cool. Some animals increase conduction, that is, by increasing the amount of their surface area that is in contact with a cooler surface. Radiation of heat from the body happens naturally if the external temperature is lower; and sweat secretion can reduce body temperature through evaporative cooling. Other animals, such as rodents in the desert, seek the shelter of shade or an underground burrow, or simply reduce activities to mitigate the heat. Panting—breathing quickly and loudly through the mouth—enhances the cooling effect in birds and many mammals, and some animals are light colored to reflect sunlight away from their bodies, preventing the absorption of too much heat. Remarkably, camels, hyraxes, and elands can fluctuate their internal body temperature throughout a 24 hour cycle, maintaining a body temperature of 35°C at dawn and 40°C during the hottest part of the day.

1. What is the purpose of paragraph 2?
    - Ⓐ to contradict the strategies in paragraph 1
    - Ⓑ to provide an opposite way how mammals in a different environment control their body temperature
    - Ⓒ to offer more examples for animals to keep them warm
    - Ⓓ to state manipulating the body temperature is more difficult in hot areas

2. The word fluctuate in paragraph 2 is closest in meaning to
    - Ⓐ augment
    - Ⓑ increase
    - Ⓒ mitigate
    - Ⓓ change

Answers p. 55

Chapter 5.
Physical Science

Chemistry
081-L
Biofuel

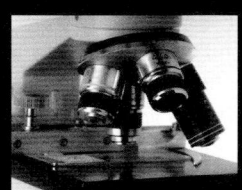

Physics
082-R
Cell discovery

Astronomy
083-R
Celestial bodies

Chemistry
084-L
Composting

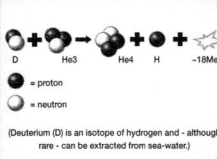

Chemistry
089-L
Helium-3

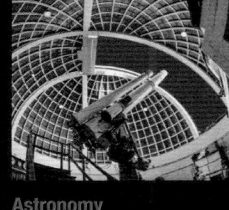

Astronomy
090-L
Hooker Telescope

Astronomy
091-R
Jupiter

Astronomy
092-L
Mars

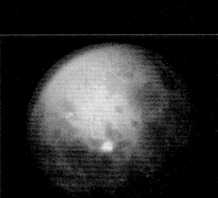

Astronomy
093-L
Mercury

Chemistry
094--R
Periodic table

Astronomy
095-R
Planets

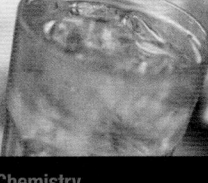

Chemistry
096-L
Properties of water

Astronomy
097-R
Stars

Astronomy
098-L
The orbits of comets

Chemistry
099-R
Origins of life

Chemistry
100-L
Trace metals

Chemistry

081

Biofuel
바이오연료

수많은 과학자들이 화석연료를 대체할 수 있는 에너지를 찾기 위해 수십 년간 연구한 끝에 생물유기체에서 연료를 얻는 방법을 개발했다. 이제 콩기름으로 자동차를 운전할 수 있는 세상이 온 것이다. 그 에너지들에 대해 알아보도록 하자.

바이오 연료는 생물유기체biomass에서 얻는 연료로 살아 있는 유기체뿐 아니라 동물의 배설물 등 대사활동에서 나오는 부산물을 모두 아우르며, 화석연료와는 다른 신재생에너지renewable energy인 바이오에탄올bio-ethanol과 바이오디젤bio-diesel 등을 포함한다.

바이오에탄올은 사탕수수 · 밀 · 옥수수 · 감자 · 보리 등 주로 녹말작물starch crop을 발효시켜 차량 등의 연료 첨가제로 사용하며 화석연료와 달리 환경오염 물질이 전혀 없고, 식물로부터 연료를 얻기 때문에 언제든지 재생이 가능하여 일찍부터 차량용 대체에너지로 주목을 받았다. 그러나 에탄올은 화석연료에 비해 에너지 전환률conversion rate이 낮아 에탄올만으로 차를 운행할 경우 화석연료보다 훨씬 더 많은 양이 필요하다는 단점이 있다. 그래서 좀더 에너지 효율성이 높은 바이오디젤에 대한 관심이 증가하고 있다. 바이오디젤은 콩기름 · 유채기름 · 폐식물기름 · 해조유 따위의 식물성 기름을 원료로 해서 만든 무공해 연료로 주로 디젤자동차의 경유 첨가제 또는 그 자체로 차량 연료로 사용된다. 바이오디젤의 50% 정도는 재배가 쉬운 유채씨rapeseed로 만들어지는데 최근에는 유채씨보다 효율성이 5배 정도 더 높은 야자유palm oil에 관심이 집중되고 있다. 그러나 야자수 재배의 증가로 인해 열대우림지역rainforest 생태계 파괴가 야기되면서 효율성이 높으며 생태 친화적인 해조algae가 새로운 바이오디젤의 연료로 급부상 하고 있다. 해조는 성장이 빨라 공급이 수월하며 몸 속의 40%가 농축된 기름으로 팜유보다도 약 30배나 효율성이 높지만 수확이 어려워 해조수확 기술의 발전이 필요하다.

필수어휘
- sugar cane 사탕수수
- fossil fuel 화석연료
- petroleum 석유
- rapeseed 유채씨
- tropical 열대의
- rainforest 우림
- ravaging 황폐하게 만드는
- algae 해조류

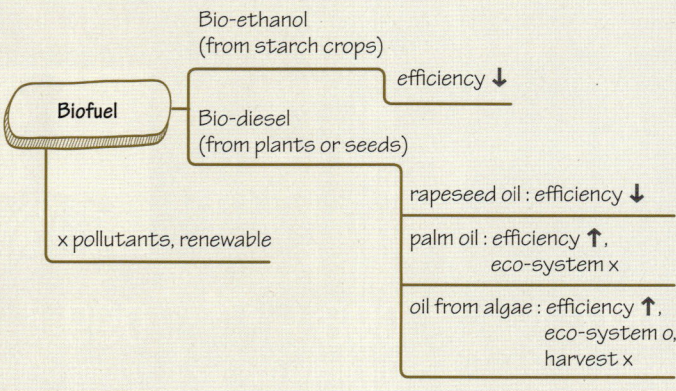

Mini Practice

Listen to part of a discussion in a chemical engineering class. 🎧 Ch5_01

1. According to the professor, what is the drawback of using ethanol as a primary energy source?

    Ⓐ Ethanol is made from staple crops such as corn or sugar cane, which are needed for food.
    Ⓑ Ethanol provides much less energy compared to fossil fuels.
    Ⓒ Ethanol can only be used when mixed with gasoline, because cars cannot run on pure ethanol.
    Ⓓ Ethanol has only been shown to provide energy in laboratory conditions.

2. Based on the lecture, what makes algae a suitable source of bio-diesel?
Click on 2 answers.

    Ⓐ Algae have a very high concentration of oil compared to other sources.
    Ⓑ Algae are fast and easy to grow.
    Ⓒ Algae can be easily harvested with existing technology.
    Ⓓ The use of algae does not damage natural ecosystems.

Listening Script

Professor: Okay, let's talk about some of the alternatives that are available to using fossil fuels. Have any of you already heard of the term bio-fuel? A bio-fuel is a fuel made from an organic and renewable source of energy such as a plant. Bio-fuel falls into two varieties: bio-diesel and ethanol. We'll start with ethanol. It is most commonly made from corn or sugar cane, which are both really common staple crops. But unfortunately, ethanol only provides about two-thirds the amount of energy that fossil fuel does. Making enough ethanol to meet all of a single car's energy requirement would need an enormous expanse of land used just for ethanol production.

In contrast, bio-diesel provides almost the same amount of energy as petroleum-based fuels and bio-diesel is, of course, used in diesel engines. Like ethanol, bio-diesel is typically made from plants or plant seeds. About 50% of all bio-diesel is made from rapeseeds. Although it's easy to grow, there are other plants that are more efficient sources of bio-diesel. Uh, for example, the oil palm tree. The oil palm provides five times more bio-diesel per acre than rapeseeds do. The problem, however, is that the oil palm only grows in tropical climates. Sections of the rainforest can be, well, have already been converted to grow this plant, but in the process, the natural habitat of the animals that lived there has been destroyed.

Fortunately, there is a plant that just might be able to provide all of the earth's energy needs without ravaging the environment. I'm talking about algae. Algae are actually 40% oil by weight, which makes it proportionally the most concentrated source of bio-diesel. They grow really quickly. Actually, algae can double in size in just a few hours. That means that compared to the oil palm tree, algae can provide 30 times more bio-diesel. Even better, it's really easy to grow in ponds or on lakes. There's just one challenge. Harvesting algae from the environment is technologically very difficult. But there is ongoing research to improve this harvesting technology.

Answers p. 56

Biology

082

Cell discovery
세포 발견

예전부터 사람들은 생물체의 기본 구성 및 그 역할에 대해 호기심이 많았다. 미생물을 확대해서 보여주는 현미경microscope은 이와 같은 궁금증을 해결하는 데에 커다란 공헌을 하였다. 현미경 발달에 크게 기여했던 사람은 '미생물의 아버지'라 불리는 레벤후크Anton Van Leeuwenhoek(1632-1723)였다. 그가 만들었던 최초의 복합 현미경은 대물 렌즈objective lens와 대안 렌즈eyepiece로 이루어졌고, 육안으로는 관찰할 수 없었던 물질과 미생물체microorganism를 발견하는데 도움을 주었다. 그는 강물이나 빗물 등을 현미경으로 관찰하면서 그 안에 들어 있는 수많은 미생물체의 존재를 발견하게 되었다.

그 후 영국의 로버트 훅Robert Hooke(1635-1703)은 복합 현미경을 통해 모든 생물체는 '세포cell'라는 가장 작은 단위로 이루어 졌다는 사실을 최초로 발견하였다. 과학에 호기심이 남달랐던 그는 1665년 현미경으로 코르크의 죽은 세포에서 세포벽으로 둘러 싸인 '작은 방' 구조를 발견하고 그것을 세포라고 불렀다. 이 발견은 생물체의 미세구조가 알려지는 계기가 되었고, 그 후 활발한 관심과 연구들을 통해 세포는 세포막cell membrane, 세포질cytoplasm, 미토콘드리아mitochondria, 리보솜ribosome, 핵nucleus 등으로 구성되었음을 알게 되었다. 또한 세포들의 역할과 크기는 다양하지만 기본 구조와 목적은 동일하다는 사실도 알려졌다. 세포는 생명체를 이루는 구조적, 기능적 단위이며 모든 세포는 세포의 증식에 의해 생명활동이 이루어지게 된다는 '세포설cell theory'이 나오게 되었다.

필수어휘

- pivotal 중추가 되는, 중요한
- organ 기관
- microscope 현미경
- tissue 조직
- cell division 세포분열
- DNA 디옥시리보핵산 deoxyribonucleic acid (유전자의 존재를 이루는 핵산)

The Development of Cell Theory

Cell theory in Biology describes the properties of cells. This theory holds that cells are the basic unit of structure of all living organisms. The three pivotal tenets are as follows: 1) All the living organisms are composed of cells; 2) The cell is the basic unit of life; 3) All the cells come from the reproduction of other, pre-existing, living cells. Discovery of the cell and development of the theory was a cornerstone in the formation of the field of Biology. Cell theory was first proposed in 1838 and is generally accredited to Matthias Schleiden and Theodor Schwann. However, from the 17th century through the early 19th century, many other scientists also contributed to the development of this theory.

In 1665, Robert Hooke was the first one to discover cells when he used a microscope to examine slices of cork. The dead cell walls that he saw reminded him of the rooms that monks lived in, cellula in Latin, and so he called them cells. Later on, in 1824, Henri Dutrochet documented the cells of plants and animals in his drawings. He asserted that cells were the fundamental or basic unit of an organism. Following this discovery, modern scientists went to learn that cells in the body operate and function individually but are also collectively the building blocks of our organs, bones, and skin tissues.

[A ■] This discovery was followed by the work of Theodor Schwann and Matthias Schleiden, whose examination of plant and animal tissues led to the development of the bulk of the cell theory. [B ■] This was a huge leap in the field of Biology because prior to that little was known about animal or human tissue due to the difficulty of studying them. [C ■] Rudolf Virchow is credited with the discovery of the third tenet in 1855. [D ■] He stated that all new cells come from preexisting living cells, which he wrote in Latin as "Omnis cellula e cellula," which means literally "every cell from a cell." Scientists were then able to discover that cells may be produced by cell division. Most importantly, they could find out that information from the original cell was passed down to the new cell in the form of DNA.

1. The word asserted in paragraph 2 is closest in meaning to
   A supported
   B claimed
   C implied
   D indentified

2. Look at the four squares [■] that indicate where the following sentence could be added to the sentence.

   They found that all living organisms were composed of cells and cell products.

   Where would the sentence best fit?

Astronomy

★★★
083

Celestial body -
comets vs. asteroid
천체 - 혜성 vs. 소행성

천문은 주제가 다양하며 내용이 다소 추상적일 수 있다. 먼저 천문학 관련 어휘를 공부하고 시작하도록 하자. 여기서는 토플에 출제된 혜성의 구성, 궤도와 소행성과의 비교에 대해 알아보자.

필수어휘

- meteoroid 유성체, 운성체
- extraterrestrial 천체의, 외계의
  [syn] celestial
- diffuse 발산하다
  [syn] release, emit
- disturbance 섭동
  [syn] perturbation
- vicinity 근처, 인접
- the Kuiper Belt 해왕성 궤도의 바깥쪽에 있는 소천체를 일컫는 지역
- rotate 공전하다
- cometary 혜성의

혜성comet은 얼음과 가스로 이루어진 천체로, 행성planet과 소행성asteroid 등과 함께 태양계solar system를 구성한다. 혜성은 태양계가 만들어 지는 초기에 태양계 끝의 오르트 구름Oort Cloud이라는 구름 벨트에서 만들어 진 후, 태양의 중력gravity이나 다른 천체의 섭동현상perturbation으로 태양계 안으로 진입한 천체로 짐작된다.

혜성의 구성

혜성은 핵nucleus과 그 주변을 감싸는 대기층atmosphere인 코마coma로 이루어진다. 핵의 크기는 지름이 작게는 수 백 미터에서부터, 수 십 킬로미터까지 다양하며 기체인 탄소carbon, 수소hydrogen, 질소nitrogen와 고체인 철iron, 규소silicon, 마그네슘magnesium 화합물로 이루어져있다. 이 물질들은 태양 형성 시 있었을 것이라고 추정되는 구성 성분과 거의 비슷하다는 분석이 있다.

혜성의 꼬리

혜성의 꼬리tail는 태양에 가깝게 이동하는 경우 태양 바람에 가스가 뒤로 밀리면서 발생한다. 꼬리의 종류에는 태양에 접근할수록 점점 길이가 길어지는 이온 꼬리ion tail와 태양 광선의 복사압radiation pressure의 영향으로 코마에서 뒤로 밀리면서 혜성의 진행 방향과 반대 방향으로 발생하는 먼지 입자로 이루어진 먼지꼬리dust tail가 있다.

혜성의 궤도

혜성의 궤도는 200년을 기준으로 장주기 혜성Long-period comets과 단주기 혜성Short-period comets으로 나뉜다. 대부분 타원형 궤도elliptical orbit를 돌지만 길어지는 경우 포물선parabola이나 쌍곡선hyperbola의 형태를 띠기도 한다. 단주기 혜성은 궤도경사orbital inclination가 작고 공전방향이 순행이다. 2년에서 200년 사이의 궤도를 가지고 있는 헬리형 혜성Halley's comet이 대표적인 단주기 혜성에 속한다. 장주기 혜성은 단주기 혜성과 달리 진행 방향을 예측하기 어렵고, 지구 대기 진입 속도가 상당히 빠르다. 궤도가 200년 이상에서 수 십 만년에 이르며 대부분 포물선 주기를 가진다.

Mini Practice

Celestial Bodies in Solar System

We have many types of celestial bodies in our solar system. A celestial body is any natural object that exists outside of the earth's atmosphere. The largest celestial object is, of course, our Sun, followed by medium sized objects like the planets, and smaller objects like dwarf planets, asteroids, comets, and smaller debris.

An asteroid is a special type of celestial body that is typically rocky and metallic and can range in size from a few meters up to nearly 1,000 kilometers in diameter. Asteroids are very cold, emit little radiation and unlike comets do not have a cloud of diffuse light surrounding them. The majority of asteroids may be found orbiting the Sun in irregular orbits between Mars and Jupiter. Some scientists believe that these asteroids between Mars and Jupiter were once a planet that exploded or collided with something, while other scientists believe that the pieces never came together in time to make a planet. Occasionally these asteroids veer off course and collide with other planets in our solar system. A collision of an asteroid with the earth during the Mesozoic Era may have caused the extinction of the dinosaurs.

Comets, unlike asteroids, are composed of ice and various gases like carbon monoxide, carbon dioxide, methane, and ammonia. Think of them like big, dirty snowballs. When a comet's orbit brings it close to the sun, it heats up and begins to melt, releasing dust and gas. This dust and gas is blown by the solar wind into a tail, which points away from the Sun. There are two main categories of comet orbits: short period and long period. Most commonly known comets are short period comets that come from the Kuiper Belt beyond the planet Neptune and may have an orbit length of between 20 and 200 years. Halley's Comet is one example of a famous short period comet. Long period comets come from the *Oort Cloud*, a massive collection of icy planetesimals. Because these comets travel a great distance, their orbits are sensitive to the movements of stars, supernova events, other comets and other celestial bodies.

1. The word massive in paragraph 3 is closest in meaning to
   A) obscured
   B) equal
   C) prevalent
   D) huge

2. According to the passage, which of following is true?
   A) Halley's comet is a long period comet.
   B) When the comet is far from the Sun, they make a tail.
   C) The size of asteroids is quite similar.
   D) Long period comets generally come from the Oort Cloud.

Answers p. 57

Chemistry

★★ 084

Composting
퇴비

우리가 버리는 음식물 쓰레기는 어떻게 다시 재활용되는 것일까? 음식물 쓰레기나 가축의 분뇨를 뿌린다고 해서 거름이 되는 것은 아니다. 퇴비화 과정을 살펴보도록 하자.

퇴비화는 음식물 찌꺼기, 축산폐기물, 낙엽 또는 하수처리장 찌꺼기와 같은 유기물organic materials을 안정한 부식토humus로 변환시키는 생물학적 공정이다. 유기물을 퇴비화한다는 것은 유기물 중에서 분해성이 있는 물질을 미생물microorganism로 분해시키는 과정을 말한다. 그렇게 유기물이 미생물 또는 박테리아에 의해 부패와 발효가 진행되면 기존 유기물이 갖고 있던 성질은 없어지고 검정색 또는 흑갈색의 부식토로 변하게 된다. 부식된 흙의 경우 (-)전기negative charge를 띠고 있기 때문에 (+)전기positive charge를 띠는 비료 양분, 즉 암모니아, 석회, 마그네슘, 칼륨 등을 끌어들이는 성질을 갖게 된다. 그래서 농경지에 부식토를 넣으면 흙 주변의 비료 양분을 단단히 끌어당기고 미생물의 먹이가 되어 조금씩 질소nitrogen를 방출하는 것이다.

부식토는 악취가 없고 영양분이 풍부하며 병원균pathogens이 거의 없는 뛰어난 토양 개량제이다. 또한 물 보유능력water retention capacity과 양이온 교환능력cation exchange capacity이 좋아 작물에 충분한 영양을 제공할 수 있는 것뿐만 아니라 토양의 수분 보유능력을 향상시키고 토양침식을 방지하는 훌륭한 토양개량제로 사용될 수 있다. 또한 유기폐기물을 부식시키는 과정에서는 많은 메탄가스가 발생하지만 퇴비화 과정은 메탄가스methane를 거의 방출하지 않으므로 지구환경에도 엄청난 이득을 가져올 수 있다.

필수어휘

- composting 퇴비화
- waste management 쓰레기처리
- organic waste 유기폐기물
- humus 부식토
- cut down on ~을 줄이다
- conversion 전환
- microbes 미생물
- microorganisms 미생물
- landfills 매립지

Composting: Organic material + O_2 → Humus + CO_2 + H_2O + NH_3 + Energy

Mini Practice

Listen to part of a lecture in a chemistry class. 🎧 Ch5_02

1. What can be inferred about the characteristics of composting? Click on 2 answers.
   - Ⓐ Composting slows down the conversion of soil into humus.
   - Ⓑ Composting happens better under warmer temperatures.
   - Ⓒ The process of breaking down organic materials is related to the activity of microbes.
   - Ⓓ Composting generates emission of greenhouse gases.

2. What does the professor imply could happen if a compost pile is turned frequently?
   - Ⓐ It can reduce the emission of methane.
   - Ⓑ It can significantly contribute to less pollution in soil.
   - Ⓒ It can lower the cost of composting.
   - Ⓓ It can increase the efficiency of composting.

Listening Script

Professor: I want to talk about composting, and how it fits into the bigger picture of recycling and waste management in general. Composting is the process of converting organic waste into a rich soil called "humus." Do any of you have a garden at home? Well, if you do, you will know that this dark, nutrient-rich soil helps plants grow better. It also cuts down on insects and disease. On its own, all organic materials will, over time, break down into humus.

But what we'll be focusing on is the benefit of separating out the organic material from the rest of our household waste and composting it to accelerate the conversion into humus. See, composting speeds up that process. Without any intervention, the process of breaking down organic materials takes place under lower temperatures. And there are some microbes that are part of the process that rely on those lower temperatures. But when we compost, we are essentially creating a warmer environment, and different microorganisms thrive in that environment.

But there's another connection between composting and landfills. It's claimed that by reducing the amount of waste ending up in landfills, the amount of methane that ends up in the atmosphere can also be reduced. Why? Well, organic waste really creates a lot of methane when buried in the ground. But if organic waste is composted properly, far less methane is produced. What do I mean by "properly"? Well, I mean the compost pile needs to be turned over frequently, introducing air so that aerobic conditions are maintained. In other words, the bottom of the pile needs to periodically get to the top where there's oxygen for those bacteria. That process of turning the compost pile prevents the formation of such high amounts of methane.

Answers p. 58

Astronomy

★★
085

Cosmic rays
우주광선

우주비행사들이 우주여행을 할 때 처하는 위험 중 하나가 바로 우주 광선cosmic rays에서 나오는 방사능radiation에 대한 노출이다. 이 방사능은 우주선 승무원들에게 암cancer을 유발할 수 있을 만큼 치명적인 수준이라고 알려져 있다. 우주 방사능은 보통 태양풍solar wind의 형태로 전달되지만 태양에서 뿜어져 나오는 방사능 외에도 태양계 밖 우주에서 방출되는 방사능도 존재한다. 지구는 자체적인 자기장 막magnetic shield으로 우주 방사능이 대기권 안으로 들어오는 것을 차단하고 있지만 이 보호막을 벗어난 우주에서는 상황이 달라진다. 따라서 우주 탐사 시 우주선spacecraft으로 쏟아지는 방사능을 막는 방법에 대한 연구가 계속되고 있다.

국제 우주정거장에 상주하는 우주인의 경우, 태양 폭발solar eruption이 일어나면 폭주하는 방사능으로부터 몸을 지키기 위해 두꺼운 벽이 둘러진 별도의 장소로 몸을 피한다. 하지만 이조차도 우주 방사능을 완전히 차단할 순 없다. 따라서 과학자들은 지구 자기장 막에서 열쇠를 얻어 우주선 선체 주위에 자기장 막으로 된 우주 방사능 보호막을 만들어내기 위해 힘쓰고 있다. 자기장 보호막은 우선 우주선이나 달 등 우주 방사능을 차단하고자 하는 대상 주변에 자기권을 형성한 후 이 안에 플라즈마plasma로 불리는 이온화 가스ionized gas를 주입하는 방식으로 만들어진다. 이렇게 만들어진 보호막 속 플라즈마는 우주 방사능을 우회시키거나 속도를 늦춰주는 역할을 하지만 이 자기장 막도 자기장의 양극poles이 방사능에 그대로 노출된다는 단점이 있다.

필수어휘

- □ manned mission 유인 (사람을 태운) 임무
- □ obstacle 장애물
- □ insurmountable 극복할 수 없는
- □ radiation 방사선
- □ dose 복용량
- □ physical shield 물리적 방패
- □ viable 실행 가능한
- □ magnetic shield 자기 차폐 (자기장을 이용한 방패)

Cosmic rays
- can cause cancer to astronauts
- to prevent radiation? → magnetic shield over spaceship → but, poles are still exposed to radiation

204

Listening

Mini Practice

Listen to part of a discussion in an aeronautics class. 🎧 Ch5_03

1. What is the drawback in covering a spaceship with water?

   Ⓐ It would be very expensive.
   Ⓑ It would significantly increase the weight of the ship.
   Ⓒ It will allow parts of the ship to be exposed to additional radiation.
   Ⓓ The technology to encase a ship in water doesn't exist.

2. According to the professor, what's the problem with using a magnetic shield?

   Ⓐ It would leave parts of the ship exposed to radiation.
   Ⓑ It's not possible to reproduce the Earth's magnetic field.
   Ⓒ It would only deflect positively charged cosmic rays.
   Ⓓ There's not enough research about this type of shield.

Listening Script

Professor: Recently, there has been a lot of interest in the possibility of a manned mission to Mars. Although a very exciting goal, there is one particularly large obstacle that is very difficult to overcome. It may even be insurmountable. See, if astronauts travel away from Earth, they will be exposed to cosmic rays. So, what are cosmic rays? Um, they are positively charged particles flying through space at incredible speeds. We really don't know very much about cosmic rays. Where do they come from? Why do they exist? These questions are currently unanswered. But one thing we do know about them is, as I said, they travel very fast. Just about at the speed of light.

Now, that means cosmic rays are essentially high-energy radiation, and we don't fully understand the effects that they would have on living tissue. A trip to Mars would take a long time. More than long enough to be exposed to a dangerous dose of radiation from cosmic rays. So, what to do about it? Well, there have been a few proposals made about how to address this problem, and that's what I want to discuss with you. Some scientists have proposed some sort of physical shield. Basically, a covering for the ship that would protect it from cosmic rays. And strange as it may seem, lighter elements are actually more effective at blocking cosmic rays than heavy elements like metals. So one option would be water. But you can imagine, covering an entire ship in water is going to take a lot of water. That's going to really significantly increase the weight of the ship. And we just don't have the technology to launch something with that kind of weight into space. So, that's really not a viable solution.

So let's look at the other options. One is to use a magnetic shield. As I mentioned, cosmic rays carry a positive charge. That means that a magnetic shield could be used to draw the cosmic rays away from the body of the ship and towards the poles of the magnet. That would protect the ship from cosmic rays, assuming the magnet was strong enough. But as you might have guessed, there's a problem with this method too. The ship would remain exposed to cosmic rays at the poles of the magnet. So parts of the ship would be protected, but parts of the ship would be constantly exposed to cosmic rays. In exposed areas, the magnetic shield would be completely useless, astronauts would be exposed to dangerous levels of radiation.

Yet another proposal is to use a static shield, but it is the least promising suggestion, so I'm not going to touch on it at this moment.

Answers p. 58

Astronomy

086
Distance from a star
별과의 거리

별의 거리 측량법과 함께 우주의 세부적인 사실들을 발견한 허블 망원경의 역사와 역할에 대해 알아보도록 하자.

필수어휘

- astronomical 천문학의
- observatory 관측소, 천문대
- instrument 도구
  - syn apparatus, implement
- spherical 구형의, 둥근
- aberration 광행차 (관찰자의 움직임에 의해서 천체의 겉보기 위치가 영향을 받는 현상)
- solar array 태양 전지판
- optics 광학
- gyroscope 자이로스코프 (항공기·선박 등의 평형 상태를 측정하는 데 사용되는 기구)

천문학자들은 별과 지구 사이의 거리를 측정할 때, 시차 parallax (관측 위치에 따른 물체의 위치나 방향의 차이)를 이용한다. 지구가 태양 주변을 공전 revolution 하기 때문에 지구 가까이에 있는 항성들은 그보다 멀리 떨어진 별들에 비해 자신의 위치를 이동하는 것처럼 보인다. 이것을 시차이동 parallax shift 이라고 부르는데 천문학자들은 그 이동 거리를 관찰하고 지구 궤도의 지름을 계산해서 하늘 위에 펼쳐있는 시차 각 parallax angle 을 계산할 수 있다.

이때 시차 이동거리가 짧을수록 별과 지구 사이의 거리는 멀어진다. 이 계산은 지구와 별의 거리가 수백만 광년 light-year 내의 별에서만 정확하다. 별들이 그 이상 멀리 있는 경우 측량하기에는 시차거리가 너무 짧아지기 때문이다.

100광년 이상 멀리 떨어져 있는 별의 거리를 측량하는 방법은 세페이드 변광성 Cepheid variable stars 을 이용하는 것이다. 여기서 변광성이란 시간에 따라서 밝기가 변하는 별을 말한다. 세페이드 변광성은 주기가 1일 미만에서 50일 가량이며, 변광 주기 period of variable star (별 밝기의 극소에서 다음 극소까지 또는 극대에서 다음 극대까지의 시간 간격)가 길어질수록 색은 밝아지기 때문에 주기와 광도의 상관관계를 통해 절대 광도 true brightness 를 알아내어 세페이드 변광성이 위치한 은하와 성단 constellation 까지의 거리를 측정할 수 있다. 천문학자들은 시간이 지나면 이 별들의 밝기가 바뀌는 성질을 이용하여 정확한 밝기를 알아내고, 겉보기 밝기 apparent brightness (주관적인 밝기)와 절대 광도를 비교해서 별과의 거리를 측정할 수 있다. 이 방법은 1912년 미국의 천문학자 헨리에타 리에빗 Henrietta Leavitt 이 발견한 것으로, 20세기 초기에 많은 구상 성단 globular cluster 의 거리를 밝혀내는데 이용되었다.

The Hubble Space Telescope

The Hubble Space Telescope (HST), the first permanent astronomical observatory above the Earth's atmosphere, is a joint mission by the ESA (European Space Agency) and NASA (National Aeronautics and Space Administration) to provide much more detailed information about the universe than the best ground-based telescopes can, including in the visible, infrared and ultraviolet ranges. The HST is the most complicated and sensitive optical telescope ever constructed, and has become astronomers' most important instrument for making new discoveries about the cosmos.

Launched into orbit by the Space Shuttle Discovery on April 24, 1990, the Hubble was capable of dealing with the problem that because of the Earth's turbulent atmosphere, clouds and light pollution, astronomers could not accurately observe cosmic details. Hubble does not travel to or circle around other stars, planets or galaxies, but while it rotates around the Earth, it takes pictures of them. Unfortunately, just two months after putting the HST into space 600 kilometers above the Earth's surface, astronomers learned that there was a problem in one of the telescope's mirrors, a spherical aberration caused by a manufacturing error, making the images almost useless. During the next three years, the usefulness of the HST was severely limited, until the first HST servicing mission from December 2nd through December 13th, in 1993. During the repair, two additional cameras were installed, which later took many of the HST's most famous photos. Hubble has been periodically serviced by astronauts so it can carry out its missions, including replacing the solar array which caused the spacecraft to shake as the panels expanded and contracted upon entering and leaving sunlight, complementing its optics, and replacing batteries and directional gyroscopes.

The Hubble Space Telescope has provided researchers with a more thorough understanding of the planets, the galaxy and the whole universe. The HST allows astronomers to see remote objects including distant galaxies that otherwise can't be detected at all by other telescopes, as well as to provide great views of our solar system's celestial bodies such as Mars and Jupiter. Therefore, on the basis of images the HST took of other galaxies, scientists were able to learn further information about star formation and the Big Bang. Also, it is possible for the HST to help astronomers to calculate the distances and ages of stars more accurately, and to know each star's stage of stellar evolution.

1. Which of the following is true in paragraph 2?
    - (A) HST has never had any mechanical problem since its first launch.
    - (B) HST circles around the earth during its mission.
    - (C) Astronauts could hardly fix limitations of HST, so still they have searched for solutions.
    - (D) Earth's turbulent atmospheric conditions help astronomers observe cosmic details.

2. The word complementing in paragraph 2 is closest in meaning to
    - (A) reducing
    - (B) comparing
    - (C) supplementing
    - (D) subjecting

Answers p. 59

Physics

★★
087

Erosion
침식

대규모 가스 흐름인 바람은 기압atmospheric pressure 차로 인해 공기가 고기압에서 저기압으로 이동하면서 생기는 현상이다. 예를 들어 해안 주변에서는 바다에서 육지로 부는 해풍sea breeze과 육지에서 바다로 부는 육풍land breeze이 발생한다. 햇빛이 있는 낮 동안 육지와 비교해 바다는 훨씬 느린 속도로 가열되는데, 이때 바다보다 육지의 온도가 상대적으로 빠르게 상승하면 그 기압 차로 대류 현상conduction이 발생한다. 낮 동안 육지의 따뜻한 공기는 주변보다 가벼워 위로 상승하고, 바다 위의 공기는 육지보다 상대적으로 차갑고 기압이 더 높아 그 기압 차로 해안에 차가운 해풍이 만들어 진다. 반대로 밤이 되면 육지의 공기는 바다보다 온도가 급격히 낮아지지만, 해수 공기의 온도에는 거의 변화가 없기 때문에 육지의 기압이 바다보다 높아지면서 육풍이 분다. 그 외 지구 바람의 대규모 패턴을 형성하는 요소로는 적도equator와 극지방pole 사이 온도 차이와 지구의 자전rotation 등이 있다. 이 때 풍향계weathervane가 바람의 방향direction을 풍속계anemometer가 속도velocity를 측정해주는 것을 도와준다.

지구의 3/4을 차지하고 있는 물은 지구상에 생물체를 존재하게 하는 결정적 물질이다. 온도와 압력에 따라 얼음, 액체, 증기 등의 다양한 형태로 강, 호수, 바닷물, 지하수, 빙하glacier, 증기steam, 구름cloud, 강수precipitation에 존재한다. 물의 지속적 움직임인 물 순환water cycle or hydrologic cycle은 강, 해수, 대기 증발evaporation, 액화condensation, 강수, 지면의 물 runoff, 침투infiltration 등의 물리적 과정들을 통해 변화한다.

필수어휘
- abrade 마멸시키다
- dune 모래 언덕, 사구
- topographical 지형학의
- windward 바람이 불어오는 쪽의
- lee 바람을 받지 않는 쪽
- scar 흉터를 남기다, 흔적을 남기다
- boulder 바위

Erosion

Erosion is a natural process which changes the landscape through the forces of wind, water, and ice along with the interaction of gravity and human activity. The land subjected to destructive forces gets worn down into fine particles which are then transported to another location and later deposited as sediments.

[A ■] When air moves, wind picks up light materials such as silt and sand and transports them to other places. [B ■] For example, in dry areas when wind containing fine particles of sand strikes rock, the surfaces of the exposed rock are abraded and break off in small pieces, wearing away gradually. [C ■] In other places, sediments blown by wind eventually settle and develop into landforms. [D ■] One example of this is a sand dune, a hill or mountain of sediment deposited by the wind, which forms when sand begins to build up behind a topographical obstacle and then more and more material is accumulated. A sand dune has two sides; on the windward side there is a gentle slope where the sand is pushed up the dune while the other is steeper as the sand builds up in the lee of the wind. The shape and size of a dune depends on the amount of sand or other sediment available, the wind speed and direction, and the amount of vegetation present.

Moving water is another agent of erosion. Rain carries away bits of soil, rushing rivers wear away their banks, and waves along seashores change the shape of the coastline. In addition, water is one of the major elements that cause dramatic changes in desert. Like other places, it openly changes the desert through the formation, by erosion, of river valleys and lakes, but more importantly, it affects the environment in the desert as a part of the tremendous temperature changes between day and night in hidden ways. The dew or mist that settles on rocks during the night is absorbed by minerals, salts and the rock itself. When the day approaches, it evaporates into the air and this cycle repeats. As rocks absorb the water at night, they expand slightly, and during the day they shrink again, sustaining minor but significant damage. Although this may seem insignificant, these subtle changes have led to gradual but dramatic changes in the appearance of rocks over a long period of time. This process can scar rocks, the results of which can be clearly seen in the Great Sphinx of Giza, and in some extreme cases, it can even break large boulders.

1. Look at the four squares [■] that indicate where the following sentence could be added to the sentence.

   One of the major erosion agents is wind.

   Where would the sentence best fit?

2. The word change in paragraph 3 is closest in meaning to
   - Ⓐ modify
   - Ⓑ scatter
   - Ⓒ form
   - Ⓓ annihilate

Chemistry

★★
088
Fuel
연료

인류는 2백 만년 전 나무를 연료fuel로 쓰기 시작한 이래로 다양한 연료를 사용해왔다. 사람들은 빛을 내는 수단으로 식물성 기름이나 동물성 지방을 활용하기도 했고, 보다 더 강한 빛과 열을 만드는 숯charcoal은 기원전 6천년 경부터 금속을 제련smelt하는 목적으로 그리스인들이 사용했다. 18세기 유럽 전역에서 사용한 목재lumber는 그 소비가 크게 증가하자 산림벌채deforestation를 야기하였고, 영국이 증기 엔진steam engine을 도입하면서 석탄coal 사용이 가속화되었으며, 20세기에는 전기와 자동차의 주 동력원으로 석유 사용이 급등했다.

석유의 사용

탄화 수소hydrocarbon로 이루어진 석유petroleum는 석탄과 함께 가장 잘 알려진 화석 에너지fossil fuel로, 재생이 불가능하다. 19세기 말 이후 자동차 몇 내연 기관internal combustion engine과 같은 화석 연료를 사용하는 기계들이 발명되면서 석유 소비가 급속도로 증가하였다. 석유는 기체 형태의 천연 가스natural gas와 정제되지 않은 액상의 흑갈색 원유crude oil로 구분할 수 있다. 석유 형성에 대한 이론은 다양하지만 해양 퇴적물marine sediment에 미생물과 같은 유기물질organic matter이 매립되어 생겼다는 설이 가장 유력하다. 수 백 만년 동안 모래, 점토mud와 같은 퇴적물과 함께 쌓인 유기물질이 높은 압력pressure과 온도를 받아 액상의 기름과 기체의 천연가스로 전환된 것이다.

한편 수 십 년 안에 석유가 고갈될deplete 것이라는 예측이 있어, 인류가 직면하게 될 여러 문제를 감안한다면 대체 에너지원의 발견과 보급이 시급한 상황이다.

필수어휘

- fossil fuel 화석 연료
- Industrial Revolution 산업 혁명
- anaerobic 무산소성의
- refine 정제하다
- pollutant 오염 물질
- combustion 연소
- exploit 사용하다
- combustible 가연성의
- marsh 늪지대 [syn] swamp
- metamorphic rock 변성암
- pore-water 공극수
- anthracite 무연탄
- lignite 갈탄
- peat 토탄

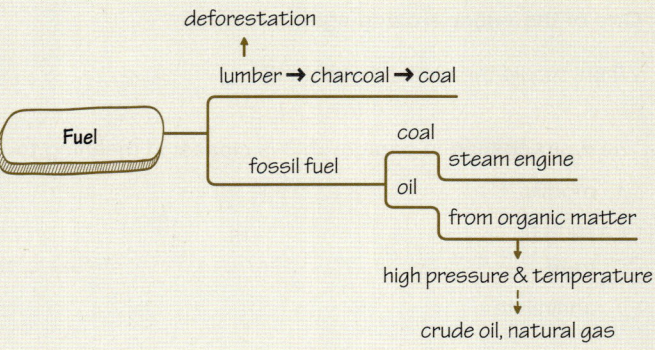

Fossil Fuel

Fossil fuels such as coal and petroleum that contain a high percentage of carbon content were formed by the anaerobic decomposition over millions of years of organic matter including plants, plankton and other forms of life. Over time, organic matter which was buried under sediment and rock eventually formed large quantities of fuel. There has been tremendous use of fossil fuels since the beginning of the Industrial Revolution. These underground resources are still our primary fuel and supply more than 90% of the world's energy sources for electricity and for powering vehicles.

Petroleum, consisting of crude oil and natural gas, is typically made when marine organisms die and settle to the seafloor in anaerobic environments where they cannot rapidly decompose. Then, the remains become buried under sediments like silt, sand or mud, and petroleum results from the chemical breakdown of these organic remains into a viscous gel called kerogen, which changes with heating into hydrocarbons, compounds consisting of carbon and hydrogen atoms. Because of high temperature and pressure, the oxygen and nitrogen in the original organics are driven off, leaving hydrocarbon compounds. The petroleum industry comprises the entire process of locating, drawing out, refining, conveying, and marketing petroleum products. This process has a lot of negative effects on the environment, such as causing water pollution through oil spills and the by-products of petroleum refining, and causing air pollution through the release of greenhouse gases and other pollutants produced by combustion.

Coal, the first fossil fuel exploited by humans on a large scale, is a combustible black or brown sedimentary rock made mostly of organic carbon, and derived mostly from land vegetation accumulation in ancient forests or marshy environments. First, vegetation is converted to peat, a loose, rich and brown soil. As more rock layers press down on the buried peat, oxidative decay uses up lots of oxygen, rendering the sediment pore water devoid of oxygen (anoxic). The process of lithification as a result of increasing burial depth removes the pore water and increases carbon content, converting it to coal. Low-grade coal called lignite can be mined with relative ease near the surface, and tends to contain minerals such as pyrite, which is formed under the reducing (low-oxygen) conditions. However, the harder, denser pure coal is called anthracite and is close to being a metamorphic rock; it can be found in more subterranean seams.

1. According to paragraph 1 and 2, which can be inferred about fossil fuels?
   - (A) Prior to the Industrial Revolution, they were not commonly used because of the black smoke.
   - (B) With low temperature and pressure, petroleum can be never formed.
   - (C) Following the Industrial Revolution, people found out coal deposits and could use them for electricity.
   - (D) Without organic matter, they almost never could form.

2. The word devoid of in paragraph 3 is closest in meaning to
   - (A) considerable
   - (B) lack in
   - (C) spectacular
   - (D) competent

Answers p. 60

Chemistry

★★
089

Helium-3
헬륨 3

최근에는 수력, 원자력, 지열 등 널리 알려져 있는 대체에너지원 외에도 신에너지원들이 많이 출제되는 경향이므로 이러한 에너지원들을 미리 공부해 놓도록 하자!

화석연료fossil fuel의 고갈과 심각한 지구온난화 문제로 다양한 종류의 대체에너지alternative energy의 중요성이 대두되고 있다. 그 중에서 미래의 에너지 자원으로 떠오르고 있는 헬륨3는 가장 이상적인 핵융합 발전nuclear fusion power generation의 원료로 평가되고 있다. 하지만 그것은 지구에는 거의 없고 오직 달 표면에서만 채취할 수 있기 때문에 헬륨3를 놓고 강대국들이 벌이는 달 개발 경쟁이 치열하다. 미국, 러시아, 일본, 독일, 중국, 인도가 최근 달 탐사에 적극 나서고 있는 것도 바로 이 헬륨3 때문이다.

에너지 전문가들은 화석 연료가 지금 추세대로라면 석유petroleum는 40년, 천연 가스natural gas는 60년 뒤 고갈될 것이라고 전망하고 있으며 몇몇은 이를 대체할 획기적인 에너지원이 핵융합 발전이라 주장한다. 이는 태양이 에너지를 만드는 것과 유사해서 '인공 태양'이라고도 불리며 이중수소deuterium와 삼중수소tritium를 결합해 헬륨을 만들 때 손실되는 질량을 에너지로 이용하는 것이 기본 원리이다. 여기서 헬륨3가 주목 받는 이유는 바로 그것을 삼중수소로 활용할 수 있기 때문이다. 보통 헬륨보다 중성자 하나가 적은 헬륨3는 핵융합을 시키기가 좋다. 만일 우주 왕복선이 30톤의 헬륨3를 싣고 온다면, 이것만으로도 미국에서 1년 동안 사용하는 전력을 생산할 수 있다. 이 만큼 효율성이 좋은 헬륨3의 가치는 1톤당 40억 달러나 되며 이는 이미 강대국들의 치열한 달 탐사 경쟁을 부추기는 원인이 되고 있다.

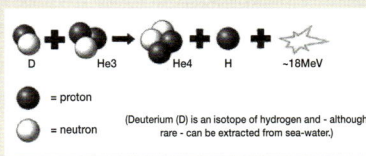

(Deuterium (D) is an isotope of hydrogen and - although rare - can be extracted from sea-water.)

필수어휘

- □ isotope 동위원소
- □ nuclear fusion 핵융합
- □ nuclear fission 핵분열
- □ variation 변화, 변형
- □ protons 양성자
- □ neutrons 중성자
- □ radioactive 방사성의
- □ hypothetically 가설에 근거해서

Mini Practice

Listen to part of a discussion in a chemistry class. 🎧 Ch5_04

1. What is an isotope?
   - Ⓐ A different type of chemical element
   - Ⓑ A variant of a chemical element
   - Ⓒ A new form of chemical element
   - Ⓓ A nuclear chemical element

2. Which of the following is true about nuclear fusion? Click on 2 answers.
   - Ⓐ It requires splitting of atoms.
   - Ⓑ It emits no radioactivity.
   - Ⓒ It is safe enough for it to occur inside cities.
   - Ⓓ It only gives off small quantities of energy in present nuclear fusion reactors.

Listening Script

Professor: Scientists and engineers have been thinking up alternative sources of energy for decades, and we've discovered some that are pretty useful. Among those, scientists have come across a gas that they think could be a potential source of energy in the future. It's a gas called helium-3, um, which is an isotope of the element helium, which I'm sure you know about, and this isotope can be used in nuclear fusion reactions. Ah, so, in case some of you aren't familiar with the terminology, an isotope is a kind of variation of a chemical element. What differentiates isotopes of a particular element is that they have a different number of neutrons from other isotopes of the same element, but, of course, they have the same number of protons.

Okay, so, in contrast to nuclear fission, which splits an atom's nucleus apart, nuclear fusion produces energy by combining nuclei. Nuclear fission has already been tested with the hydrogen isotopes deuterium and tritium, but those reactions give off most of their energy in the form of radioactive neutrons, raising concerns about both safety and production. On the other hand, helium-3 is perfectly safe. It doesn't pollute or emit radiation, and so it poses no danger to surrounding areas. If we were able to create a nuclear fusion reactor using helium-3, it could hypothetically be located right in the middle of a city and there wouldn't be any risk.

So, let's get back to the potential this gas has for fueling the world. An isotope of the element helium, as we've mentioned, helium-3 has the usual two protons but it has only one neutron. When heated to very high temperatures and combined with other chemical elements, a reaction occurs which releases incredible amounts of energy. If approximately two pounds of helium-3 were to undergo nuclear fusion, it would release about nineteen megawatt-years of energy. Let me put that into perspective for ya: a mere 25 tons of the stuff could power the entire United States for a whole year! Incredible, isn't it?

Answers p. 61

Astronomy

★★
090

Hooker Telescope
후커 망원경

토플시험에 가장 많이 출제된 망원경에는 허블우주망원경과 후커망원경이 있다. 후커망원경으로 빅뱅이론이 탄생하게 되었고 허블우주망원경으로 웬만한 행성을 관찰할 수 있게 되었으므로 이 두 망원경에 대한 지식은 반드시 알아놓도록 하자!

천문학 발전에 가장 큰 공헌을 한 사람으로 미국 천문학자 에드윈 허블을 꼽는 이들이 많다. 허블은 1929년 후커 망원경Hooker Telescope을 이용해서 "우주팽창은 가속화되며, 은하galaxy 거리가 멀수록 더 빨리 멀어진다"는 '허블의 법칙Hubble's law'을 발표했다. 이것은 우주상에 존재하는 모든 은하가 현재 우리가 살고 있는 은하로부터 거리에 비례하는 속도로 점점 멀어지고 있다는 법칙이다. 허블은 100인치 반사 망원경인 후커 망원경과 윌슨산 천문대의 60인치 망원경으로 우리 은하에서 안드로메다 은하까지의 거리를 측정하는데 성공했다. 뿐만 아니라 우주의 나이를 거꾸로 계산할 수 있는 공식을 제시하고 은하 분류를 처음으로 시도하기도 했다. 이러한 연구결과는 빅뱅 이론Big Bang Theory과 우주 팽창론theory of expanding universe에 설득력을 더해주었으며 천문학 역사에 위대한 성과를 올리는데 기여하였다.

이로부터 오랜 세월이 지난 1990년, 허블의 이론을 입증하기 위해 우주로 발사된 망원경이 바로 허블Hubble Space Telescope 망원경이다. 우주 개발 역사의 첫 장을 장식한 허블 망원경의 발사 및 관측을 통해 허블이 제시했던 우주의 나이는 물론 우주가 팽창하는 속도까지 증명할 수 있게 되었으며, 혜성과 목성의 충돌관측, 블랙홀의 발견 등 천문학 분야에 무수한 성과를 안겨주었다.

필수어휘

- □ evolution 진화
- □ Milky Way 은하계
- □ galaxy 은하수
- □ current 최신의
- □ interferometer 간섭 관측기
- □ pipe 수송하다 보내다
- □ synchronize 동시에 일어나다, 동기화시키다
- □ precise 정확한
- □ blurry 흐릿한, 불명확한
- □ rudimentary 가장 기본적인

Listening

Mini Practice

Listen to part of a discussion in an astronomy class. 🎧 Ch5_05

1. What was significant about the Hooker Telescope?
   - Ⓐ It revealed that galaxies outside the Milky Way were being attracted to each other.
   - Ⓑ It was powerful enough to determine the number galaxies outside of the Milky Way.
   - Ⓒ It led to the formulation of the Big Bang Theory.
   - Ⓓ It led to increased interest in the development of the telescope.

2. What is one benefit interferometers have over conventional telescopes?
   - Ⓐ They provide much clearer and more accurate pictures.
   - Ⓑ Using computers, they create images that are viewable from different angles.
   - Ⓒ They can examine much greater distances than normal telescopes.
   - Ⓓ They have discovered planets which may contain life.

Listening Script

Professor: In astronomy, the telescope is a fantastic example of a technology that changed how we perceive the universe. To start with, I want to talk about the Hooker Telescope. I think it was the most significant step in the evolution of the telescope, because it made it possible for scientists to see beyond the Milky Way and to discover that many of what they previously thought were actually countless other galaxies existing outside of the Milky Way. Even alone, that's a huge discovery. But it's only the beginning. Because it was through the Hooker Telescope that the astronomer Edwin Hubble was able to determine that these other galaxies were moving away from us, and from each other; in other words, that the universe was expanding. And this became the basis of what important theory? You guessed it... I'm talking about the Big Bang Theory. So, with this important advance in technology, that is, with the Hooker Telescope, scientists were able to come up with what is possibly the most significant theory about the creation and early development of the universe. And, once this theory was generally accepted, it quite literally changed the whole way that we look at the universe.

Ok, so let's move on to something a little more current, the Interferometer. Astronomical interferometers use multiple telescopes, and those telescopes could be thousands of meters apart. The data from those telescopes is piped back to a computer, and then the images have to be synchronized so that the computers show the same thing. Obviously, the process is very complicated, so you might wonder, what's the benefit of using interferometers? Can we see further using them? Not significantly. It's not so much being able to see further, but rather the images that are produced are considerably sharper than those produced by traditional telescopes. Using an interferometer, we can get fairly precise images of things that previously were blurry or unclear. That makes it easier for us to find more planets, including some that may have been missed using the older, unclear images from traditional telescopes. And with every additional planet we find, the chance increases that we may actually be able to find a planet with life on it. Even if such a planet did not have intelligent life, merely discovering a planet with very rudimentary life would be incredible.

Answers p. 62

Astronomy

091

Jupiter
목성

태양으로부터 다섯 번째로 멀리 위치한 목성Jupiter은 지구 지름의 11배에 달하는 크기로 태양계 내에서 가장 큰 천체이다. 밝기는 달, 금성 다음으로 밝다. 목성은 다른 목성형Jovian 천체들과 마찬가지로 90% 가량의 수소와 10% 정도의 헬륨으로 이루어져 있으며 약간의 메탄, 암모니아가 섞여있다. 토성Saturn도 이와 비슷한 구성이며, 천왕성Uranus과 해왕성Neptune은 수소와 헬륨의 양이 훨씬 적다. 목성은 대부분 기체로 구성되어 있어서 태양처럼 지역에 따라 자전 속도가 상이하므로 적도는 빠르게, 극지방은 상대적으로 느리게 자전한다.

목성의 대기는 위도에 따라 여러 개의 띠band로 분리되는데, 적갈색, 하얀색의 띠와 흰색의 타원형이 있다. 남위 23°에는 난기류와 폭풍이 만드는 대적점Great Red Spot이라는 커다란 붉은 점을 볼 수 있다. 목성의 소용돌이라고 불리는 대적점은 타원형이며, 가장 작은 크기조차 지구보다 훨씬 크다. 남반부의 이 대적점은 두 개의 대기 띠 사이에 놓여있고 대적점 주위의 대기층은 반시계 방향으로 순환하는 복잡한 대기 흐름을 그대로 반영한다.

목성 주변에는 흐릿한 행성 고리와 강력한 자기장이 존재하며, 이러한 강한 자기장 현상으로 인해 지구의 오로라와 같은 현상이 목성에서도 관측된다. 1610년 갈릴레오가 망원경으로 발견한 4개의 위성 이오Io, 유로파Europa, 가니메데Ganymede, 칼리스토Callisto를 포함, 목성은 총 67개의 위성이 있다. 이 중 지구의 달보다 약간 큰 이오는 목성에 가장 가깝게 위치하고 있어서 자기장 영향을 많이 받아 화산 활동이 활발한 천체로 알려져 있다. 실제로 용암류lava flow, 용암호lava lake, 거대한 칼데라caldera 화산 활동으로 생긴 화산 꼭대기에 푹 패인 지형 등 화산 활동의 흔적이 보이며 황산 기둥sulfurous plume이 500km정도로 뿜어져 나오기도 한다. 이 화산들은 많은 양의 황산 가스를 대기로 발산하여 붉은 색, 노란 색, 주황 색으로 아름다운 이오의 색을 만들어 낸다.

필수어휘

- interstellar 성간의
- nebula 성운
- accretion 부착
- clump 덩어리
- mass 질량
- coalesce 합치다
- disk 원반

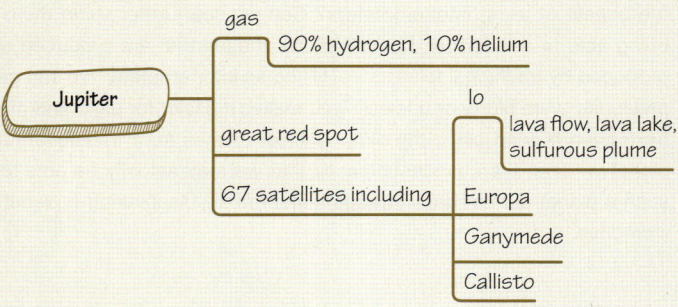

Formation of the Planet Jupiter

Some scientists theorize that about 4.6 billion years ago, our solar system was just a collection of interstellar dust and gases, sometimes referred to as a solar nebula. The formation of Jupiter, the fifth planet from the sun in our solar system, has puzzled scientists. This planet is of a type called a gas giant and is primarily composed of hydrogen gas with a dense core. Scientists mostly rely on either the *core accretion model* or the *disk instability model* to explain the formation of Jupiter.

The core accretion model suggests that interstellar dust and particles slowly accumulated and were drawn together by gravity until they coalesced into dense rocky masses of the inner planets. The collision of these particles and clumps may have raised temperatures and could have created a hot molten core. The core may have collapsed in on itself, becoming very dense, while the lighter gasses like hydrogen and helium were swept away by solar winds. However, when the distance from the sun was great enough these lighter gasses could have been captured by dense mass of the cores. When Jupiter was forming, its core was almost ten times the size of earth and became very dense. This allowed the planet to capture hydrogen, which now forms the bulk of the planet's mass. However, this process had to happen very quickly before the solar winds could carry away the hydrogen.

The disk instability model is another theory proposed by scientists to explain the creation of Jupiter. Scientists propose that the density of Jupiter's core is not sufficient to acquire the current mass that it has and that it would take hundreds of millions of years to form by accretion. The presence of moons and the asteroid belt seem to suggest that Jupiter's formation happened at a much quicker pace. The disk instability model proposes that Jupiter formed as a whole object and not piece by piece. This theory suggests that early on in the creation of the solar system, massive disks or clumps of hydrogen gasses formed and eventually joined. As many of these massive disks merged, the mass of the planet increased, thereby accelerating the speed at which the planet formed.

1. The word merged in paragraph 3 is closest in meaning to
   - (A) modified
   - (B) combined
   - (C) duplicated
   - (D) enhanced

2. According to the passage, which one is true?
   - (A) The disk instability model proposes that Jupiter gradually formed by accretion.
   - (B) Jupiter is the fourth planet from the Sun.
   - (C) Jupiter has a sparse core.
   - (D) In the accretion theory, the process of coalescence resulted in higher temperatures and a molten core.

Answers p. 62

Astronomy

★★★

092

Mars
화성

화성에 생명체가 존재할 것이라는 주장은 수십 년간 꾸준히 제기되어오면서 토플시험에서도 가장 자주 출제된 행성으로 꼽힌다. 따라서 화성 생명체에 대한 가능성을 불러일으킨 여러 이유들을 알아두도록 하자.

화성Mars은 로마의 신 마르스(그리스 신화의 전쟁의 신 아레스)에서 따온 이름이다. 이는 화성의 붉은 모습이 전쟁의 불길, 또는 피를 연상하기 때문에 지어진 것이다. 이러한 이유로 화성은 동양에서도 불길한 징조로 여겨졌다.

화성에 생명체가 있을 것이라는 주장은 1877년 이탈리아의 한 천문학자가 화성에 수로canal가 있을 것이라고 추측하면서 시작되었다. 또한 계절에 따른 화성 표면의 색 변화는 화성에 있는 초목vegetation이 만개bloom하거나 시드는 것wither에 의한 것이라는 가설도 있었다. 그로부터 수많은 화성 탐사exploration of Mars가 시작되었으며 이는 화성에 대한 여러 흥미로운 사실을 밝혀냈다. 우선 화성에는 물이 흘렀던 자국이 존재하지만 물이 얼음으로만 존재했다는 이론이 팽배하며 이런 얼음의 존재가 생명체의 존재 여부와 직결될 수 없다고 과학자들은 생각한다. 또한 화성의 대기atmosphere 대부분을 이산화탄소carbon dioxide가 구성하고 있으며 활발한 화산활동volcanic activities으로 많은 협곡canyons이 존재하고 있음이 밝혀졌다. 그러나 이렇게 대기 중 높은 이산화탄소의 농도나 화산활동이 활발한 환경에서 생명체가 있을 가능성이 거의 없음에도 불구하고 현재까지도 화성에 대한 연구는 끊임없이 지속되고 있으며 여전히 생명체가 있을 가능성이 가장 높은 행성으로 간주되고 있다.

필수어휘
- speculation 추측, 가설
- canals 수로
- polar ice caps 극지방 만년설
- varied 다양한
- primitive 원시의
- dwarf 왜소해 보이게 하다
- labyrinthine 미로와 같은
- peer 자세히 들여다 보다

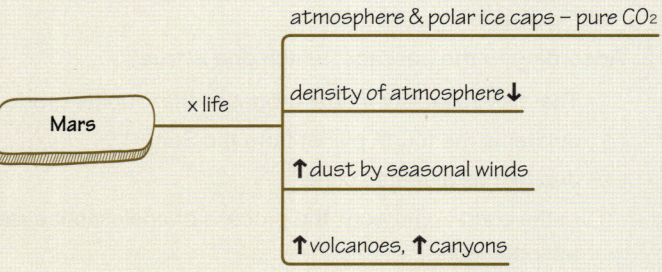

Mini Practice

Listen to part of a discussion in an astronomy class. 🎧 Ch5_06

1. What initially led to interest about researching Mars?
   - (A) Measurement of the height of Olympus Mons
   - (B) A map of Martian canals created by an Italian astronomer
   - (C) Color changes caused by Martian activities
   - (D) A series of experiments conducted on the surface

2. Which of the following is NOT true about Mars?
   - (A) It supports a form of blooming plant life.
   - (B) It has tremendous volcanoes.
   - (C) There may have been flowing water on the surface once.
   - (D) It has an extensive maze of canyons.

Listening Script

Professor: You may have noticed the planet Mars in the news recently, because it is going to pass nearby us soon. So I figure this is a good time to talk about the Red Planet. Could there be life on Mars? That's been a topic of speculation for over a century and a half, ever since the Italian astronomer, Giovanni Schiaparelli mapped its "canals," back in 1877. Despite being supported by very few serious astronomers, the idea of a somewhat Earth-like planet, although colder and drier and free of any Martians, endured right up to the beginning of the Space Age. At that time, Mars was still thought to have polar ice caps and a reasonable atmosphere. The Red Planet also showed color changes that varied seasonally, and which some thought might be the flowering of some kind of primitive plant life. But the images sent back in the 1960s by NASA's Mariner missions painted a very different picture; that of a cratered, moon-like Mars. The atmosphere turned out to be composed of almost pure CO_2, as did the polar ice caps. And the density of that atmosphere was very low, barely one-hundredth that of Earth's.

As for the flowering plant life? Well, that turned out to be nothing more than dust. Lots and lots of dust, blown around here and there by the Red Planet's strong seasonal winds. Nevertheless, Mars also became more interesting in some ways. It was discovered that Mars has massive volcanoes, some of which dwarf even Earth's tallest mountains. Olympus Mons on Mars, for example, is much more than twice as tall as Earth's Mt. Everest. It was also discovered to have a vast labyrinthine network of canyons. And it showed evidence that sometime in its distant past, water may have flowed on its surface. And still, the possibility of finding some sort of living organism could still not be ruled out.

See, you need to understand that it's much easier to prove the existence of something than it is to prove that it doesn't exist. So even today, scientists continue to peer under the Martian rocks. Lots of experiments have been conducted to try and detect any signs of life on the planet's surface, but so far none of them have been successful. Scientists generally now agree that those experiments were all flawed. Even if a positive result were to be reported, it could easily be explained as purely chemical processes, none of which necessarily require the presence of life.

Answers p. 63

Astronomy

★★★
093

Mercury
수성

> 화성 다음으로 자주 토플에 출제되는 행성으로는 수성 Mercury, 목성Jupiter, 명왕성 Pluto 등이 있으니 잘 알아두재!

수성은 태양계 행성 중 가장 태양에 가까운 행성이다. 공전주기orbital period는 88일, 자전주기rotation cycle는 58일이며 수성의 핵은 전체 반지름의 70% 이상을 차지하는데, 이 핵core은 대부분 철Fe로 이루어져 있다고 추정된다. 철을 둘러싸는 맨틀mantle은 규산염으로 구성되어 있으며 그 표면은 달과 같은 크레이터craters로 가득 덮여있다. 또한 나트륨, 칼륨 등으로 이루어진 대기atmosphere와 약한 자기장magnetic field도 존재하는 것으로 확인되었다. 수성의 궤도는 태양의 강력한 중력에 의해 매년 조금씩 움직인다.

수성은 핵core에 있는 풍부한 철 때문에 밀도density가 굉장히 높아 다른 행성에 비해 상당히 무겁다. 이렇게 밀도가 높은 이유로는 세 가지 주장이 있다. 첫 번째는 태양 주위를 떠다니는 무거운 성분들이 뭉쳐져서clump together 그렇다는 이론과, 두 번째로 소행성 충돌로 인해 밀도가 낮은 표면이 날아가고 중심부에 있던 철만 남아서 그렇다는 이론이 있다. 마지막으로 태양이 표면 수분을 증발시키고 그 강렬한 태양빛에 의해 타고남은 토질의 밀도가 높아졌을 것이라는 이론이 있다. 하지만 1970년에 보낸 탐사선에서 얻은 정보 외에는 수성에 대한 충분한 정보가 존재하지 않아 아직은 어떠한 결론도 내릴 수는 없다.

필수어휘
- iron core 철핵
- clump 뭉쳐지다
- asteroid 소행성
- collision 충돌
- knocked off 털어내다
- proximity 근접
- vaporize 증발하다
- probe 우주탐사선

Mercury — ↑density (Fe↑)
- theory ①: heavy elements clumped together
- theory ②: asteroid crash left dense core
- theory ③: Sun vaporized the land

Mini Practice

Listen to part of a discussion in an astronomy class. 🎧 Ch5_07

1. What is unusual about the makeup of the planet Mercury?
   - Ⓐ It's denser for its size than other planets.
   - Ⓑ Its location is in close proximity to the Sun.
   - Ⓒ It has lots of very dense gases.
   - Ⓓ Mercury is composed of elements that are not found on Earth.

2. Which possible theories were given about how Mercury was formed? Click on 3 answers.
   - Ⓐ It collided with an asteroid or another planet.
   - Ⓑ The Sun vaporized less dense material from the surface.
   - Ⓒ In the early solar system, heavy elements near the sun clumped together.
   - Ⓓ 2/3 of the planet is composed of iron particles leftover from the formation of other planets.
   - Ⓔ Magnetic material left over from the formation of Venus and Mars drifted together.

Listening Script

Professor: Today we'll be discussing Mercury, the planet in our solar system which is closest to the Sun. So, Mercury isn't particularly big, but it has an interesting property that you might not expect from such a small planet; it's really dense, it's actually the densest planet in our solar system. That means, for its size, it's very heavy. Why is it so dense? Well, the density is due to its iron core. And it really does have a lot of iron. Iron makes up something like two thirds of the planet. Amazing, right?
So, now you're wondering what caused Mercury to have a core of iron that makes up such a large portion of the planet, right? Well, it's really close to the Sun, so some people think it's because of heavy elements that were floating close to the Sun when the solar system formed. So, in the early solar system, these heavy elements would clump together, and maybe you would end up with a dense planet like Mercury. But that's just one theory. Another says that maybe something, like an asteroid or a small planet, crashed into Mercury. A violent collision could have knocked the lighter elements from the surface off of Mercury and left behind only the dense core.
Yet another theory considers Mercury's very close proximity to the Sun. You see, many people think that being so close to the Sun could have caused the land on Mercury to vaporize, and again, just left behind a dense core. Perhaps at some point, Mercury did have some land that wasn't as dense, but the incredible heat from the Sun just burned it all away. Why don't we know how Mercury ended up the way it is? Well, we simply don't have enough data on Mercury. The only time we ever sent a probe to Mercury was in the 1970s. That was a long time ago, and there hasn't been another probe since.

Answers p. 64

Chemistry

094

Periodic table
주기율표

화학에서 원소chemical element는 모든 물질의 기본이 되는 물질로 다른 물질로 분해, 합성, 전환이 불가능하다. 원자atom는 원소의 가장 작은 부분이다. 과거 원자는 더 이상 쪼갤 수 없는 것으로 알려져 있었으나 20세기 초반 화학자들이 세 개의 미립자가 원자 안에 존재한다는 사실을 발견하게 되었다. 원소의 중심인 원자 핵atomic nucleus은 양의 전기를 지닌 양성자proton와 전기를 띠지 않는 중성자neutron로 이루어지며 이 핵 주변을 선회하는 음의 전기를 띠는 전자electron가 원자를 구성하고 있다.

오늘날의 주기율표periodic table는 화학 원소들이 주기성을 띠면서 원소의 원자 번호인 양성자 수의 순서대로 배열되고, 물리적, 화학적 성질이 비슷한 원소들이 같은 족으로 배열되어 있다. 즉 주기율표의 표준 형식은 7개의 가로 열row의 주기period와 18개의 세로 행column의 족group으로 구성되어 있다. 현재 자연계에 존재하는 원소 98개, 인공적인 원소 20개로 모두 118개가 존재하는 것으로 알려져 있다. 원소는 크게 금속metal, 비금속non-metal, 준금속metalloid으로 분류된다. 19세기 이후 여러 과학자들의 노력으로 이루어진 주기율표는 순환하는 성향으로 인해 원소의 주기성 또는 반복성을 보여주는데 사용될 뿐 아니라 화학적 활동을 분석하는데 유용하며 또한 아직 발견되지 않았거나 합성될 수 있는 새로운 원소들의 성질을 예측하는 용도로 사용되기도 한다.

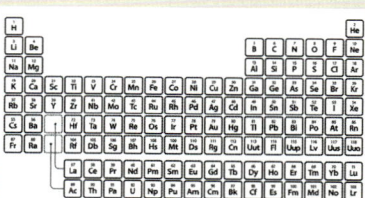

필수어휘
- period 주기
- row 열
- column 세로 열
- element 원소
- triad 3가 원소
- electronic 전자의
- valence 원자가
- proton 양성자

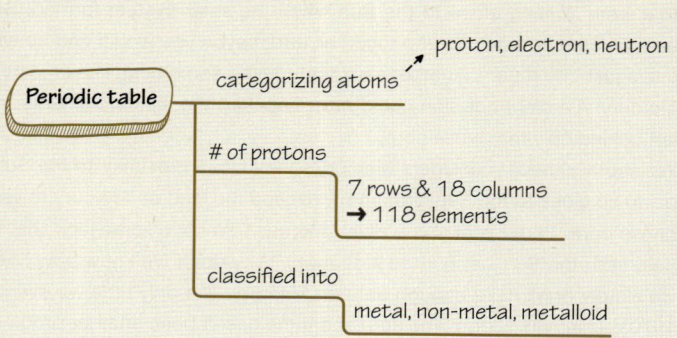

Periodic Table of Elements

Dmitri Mendeleev (1834-1907) is generally credited with the creation of the modern periodic table of elements. This table consists of rows called periods and columns called groups in which all the known chemical elements are organized based on their atomic numbers, electron configurations, and chemical properties. In 1869, Mendeleev presented his finished work, *The Dependence Between the Properties of the Atomic Weights of the Elements*, to the Russian Chemical Society. The periodic table would earn a greater reputation after it was re-published in a German academic journal. His presentation of the periodic table was the most complete and because of its accuracy, it gained him the lion's share of notoriety as the creator of the table. Mendeleev built upon the work of many other scientists who laid the foundation for the categorization of chemical elements.

Johann Dobereiner (1780-1849) was one of the earliest scientists who grouped chemical elements with similar characteristics into groups, which he called triads. He proposed the idea that the middle element of the triad was the average of the other two elements. Further research would reveal that larger groupings could be created of elements with similar properties.

John Newlands (1837-1898) was the first scientist to assign elements based on an atomic weight. When he published the Law of Octaves, another grouping theory, he proposed the idea that elements repeat their properties every eighth element based on their atomic weight. He was ridiculed for his ideas, but several years after the work of Mendeleev was published his theories were indeed proved correct.

Lothar Meyer (1839-1895) published a periodic table of elements around the same time as Mendeleev, but he has received less credit because his table only contained 28 elements and was not as insightful as Mendeleev's work. His table arranged elements into six families according to their valence or bond-forming power.

Following the work of Mendeleev, the British physicist Henry Moseley (1887~1915) discovered that by the X-ray measurement, the number of positive charges in atoms are closely related to the chemical properties of elements. With the number of protons, he was able to move and properly sequence elements that were out of place. With his discoveries, the periodic table was rearranged based on the number of protons in the atomic nucleus rather than the atomic weight.

1. The word properties in paragraph 1 is closest in meaning to
   - (A) holdings
   - (B) clues
   - (C) attributes
   - (D) enigmas

2. The word proposed in paragraph 3 is closest in meaning to
   - (A) precluded
   - (B) postulated
   - (C) orchestrated
   - (D) prevailed

Answers p. 64

Astronomy

095

Planets
행성

태양계의 8개의 행성을 크게 내행성과 외행성으로 나눌 수 있다. 각 범주의 특징을 기억하고, 지구 외에 다른 행성에서 물의 흔적과 생물체의 존재 여부에 대한 가설들을 숙지하자.

우리 태양계의 8개 행성planet은 질량과 구성성분 등의 물리적 특성에 따라 크게 지구형 행성Terrestrial Planet(수성Mercury, 금성Venus, 지구Earth, 화성Mars)과 목성형 행성Jovian Planets(목성Jupiter, 토성Saturn, 천왕성Uranus, 해왕성Neptune)으로 나뉜다.

지구형 행성 Terrestrial Planet

태양 가까이에 위치한 지구형 행성은 목성형 행성과 비교해 밀도density가 훨씬 높지만 질량mass과 크기volume는 다소 작으며, 철Fe, 규소Si, 마그네슘Mg 등의 단단한 암석 재질의 고체로 구성되어 있다. 이러한 구성 성분들이 모이면coalesce 압력과 온도가 높아지면서 지질 분화differentiation 단계를 겪는데, 이 때 중심에서부터 금속 성질의 단단한 핵core, 맨틀mantle, 가장 외부의 지각crust 등이 내부 층들을 형성한다. 각 행성에는 얇은 대기층이 있고 위성moon의 수가 아주 적거나 아예 없으며, 행성 주변의 고리ring는 존재하지 않는다.

목성형 행성 Jovian Planets

목성형 행성들은 지구형 행성보다 먼저 생성된 천체들로 태양에서 훨씬 멀리 떨어져 있어 그 영향을 적게 받으면서 태양이 흡수하지 않은 가스 구름들을 쉽게 끌어 모을 수 있었을 것이라 추정된다. 그렇게 낮은 온도와 여러 물질들로 형성되면서 부피와 질량이 커졌다. 하지만 암석과 철로 이루어진 얇은 내핵을 제외하고 대부분 수소hydrogen와 헬륨helium 등의 가벼운 휘발성 가스로 형성되어 밀도는 낮다. 대기의 두께가 지구형 행성에 비해 상당히 두껍고 외행성이 가지고 있는 위성의 개수는 많으며, 얼음과 암석으로 된 고리를 가지고 있으며 자전rotation 속도가 지구형 행성에 비해 훨씬 빠르다.

필수어휘

- prerequisite 전제 조건
- crater 분화구
- lava flow 용암류
- trace 흔적, 자취 syn track
- probe 우주 탐사선
- Martian 화성의
- channel 해협
- canyon 협곡

Mini Practice

The presence of water on other planets

Because water is a key prerequisite for life, people have been searching for the presence of liquid water on other planets in our solar system as a major part of the search for signs of life outside of the Earth. We know that Mars and Venus had traces of liquid water in the past, but so far, the Earth is the only plant known to currently have liquid water.

Venus once had the greatest number of active volcanoes of any planet in the solar system and volcanic activity shaped its surface into forms such as craters and lava flows, but now, most volcanoes on Venus have long been extinct. Due to that volcanic activity, Venus has a very thick atmosphere composed almost entirely of carbon dioxide. That atmosphere generates a strong greenhouse effect, making Venus hotter than Mercury, even though Mercury is closer to the sun. Therefore, although Venus has some traces of water vapor in its atmosphere, it is much too hot for liquid water to survive there. If there were any oceans of water on its surface when it was young, they must have evaporated quickly, and even if life once began there, no traces would be left now.

The dark markings on the Martian surface in the northern hemisphere may have been caused by liquid water on Mars in its remote past, and photos taken by several probes suggest that liquid water once existed in great quantities on the surface of Mars. The Viking orbiters and the Mars Global Surveyor have relayed images back to Earth of surface features such as channels and canyons that seem to have been formed by flowing water. Researchers theorize that small amounts of liquid water have flowed on and just below the surface and that liquid water may still be present in parts of the subsurface. Furthermore, it is believed by some that the observed channels were once completely filled with flowing water. These channels closely resemble Earth's river systems and geologists believe that they are remnants of long-gone rivers that once carried Mars' rainfall from the mountains down into the valleys. The flowing marks on the ground indicate that the atmosphere was once thicker, the surface warmer, and there was once an abundance of water.

1. The word remnants in paragraph 3 is closest in meaning to
   - (A) traces
   - (B) areas
   - (C) remains
   - (D) refinement

2. According to the passage, which of the following is true?
   - (A) Volcanoes on Venus have been active recently.
   - (B) There was never water on Venus.
   - (C) The atmosphere on Mars was thicker than on the Earth.
   - (D) On the Martian surface, there are traces of liquid water in the past.

Answers p. 65

Chemistry

★★★
096

Properties of Water
물의 특성

왜 얼음은 물위에 뜰까? 만약 얼음이 물아래 가라앉았다면 어떤 현상이 일어났을까? 지구 내 생명체 존재를 가능케 한 이 신비로운 물의 특성을 파헤쳐 보도록 하자.

물은 지구상에서 유일하게 고체의 부피가 액체보다 큰 물질이다. 이것은 물이 수소 결합hydrogen bond이라고 하는 상당히 강한 분자 사이의 인력attraction을 갖기 때문이다. 이렇게 강력한 수소결합으로 이루어진 물 분자 사이의 인력을 끊을 때는 많은 에너지가 필요하다. 때문에 물은 다른 물질에 비해 끓는점boiling point이 높으며 비열specific heat(온도를 높이기 위해 소비되는 에너지)도 대단히 큰 물질이다. 따라서 물을 끓이려면 많은 연료를 사용해야 하는 불편함이 있기도 하지만 생물체가 살아가는 데 있어서 중요한 역할을 하기도 한다. 예를 들어 덥거나 추운 날에도 체온을 일정하게 유지할 수 있는 것은 바로 물의 비열이 크기 때문이다.

물 분자의 수소 결합으로 인한 특성 중 가장 신기한 것은 고체 상태인 얼음이 액체 상태인 물에 뜬다는 사실이다. 대부분의 물질은 액체에서 고체로 바뀌면서 부피volume가 줄어들고 밀도density가 커지게 되는 반면에, 물은 고체가 될 때 수소 결합수가 늘어나고 그 사이에 빈 공간이 생기면서 부피가 늘어나게 된다. 그렇게 되면 얼음의 밀도는 물보다 작아져서 물 위에 뜨게 되는 것이다. 물이 얼음으로 변할 때 수소 결합은 강해지면서 물 분자들이 육각형hexagon의 구조를 이루게 되는데 그 사이에 빈 공간이 생겨 부피가 10% 정도 증가하게 된다. 따라서 밀도가 감소하는 반면 얼음이 녹을 때에는 수소 결합의 일부가 끊겨 빈 공간을 채우므로 물 분자 사이의 간격이 줄어들어 부피가 작아지고 밀도가 커진다. 그렇기 때문에 강이나 호수가 수면위에서부터 얼어 한 겨울에도 호수의 물고기들이 생명을 유지할 수 있게 되는 것이다.

필수어휘
- freezing point 어는점
- density 밀도
- molecules 분자
- aquatic organisms 수중생물
- insulation 단열
- spell 주문을 걸자
- specific heat index 비열지수

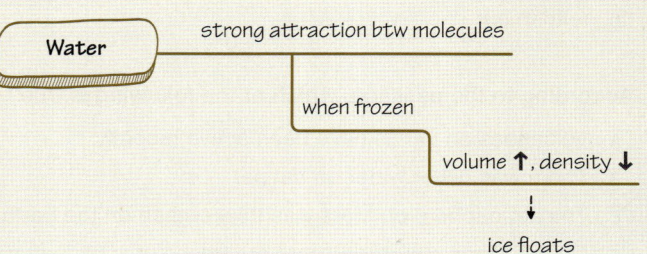

Listening

Mini Practice

Listen to part of a discussion in a chemistry class. 🎧 Ch5_08

1. According to the professor, what is true about iron and water?
   - Ⓐ A large quantity of water is needed to achieve heating at the same rate as iron.
   - Ⓑ It takes a lot of energy to heat water, compared to iron.
   - Ⓒ Iron is harder to heat than water of equal mass.
   - Ⓓ Like water, iron has a high specific heat index.

2. Based on the lecture, which is not a result of the of properties of water?
   - Ⓐ Fish can survive in lakes, even in freezing weather.
   - Ⓑ A can of soda can explode if frozen.
   - Ⓒ In coastal areas, temperature changes in the air occur more gradually.
   - Ⓓ It takes more energy to cool down the ocean than to heat it up.

Listening Script

Professor: Let's talk about the chemistry of water, the most abundant liquid on our planet. As I'm sure you know, most substances, when they are frozen, they contract and become denser. But not water. As the temperature of water approaches zero degrees Celsius, that is, the freezing point of water, its density actually decreases. In other words, it starts expanding. What do I mean when I say density decreases? Well, it means the water molecules start moving apart. And of course, as the water changes into ice and the distance between molecules increases, the water expands. If you think about it, that explains why cans of soda explode if you leave them in the freezer a long time. The soda is mostly water, so it expands and literally grows larger than its container. And since frozen water, or ice, is less dense than the liquid form, ice floats, which is the key to the survival of many aquatic organisms. You see, in the winter, when bodies of water freeze, the ice floats on top of the water, and actually serves as insulation, keeping the water beneath warm enough to remain liquid.

Most substances don't expand when frozen. If water behaved like that too, ice would sink rather than float. Consider the consequences; the ice would build up on the bottom of lakes and bodies of water until the whole thing froze solid. That would spell the end of most aquatic life in the water. Additionally, water has a high specific heat index. That means it takes a lot of heat to raise the temperature of water, or, in other words, water can absorb a lot of heat. This can be easily observed. If you take some volume of water, and some iron, um, a piece of equal mass to the water, and you try heating both of them, well, it would require about ten times as much energy to heat the water to the same temperature as the iron. What does that mean for life on Earth? Well, the oceans are all made of water. So of course, that means it takes a lot of energy to heat them up. But it also means they cool down quite slowly. By absorbing and releasing heat in this way, the oceans smooth out changes in temperature in the surrounding environment, essentially regulating global air temperature. This explains why temperature changes from season to season are generally quite gradual, especially in coastal areas.

Answers p. 65

Astronomy

097

Stars
별

대부분의 항성들은 인간과 마찬가지로 탄생, 성장, 죽음을 경험하는 생명주기를 경험한다.

탄생

먼저 성간 물질interstellar matter인 가스나 먼지가 모이면서, 별들의 공장으로 알려진 성운nebulae이 만들어 진다. 이때 서로 잡아 당기는 인력gravity 작용으로 생긴 중력 수축현상gravity contraction으로 인해 내부 압력이 증가하게 되고 별 이전 단계인 고밀도와 고온의 원시성protostars이 생성된다. 이 원시성은 더 많은 물질을 모으며 회전하면서 밀도가 계속 상승하다가 어느 시점에 이르러 원자 열 핵융합atomic thermonuclear fusion을 거쳐 스스로 빛과 열을 방출하는 별이 된다.

성장

그 후 별은 일생 중 90%의 시간을 보낸다는 주계열성main sequence star 단계를 거치는데, 이 때 별의 중심에서 수소를 헬륨으로 전환하는 핵융합hydrogen core fusion이 일어난다. 이 단계의 특징은 중심부로 수축하려는 중력과 외부로 팽창하려는 기체 압력force of pressure 사이의 힘이 비슷해지면서 정역학적 평행상태statics equilibrium를 경험한다는 것이다.

죽음

주계열성 단계 이후 태양과 비슷한 크기의 별은 핵에서 융합하던 수소가 거의 다 소진되어 핵 융합이 정지되며 별 생애 마지막 10% 가량을 차지하는 적색거성red giant star이 된다. 이 단계에서는 별의 부피가 팽창하면서 에너지 파동pulsation으로 바깥 부분이 없어지고 중심부의 핵만 남아 백색왜성white dwarf을 형성한다. 태양의 직경보다 적어도 3배 이상 큰 적색 거성은 적색 초거성red supergiant으로 분류되며 내부의 핵반응이 멈추고, 온도와 압력의 감소로 인한 수축현상으로 폭발해explode 우주 도처에 많은 물질을 퍼뜨린다.

필수어휘

- □ nuclear fusion 핵융합
- □ birthplace 발생지, 근원지
- □ explode 폭발하다　[syn] burst
- □ supernovae 원시성
- □ finite 유한한
- □ faint 흐릿한, 희미한　[syn] dim
- □ condense 응축하다
  　[syn] compress, compact
- □ radiate 발산하다, 내뿜다
  　[syn] give off, release
- □ shockwave (지진이나 폭발로 인한) 충격파
- □ orbit 궤도

Final Stages of Stars

A star is a luminous globe of gas generating its own heat and light as a result of nuclear fusion deep in its interior. Stars are born from nebulae, clouds known as the birthplaces of stars, and can live for billions of years. Generally, however, stars live for shorter periods of time before their death and the most massive ones die with an explosion, known as a supernova.

After the birth of a star through the initiation of nuclear fusion, the star goes through several stages in its lifecycle and faces death, after all. Because stars in the universe have a finite supply of hydrogen fuel, they eventually consume all of their fuel and the energy flow from the core of the star ceases. However, stars do not expire and disappear at once, but instead, undergo a sequence of events that continue for quite some time before completely burning out.

In case, the dying star has a similar or larger mass to the sun, nuclear reactions outside the core can cause an extremely massive dying star, known as a "red giant," before it begins its unavoidable collapse. Instead of becoming fainter, they become more luminous, consuming their last remaining hydrogen at a greater rate. At this moment, the stellar material divides into two zones—the inner zone and the outer zone. The outer zone or shell will expand outwards because the star's gravitational field is no longer strong enough to pull it to the core. [A ■] There is still some hydrogen left in the outer zone at this point so it will continue to burn. [B ■] As it collapses, the inner zone will form a very dense white core and will no longer produce energy but will still radiate trapped heat, and send violent shockwaves outwards that push on the outer zone forcing it to expand at an even faster rate. [C ■] The outer zone will grow to hundreds of times its original size, eventually engulfing an area larger than the Earth's orbit, while at the same time, cooling down by thousands of degrees and becoming so bright that it is visible to the naked eye thousands of light-years away. [D ■] This giant red star will then become progressively dimmer and cooler before blinking out entirely. It will expand in all directions, finally sending its remains into space, most likely to be picked up later by other newly formed stars.

In contrast, stars with lower masses may not supernova, instead form white dwarf stars that cool very slowly, remaining for a few billion more years before eventually dying out completely. White dwarf stars can also form from the remnants of a supernova.

1. The word luminous in paragraph 1 is closest in meaning to

    (A) notable
    (B) momentous
    (C) brilliant
    (D) modest

2. Look at the four squares [■] that indicate where the following sentence could be added to the sentence.

    In contrast, the inner zone will begin to collapse in upon itself under its own gravity.

    Where would the sentence best fit?

Astronomy

098

The orbits of comets
혜성의 궤도

천문학에서 태양계 행성 다음으로 토플에 많이 출제되는 주제는 혜성 또는 소행성이다. 그 중에서도 핼리혜성이 자주 나왔으므로 핼리혜성을 비롯한 혜성의 공통적인 특징을 알아두자.

혜성 대부분은 중심부에 핵core을 가지고 있으며 얼음ice과 암석rock 그리고 먼지입자dust particles들로 둥글게 이루어졌다. 핵 주변에는 핵을 둘러싼 먼지와 가스인 코마coma가 존재하는데 혜성이 태양 가까이에 가면 코마의 물질이 태양빛과 태양에서 날아오는 입자에 의해 뒤로 밀려 나가는 긴 꼬리를 형성한다.

혜성의 궤도는 대부분 행성과 같은 타원 궤도elliptical orbit이다. 그러나 때로는 타원이 무한히 길어져 포물선이나 쌍곡선의 형태parabolic orbit를 가지기도 한다. 혜성은 생성 초기 태양계 바깥 대열에서 태양의 중력으로 인해 태양계 내로 진입을 하게 되는데, 목성Jupiter과 같은 큰 질량을 가진 행성으로부터도 영향을 받아 궤도요소가 매우 잘 변하는 편이다. 그래서 어떤 혜성들은 태양계solar system 내에 진입한 후 태양이나 다른 행성에 부딪혀서 부서지기도 하고, 아예 태양계 밖으로 빠져나가 버리기도 한다.

우리에게 가장 잘 알려진 핼리혜성Halley's comet은 75년마다 한 번씩 돌아오는 정기적 주기periodic orbit를 갖고 있으며 대부분의 시간을 태양계 밖에서 보낸다. 또한 태양에 가까워지면 태양의 거대한 중력gravitational force으로 인해 회전속도가 증가하고 중심부의 먼지와 얼음은 기화되어 꼬리를 형성한다. 그러나 태양을 벗어나면서 빠른 속도로 태양과 멀어지는 특징을 지닌다.

필수어휘
- stable 안정된
- eccentric 기이한
- upwards 위쪽의
- elongated 길쭉한
- furthest 가장 먼
- immense 엄청난
- gravitational pull 중력
- be consumed 소비되다, 먹히다
- Jupiter 목성

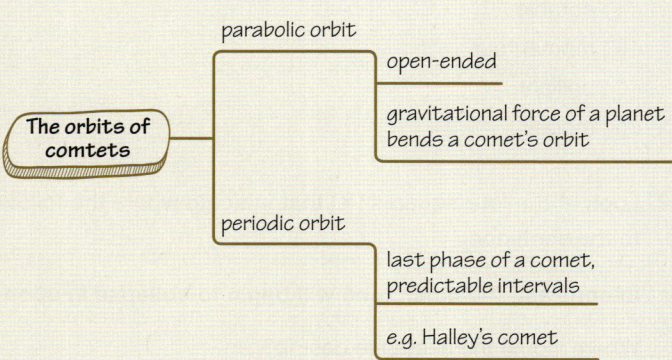

Mini Practice

Listen to part of a discussion in an astronomy class. 🎧 Ch5_09

1. According to the professor, how are comets influenced by the sun? Click on 2 answers.
   - Ⓐ Some of the solid material of the comet is vaporized by the sun.
   - Ⓑ The sun's gravity alters the velocity of the comet.
   - Ⓒ Parabolic orbits are bent into periodic orbits by the sun.
   - Ⓓ The sun causes the comet to go towards unknown areas of the solar system.

2. Based on the lecture, which of the following is likely to be true about Halley's Comet?
   - Ⓐ It is a long period comet and it has a circular orbit.
   - Ⓑ The exact age of Halley's Comet can be determined by comparing it with other comets.
   - Ⓒ It is one of the oldest comets in our solar system.
   - Ⓓ The gravitational force of other planets has affected its orbit.

Listening Script

Professor: Today, I want to focus on the orbits of comets. We differentiate between comets by their type of orbit, whether they are short period or long period orbits. Short period comets generally remain within our solar system and have very stable orbits that allow us to predict the length of their orbit and when they will return. Long period orbits are very eccentric and it takes them at least 200 years and even upwards of a thousand years to fly back towards the sun.

Let's talk about perhaps the most famous of short period comet, Halley's Comet. Halley's Comet is a short period comet that passes by the sun once every 75 years. It has a stretched out and elongated orbit that's very different from the circular orbit of the earth. At its closest point to the sun, it is actually ½ the distance from the sun that the Earth is. At its furthest point, it's almost 3,500 times as far from the sun as Earth is. As it gets closer to the sun, the sun's immense gravitational pull speeds the comet up and the heat from the sun will vaporize some of the ice and dust on the comet. Every time the comet passes the sun it gets smaller and smaller. But how is it that Halley's Comet has not yet been consumed by the sun? The answer to that is that Halley's Comet was not always a short period comet but was captured in the past.

Many long period comets originate from the Oort Cloud and they have extremely long orbital paths. Because these comets' orbits cover unimaginable distances, it may take tens of thousands of years for the comet to return. So, scientists rarely track the paths of long period comets. So, how does a long period comet turn into a short period comet? Well, we have many other planets in our solar system and these planets all have their own gravitational pulls. So if a long period comet happens to pass by, let's say Jupiter, in just the right way, then the gravitational pull of Jupiter may be just enough to capture the comet and bring it into a shorter orbit around the sun.

Answers p. 67

Chemistry

099

Origins of life
생물의 기원

생물 기원에 대한 이론은 신의 만물 창조로 시작했다는 창조론 creationism 등을 비롯하여 여러 가지 가설이 제기되고 있다.

원시수프 이론primordial soup은 생물이 유기물 혼합 용액에서 시작되었다는 화학 합성chemosynthesis이론을 주장한다. 이 이론에 따르면 화학 합성물(생물체)은 38억 년 전 경 아미노산amino acids으로 이루어진 따뜻한 연못pond 혹은 해수에서 발생되었다. 이 아미노산 덩어리는 따뜻한 연못에서 빛 에너지를 받으며 단백질 등의 복잡한 분자들을 형성한 것을 의미한다. 하지만 단백질은 자연적으로 합성될 수 없으며, 그 당시 단백질로 만들어 질 수 있는 어떤 구조나 상황도 없었다는 반박이 있다.

자연 발생설Spontaneous Generation은 생물체가 무기물로부터 자연적으로 발생했다고 주장한다. 초기 과학자들은 썩은 고기에 생기는 구더기를 언급했지만 1668년 이탈리아 물리학자 Francesco Refi에 의해 반박 당하는 등 끊임없는 논란이 있었다. 결국 19세기 프랑스 미생물 학자인 파스퇴르Louis Pasteur가 끓인 고기 즙 실험에서 생물은 결코 자연 발생하지 않는 다는 결론을 내리게 된다.

범종설 혹은 포자설Panspermia은 생물체는 지구가 아닌 외계outer space에서부터 운석meteor이나 행성planet 내부에 있던 생물체의 '씨앗seed'이 지구 내부에 떨어지면서 시작되었다는 이론이다. 하지만 오랜 시간 동안 생물체가 운석 안에서 존재할 가능성이 희박하고 지구 내부로 진입할 때의 충격을 이겨낼 가능성도 높지 않다는 반박이 있다.

필수어휘
- collision 충돌 [v] collide
- bombardment 폭격
- stabilize 안정시키다
- ocean ridge 해양 융기
- crack 균열
- pore 구멍
- spew out 분출하다
- linger 잔류하다
- mutate 돌연변이가 되다

Origin of life

Scientists widely accept that life could not have existed during the heavy asteroid collisions which pelted the Earth for millions of years, up to about four billion years ago when the most of the bombardment ceased and the earth's plates began stabilizing. It was only after this stabilization that the first forms of life were able to slowly take shape, and much of the evidence scientists have gathered points to ocean ridges situated just above the Earth's mantle as the place where life originated. The ocean ridges have cracks and pores where rich minerals from the mantle below spew out with temperatures of 100 degrees Celsius and above. The hot water that escaped through these crevices provided the right elements for life to spring up through the seas.

The first organisms that formed were almost certainly similar to bacteria, microscopic organisms which found ways to obtain energy without sunlight or minerals from the atmosphere. The chemical reactions that were taking place on the ocean floor allowed bacteria to thrive as they took advantage of the naturally generated energy. Early bacteria could not have produced their own energy; instead they directly consumed the chemicals that gushed out of the Earth into the ocean. For a very short period of time after emerging, these raw chemicals do not undergo any chemical reactions. Lingering near the ocean floor, bacteria take this opportunity to ingest the chemicals and allow the reactions to happen inside, releasing energy directly inside the cells.

Fossil records indicate that the first forms of life were most likely the Archaea, singled-cell bacteria-like organisms that are still in existence today. Geneticists mapped out the DNA of the Archaea along with the DNA of hundreds of bacteria and they compared them to find the similarities and differences in their genomes. Just recently, they made a fascinating discovery that solidified the theory that Archaea were the first inhabitants of the earth. By comparing the genomes, they were able to conclude that most Archaea and bacteria share similar DNA sequences, while only a few bacteria strains have deviations in their DNA, representing more recent stages of evolution. It could therefore be concluded that the majority of the DNA in the population all stemmed from a common ancient ancestor, the Archaea.

1. The word crevices in paragraph 1 is closest in meaning to
   - (A) sides
   - (B) gaps
   - (C) holes
   - (D) places

2. Which of the sentences below best expresses the essential information in the highlighted sentence in the passage? *Incorrect* choices change the meaning in important ways or leave out essential information.
   - (A) The energy from the chemical reactions is released inside bacteria after the chemicals have been consumed.
   - (B) Chemical reactions occur inside bacteria after they have been engulfed near the ocean floor.
   - (C) Chemical reactions near the seabed are swallowed by opportunistic bacteria so that the energy can be released inside for used by the cells.
   - (D) Energy from chemical reactions is released inside bacteria after they have been consumed near the ocean floor

Chemistry

100
★★

Trace metals
소량금속

범세계적인 지구 온난화 문제의 주범인 대기 내 이산화탄소를 줄이기 위한 방법 중 물리과학분야의 기술을 이용한 방법을 살펴보자.

동식물 세포 내에서 이산화탄소carbon dioxide를 탄산carbon acid으로 전환시켜주는 금속metals이 있다면 동식물의 체내에서 발산되는 이산화탄소를 상당부분 줄일 수 있을 것이다. 이러한 금속들은 소량금속 또는 미량금속trace metals이라 불리는데 그 이유는 이름에서도 알 수 있듯이 동식물 내에 존재하는 정말 소량의 금속을 의미하기 때문이다.

이러한 소량금속은 동식물 내에서 이산화탄소를 탄산carbon acid으로 바꾸어 주는 효소enzyme 역할을 하며 대표적으로는 철iron, 마그네슘magnesium, 아연zinc, 구리copper, 망간manganese 등이 있다. 아연은 효소 안에서 탄소순환carbon cycling을 촉진시켜 독성인 이산화탄소를 탄산으로 바꾼 뒤 폐lung에 보내어 그곳에서 혈액이 다시 탄산을 이산화탄소로 전환시켜 체내에서 안전하게 배출시키는 역할을 한다. 반면 식물인 돌말diatom은 아연이 없는 물속에서 살기 때문에 대신 카드뮴cadmium을 이용하여 체내 탄소 순환을 촉진시킨다. 이렇게 이산화탄소를 흡수하여 탄산으로 바꾸는 소량금속에 대해 더 많은 연구가 진행된다면 지구의 이산화탄소 발생을 줄여 궁극적으로는 지구온난화 해결에도 기여를 할 수 있을 것이라 기대된다.

필수어휘

- trace metal 소량금속
- enzyme 효소
- zinc 아연
- carbon cycling 탄소 순환
- byproduct 부산물
- cellular 세포의
- carbon acid 탄산
- micro-photosynthetic 미세광합성의
- diatom 규조 (바다식물)
- catalyze 촉진시키다
- cadmium 카드뮴

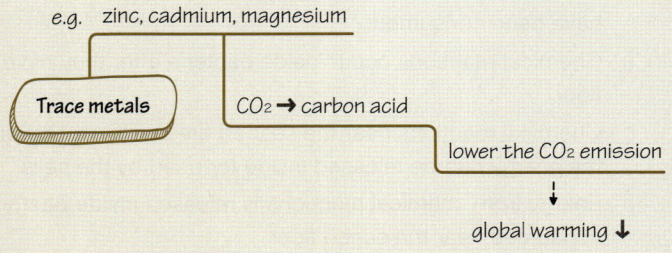

Listening

Mini Practice

Listen to part of a discussion in an environmental science class. 🎧 Ch5_10

1. According to the professor, how is zinc involved in the human metabolic process?
   - Ⓐ It is part of an enzyme for converting between carbon dioxide into carbonic acid.
   - Ⓑ It inhibits formation of carbonic acid, which is toxic to humans.
   - Ⓒ It cycles carbon, allowing for efficient oxygen metabolism in the lungs.
   - Ⓓ It allows humans to safely breathe carbon dioxide.

2. Why does the professor talk about diatoms?
   - Ⓐ To give an example of another way carbon can be moved around in an ecosystem
   - Ⓑ To emphasize their role as the fundamental element of a marine ecosystem's food chain
   - Ⓒ To show the difference between how zinc is used in plants compared to humans
   - Ⓓ To point out that diatoms are needed to process zinc in marine ecosystems

Listening Script

Professor: Let's get started. Today, we'll talk about trace metals. What are they? Trace metals are tiny amounts of metal which can be found in living cells. They are used by enzymes. This time, the trace metal that I want to talk about is zinc. Zinc is used in an enzyme to increase the speed of a process called carbon cycling. Carbon cycling, um, is the process of changing one kind of molecule containing carbon into a different kind of molecule also containing carbon. I guess maybe that's not really clear, so I'll try to explain it in terms of humans. So, in humans, as you know, carbon dioxide is a byproduct of many cellular processes. But did you know that it's toxic to humans? So, that enzyme, containing zinc, changes or "cycles" carbon dioxide to carbonic acid. That is, the enzyme takes the carbon-containing CO_2 molecules and reforms them into molecules of carbonic acid. Carbonic acid can be safely transported, through blood, to the lungs. And in the lungs, it is one again cycled back to carbon dioxide so it can be exhaled safely.

Now let's consider a specific type of plant: diatoms. Um, diatoms are micro-photosynthetic plants that make up the first step of the food chain in many different ecosystems. They are found in water, where they are eaten by baby fish or other small creatures. These tiny little plants play a very important role in transporting carbon molecules throughout an ecosystem. And this transportation happens in several ways. For example, maybe a fish eats a diatom and then travels to another part of the ocean. Or, maybe a diatom dies, and it sinks and carries its carbon to the ocean floor.

So, this is very interesting. Although zinc can be found in a variety of places all over the world, there is no zinc to be found in lakes, rivers, or ocean shallows. In other words, just about any place where the water is not particularly deep. And yet, you can find diatoms in these areas. How? Well, since those places contain no zinc, the diatoms in shallow areas use a different trace metal, cadmium, to catalyze their carbon cycling.

Answers p. 68

Chapter 6. Environmental Science

Ecology
101-L
Allopatric speciation in Amazon

Geology
102-L
Channeled scabland

Environmental Studies
103-R
Cold environment

Ecology
104-L
Competitive Exclusion Principle

Environmental Studies
105-R
Environmental problems

Ecology
106-R
Extinction

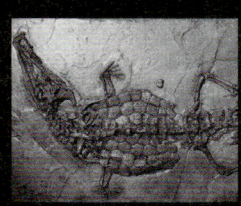

Paleontology
107-R
Fossilization

Geology
108-L
Geothermal energy

Ecology
109-L
Global warming and ocean acidification

Geology
110-R
Groundwater

Environmental Studies
111-L
Little ice age

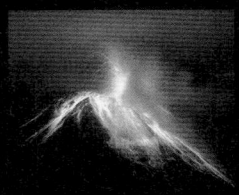

Geology
112-R
Magma

Meteorology
113-L
Northern Lights

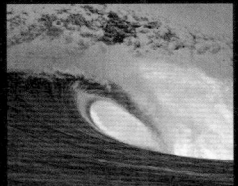

Environmental Studies
114-R
Ocean energy

Geology
115-R
Predicting volcanoes

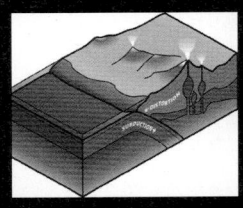

Geology
116-L
Seismic waves

Ecology
117-R
Soil

Environmental Science
118-L
Stalagmite

Paleontology
119-L
Uranium-Lead Dating

Environmental Studies
120-R
Wildfire

Ecology

★★★

101

Allopatric speciation in Amazon
아마존내의 종분화

아마존이 처한 환경문제들은 토플시험에도 다양한 분야에서 예로 많이 등장하기 때문에 아마존에 대해서 좀더 관심을 가져보도록 하자!

아마존은 지구상의 동식물 중 40%가 서식하고, 1헥타르 당 약 7,000여 종의 식물이 서식하는 지구상에서 가장 다양한 생물종various species을 자랑하는 생태계의 보고이다. 참고로 그 다음으로 생물종이 다양한 지역은 산호초coral reefs이다. 다양한 생물종이 있다는 것은 한 지역에 활발한 종분화speciation가 있었다는 것을 의미한다. 그렇다면 왜 유독 아마존의 생물들은 다양한 종으로 분화하게 된 것일까?

열대 우림의 높은 온도와 습도가 식물의 번식을 활발하게 만드는 것은 사실이지만 생물들이 분화하는 원인이 될 수는 없다. 다양함과 풍부함은 별도이기 때문이다. 우선 종이 다양한 형태로 분화하기 위해서는 지리적 격리geographical isolation가 존재해야 하며 이러한 고립이 생리적인 격리biological isolation로 이어질 만큼의 시간이 존재해야 한다. 그러나 아마존에는 산이나 바다와 같은 지리적 장애물barrier이 존재하지 않기 때문에 많은 생물학자들은 아마존의 종분화에 대해 많은 의문점을 갖게 되었다. 그 중 알프레드 월리스Alfred Wallace라는 박물학자가 여러 갈래로 뻗어있는 좁고 긴 강들이 바로 종분화를 이끈 주역이라 주장하면서 절엽 개미leaf cutter ants의 종분화를 그 예로 보여주었다. 그에 따르면, 아마존에 새로운 강이 형성되면서 개미의 일부 종들을 떠내려 보내거나 이들을 영구적으로 분리 및 분산시켜 그들은 다시 뭉치는 것이 불가능하게 되었다. 이렇게 강에 의해 분리된 개미들은 시간이 지남에 따라 각기 다른 종으로 진화하며 여러 다른 종의 절엽개미들을 형성하게 되었다. 따라서 작고 큰 수많은 강들이 바로 아마존의 종분화의 비밀을 푼 열쇠가 된 것이다.

필수어휘
- biodiversity 생물다양성
- evolutionary 진화적인
- allopatric speciation 이지역 종형성
- terrain 지형
- leaf cutter ants 절엽개미
- deterred 제지된

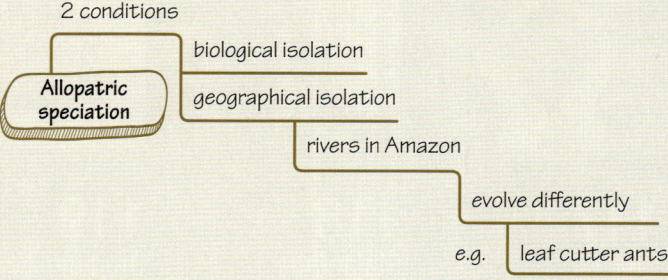

Listening

Mini Practice

Listen to part of a lecture in an ecology class. 🎧 Ch6_01

1. What two events must occur in order for allopatric speciation to take place?

   Ⓐ Interaction with members of another species
   Ⓑ Passage of time
   Ⓒ Large rivers or mountains must form
   Ⓓ Separation by geographical barriers

2. Why doesn't the Amazon Rainforest have the usual conditions for allopatric speciation?

   Ⓐ It extends over too great an area for it to be occupied by a single species.
   Ⓑ It doesn't possess any of the features traditionally considered to be barriers.
   Ⓒ Its trees preclude the formation of large mountains and rivers.
   Ⓓ There is too much diversity among existing species.

Listening Script

Professor: The Amazon is an amazing place with a tremendous amount of biodiversity. Biodiversity refers to the richness and a variety of animal and plant species in an area. Do you know why the Amazon is so rich in animal diversity? Well, the evolutionary process that creates new species known as speciation is responsible for the diversity in animal life. There are four types of speciation but today we will focus on allopatric speciation. Allopatric speciation begins when a single species is separated from each other due to a geological barrier. Geological barriers can be mountains, oceans, deserts, or other types of terrain. If this separation happens over a long time with no intermixing, the separated species will evolve differently. This leads to the creation of entirely new species. However, there are no deserts or mountains in the Amazon. How did these animals evolve differently to create new species? This question puzzled many scientists and they could not figure out how so many species evolved in one place.

It wasn't until the naturalist, Alfred Wallace, explored several remote places in the Amazon that the mystery was solved. He discovered that there were geographical barriers that seemed insignificant to humans but were important barriers to animals in the Amazon. The answer was in the rivers! There are many small and large rivers that can separate species. How did he discover this? During his study of the leaf cutter ants, he found that they were deterred by rivers. New rivers might form and carry some species off and this would create a permanent separation. In the Amazon, the rivers are geographic barriers that block species from meeting and transport species to new places, leaving them to evolve differently over time. This is why there are so many species in the Amazon. Although the answer was simple, the scientific community was unable to discover the answer because the Amazon is so unique and different from the other regions that they had investigated.

Answers p. 70

Geology

★★
102

Channeled scabland
화산용암지

지질학 역사에서 가장 흥미로운 논쟁 중의 하나는 워싱턴주 동부의 가장 젊고도 독특한 절경인 그랜드쿨리Grand Coulee의 기원에 관한 것이다. 그랜드쿨리는 죽기 전에 꼭 봐야 할 자연절경 중 하나로 꼽히는 신비로운 화산지대이다.

그랜드쿨리의 지질학적 이름은 '수로가 있는 화산용암 지대Channeled scabland'로 현무암을 덮고 있는 황토loess나 토양의 '딱지scab' 사이로 흐르는 거대한 수로channel가 형성된 지형을 의미한다. 이 신비로운 지형은 과연 수백만 년에 걸친 강의 침식 때문이었을까 아니면 현대판 노아의 홍수Noah's flood의 결과물일까? 그랜드쿨리의 가파른 수직 절벽과 울퉁불퉁한 지형은 이곳이 비교적 최근에 형성되었음을 보여준다. 그러므로 이 지형이 수백만 년은 족히 걸리는 강의 침식작용erosion으로 만들어진 것은 아님을 짐작할 수 있다.

또한 컬럼비아 고원plateau에서 주로 바닥이 아래로 경사가 진 것과 반대로 쿨리의 바닥은 위로 경사져 있다는 점도 특이한데, 실제로 그랜드쿨리에는 처음부터 물이 없었으며 강도 없었다고 한다. 이처럼 그랜드쿨리 협곡canyons은 오랫동안 수수께끼만을 남긴 채 탄생의 실마리를 제공하지 않아 과학자들의 골머리를 아프게 했다. 그러던 중 하렌 브레츠라는 과학자가 그랜드쿨리는 최대 규모의 홍수가 발생한 마지막 빙하기last ice age에 형성되었음을 밝혀냈다. 그 당시 약 50년을 주기로 610미터가 넘는 물기둥이 로키 산맥의 얼음 댐을 뚫고 들어와 워싱턴을 통해 태평양으로 빠져나갔다. 그 물살의 세기가 어찌나 셌던지 기반암bedrock을 산산조각 낼 정도였고 그 결과 오늘날 쿨리(물 마른 협곡)들이 만들어진 것이다.

필수어휘
- channeled 수로화 된
- scabland 화산용암지
- barren 황무지의
- soilless 흙이 없는
- ravine 협곡
- petering out 점점 작아지는
- erosion 침식
- magnitude 규모
- pinpoint 정확히 찾아내다
- ripples 잔물결
- indicative ~를 나타내는
- dammed 댐으로 막아진
- viciously 맹렬하게
- painstakingly 공들여

Mini Practice

Listen to part of a lecture in a geology class. 🎧 Ch6_02

1. What is implied about how the scablands were formed?
   - Ⓐ The whole process took just a few hours.
   - Ⓑ Several different kinds of erosion were involved.
   - Ⓒ The process took a long time and did not end until the 1900s.
   - Ⓓ Their formation was proof that natural forces shape the landscape very slowly.

2. At the end of the lecture, the professor describes the formation of the scablands. Indicate whether each of the following steps was part of the process he described.

	YES	NO
Ⓐ The water was prevented from flowing by an ice dam.		
Ⓑ The glacier began breaking apart gradually, over an extended period of time.		
Ⓒ The ice dam collided with another glacier, and the resulting damage caused it to break apart.		
Ⓓ The melting glacier caused the river to overflow.		

Listening Script

Professor: The Channeled Scablands in the state of Washington have puzzled geologists for a long time. The Scablands which are barren and generally soilless are a unique geological feature peculiar to the state of Washington. As you can see from this picture, the Scablands are full of steep ravines and massive channels cut into the landscape. Some researchers have estimated that the Scablands cover an area of about 5,000 km^2 beginning in northern Idaho and petering out along the border of the Oregon. Scientists previously believed that a slow erosion process occurred over millions of years and this caused the channels and ravines, but in 1922, American geologist J Harlen Bretz presented a new theory.

Bretz observed that there were no rivers within 90 kilometers of the Scablands that were capable of creating erosion of this magnitude. Glaciers were also out of the question because the ice sheet never reached this part of Washington during the Ice Age. After studying the Scablands, Bretz concluded that neither glaciers nor slow water erosion was responsible for these channels. He concluded that at one time, there was a sudden mega-flood that swept through the region and that this flood created the channels and ravines in a matter of hours. When he presented these findings to the Geological Society of America, he was instantly attacked and criticized for his theory. Because Bretz was unable to pinpoint a source for the flood, so he faced heavy opposition. It wasn't until another geologist, Joseph Pardee, conducted his own research that a source was located. By flying over the Scablands, Pardee noticed that the ravines and channels formed distinct ripples that were indicative of a past giant current. He believed that a glacier might have dammed a glacial lake up in the past and when that glacier moved or melted, it created a massive flood. This mega flood would have viciously swept through the landscape carving out the channels and creating giant ripple marks on the landscape. He eventually settled on Lake Missoula as the glacier lake and shared his findings with Bretz. Together they painstakingly collected data and evidence to support this theory. Finally, after many years of hard work, their work was recognized in 1979 by the Geological Society of America as significantly contributing to the field of earth sciences.

Answers p. 71

Environmental Studies

★★★
103

Cold Environment
한랭 환경

빙하glacier는 오래 동안 눈이 쌓여 만들어진 육지를 덮고 있는 두툼한 얼음 층이다. 이것은 삭마ablation(풍화나 침식 작용으로 얼음이나 눈이 깎여 나가는 현상) 보다 쌓이는 눈이 더 많은 지역에서 만들어지는데, 특이한 점은 이 빙하가 천천히 흐르는 강처럼 움직이며 그 무게로 암석을 침식시키기도 한다는 것이다. 빙하는 두께가 얇은 해빙sea ice이나 물 표면에 생기는 호수 얼음lake ice과는 다르다. 전 세계 대륙의 10% 가량을 덮고 있는 빙하 대부분은 남극Antarctic과 그린란드와 같은 극지방polar regions에 대륙 빙하ice sheet의 형태로 존재한다. 간혹 히말라야 산맥이나 로키 산맥, 멕시코 등의 고원 지대에서 산악 빙하mountain glacier가 발견되기도 한다.

빙하는 내린 눈이 녹지 않고 일 년 동안 쌓이다가 그 위에 또 다시 눈이 내리고, 녹고, 어는 현상이 반복되면서 얼음으로 재결정 작용recrystallization이 일어나면서 생긴다. 빙하는 시간이 흐를수록 얼음 알갱이들이 점점 커지고, 얼음 사이에 있던 공기 포켓이 작아지면서 밀도가 높아진다. 이런 현상들이 반복되면 눈과 빙하 얼음의 중간 단계인 만년설firn이 된다. 그렇게 크기가 더 커진 얼음 수정체가 압력을 받아 얼음 사이의 공기가 거의 없어지면서 빙하 결정체가 생성되고, 엄청난 두께로 쌓이면서 빙하를 형성하게 된다. 이러한 과정을 통해 형성된 빙하는 엄청난 두께로 인해 위에서부터 강한 압력이 가해지고, 이로 인한 온도 상승현상과 중력 작용gravity이 함께 작용하여 빙하를 움직이게 만든다.

필수어휘

- harsh 혹독한, 심한 [syn] severe
- biome 생물 군계
- equator 적도
- elevation 고도 [syn] altitude
- precipitation 강수
- permafrost 영구동토층 (1년 내내 얼어있는 토양층)
- latitude 위도 cf. longitude 경도
- hinder 방해하다 [syn] impede, hamper
- shrub 관목
- indigenous 토착의 [syn] native

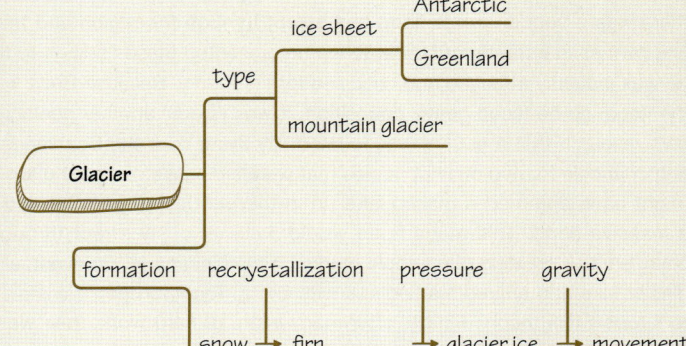

Mini Practice

Tundra

Tundra is a harsh, treeless biome with freezing winter temperatures and short cool summers. This ecosystem is primarily found in the Arctic, Antarctic, on high-elevation plateaus in Alpine regions, and occasionally near the equator if the elevation of the mountains is high enough. It is very windy and receives about 4-20 inches of precipitation a year, a similar amount to desert climates, which typically get less than 10 inches a year. There is often an underground layer called permafrost where the soil is permanently frozen. During the summer in the southern Arctic regions, the top surface of the soil melts and becomes marshy. This marshy land briefly supports animal life such as insects or migrating birds.

Tundra ranges begin at the tree line, beyond which trees cannot grow, and end at the latitudes where snow and ice permanently cover the landscape. [A ■] The bitter cold temperatures and lack of moisture hinder tree growth. [B ■] However, there are shrubs, grasses, mosses and lichens, which do manage to grow. [C ■] Most of them grow thick, waxy leaves to keep the moisture from evaporating. [D ■] Some grow very low to the ground to prevent frost damage, and others grow in clusters to withstand frigid temperatures. There are also animal species that find their home in the tundra. The caribou, arctic foxes and bears in the polar tundra; and the mountain goats and sheep that live in alpine tundra have adapted to this environment and found ways to thrive. Almost all of them are warm blooded animals and have insulating systems such as layers of fur and fat to keep their bodies warm. During the short breeding season, animals breed and raise their young quickly. Some migrate to avoid the severe cold and others stay in burrows to protect themselves against strong winds.

Nowadays, the Arctic tundra is threatened by global warming. The rise in temperatures has encouraged nonnative species of animals to migrate to the region where they compete with the indigenous animals for food. In addition, melting of the permafrost and migration of new animals have introduced nonnative plants, which are crowding out native plant species.

1. Look at the four squares [■] that indicate where the following sentence could be added to the sentence.

   These plants developed adaptation systems that help them endure this harsh climate.

   Where would the sentence best fit?

2. The word threatened in paragraph 3 is closest in meaning to
   - Ⓐ shunned
   - Ⓑ menaced
   - Ⓒ transformed
   - Ⓓ triggered

Answers p. 71

Ecology

★★

104

Competitive Exclusion Principle - Gause's law
경쟁배타원리 - 가우스이론

생물들이 다투어야 하는 경쟁에는 적어도 두 종류가 있다. 종 내에서 여러 개체들은 먹이, 자원, 공간, 그리고 짝짓기를 두고 경쟁한다. 이러한 종 내 경쟁의 효과는 직선적으로 나타난다. 1930년대 러시아 생태학자 가우스G.E. Gause는 배양액에서 자라는 두 종의 짚신벌레 개체군paramecium을 가지고 실험을 하였다. 두 종의 짚신벌레를 따로 키웠을 때, 각 종의 개체군은 예상대로 S 모양 개체군 생장 곡선을 보였다. 같이 키웠을 때 처음에는 두 종 모두가 S 모양으로 생장하다가 시간이 지나자 한 종은 생존하고 다른 종은 소멸했다. 이후 30년 동안 유사한 실험을 실행한 결과 여러 생물군에서 동일한 결과가 나타났다. 이 결과에 기초하여 1960년에 생태학자 하딘Garret Hardin은 "제한된 자원을 공동으로 이용하는 두 종은 공존할 수 없다"는 경쟁배타의 원리Competitive Exclusion Principle를 제안하였다.

그러나 실험실 밖에서는 이러한 경쟁배타의 원리가 적용되기는 힘들다는 것이 밝혀졌다. 1950년대 맥아더Robert MacArthur는 미국 북동부, 그리고 캐나다 남동부 침엽수림에 사는 울새warblers를 연구하고 있었다. 그가 보기에 5 종이 동일한 나무에서 살고 있었는데 자세한 관찰 결과 종 간의 경쟁은 최소였다. 일부 중복되기는 하였으나 같은 나무 안에서 자기가 좋아하는 구역이 구분되어 있었다. 이 경우 심한 경쟁이 종의 배제를 초래하지 않은 것이다. 그 대신 자원이 종들 사이에 분배되었다. 여러 종류의 생물에 대한 많은 연구는 자원의 분배resource partitioning에 의하여 경쟁이 최소화된다는 것을 입증하고 있다.

필수어휘

- Competitive Exclusion Principle 경쟁배타원리
- ecological factors 생태학적 요소
- paramecium 짚신벌레
- protozoa 원생동물
- warblers 휘파람새
- forage 먹이를 찾아 다니다
- microhabitats 미소서식지
- stimulant 자극제

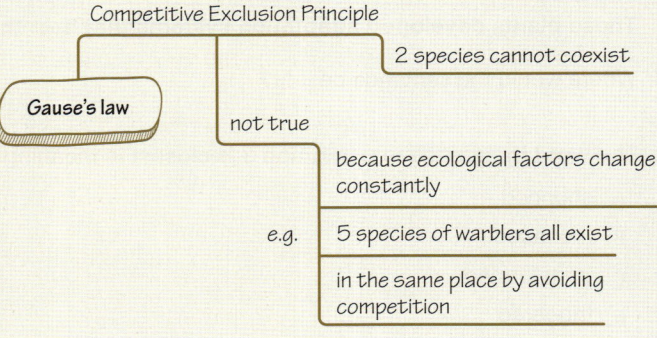

244

Mini Practice

Listen to part of a lecture in an ecology class. 🎧 Ch6_03

1. According to Gause's law, what can be expected to happen if two species are in a confined space with limited resources?
   - Ⓐ The species will divide the resources between them.
   - Ⓑ One species will become extinct.
   - Ⓒ The inferior species will be consumed by the superior species.
   - Ⓓ The inferior species survives through evolution.

2. What unique characteristic makes it possible for the warbler birds to coexist?
   - Ⓐ All of them are from the same species.
   - Ⓑ They forage in distinct and separate microhabitats.
   - Ⓒ Their flight patterns are significantly different.
   - Ⓓ They provide mutual assistance in foraging for resources.

Listening Script

Professor: In the animal kingdom, various species sometimes compete for the same resources and food. According to Gause's law, also known as the competitive exclusion principle, in situations where ecological factors are constant, two species cannot coexist with each other if they compete for the same resources. He asserted that if one species acquired even a slight advantage, then the other species would die out in the long term.

This principle came from his experiments with two species of paramecium, a type of protozoa. He provided the paramecium with food and water every day and eventually one species was able gain a competitive advantage over the other. After a few days, only one species survived. The problem with this principle is that ecological factors must be constant and controlled. However, in nature, habitat changes, predators, food availability, shelter, and other ecological factors are constantly shifting and changing. It would be rare to see this principle in action in a natural environment.

In nature, it seems that species find a way to coexist even if they depend on the same resources. One study in the Belize jungles examined the way that five species of warblers were able to live in a single ecological community. After carefully observing the warbler communities for several weeks, the researchers found that each species had a different foraging style that led to their ability to coexist. All species fed on the same crawling and flying insects, but one species would forage near the crown of the tree, several others below that, another around the trunk, and one species would forage near the ground. By foraging in different microhabitats, the warblers were able to avoid competition for resources.

Although it is rare to find an example of Gause's law in nature, it has been an important stimulant of research in the field of ecology. Not only was this an early attempt to mathematically model ecological phenomena, it encouraged scientists to experiment and observe nature to test the validity of the principle.

Answers p. 72

Environmental Studies

105
Environmental Problems
환경 문제들

환경 문제에 대한 내용은 기후 변화로 인한 해수 상승과 생태계에 끼치는 영향이 출제된다. 열섬효과와 사막화의 원인과 그 과정을 알아두도록 하자.

필수어휘

- vegetation 식물
- modification 변형, 변화
- metropolitan 대도시의
  - [syn] urban [ant] rural 시골의
- pavement 포장 도로
- shade 그림자, 그늘지게 하다
- contributor 원인(제공자)
- deforestation 산림 벌채
- drought 가뭄
- overgrazing 과도 방목
- deplete 감소하다, 고갈시키다
  - [syn] exhaust
- salinity 염분, 염도
- waste heat 여열

지구 온난화global warming는 온실효과greenhouse effect의 주요 원인인 이산화탄소carbon dioxide의 양이 대기층에 지속적으로 증가한 결과 나타나는 현상으로, 19세기 후반 이래로 전 세계적인 기온 상승을 야기했다. 온난화의 원인은 정확하게 규명되지 않았지만 산업화와 더불어 많은 양의 화석 연료를 연소하고 산림forest을 목축과 농업을 위해 과도하게 개간한 결과, 대기 중에 탄소가 대량으로 축적되었고, 폐기물 관리waste management나 농업 생산 과정에서 메탄이나 아산화질소nitrous oxide 등이 배출되면서 지구 온난화 현상이 더욱 악화되었을 것으로 추정된다.

지구 온난화 결과는 지구 곳곳에서 나타나고 있다. 온도 상승으로 인해 극지방pole의 빙하glacier, 빙상ice sheet, 해빙sea ice까지 점점 녹아내리고 있다. 때문에 지난 세기 동안 해수면sea level은 급격히 상승하여 해안이 심각하게 침식되었다. 전 세계적으로 강수precipitation의 패턴 변화와 폭염, 가뭄, 허리케인, 사이클론과 같은 극심한 자연 현상이 빈번하게 발생하는 것 역시 지구 온난화의 또 다른 결과이다.

생물의 움직임에서도 온난화의 영향을 볼 수 있다. 한 조사에 따르면, 남극의 아델리 펭귄Adélie penguins의 수가 암수 32,000쌍에서 향후 30년 안에 11,000쌍으로 그 수가 감소할 것이라고 예측했고, 특정 동, 식물 종들은 추운 지역을 찾아 더 높은 위도latitude로 이동하고 있다. 더구나 온난화의 결과로 2050년에는 생물 수백만 종이 멸종되어 인간을 위협하는 결과를 초래할 것이라는 예측도 있다.

Urban Heat Islands & Desertification

Humans have been very successful, perhaps unintentionally, at altering their physical environments on the earth. Sometimes this can negatively affect the environment and the places where people live. Urban Heat Islands (UHI) and desertification are two examples of how the removal of green vegetation and the modification of human dwellings have harmed the environment.

The Urban Heat Island (UHI) is generally found in a large metropolitan area like Seoul or New York City, where the surface temperature of the city is significantly higher than the nearby rural areas. In general, the difference in temperature is greater during the night than during the day. The temperature disparity between the two regions comes from man-made modifications which trap or store heat. The type of materials used to build buildings and materials like tar, asphalt and concrete that are used for pavements and roofs are all major heat storage reservoirs. These all absorb solar heat, which is gradually released at night. Vegetations and trees provide valuable shade and thus, have a cooling effect. Rural areas that have larger amounts of earth and vegetation are therefore cooler, whereas a city that lacks vegetation and trees is more likely to become a UHI. The second contributor to the increased temperatures is waste heat. Cooling during the summer, heating in the winter, factories and transportation are burning off energy. The energy people burn off usually escapes in the form of heat and increases greenhouse gases. This leads to a temperature difference that is the greatest in winter and summer when energy consumption is at its highest.

Desertification is a process by which fertile regions are transformed into deserts by the loss of vegetation and topsoil due to deforestation, drought and harmful agricultural practices. Deforestation removes trees to produce timber that can be turned into wealth, but at the same time does away with the vegetation and trees that maintain the balance of life. Over-cultivation of cash crops and overgrazing by livestock can deplete water sources in the region. Also, harmful and irresponsible irrigation practices may further diminish available water and increase the salinity of the soil. Even gathering firewood for cooking and heating can exhaust vegetative resources. As the soil becomes exposed to the environment, it dries up and may be blown away by the wind or washed away by the rain. The removal of topsoil means nothing can grow and the region becomes inhospitable and eventually, a desert.

1. The word disparity in paragraph 2 is closest in meaning to

    A increase
    B expansion
    C diffusion
    D difference

2. The word harmful in paragraph 3 is closest in meaning to

    A robust
    B modest
    C detrimental
    D profitable

Answers p. 73

Ecology

106

Extinction
멸종

지구상의 생물들은 다른 생물이나 환경 등 비생물적 요소들과 상호 영향을 주고 받으며 살아가며, 이러한 생물, 비생물적 환경 요인들과의 균형이 종의 생존에 큰 영향을 미친다. 유전적 동종 교배, 번식 결핍, 개체 수 감소와 같이 종 내의 진화 차원의 변화 요인 뿐 아니라, 주변의 다른 생물이나 환경적 요소들이 급격하게 변화하며 나타나는 영향으로 인해 특정 종이 지구 상에서 완전히 사라진 현상을 멸종extinction이라고 한다. 다시 말해 멸종은 특정 생물 종의 마지막 개체가 죽어 지구상에 더 이상 자취를 찾을 수 없게 된 현상을 의미한다.

대량 멸종mass extinction은 많은 종류의 생물들이 급격한 환경변화에 의해 단기간 내에 지구상에서 사라져버린 현상을 지칭하며, 그 원인으로 기후나 해수면 변화, 화산 활동과 같은 지구 환경 변화와 소행성 등의 천체celestial bodies와의 충돌로 인한 외부 요인설 등이 지목되고 있다. 지구 역사상 자연 발생 대량 멸종 사건은 5차례 있었으며, 그 중 가장 최근 사건은 7천만 년 전에 발생하였으며 당시 공룡을 비롯한 75%의 생물 종이 멸종하였다.

최근에 사라진 생물 종의 멸종 원인 분석에 따르면, 생물 종의 멸종과 인류의 등장이 관련 있다고 한다. 홍적세Pleistocene Epoch 중기 말엽에 등장한 호모 사피엔스Sapiens 등장 이후 인간은 자신들의 필요에 따라 지구 자원을 과도하게 착취하였다. 인구의 급격한 성장은 생물들을 과다하게 착취하고 생물 개체 서식지를 파괴하는 등 생태계 균형 파괴의 주요 원인의 하나로 간주된다. 홍적세 후기 십만 년 동안 아프리카 대륙의 거대 포유 종의 약 40%, 신대륙New World과 호주에서는 70% 이상이 멸종되었다.

필수어휘

- sheer (양, 크기를 강조하여) 순전한
- game 사냥감
- epidemics 전염병

Extinctions of the New World

Shortly after the Pleistocene epoch, about ten thousand years ago, many mammal species including mammoths and mastodons vanished quite abruptly from the North and South America. At the same time as this mass extinction, human hunting and gathering societies such as the Clovis society were spreading through the same region. In combination with the rapid rate of extinction, which occurred over a geologically brief 2000-year period, the sheer number of species involved has led many researchers to theorize that human activity may have caused the extinctions.

But although some big game species that became extinct lived in human-populated areas, it is now widely thought that humans could not have been the sole cause of the extinctions. [A ■] Anthropologists examining Clovis hunting sites have only found bones from a handful of the extinct species, and as the vast majority of the species that died out were not game species that would have been hunted by humans, it seems unlikely that humans were a significant factor in the extinctions. [B ■] Further supporting the theory that humans were not solely responsible is the fact that the Clovis people simply had not developed the appropriate technology. [C ■] Lacking the ability to store food for significant periods of time, they relied principally on their hunting abilities, which allowed them to move from place to place as they exhausted resources in one region. [D ■]

Ruling out human hunting, it is hard to find an alternative key factor. The period following the Pleistocene epoch was a time of sweeping climate change, and clearly, this was of some significance. However, it is hard to point the finger solely at climate change because most of the mammals that went extinct had previously been able to adapt to survive even more severe climate changes in the past. Disease has been considered as another factor, perhaps crossing from Asia via the Bering land bridge, but usually such epidemics leave a few individuals who are resistant and can reestablish the species.

These post-Pleistocene extinctions are likely the result of complex interactions between human hunting and gathering activities and climate change. These interactions may have been very subtle, so further research is needed, in particular focusing on each species and its ecological requirements individually.

1. Look at the four squares [■] that indicate where the following sentence could be added to the sentence.

   As a result, it is unlikely they would have hunted all of these species to extinction.

   Where would the sentence best fit?

2. The word solely in paragraph 3 is closest in meaning to
   - (A) finally
   - (B) exclusively
   - (C) ultimately
   - (D) accurately

Paleontology

★ 107
Fossilization
화석화

화석화 과정과 화석을 통해 발견된 사실들을 기억하자.

화석fossil은 지질 시대의 식물과 동물의 잔해remnant나 흔적trace이 자연적인 보존 과정을 통해 남아 있는 과거의 '증거 자료'이다. 화석은 주로 퇴적암sedimentary rock에서 발견되고, 때로는 석탄, 빙하, 호박amber 등에서도 발견된다. 퇴적암에서 발견된 화석들은 고대 생태계의 모습을 그대로 담고 있기 때문에 화석에서 볼 수 있는 지질학적 암석의 특징과 생물학적 특징이 고대 생태계ecosystem뿐 아니라 그 당시의 기후, 지질topography, 환경 등의 다양한 정보를 제공해 줄 수 있다. 화석은 크게 체 화석body fossil과 흔적 화석trace fossil 두 종류로 나뉜다. 먼저 체 화석은 뼈, 조개shell, 꽃가루pollen grain와 같이 생물체의 광물화된 조직이 직접 남아 있는 형태이고, 흔적 화석은 벌레가 남겨놓은 구멍이나 동물의 발자국, 둥지nest, 도구 등의 생물체의 활동이 그대로 남아 있는 흔적을 의미한다. 형태학적으로morphologically 동일 종의 일련의 연속적인 화석을 통해 그 종의 계보lineage를 알 수 있고, 이러한 연속적인 모습은 종의 형태학적인 변화에 대한 정보를 제공하기도 한다. 게다가 개별적인 여러 화석들의 증거를 통해 특정 장소와 특정 시간에 발생했던 생태 군락의 전체 모습도 그려볼 수 있다.

화석은 오랜 시간 동안 사람들의 관심을 불러 일으켰으며, 17세기부터 고생물학paleontology을 통해 과학적으로 밝혀지기 시작했다. 이 때부터 지구의 46억 살의 나이와 다양한 생물 종의 발생과 멸종에 관련된 사실 또한 밝혀 지고 있다. 19세기 다윈의 종의 기원On the Origin of Species이 고생물학의 연구에 박차를 가하는 원동력이 되었고, 현대 고생물 학자들은 다양하고 발전된 과학적 기술을 통해 화석에 관한 조사를 면밀히 하고 있다.

필수어휘

- □ **exoskeleton** 외골격
- □ **conducive to** ~에 유리한
- □ **entomb** 매장하다
  - n entombment
- □ **scavenger** 죽은 동물을 먹는 동물
- □ **estuary** 강어귀 (강 하구)
- □ **decomposition** 분해
  - syn breakdown, decay
- □ **stratum** 층 syn layer pl strata
- □ **subject to** ~을 당할 수 있는

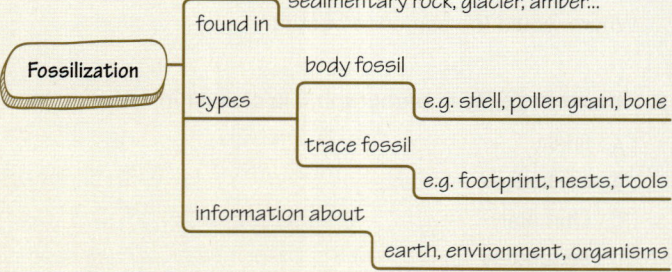

Fossilization
- found in — sedimentary rock, glacier, amber...
- types
  - body fossil — e.g. shell, pollen grain, bone
  - trace fossil — e.g. footprint, nests, tools
- information about — earth, environment, organisms

Fossilization

The term fossilization refers to a complex process that preserved the remains and traces of ancient animal and plant life within the earth. Fossils are usually found in sedimentary rock and on the earth's surface after being uncovered by the geological movement of the earth's crust. Geologists and paleontologists use a variety of research techniques like absolute dating and relative dating to determine the age of fossils. Through the analysis of fossils and the fossilization process, paleontologists have been able to learn about the lives of ancient animal and plant species and have learned about the type of physical environment that existed in ancient times.

There are several stages in the fossilization process. First, a plant or animal must have died in an environment conducive to fossilization. Organisms that have hard parts, like the bones and teeth of vertebrates or the seashells and exoskeletons of invertebrates, have increased chances of fossilization. Although soft tissues usually decompose, in very rare occasions soft parts of animals such as flesh and skin have been preserved in fossils.

Second, organisms must be rapidly entombed within sediments like sand, mud or silt in order to be better preserved and protected from physical elements. This favorable entombment protects the dead organisms from interruption by predators and scavengers. This also lowers the chance of bacteria prematurely causing the body to decompose. The sediments also reduce environmental effects like temperature fluctuations, which could destroy or damage the remains. Hence, the ideal locations for fossilization are the bottoms of riverbed, lakes, and estuaries, or the seabed. Deposited beneath water, they are less likely to be disturbed during the process. On the other hand, in relatively dry continental environments, organisms could be subject to erosion and are less likely to be preserved before decomposition.

Third, over millions of years, the organisms are buried deeper and deeper by a buildup of sedimentary strata. The weight and pressure ultimately turns the sediment into solid rocks. Then, groundwater rich in minerals can enter the remaining organism-shaped space, and the minerals in the groundwater fill the pores. As this process occurs, minerals in water gradually replace the original material in the skeleton and change the chemical composition.

1. The word fluctuation in paragraph 3 is closest in meaning to
    - (A) increment
    - (B) variation
    - (C) extent
    - (D) fragmentation

2. According the passage, which one is NOT true?
    - (A) Some environmental effects are not favorable for fossilization.
    - (B) Soft portions of the body are less likely to become fossilized than hard parts.
    - (C) The best place for the fossil is on land.
    - (D) Absolute dating is used by geologists to date fossils.

Answers p. 74

Geology

★★★
108

Geothermal energy
지열에너지

지열은 지구의 내부에서 외부로 나오는 열을 말한다. 이러한 지열은 수증기water vapor, 온수hot water 및 화산 분출volcanic eruption 등에 의해서 지표로 유출된다. 지열은 지구의 모든 표면에서 방출되지만 그 양은 지역에 따라 크게 다르다. 이 에너지는 지구 자체가 가지고 있는 에너지이므로 굴착하는 깊이에 따라 잠재력이 무한하다고 할 수 있다. 현재 지열 에너지는 온천hot spring 등의 관광 자원이나 난방의 열원 등으로 직접 이용되는 경우가 많다.

지열에너지는 잠재력이 무한하고unlimited, 깨끗하고clean, 발전비용이 저렴하다는inexpensive 등 다양한 이점을 지니고 있다. 또한 날씨의 영향을 받지 않는 점과 폐기물이 없다는 점도 큰 장점이다.

하지만 고열을 끌어 모으기에 적합한 지역이 많지 않아 여러 곳에서 에너지를 얻을 수 없다는 단점이 있는데 때문에 화산이 없는 우리나라의 경우 지열 에너지를 얻는데 어려움이 따르기도 한다. 세계적으로 지열에너지 발전 용량이 많은 나라는 미국, 필리핀, 인도네시아, 멕시코, 이탈리아가 있으며, 나라 전체 에너지 생산율 중에 지열에너지가 차지하는 비율이 가장 높은 나라는 아이슬란드이다.

필수어휘
- geothermal energy 지열에너지
- thermal 열의
- earth's crust 지각
- molten rock 용암
- geysers 간헐천
- fissure 길게 갈라진 틈
- steam vents 증기배출구
- hydrothermal power 열수발전소
- determinant 결정요인

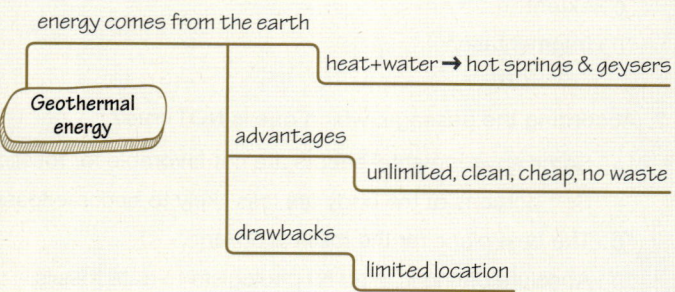

Mini Practice

Listen to part of a lecture in a geography class. 🎧 Ch6_04

1. According to the professor, what is the most problematic aspect of using geothermal energy?
   - Ⓐ Access to suitable locations is limited by the geography.
   - Ⓑ Costs related to installation and maintenance are very high.
   - Ⓒ It isn't yet possible to drill deep enough into the earth.
   - Ⓓ The amount of geothermal energy available is limited.

2. Why is geothermal energy superior to other renewable sources like wind and solar?
   - Ⓐ It generates consistent output.
   - Ⓑ It generates more energy per hour.
   - Ⓒ It is far less expensive than wind or solar energy.
   - Ⓓ Less energy is wasted compared to other sources.

Listening Script

Professor: Geothermal energy is a form of thermal energy or heat energy that comes from the earth. This heat comes from the massive molten rock ocean that sits at the center of the earth. When the earth's crust is thin, the heat can escape and when it meets with water it forms hot springs and geysers. In the ocean, the earth's crust is thinner and there may be large cracks or fissures at the bottom of the ocean. When the molten rock escapes from these fissures and meets the water, it creates massive steam vents in the ocean. When these vents are near the shore or on land, some people use them to make electricity. They build hydrothermal power plants on these vents to take advantage of the natural steam. This steam is collected and then used to turn turbines, which produces electricity. The unlimited supply of steam makes this a very efficient source of energy. However, the biggest drawback is limited land based locations and difficulty in utilizing ocean steam vents that are not close to the shoreline. Local geology is a crucial determinant in the use of geothermal energy.

Some people have found a way to drill into the earth and create an artificial steam vent. The further they drill into the earth the hotter it gets. Once they have drilled deep enough into the earth's crust they flood the well and this creates fractures at the bottom. This creates an artificial hydrothermal vent and they use the hot water or steam from this vent to turn turbines like natural hydrothermal plants. What's great about this system is that there is no waste and the power plant can recycle the water and use it again. This type of energy production is called enhanced geothermal heating system. As this system improves more and more people may try to capture geothermal energy to power our future.

Answers p. 74

Ecology

109

Global warming and ocean acidification
지구온난화와 바다산성화

최근 지구 온난화의 원인인 대기 중 이산화탄소의 방출량 증가로 인해 해양의 산성화acidification가 지난 수 십만 년 중 가장 빠르게 진행되고 있다고 보고된다. 바다의 화학물질 조성이 전례 없이 빠른 속도로 변화되고 있는 가장 큰 이유는 대기 중 이산화탄소의 약 3분의 1에 해당하는 양을 바다가 흡수하기 때문이다. 이것은 대기 중 온실가스의 양을 줄여주는 역할을 하기도 하지만 바다 속의 화학성분 chemical composition 변화와 생물에게는 악영향을 일으키는 문제점을 발생하게 된다. 이산화탄소가 바다에 녹아 들게 되면 부식corrosion이 발생하고 바닷물과 반응하여 탄산carbonic acid이 만들어지는데 이때 수소이온hydrogen ion이 증가되어 ph가 점점 낮아지게 되는 것이다.

이러한 해수 농도의 변화는 인간에게는 미비해 보이지만 실제로 해양생물들이 받아들이는 충격은 엄청나다. 바다의 산성화가 진행되면 물고기 유생의 후각기능이 떨어져 물고기가 포식자predator의 냄새를 구별할 수 없을 뿐 아니라 스스로 포식자에게 다가가는 위험한 행동을 하게 되기도 한다. 또한 탄산염carbonate으로 인해 패류껍질의 경도가 낮아지거나 생성자체를 어렵게 하며 산호초coral reefs들을 잠식시켜 어류의 먹잇감을 없애고 물고기들이 자신의 집을 찾는 능력을 방해한다. 바다의 산성화는 물고기의 호흡, 바다 생물 유체의 성장, 그리고 영양분과 독소를 흡수하는 바다의 기능에 영향을 주게 될 것이며, 어류, 조개 등 인간생활에 중요한 먹이사슬에도 직접적 영향을 주게 될 것이다.

필수어휘

- carbon dioxide 이산화탄소
- phytoplankton 식물성 플랑크톤
- algae 해조류
- molecular bonds 분자결합
- acidification 산성화
- carbonic acid 탄산
- calcium carbonate 탄산칼슘
- crustaceans 갑각류
- chalky 백악질의
- residue 잔여물
- depleted 고갈된
- dismiss 무시하다

Listening

Mini Practice

Listen to part of a lecture in an oceanography class. 🎧 Ch6_05

1. What is the result of carbonic acid reacting with calcium carbonate?

    Ⓐ Ocean water acidity increases.
    Ⓑ The substance produced from the reaction is used by crustaceans creating their shells.
    Ⓒ The reaction produces carbon dioxide which is absorbed by the water.
    Ⓓ Land temperatures are reduced.

2. Why are plankton and sea snails mentioned?

    Ⓐ If they disappear, it would catalyze catastrophic deterioration of the particular ecosystem.
    Ⓑ They have been able to adapt to increasingly acidic water by making harder coverings.
    Ⓒ Larger marine animals depend upon them as a primary food source.
    Ⓓ They are not affected very much by global warming.

Listening Script

Professor: Last week we discussed various ways that humans produce carbon dioxide (CO_2) and its contribution to global warming. Today we will continue that discussion by looking specifically at how human produced carbon dioxide has negatively affected the ocean. The ocean is a great absorber of carbon dioxide. Plants like phytoplankton and algae absorb most of the CO_2 and then release oxygen into the air. Because the ocean absorbs the majority of CO_2, it reduces the impact that pollution has on the air we breathe. Because of water's tight molecular bonds it absorbs a lot of energy and stabilizes the temperatures that we feel on land. In fact, the ocean has been a great help in balancing out our world ecosystem.

However, as CO_2 levels increase there is a greater risk of ocean acidification. When the ocean absorbs carbon dioxide it reacts with the water, which creates carbonic acid. This acid then reacts with naturally existing calcium carbonate and this creates a chalky white residue. This residue is important for many crustaceans because it helps them build their shells. Normally this acid production process is a good thing but the danger is that there is too much carbonic acid being produced. Currently this increase in acid does not affect the majority of ocean life but we are beginning to see it impact phytoplankton, plankton, and small animals like sea snails. These small life forms are crucial to the entire ocean ecosystem. If the phytoplankton populations are depleted then we lose our number one producer of oxygen. When the plankton and small animals die other larger fish and animal species that depend on them for food will begin to disappear. The die off of these larger species would spell disaster for many of the world's economies and the negative chain reaction would result in almost cataclysmic destruction of the world as we know it. I know it is easy to dismiss a little acidity and think it is not important. However, little changes keep building up and if left unchecked, the consequences for the human species could be disastrous.

Answers p. 75

Geology

110

Groundwater
지하수

지하수의 구성과 오갈랄라 대수층이 출제되는데 지하수와 관련된 어휘들은 다소 생소하다. 관련 어휘부터 꼼꼼히 체크하자.

필수어휘

- **Pliocene** 선신세의 (500만–1700만년 전)
- **unconsolidated** 굳지 않은, 결합되지 않은
- **aquifer** 대수층
- **irrigation** 관개
- **inexhaustible** 고갈되지 않는, 무궁무진한
- **drought** 가뭄
- **replenish** 다시 채워 넣다
- **unprecedented** 전례 없는
- **deplete** 감소하다, 고갈하다
- **pollutant** 오염물질
- **exploit** 이용하다, 활용하다

지하수groundwater는 유동물질이 지표 아래 토양의 빈 공간인 공극pore space과 암석의 균열fracture에 유입infiltration되어 형성된 물이다. 이 물은 지구 전체 물의 0.6%를 차지하고 있으며, 지표에 내린 강수precipitation가 계곡이나 호수로 흘러 바다로 가는 경우도 있고 일부는 지면 위를 흐르다가runoff 흡수되어 지하수를 형성하기도 한다.

암석의 공극 크기에 따라 지하수가 내려가는 속도velocity가 다양해진다. 지하로 내려간 물이 일정 영역의 모든 구멍들을 채우게 되면 그 지역을 포화대saturated zone라고 부르고, 이 포화대 위의 지하수면water table을 경계로 그 아래에는 불포화대unsaturated zone가 위치한다. 공극률porosity은 암석, 퇴적층 또는 토양의 전체 부피에서 구멍opening과 빈 공간void이 차지하고 있는 비율을 의미하며, 물을 얼마나 함유할 수 있는지 알 수 있는 지표이기도 하다. 투과성permeability은 구멍이나 균열에 물이 통과할 수 있는 능력을 말한다. 사암sandstone의 경우 구멍이 많고 투과성도 좋다. 반면 화강암granite은 투과성이 좋지 않다. 퇴적암의 일종인 셰일shale의 경우는 공극률은 높으나 투과성은 좋지 않다.

대수층aquifer은 물을 보유하고 담아 놓을 수 있는 공극의 지층을 말하며, 지하수로 포화된 투과성이 좋은 영역이다. 이 곳은 우물well이나 샘spring 등 지표에 물을 공급하며, 경제적 가치가 큰 지역이다. 이 지역은 물의 움직임이 자유로우며 균열이 많은highly fractured 바위층이나 사암, 역암conglomerate 등이 대수층을 이루고 있는 암석들이다. 지하수가 주변의 마그마에 의해서 고온으로 상승된 물을 온천hot spring이라고 부르고, 그 뜨거운 물이 지하의 압력을 받아 일정 간격을 두고 분출하는erupt 온천을 간헐천geyser이라 부른다.

The Ogallala Aquifer

The Ogallala aquifer is the largest groundwater reserve in America and is located under the Great Plains. It covers about 450,000 square kilometers and lies beneath eight states including South Dakota, Nebraska and Texas. The Ogallala Aquifer was formed near the beginning of the Pliocene era by sediment from streams that flowed eastward from the Rocky Mountains. It consists of unconsolidated, poorly sorted clay, silt, sand and gravel with groundwater filling the spaces.

Beginning in the early 1900s, this aquifer has long been a major source of water in the region for agricultural, industrial, and residential development. Due to large-scale irrigation and farming, this region became the most agriculturally productive area in the world. Eventually, this would encourage many immigrants to settle down and water consumption to sharply increase in the area. Settlers believed that the water supply that lay in the aquifer was inexhaustible, but this valuable source of water is now in danger of disappearing.

The aquifer is primarily replenished by precipitation, including rain and snow. However, severe cycles of drought in the 1930s and 50s reduced the water replenishment rate in the aquifer. In addition, because of the semiarid climate in the Great Plains, the annual evaporation rate exceeds that of the average annual rainfall each year. Another danger is the unprecedented expansion of commercial farming industries. According to research, it is estimated that the yearly rate of groundwater withdrawals for agricultural use multiplied five times between 1949 and 1974. Annually, the aquifer is capable of recharging itself by about half an inch, but farmers were withdrawing four to six feet a year and at the current rate, the aquifer will be 70 percent depleted by 2060. It is possible that there will be no accessible groundwater in the area in the next 50 to 100 years. This has been further complicated by the contamination of the aquifer by pesticides, herbicides, and other industrial pollutants.

Recent conservation efforts for the Ogallala Aquifer seek to limit contamination and depletion of the aquifer. Farmers have strived to reduce their consumption of water and utilize new irrigation technology that increases efficiency and reduces water waste.

1. The word exceeds in paragraph 3 is closest in meaning to
    A) modifies
    B) magnifies
    C) trespasses
    D) surpasses

2. What can be inferred from the passage?
    A) The problem of Ogallala Aquifer will be solved in the near future.
    B) Prior to the twentieth century, Ogallala aquifer was not a main source of water.
    C) Without farming, settlers there have never experienced problems.
    D) Conservation efforts could deal with all of the predicaments.

Answers p. 76

Environmental Studies

★★★
111

Little Ice Age
소빙기

기후변화는 토플시험에서 가장 뜨거운 주제 중 하나이다. 지구 온난화에 대한 우려가 점점 높아지는 가운데 오히려 지구는 또 다른 빙하기를 맞을 수도 있다는 이 가설의 근거가 무엇인지 살펴보도록 하자!

빙하기는 수 만년 전 선사시대prehistoric era에 있었던 단순한 기후현상이 아니라 인류역사와 문명에 지대한 영향을 끼쳐온 기후현상 weather phenomenon임이 여러 증거를 통해 밝혀졌다. 지구상에서 추운 계절과 더운 계절이 반복되듯, 지구도 추위와 더위를 오고 간다. 1450년부터 1850년까지 약 400년간 지구는 매우 추웠으며 이 시기는 1억~3억 년 혹은 몇 천만 년 동안 추위가 계속되는 빙기(氷期)보다 훨씬 짧아서 소빙기Little Ice Age라고 부른다. 소빙기였던 17세기의 추위는 1만 년 전 인류가 농경agriculture을 처음 시작한 이래 가장 혹독했으며 여름에도 서늘하거나 심지어 눈이 내렸고, 아열대의 양쯔강과 런던의 템스강이 얼어붙기까지 했다. 또한 흉작과 기근이 속출하여 전세계적인 대기근great famine이 시작되었고 이는 국가지배체제의 붕괴를 일으키는 봉기와 반란으로 이어졌다. 유럽 국가는 국민의 불만을 잠재우기 위해 강력한 군사력으로 사회적 공포를 조장하거나 대대적인 탄압crackdown을 자행했으며 식민지 쟁탈전에 몰입함으로써 국민의 불만을 다른 곳으로 돌렸다. 또한 유럽국가들은 정통 종교를 강화하고 다른 종파를 이단으로 규정하여 순종을 강요하면서 이 시기에 많은 사람이 이단과 마녀로 몰리면서 처형되었다. 이러한 역사적 사료들은 기후현상이 삶의 방식뿐 아니라 문화, 종교, 예술, 정치 등 모든 분야와 밀접한 관계를 맺을 수 있음 보여준다.

필수어휘
- climatic 기후의
- social disruption 사회적 붕괴
- fierce 맹렬한
- erratic 불규칙한
- northern hemisphere 북반구
- unequaled 무적의
- famine 기근
- plummet 곤두박질치다
- profound 심각한
- dire 대단히 심각한
- malnutrition 영양결핍
- Bubonic Plague 림프절 페스트
- blistering 지독히 더운
- hailstorm 우박을 동반한 폭풍
- ensued 뒤따랐다

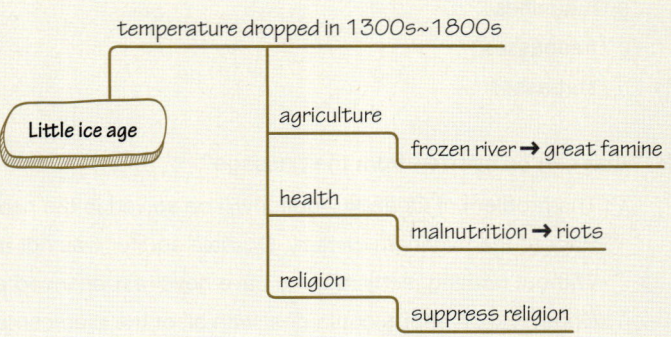

Mini Practice

Listen to part of a lecture in a climatology class. 🎧 Ch6_06

1. Why is New York Harbor mentioned?
   - Ⓐ As an example of the impact of the LIA's on human health
   - Ⓑ As an example of the effects the LIA's had on agricultural production
   - Ⓒ As an example of the impact the LIA's had on the global climate
   - Ⓓ As an example of how the LIA's affected global politics

2. What can be inferred about the people in France in 1788 who were rioting?
   - Ⓐ They didn't have enough food.
   - Ⓑ They suffered from the Bubonic Plague.
   - Ⓒ They approved of Queen Marie Antoinette.
   - Ⓓ They didn't have enough warm clothing.

Listening Script

Professor: Today I want to talk about a period of severe climatic and social disruption, the Little Ice Age or LIA, which brought fierce winters and erratic weather to many parts of the northern hemisphere, especially Northern Europe. There's a lot of disagreement among scientists about exactly when the LIA began and ended, but documented reports of abnormal weather date from the early 1300s through the middle of the 1800s, and it significantly influenced agriculture, health, and of course through that the economy and politics, and it gave rise to weather phenomena that have been unequaled since. For example, in 1780 the whole of New York harbor froze over, allowing people to walk across the ice from Staten Island to Manhattan! And in London, the Thames River froze twice!

Changes in the weather leading to LIA began somewhere around 1250, as icepacks in the North Atlantic and glaciers in Greenland started to spread south. By 1300, summers in Northern Europe were getting colder, and starting in 1315 there were three years of continuous rain that led to a famine throughout Europe. With glaciers growing worldwide, by 1650 the global temperature plummeted to a record low. At that time, farmers didn't have the seeds available today that can endure harsher weather, so the low temperatures had a profound impact. In France, one failed harvest in 1693 led to a famine that killed millions. Although that was the second famine attributed to the LIA, and agricultural and economic consequences were dire, the worst impact was on human health. General malnutrition left people with weakened immune systems, vulnerable to a wide range of diseases, including influenza, malaria, and famously, the Bubonic Plague, which killed around 25 million Europeans. In England, the death rate exceeded the birth rate for most of the 1550s. There's a famous quote I'm sure you've heard, which maybe attributable to the LIA. In 1788 in North France, there was a particularly harsh winter followed by a blistering summer and a hailstorm in July, withering the grain and causing a lack of bread. Riots ensued the following year, during which Queen Marie Antoinette allegedly said, "Let them eat cake!" words which helped spark off the French Revolution.

Answers p. 76

Geology

112
Magma
마그마

마그마는 지구 깊숙한 곳에서 발견되는 고온의 용융 암석molten rock과 가스의 혼합체이다. 마그마의 온도는 대부분의 경우 대략 700-1300°C이고, 카보나타이트carbonatite 마그마의 경우 600°C로 상대적으로 온도가 낮다. 마그마는 주로 커다란 지하 웅덩이인 마그마 챔버magma chamber에 모여 있는데, 그 안에 있는 용융 암석은 오랜 기간 동안 엄청난 압력을 받다가 이 압력이 챔버 주변의 암석에 균열을 만들고 그 균열 사이로 마그마가 빠져 나가는 화산 폭발로 인해 챔버 위에 화산이 생겨나게 된다. 마그마 챔버를 발견하기는 쉽지 않지만, 발견되는 대부분의 챔버의 깊이는 주로 지표면으로부터 1-10km 아래에 존재한다. 마그마가 형성되는 환경은 섭입대subduction zone(오래된 대양저ocean floor가 지각 아래로 밀려들어가는 해구trench 지역), 대륙 단층 지역continental rift zone 등이 있다.

마그마는 용암lava의 형태로 화산으로부터 분출하는 경우도 있고 지표 아래에서 냉각되어 응고되기도 한다. 마그마로부터 형성된 암석은 화성암igneous rocks으로 분류되고, 화강암granite과 현무암basalt 등이 가장 잘 알려져 있다. 화강암의 경우 분출 후 서서히 냉각되면서 입자가 굵은 형태를 띠며, 반대로 현무암의 경우 용암 분출 후 급격히 냉각되어 입자가 작은 광물질 구조를 지녔다. 그리고 마그마의 온도에 따라 생성되는 광물이 달라지는데, 감람석olivine은 고온에서 다른 물질과 결합 없이 생성된 형태이고 석영quartz은 다른 성분들과 결합되면서 복잡한 구조를 이루는 암석이다.

필수어휘
- behave 움직이다, 반응하다
- be subjected to ~을 당하다
- silicate 규산염
- tetrahedron 사면체
  - pl tetrahedra
- granitic magma 화강암질 마그마
- basaltic magma 현무암질 마그마
- viscous 점성이 있는, 끈적거리는
- solidify 굳어 지다
- solidification 응결

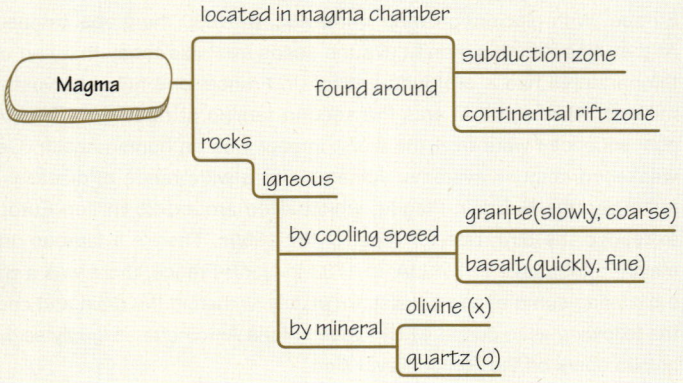

Properties of Magma

Why do certain kinds of magma behave in one way while other kinds of magma behave entirely differently? One must first understand the composition of magma and what happens to it as it forms in order to understand its behavior. There are two main types of magma in the world: basaltic magma, which contains 50 percent silicate and one or two percent water, and granitic magma, which contains 70 percent silicate and about 10 percent water. The difference in magma composition is the reason why different magmas behave differently in the same environment. This is because the proportion of silicate and water contained within the magma largely determines the manner in which the magma will behave.

The silicate in magma forms tetrahedral bonds that join to form chains or frameworks within the magma. With a higher amount of silicate, the chains become longer. Because granitic magma has a high amount of silicate, the chains are very long and tend to tangle with each other, which limit movement. Basaltic magma has lower amounts of silicate, which means it forms shorter chains, making it less viscous so it behaves more like a liquid. This allows basaltic magma to flow and move about more freely.

The water content in magma is another important component affecting its behavior. Water greatly lowers the point at which magma will solidify. In very dry granitic magma, the solidification point will be around 700°C. However, with granitic magma composed of 10% water, it will still remain in a liquid form at a much lower temperature—600°C. Due to the immense pressures deeper in the earth, the water has nowhere to escape, but as the magma rises, the pressure decreases and the water will escape in the form of steam, giving the magma more than enough time to solidify before reaching the surface of the earth. Therefore, granitic magma typically solidifies about 5-20 kilometers below the earth's surface. With basaltic magma, as it contains almost no water, any water that does escape as steam has almost no effect on the way that the magma behaves. Therefore, most basaltic magma erupts from the earth violently, which can be seen in the many basalt volcanoes that are common around the globe.

1. The word viscous in paragraph 2 is closest in meaning to
    - (A) thick
    - (B) widespread
    - (C) various
    - (D) moist

2. The word it in paragraph 3 refers to
    - (A) surface
    - (B) steam
    - (C) pressure
    - (D) magma

Answers p. 77

Meteorology

★★
113

Northern Lights
북극광 - 오로라

지구상에서 가장 신비하고 아름다운 기상현상 중 하나라 여겨지는 오로라aurora는 라틴어로 '동틀녘, 일출'이라는 뜻으로 극광the polar lights 또는 북반구에서는 노던 라이트northern lights라 불린다.

오로라는 다양한 색의 빛들이 아름다운 형태를 취하며 밤하늘을 신비롭게 수놓는 태양의 작품이며 극지방에서 볼 수 있지만 남극the South pole보다는 북극the North pole에서 훨씬 더 많이 관측된다. 오로라의 원리를 이해하려면 태양의 성질을 간단하게 알아야 한다. 태양에는 자기장magnetic field이 존재하는데 이 자기장들은 강력하면서도 불안정하여 쉽게 폭발하고 여러 형태로 에너지를 방출한다. 자기장 방출의 한 종류가 바로 플레어flare 인데 이 방출로 이온화 된 가스, 즉 플라즈마plasma를 우주 공간으로 방출한다. 이때 태양에서 방출된 플라즈마의 일부가 지구 자기장에 이끌려 대기로 진입하면서 공기 분자와 반응하여 빛을 내는 현상이 바로 오로라다. 하늘은 늘 태양풍solar wind에 노출되어 있지만 지구를 둘러싸고 있는 자기장으로 인해 대부분은 자기권 밖으로 흩어진다. 그러나 지구의 양 극지방은 자기력이 가장 강력하므로 이곳에 태양풍 입자들이 모이는 현상이 발생하기도 한다. 이 입자들과 대기 속의 공기 분자air morecule가 충돌하면서 오로라가 생성되는 것이다. 이러한 오로라는 거대한 커튼 모양으로 하늘을 가로질러 출렁이는 것처럼 보일 때가 있다. 주로 위도 65~70° 사이, 지표로부터 65~100km 사이에서 많이 나타난다. 오로라는 녹색 혹은 황록색이 가장 많이 보이지만 때때로 적색, 황색, 청색, 보라색을 띠기도 한다.

필수어휘

- □ unrelenting 끊임없는, 수그러들 줄 모르는
- □ ejected 방출된
- □ solar flare 태양폭발
- □ deflected (무엇에 맞은 후) 방향이 바꿔진
- □ radiation 방사선, 복사
- □ superheated 과열된

Mini Practice

Listen to part of a lecture in a meteorology class. Ch6_07

1. What makes the aurora visible only from extreme latitudes?
   - Ⓐ Solar flare material is drawn magnetically towards the Earth's poles.
   - Ⓑ There is much less light pollution near the North and South poles, compared to more populated areas.
   - Ⓒ Interference that would normally impede the path of charged solar particles is lessened at the extreme latitudes.
   - Ⓓ The Earth's gravity draws charged particles to pass at very high speeds.

2. In the lecture, what is implied about the Earth's magnetic field?
   - Ⓐ Without the field, the Earth would be exposed to possibly very hazardous effects from solar flares.
   - Ⓑ The field serves as a barrier, separating the atmosphere from the surface.
   - Ⓒ By creating magnetic zones, electrical equipment on Earth can be isolated and kept safe from solar radiation.
   - Ⓓ Few people understand how much the earth is protected by such a fragile magnetic field.

Listening Script

Professor: How many of you have witnessed the northern lights? These auroras, most famously known as the aurora borealis, produce amazing and beautiful displays of light. These northern lights are only visible in the extreme northern regions of the Earth in places like Alaska, northern Russia, Canada, Greenland, and northern Scandinavia. Many people make trips to these regions to see the amazing phenomena. So what causes the aurora? It starts with a collision of solar winds and magnetically charged particles with the high altitude thermosphere. Solar winds are superheated plasma particles composed of electrons and protons that are released from the Sun. These particles fly out at tremendous speeds throughout the galaxy and some of them collide with the Earth. Thankfully, these particles are mostly deflected away from the Earth by our magnetic field. If we were exposed directly to these particles it would be difficult to survive.

Some of these particles from the solar wind are trapped by the magnetic field and carried away to the poles. The trapped particles are drawn into the uppermost layers of the atmosphere known as the thermosphere. When magnetospheric levels and solar wind activity are high there is a greater chance of an aurora occurring. The emissions of photons, the ionization of nitrogen atoms and the change in electrical states of oxygen and nitrogen atoms caused by a collision with the solar winds and magnetic particles create the colorful display. Different collisions, ionizations, and changes in electrical states of nitrogen and oxygen atoms create the five major colors witnessed in the auroras. Red colors usually appear at high altitudes and are caused by excited oxygen atoms. Green happens at lower altitudes where collisions are more frequent. Blue happens in the lowest altitudes where oxygen is not common and nitrogen is more plentiful. A mixture of these colors produces yellows and pinks. Auroras usually appear as a diffuse glow or like curtains that are constantly shifting. The parallel rays in the curtains seem to suggest that Earth's magnetic field shapes the display that we see.

Answers p. 78

Environmental Studies

★★ 114
Ocean energy
해양 에너지

해양 에너지원의 형태는 여러 가지이다. 각 형태들의 장단점과 특히 OTEC에 포인트를 두고 공부하자.

인간의 에너지 소비로 화석 연료fossil fuel는 빠르게 고갈되고 있다. 이런 상황에서 에너지원을 확보하고 자급력을 키우기 위해 여러 대체 에너지원alternative energy에 대한 연구와 조사가 전 세계적으로 진행되고 있다. 그 중 재생 가능한renewable 청정에너지clean energy인 해양 에너지는 부수적으로 화석 원료가 거의 필요하지 않기 때문에, 지구 온난화global warming와 같은 환경오염을 유발하는 온실 가스greenhouse gas의 배출 감소에 기여할 수 있다. 이러한 장점이 있기 때문에 해양 에너지에 관심을 가지는 나라들이 많이 지고 있다.

조력 발전 tidal power generation
주변 천체들의 인력 작용gravity으로 주기적으로 발생하는 밀물high tide과 썰물low tide의 차를 활용한 발전으로 에너지원인 조력 에너지tidal energy는 방조제tidal embankment를 쌓아 바닷물을 가두었다가 썰물 때 흘려 보내는 힘으로 터빈을 돌려 전기를 발생시킨다.

조류 발전 tidal current power generation
조수tide현상으로 인한 바닷물의 수평적 운동인 조류는 지속적인 일반 해류ocean current와는 구분된다. 조류는 특정 시간에만 발생하는 현상으로, 조류가 센 곳에 터빈을 설치해 전기를 생산할 수 있다.

파력 발전 wave power generation
파도wave의 힘을 이용하는 파력 발전은 파도의 운동에너지kinetic energy를 전기 에너지의 형태로 바꾸는 방법이다.

해양 온도 차 발전 Ocean Thermal Energy Conversion
해양 표층의 온수와 심층의 냉수 온도 차로 에너지를 만들 수 있는 해양 온도 차 발전(OTEC)은 암모니아ammonia등의 냉각제refrigerant를 활용하여 터빈을 가동시켜 전기를 만들어 내는데, 이 때 폐쇄 사이클closed-cycle과 개방 사이클open-cycle의 두 가지 방식을 사용한다.

필수어휘
- exhaust 고갈하다
- geothermal 지열의
- extract 추출하다
- hydropower 수력
- generator 발전기
- velocity 속도
- working fluid 작동 유체
- water culture 수경 재배
- refrigerant 냉각제
- hydroponics 수경재배

Ocean Energy

Because fossil fuels are a non-renewable, finite resource that will be exhausted in the future, we have to find alternative energy sources that can be continuously replenished and will never be used up. Besides well-known renewable energy sources such as wind, geothermal and solar energy, one emerging renewable energy source is the ocean, which carries a vast amount of energy in the form of waves, tides, and ocean thermal energy conversion (or OTEC), all of which are forms of hydroelectric power.

Waves are indirectly created by the interaction of wind with the surface of the sea. In order to extract wave energy, wave energy conversion devices must create a system of reacting forces at a particular depth range, in which two or more bodies of devices move relative to each other while at least one body interacts with the waves. However, due to the high price of construction, these devices are generally built on small scales and cannot produce enough energy to be economically viable.

Tidal energy, driven by the gravitational pull of the Moon and Sun combined with the Earth's rotation, is typically converts hydropower into electricity by forcing water through turbines, activating a generator. While coming into shore, water from high tides can be trapped in reservoirs behind dams, and at low tide, the water behind the dam can be discharged to generate power. In the past, tidal power had disadvantages, such as high cost of construction, limited sites with high tidal ranges or flow velocities, and environmental impact on the marine life. However, despite these drawbacks, today it has technologically developed and improved to become a practical energy source.

Electricity can also be extracted from the ocean in the form of thermal energy. The sun heats up the surface of the ocean a lot more than it does to the deep ocean water, creating a thermal difference that can be used to produce energy. There are two types of OTEC systems: closed-cycle and open-cycle. Closed-cycle systems employ the ocean's warm surface water to evaporate a working fluid such as ammonia, which has a low boiling point. The vapor expands, turning a turbine which turns a generator and produces electricity. [A ■] Open-cycle systems directly utilize the ocean water as the working fluid, producing steam that passes through a turbine generator. [B ■] OTEC plants almost never produce carbon dioxide or other polluting chemicals, and they supply the nutrient-rich deep ocean water for hydroponics. [C ■] In addition, the only ideally suitable location for OTEC technology is equatorial water because of the greater difference in water temperature. [D ■]

1. The word employ in paragraph 4 is closest in meaning to
   - (A) hire
   - (B) enhance
   - (C) use
   - (D) clear

2. Look at the four squares [■] that indicate where the following sentence could be added to the sentence.

   However, the problem is that manufacturing of long cold-water pipes in coastal waters is extremely costly and is harmful to marine life.

   Where would the sentence best fit?

   Answers p. 78

Geology

★★
115

Predicting volcanoes
화산 폭발을 예측하는 방법

화산은 지구 내부에 녹아 있는 마그마magma와 가스가 한데 모여 내부의 강한 압력에 의해 지각의 벌어진 틈fissure으로 분출erupt하여 형성된다. 화산 분출물은 기체, 액체, 고체 등의 여러 형태로 뿜어져 나오는데, 때로는 주변 생태계와 인간과 그들의 거주지까지 파괴시킬 만큼 위력이 강하기 때문에 폭발을 예측하는 것은 중요하다.

화산 폭발이 임박한 지역에서는 지진활동seismic activity, 지표면의 변형ground deformation, 가스 분출gas emission, 온도 변화thermal monitoring 등이 발생하기 때문에 이러한 현상을 복합적으로 관찰함으로써 폭발을 예측할 수 있다.

먼저 마그마가 지표면 가까이로 상승하는 움직임은 지진earthquake을 일으킨다. 이 지진은 움직임을 기록하는 기계인 지진계seismometer에 의해 감지되고 기록될 수 있는데 지구 내부 또는 표면을 따라 전파되는 지진파seismic wave는 먼저 도착하는 P-wave(primary wave)와 나중에 도착하는 S-wave(secondary wave)로 나뉜다.

또한 지표면이 변형되는 현상은 마그마가 지표 아래에서부터 상승하면서ascend 화산의 정상summit과 경사면에 변화를 유발하기 때문에, 폭발의 중요한 징후가 된다. 1980년에 발생한 미국 세인트 헬렌 산 St. Helen의 화산 폭발은 지표면 융기를 감지해서 폭발을 예측했던 좋은 사례이다.

또 다른 예측 수단은 아황산가스Sulfur dioxide gas 등의 가스 분출gas emission이다. 화산 폭발 전 높은 수치의 아황산가스가 측정되는데, 이는 지표 근처로 상승한 마그마로부터 나온 것으로 예측의 좋은 수단이 된다. 그 예로 1991년 필리핀의 피나투보 화산의 경우, 폭발 전 아황산가스 수치가 증가하였다.

마지막으로 뜨거운 마그마와 가스가 움직이면서 지표 부근의 암석 온도가 상승하는데 이때 발생한 열 감지thermal detection를 이용해 폭발의 가능성을 예측할 수도 있다.

필수어휘
- volcanologist 지진학자
- erupt 폭발하다
- impending 임박한 [syn] imminent
- geophysical 지구 물리학의
- precede 선행하다
- chamber 방
- conduit 도관, 통로
- deformation 변형
- slope 경사면, 기울기
- vent 구멍
- fumarole 분기공
- proximity 근접

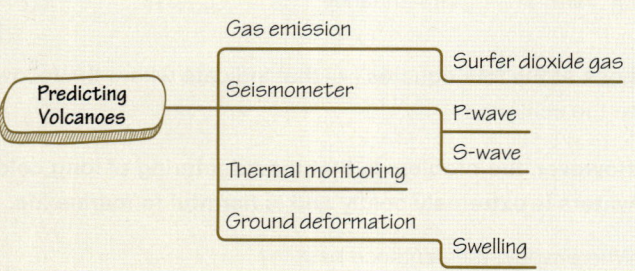

Predicting Volcanoes

Before a volcano erupts, it gives off a number of warning signs which are meticulously investigated by volcanologists. Intensive monitoring of volcanic eruptions has produced data leading to several successful warnings being issued for impending eruptions. There are processes and interactions that result in geophysical and phenomenological effects, which precede and accompany eruptions.

First, magma moves through magma conduits into the area beneath the volcano and collects in a magma chamber. While moving through the conduit, the magma changes pressure, leading to the deformation of the ground, such as the swelling of the volcano's slopes. Because this deformation is very subtle, researchers need precise surveying equipment like tilt-meters to measure the change. Also, measuring changes in the quantity and makeup of gas is helpful in predicting the likelihood of an eruption, since the percentage of certain elements, like sulfur dioxide (SO_2) or hydrogen chloride (HCl), often increases in the gas emitted from volcanic vents and fumaroles just prior to an eruption. Other clues to an impending eruption are earthquakes or seismic vibrations in the proximity of the possible eruption area. While molten rock rises up to the surface or moves through the conduit, it exerts pressure on the underground rock formation, which disturbs stress distributions and often leads to cracking or small earthquakes in the crust. Seismometers are used to detect seismic waves generated by earthquakes.

Prior to the impending eruption, active magmatic systems interact strongly with their surroundings causing ground deformation and the pressure and thermal pattern changes. However, in general, no single event can be used to predict a volcanic eruption, so the techniques available for predicting volcanic activity involve the meticulous monitoring of diverse precursors so that, when taken in total, an eruption can often be foretold. For example, in the weeks prior to an eruption of Mount St. Helen on March 19, 1982, the amount of seismic energy released increased, swelling in the slope occurred, and SO_2 emissions increased, so people were successfully evacuated and the death toll was lower. However, eruptions occur in a different way for each volcano, and until patterns are recognized for individual volcanos, predictions vary in their reliability and sometimes a volcano can erupt with no recognizable precursor events at all.

1. The word predict in paragraph 3 is closest in meaning to
   - (A) precede
   - (B) foretell
   - (C) propose
   - (D) prevent

2. The author discusses Mount St. Helen in order to
   - (A) demonstrate the importance of predicting eruptions
   - (B) emphasize the precision of eruption predictions
   - (C) exemplify how it is necessary to examine various precursors when predicting eruptions
   - (D) show the difficulty of predicting eruptions

Answers p. 79

Geology

★★★

116

Seismic waves & the interior of the Earth
지진파와 지구내부구조

판 구조론은 다양한 주제에 배경이 되는 필수 배경지식 중 하나이다. 판 구조론의 원리로 지진, 화산, 산맥형성 등과 같은 지질현상이 설명되며 특히 지진과 화산활동은 토플에서 빈출되는 주제들이므로 이와 관련된 지식과 어휘는 반드시 숙지하도록 하자.

판 구조론plate tectonics은 대류이동을 설명하는 지질학 이론이다. 판 구조론에 따르면 지구 내부의 가장 바깥부분은 암석권lithosphere과 연약권asthenosphere 두 층으로 이루어져 있으며 암석권은 지각과 식어서 굳어진 최상부의 맨틀로 구성되며 그 아래의 연약권은 점성물질인 맨틀로 구성된다. 따라서 암석권은 연약권 위에 떠 있게 되며 판plate이라 불리는 몇 개의 조각으로 나누어져 있다. 10개의 주요 판으로는 아프리카판, 남극판, 오스트레일리아판, 유라시아판, 북아메리카판, 남아메리카판, 태평양판, 코코스판, 나즈카판, 인도판이 있다. 이 판들과 더불어 다수의 작은 판들은 서로 움직이면서 보존경계transform boundaries, 발산경계divergent boundaries, 수렴경계convergent boundaries를 형성하여 지진, 화산, 조산운동, 해구 등을 발생시킨다. 세계에서 가장 활발한 화산들은 판의 경계에 존재하고 있으며 특히 태평양 주변의 환태평양 조산대에서 일어나는 현상이 활발하며 널리 알려져 있다.

판은 대륙지각continental crust과 해양지각oceanic crust을 포함하며, 하나의 판에 둘 모두가 존재하기도 한다. 예를 들면 아프리카판은 대륙과 대서양, 인도양의 해저 부분을 포함하고 있다. 판에는 일반적으로 대륙지각과 해양지각 아래 맨틀의 최상부 부분이 포함되며 이 모두를 통틀어 암석권이라고 한다. 해양지각과 대륙지각을 구분하는 기준은 구성물질의 밀도차이이다. 해양지각은 대륙지각보다 밀도가 높아 무거운데 그 이유는 구성 원소의 차이 때문이다. 해양지각에는 무거운 원소들이 대륙지각보다 더 많은 반면 대륙지각에는 가벼운 원소들이 더 많다. 그 결과 해양지각은 대체로 해수면 아래에 위치하게 된다.

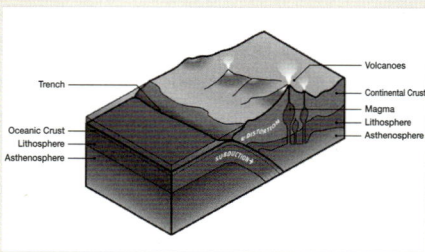

필수어휘
- seismic waves 지진파
- deduce 추론하다
- seismologists 지진학자
- velocity 속도
- lithosphere 암석권
- asthenosphere 연약권

Mini Practice

Listen to part of a lecture in a geography class. 🎧 Ch6_08

1. What are some traits of the lithosphere? Click on 2 answers.
   - Ⓐ It has a non-uniform thickness.
   - Ⓑ It is the outer part of the crust.
   - Ⓒ It has a low-velocity zone for seismic waves.
   - Ⓓ It is composed mainly of rigid material.

2. Based on the lecture, why are earthquakes significant?
   - Ⓐ They help scientists improve instruments to better monitor further earthquakes.
   - Ⓑ The waves they produce reveal clues about the Earth's deep structure.
   - Ⓒ They explain the structure of the lithosphere.
   - Ⓓ They cause the earth to bend or break.

Listening Script

Professor: Much of our knowledge of the earth's interior has come from the study of earthquakes, or more precisely, by monitoring seismic waves. Seismic waves are waves of energy caused by the sudden breaking of rock, and they're often generated by earthquakes. We have instruments at various points around the earth that monitor seismic waves, and by studying how the waves behave, we've deduced quite a lot about the interior of the earth.

When examining seismic waves scientists noticed that the density of geological material in the earth altered the speed and direction of the waves. Depending on the density of material encountered seismic waves may change direction, reflect back, or bend. When the waves hit areas of high density they speed up but when they hit low areas of density they slow down.

In 1960, there was a major earthquake, and seismologists at the time monitored the seismic waves as they moved through the earth. Their analyses showed that these waves were moving relatively slowly, until they got to what we now know as the base of the lithosphere. At that point, they changed direction and their velocity slowed down. So what did that tell us? It demonstrated that the waves had passed through a zone of less dense material just before reaching the lithosphere. This less dense zone was called the "low-velocity zone" and was later renamed the asthenosphere. In addition, the data from that 1960 quake also provided support for the tectonic plate theory, which asserts that the lithosphere is divided into giant plates. The discovery of a less dense layer below the lithosphere provided a clue as to how these plates could be moving around; they're kind of floating on top of the asthenosphere. This idea had been previously proposed but until 1960 there was a lack of significant supporting evidence.

Additionally, the seismologists noticed that, even deeper inside the earth, the seismic waves moved at a higher velocity than they did in the asthenosphere. They eventually concluded that there must be even more dense material below the asthenosphere, and so on. That's how we've mapped out the interior of the earth.

Answers p. 79

Geology

117

Soil
토양

토양의 형성 요인과 과정 그리고 그 특성에 대한 내용들을 기억하도록 하자.

토양soil은 여러 생물체의 물리, 화학적 작용으로 형성된다. 이때 가장 결정적인 역할을 하는 것은 토양 내에 존재하는 무수한 박테리아bacteria이다. 미생물체는 죽은 유기물organic matter이나 흙의 모체가 되는 물질이나 암석 등을 분해할 수 있는데, 이 분해 과정에서 영양이 풍부한 부식토humus soil가 만들어지며 또 다른 부산물인 염기성 아미노산basic amino acid은 다른 생물체의 생존을 돕기도 한다.

나무, 관목, 풀 등의 식물vegetation들은 흙의 성질을 좌우하는 역할을 하는데 낙엽수deciduous tree의 경우, 뿌리를 통해 영양분을 흡수해서 여름 동안 나뭇잎이 무성하게 자라게 하고 동절기가 되면 땅에 떨어뜨려shed 박테리아의 분해 작용으로 나뭇잎의 영양분이 토양에 되돌아가게 한다. 또한 질소 고정nitrogen fixation 과정에서 뿌리 혹은 박테리아에 의해 대기중의 질소가 식물에 필요한 질소 형태로 전환되면서 식물뿐 아니라 토양도 건강하게 유지해주는 역할을 한다.

그밖에 지렁이earthworm가 토양을 섭취하고 배설excrete한 배설물이 천연 비료fertilizer가 되며, 지렁이가 토양 안에서 지나간 자리 뒤로 만들어진 구멍에서 미생물체가 배설물을 분해할 공간을 확보하게 된다. 이와 같은 지렁이의 활동으로 토양은 더욱 비옥해지고, 다른 나무와 식물들이 영양을 얻는데 조력자의 역할을 하기도 한다. 포유류mammal 역시 토양에 영향을 준다. 방목하는grazing 초식 동물이 땅 위에서 활동하면서 흙을 밟아 부숴줌으로써 물리적으로 토양에 영향을 주고, 땅을 파는 습성을 지닌 설치류rodents과는 토양과 함께 영양분도 다양한 장소로 운반해준다.

필수어휘

- **porosity** 다공성 (고체 내/외부에 작은 구멍을 많이 가지고 있는 상태) cf. porous 구멍이 많은
- **coarse** 입자가 굵은
- **silt** 토사
- **clay** 점토
- **quartz** 석영
- **feldspar** 장석
- **permeable** 투과성의 cf. permeability 투과성 (투과하는 성질)
- **spatial** 공간의
- **aggregate** 혼합(체)
- **geomorphic** 지형의
- **humus** 부식토

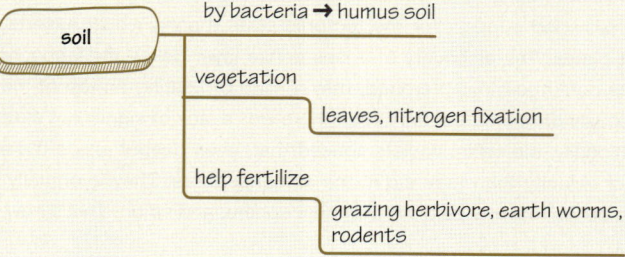

Properties of Soil

Soil generally consists of minerals, organic matter, water and air. The structure and proportion of these components greatly influence the physical properties of soil, such as texture, structure, porosity, and color. The character and make-up primarily determine the behavior of soils and how they are utilized.

Apart from gravel and other rocks soil can be classified into three categories: sand, silt, and clay. Sand is the coarsest and largest size and is composed of finely ground minerals and rocks. The composition varies from location to location. Silt is intermediate in size and is commonly composed of quartz and feldspars. Clay is the smallest and is composed of secondary minerals, clay minerals and metal oxides. Soil texture depends on the relative proportion of sand, silt and clay. If the soil consists of coarse textured particles like sand, it becomes very permeable, holds very little water, and contains few nutrients. Soils that have high concentrations of silt or clay have a low permeability and can hold large amounts of nutrients and water. However, both silt and clay restrict airflow causing many plants to suffocate and die. A balance of all three creates healthy soil where plants can thrive.

Soil structure is determined by the spatial arrangement of solid soil particles into aggregates, and the arrangement of pores or spaces between the aggregates. This spatial arrangement depends on the solid composition and texture of the soil, biological activity, geomorphic processes and climate. The distribution and arrangements of soil particles determine the soil's water-holding capacity, permeability, plant root penetration and the rate of seedling emergence.

Soil comes in a variety of colors and the colors provide clues about the properties of the material contained within the soil. Humus is a type of soil which consists of organic matter and is usually brown to almost black in color. Soils with darker colors usually indicate higher levels of organic matter. On the other hand, soils that are high in iron vary greatly in color including shades of red, yellow and light brown. The iron in the soil reacts with oxygen to form iron oxides within the soil, which create the various hues.

1. The word arrangement in paragraph 3 is closest in meaning to
   - A appearance
   - B advent
   - C configuration
   - D assignment

2. All of the following are mentioned in the passage EXCEPT
   - A Highly permeable soil holds lower amounts of water.
   - B The color of soil affects soil structures.
   - C Because of organic content, humus looks darker.
   - D Iron in the soil is one of the determinants of soil color.

Answers p. 80

Environmental Science

118
Stalagmite
석순

석순stalagmite은 동굴의 지붕 부분으로부터 떨어지는 지하수ground water가 침전deposit되면서 생긴 탄산칼슘calcium carbonate으로 만들어지며 석순의 산소구성의 형태와 동위원소의 세밀한 다양성은 동굴 근처의 강우량rainfall을 잘 반영해준다. 또한 퇴적물의 방사선 요소 radioactive element인 우라늄uranium의 비율을 통해 석순의 정확한 나이 또한 측정할 수 있다. 이러한 석순의 특징을 바탕으로 중국 란조우 대학Lanzhou University의 연구팀은 석순이 기록한 강우량과 중국의 역사적인 사건들을 비교하여 중국을 지배하던 왕조의 쇠퇴는 장마 monsoon의 강도와 연관이 있음을 주장하였다.

이와 같은 주장은 중국의 북서부 지역의 간쑤성에 위치한 왕시앙 Wangxiang 동굴에 생성된 석순의 분석을 통해 뒷받침 되었다. 연구가들은 석순을 통해 아시아 지역의 몬순강우에 대한 1,800년에 걸친 기록을 분석하였고 과거 기후변화 중에서도 장마시기의 강도를 알아낼 수 있었다. 여름장마를 일으키는 몬순풍은 인도양에서 시작되어 중국 전체를 지나가는데 이러한 습기가 풍부한 바람은 쌀을 재배하는데 필수적인 비를 가져오지만 약한 장마시기에는 쌀 수확이 적어지고 사회불안이 증가하게 된다고 연구자들은 추정했다. 따라서 수 백년 동안 중국을 지배한 다섯 개 왕조 중에서 당Tang, 원Yuan, 명Ming은 수 십년에 걸친 약한 여름장마와 건조한 기후 이후에 쇠퇴하였다는 연구결과가 밝혀진 것이다. 따라서 기후변화가 인류 문명사에 매우 중요한 역할을 했으며 석순을 통해 드러난 850년과 940년 사이의 건조한 기후는 중국의 왕조뿐만 아니라 마야문명Mayan civilization의 몰락과도 연관이 있음을 보여주었다. 이러한 사실을 통해 과학자들은 지구 기후변화가 인류문명과 인구변화에 치명적인 영향을 줄 수 있음을 다시 한 번 확인할 수 있게 된 것이다.

필수어휘
- stalagmite 석순
- paleoclimatology 고기후학
- monsoon 폭우, 장마
- temperate 온화한
- radioactive decay 방사능 붕괴
- exacerbated 악화된
- millennia 천년 (millennium의 복수)

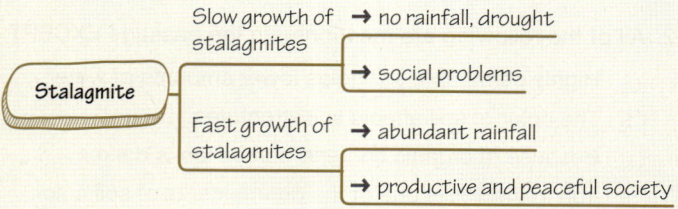

Listening

Mini Practice

Listen to part of a lecture in an earth science class. 🎧 Ch6_09

1. What can be inferred about a cave that shows a period of slow growth of a stalagmite?
   Click on 2 answers.
   - Ⓐ The cave is not located in a region with a monsoonal climate.
   - Ⓑ The cave is located in a region with frequent and heavy rainfall.
   - Ⓒ The cave is located in a region that experienced a drought at the time.
   - Ⓓ The cave is located in a very dry region.

2. What role did uranium play in the study of Paleoclimatology?
   - Ⓐ Uranium preserved the stalagmites, preventing their decay.
   - Ⓑ Examination of caves was hindered by the danger of radiation from uranium.
   - Ⓒ Consistent radioactive decay allowed researchers to determine the age of stalagmites containing uranium.
   - Ⓓ The analysis of radiation for the radioactive decay of the uranium made it possible to locate the cave.

Listening Script

Professor: Humans have been keeping precise climate records for the last few centuries, but sometimes we want to know what the climate was like before that. That's where Paleoclimatology comes in. It looks at geological records for clues about what the earth's climate was like in the distant past. Recently, analysis of a stalagmite found in a cave in western China was able to offer insight into the connection between global climate change and human society. But first, let's consider the formation of a stalagmite. As ground water carrying calcium and other minerals drips from a cave ceiling, it leaves behind deposits that build up over thousands of years to form various kinds of stalagmites. So the speed of stalagmite formation depends on the amount of ground water, which comes from rainfall.

Now, the cave I mentioned earlier is located between two climatic regions. In the southeast, there are seasonal rains, or monsoons, while the climate to the northwest is drier and more temperate. This means the area where the cave is located experiences period of both drought and rain. If the cave were located fully within the monsoonal climate, it would be less affected by drought and less useful to the study. Even more importantly, the water from that rain seeps through deposits of uranium. The consistent rate of radioactive decay of that uranium makes it possible for us to accurately calculate the age of the stalagmite, so based on analysis of the cave it has been possible to produce a particularly accurate record of the climate, dating back nearly two millennia.

By comparing the stalagmite with historical Chinese records, researchers discovered a strong correlation between the rainfall and the state of society at the same time. In years where the stalagmite indicates abundant rainfall, society in China was more peaceful and culturally productive. Drought, on the other hand, brought periods of reduced productivity and exacerbated social problems, possibly even leading to the downfall of several Chinese dynasties. The popular theory, therefore, is that a period of reduced rainfall and perhaps drought existed in China during the decline of some ancient empires. But this link we're discussing, between climate change and societal decline, is much too complicated to admit of a simple cause-and-effect relationship. This is just one piece of evidence from just one cave on a vast continent. It seems certain that climate played a role, but it's not yet clear exactly how much of a role that was.

Answers p. 81

Paleontology

119
Uranium-Lead Dating
우라늄-납 연대측정법

토플에 고생물학 분야가 출제될 때 항상 등장하는 용어 중 하나가 화석의 나이를 측정하는 탄소 또는 우라늄-납 연대측정법이다. 물론 이 측정법을 완전히 이해하는 것은 어렵지만 대략적으로라도 이론을 알아두도록 하자!

탄소연대측정법은 인류학anthropology, 고고학archaeology 분야에서도 자주 사용된다. 생물이 죽으면 더 이상 대기 중의 이산화탄소를 흡수하지 못하게 되면서 동물, 식물, 박테리아 안의 방사성 탄소인 C14는 붕괴되어 그 양이 점점 줄어들게 된다. 반면 C12 또는 C13은 비방사성non-radioactive이므로 유기체가 죽어도 그대로 그 안에 남아 있게 된다. 다시 말하면 C14 대 C12, C13 비율은 유기체가 죽은 뒤 시간이 지남에 따라 감소하므로 일단 한 번 살아있었던 생물이라면 이 비율을 측정하여 생명체가 언제 죽었는지를 알 수 있다.

지질연대 측정에 가장 많이 쓰이는 우라늄-납 연대측정법은 다음과 같은 원리를 이용한다. 우선 광물에서 우라늄과 납 샘플을 얻기 위해서는 지르콘zircon 결정이 추출되어야 한다. 지르콘은 특히 화성암igneous rock, 변성암metamorphic rock과 같은 화산암volcanic rock 속에서 잘 발견되며 열과 풍화작용에도 잘 살아남기 때문에 추출이 가능하다. 이러한 지르콘 결정 내부에는 납이 포함되어 있는데 이것이 바로 우라늄 붕괴 생성물이다. 우라늄은 방사능 붕괴를 통해서 납으로 변하게 되는데, 우라늄이 납으로 변하는 시간을 알고 있기 때문에 광물 속의 우라늄과 납의 비율을 측정하여 암석 생성연대를 측정하는 것이 가능해 진 것이다.

필수어휘
- zircon 지르콘
- sandstone 사암
- radioactive 방사성의
- molten rock 용암
- crystallize 결정화하다
- glimpse 얼핏 봄

Uranium-Lead Dating
- can guess the age of organisms
- process
  - extract zircon from particles of a stone
  - measure the amount of lead
  - determine the age of a stone

Mini Practice

Listening

Listen to part of a lecture in a paleontology class. 🎧 Ch6_10

1. In the lecture, the professor explains the uranium-lead dating process. Summarize the process by arranging the events in the proper order.

   (A) The sample is matched with other mountain ranges.
   (B) The zircon grains are examined to determine the amount of lead.
   (C) The age of a sample of sandstone is established.

1	
2	
3	

2. According to the lecture, where do geologists look to find the origin of a sample of sandstone?

   (A) Particles within the sample
   (B) The level of radioactivity of the sample
   (C) The amount of erosion evident in the sample based on its shape
   (D) The time it takes the sandstone in the sample to crystallize

Listening Script

Professor: Okay, so we're always talking about how old some land or other geologic feature is. But how do geologists know that? Well, today I'm going to talk about one technique we use, called Uranium-Lead Dating. This technique has produced a few surprises. For example, two geologists found that amazingly, something like half the sand in the Grand Canyon originally came from thousands of kilometers to the east, in the Appalachian Mountains. How did that sand end up so far away from where it started? Well, we think wind and huge rivers transported it west, where it mixed with existing sand in the Grand Canyon.

So, those two geologists found this out by looking at grains for zircon in sandstone. Zircon contains uranium, which is radioactive, and that makes it quite useful for dating purposes. See, it starts off as magma, well, molten rock from volcanoes. As it hardens, it crystallizes, and once zircon crystals form, the uranium inside them begins to change into lead. That means by measuring how much lead is in a zircon grain, you can figure out when it was formed, and that way you know the age of zircon from different mountain ranges. Then you compare the age of the zircon in the sandstone from the Grand Canyon with the age of zircon in the mountains. If the ages are the same, it means the sandstone used to be part of those mountains.

So, through Uranium-Lead Dating, we know the sandstone was formed at the same time as the granite in the Appalachian Mountains. So, through this technique, we are able to determine the age of various geological features, and gain a glimpse into our planet's early geologic history.

Answers p. 81

Environmental Studies

★★
120

Wildfire
산불

야생에서 발생한 산불wildfire의 피해는 불의 세기와 지속 시간에 따라 다양하지만 큰 화재의 경우 야생의 다양성biodiversity이 줄어들 뿐 아니라, 그들이 살고 있는 서식지habitat까지 파괴devastate되는 탈산림화로 생태계 전반을 위협하기도 한다. 게다가 심한 경우 토양의 영양분까지 함께 연소되면서 산림을 복원하기가 쉽지 않고, 재와 연기로 인해 대기 오염air pollution과 산성비acid rain가 발생한다.

하지만 불의 규모가 크지 않고 통제가 가능하다면 산불이 부정적인 것만은 아니다. 오히려 생태계ecosystem의 순환적 측면에서 긍정적 역할을 하기도 한다. 불에 탄 식물들이 거름이 되어 새로운 식물vegetation들이 자라나 무성한lush 숲을 이룰 수 있기 때문이다. 또한 그 지역에 오랜 기간 동안 쌓여 있었던 죽은 나뭇가지branch와 낙엽들이 불에 타면서 그 자리에 새로운 식물이 싹을 틔우며 성장할 수 있는 여분의 공간을 제공하기도 한다.

1990년대 애팔래치아 산맥의 한 지역에 화재가 발생한 후 그 지역의 생태군락이 화재 전 보다 더 강하고stout, 다양한diverse 모습을 보여준 사례가 있는데, 화재 발생 지역에 생태 천이ecological succession가 발생하면서 식물 군락colonization이 형성되었다. 화재 직후에는 남아 있는 식물의 씨앗이나 그 지역으로 새롭게 이동한 씨앗에 의해 개척 종pioneer species이 나타나고 시간이 지날수록 태양에 강한 초본 식물herbaceous plants과 나무 종woody species이 차례대로 발생하면서, 토양의 상태는 더욱 호전되었다. 식물들이 무성해질수록 벌과 같은 수분 매개체pollinator, 초식herbivorous, 육식carnivorous 동물들까지 그 지역으로 이동하면서 더욱 다양한 생태계가 형성되었다.

필수어휘

- wildfire 산불
- habitat 서식지 [syn] dwelling
- devastate 파괴하다 [syn] decimate
- ecosystem 생태계
- branch 나무 가지
- sprout 싹을 틔우다
- timber 목재
- fertilizer 비료
- extinguish 진화하다
- suppression 억압, 진압
- implement 시행하다, 이행하다

Wildfires

Many people view forest wildfires as terrible events that devastate animal and plant ecosystems. However, various studies of historical wildfires show that the ecosystem may benefit from smaller periodic fires by renewing vegetation and reducing the potential for massive fires.

Wildfires can be both directly and indirectly helpful to plants. Some species of plants and trees can only sprout after a fire. If the forest floor has a heavy buildup of dead vegetation, branches and leaves, new vegetation will have no space to shoot. Therefore, burning allows new trees and plants to grow and reduces the competition among vegetation for sunlight. Moreover, it normally takes several decades for dead branches or leaves to become a nutrient-rich organic material, but burnt branches and timbers decay much more quickly and this speeds up the production of natural fertilizer that encourages plant growth.

A heavy buildup of dead plants and trees means more fuel for fires, which can lead to severe fires. The Yellowstone National Park Fire of 1988 in the United State is a good example of why periodic fires are beneficial for the ecosystem and why fire suppression may lead to devastating results. Beginning in the 1940s, it was the U.S. government's policy to quickly suppress fires as soon as they were discovered. [A ■] During a 48 year period, any fire that started in or near the park was extinguished as quickly as possible. [B ■] In the summer of 1988, a series of small fires surrounding the park eventually formed the greatest conflagration in the recorded history of Yellowstone National Park. [C ■] Because of drought and strong winds, the fire burned for several months ultimately consuming over 1.4 million acres of forest in and around the park. [D ■]

This fire caused the U.S. government to reevaluate fire suppression and instead implement new systems and methods to manage forests and protect natural environments. Controlled burning is a technique used in forest management, farming, and prairie restoration to reduce the potential hazards of severe fires. Now, most park management services rely on controlled burning to remove combustible vegetation and reduce the risk of uncontrolled wildfires that could threaten wildlife, human safety, and personal property.

---

1. The word hazards in paragraph 4 is closest in meaning to
   - Ⓐ events
   - Ⓑ operations
   - Ⓒ risks
   - Ⓓ archetypes

2. Look at the four squares [■] that indicate where the following sentence could be added to the sentence.

   This led to the substantial accumulation of combustible debris on the forest floors.

   Where would the sentence best fit?

TOEFL Vocabulary

History
280

Arts
286

Social Science
294

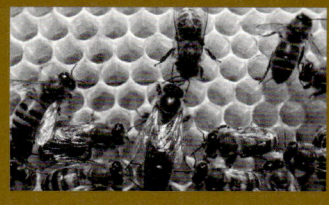
Life Science
301

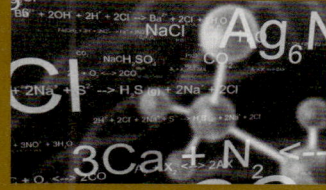
Physical Science
309

Environmental Science
315

History | Arts | Social Science

01 Anthropology I (인류학 I)

01	aristocracy [ˌærəˈstɒkrəsi]	n. 귀족 (정치)
02	biological anthropology	n. 생물학적 인류학
03	city-state [ˈsɪtiˌsteɪt]	n. 도시 국가
04	civilization [ˌsɪvələˈzeɪʃən]	n. 문명
05	clergy [ˈklɜrdʒi]	n. 성직자
06	crop rotation	n. 윤작 → 곡식 돌려짓기
07	cultivation [ˌkʌltəˈveɪʃən]	n. 경작
08	cultural anthropology	n. 문화 인류학
09	descendant [dɪˈsɛndənt]	n. 후손
10	folk story	n. 민간 설화
11	hereditary [həˈrɛdɪˌtɛri]	a. 세습적인
12	industrial revolution	n. 산업혁명
13	livestock [ˈlaɪvˌstɒk]	n. 가축
14	medieval [ˌmidiˈivəl]	a. 중세의
15	merchant class	n. 상인 계급
16	monarchy [ˈmɒnərki]	n. 군주제
17	myth [mɪθ]	n. 신화
18	nobility [noʊˈbɪlɪti]	n. 귀족
19	patronage [ˈpeɪtrənɪdʒ]	n. 후원 cf. patron 후원자
20	patronize [ˈpeɪtrəˌnaɪz]	v. 후원하다
21	primitive people	n. 원시인
22	radical [ˈrædɪkəl]	a. 근본적인, 급진적인
23	status [ˈsteɪtəs]	n. 신분 [syn] standing
24	tribe [traɪb]	n. 부족
25	urbanization [ˌɜrbənəˈzeɪʃən]	n. 도시화

02 Anthropology II (인류학 II)

01 ☐ **arid** [ˈærɪd]	a. 건조한
02 ☐ **boost** [buːst]	v. 올리다
03 ☐ **cavemen** [ˈkeɪvˌmæn]	n. 석기시대인
04 ☐ **defender** [dɪˈfendə(r)]	n. 옹호자
05 ☐ **deforestation** [diːˌfɔrɪˈsteɪʃ(ə)n]	n. 삼림벌채
06 ☐ **demise** [dɪˈmaɪz]	n. 소멸, 멸망
07 ☐ **deplete** [dɪˈpliːt]	v. 고갈시키다
08 ☐ **desert** [ˈdezə(r)t]	v. 버리다, 유기하다
09 ☐ **disturbance** [dɪˈstɜː(r)bəns]	n. 방해
10 ☐ **downfall** [ˈdaʊnˌfɔːl]	n. 몰락
11 ☐ **erosion** [ɪˈrəʊʒ(ə)n]	n. 침식
12 ☐ **ground cover**	n. 지표
13 ☐ **immense** [ɪˈmens]	a. 거대한
14 ☐ **infertile** [ɪnˈfɜː(r)taɪl]	a. 불모의
15 ☐ **noble** [ˈnəʊb(ə)l]	a. 웅장한, 귀족의
16 ☐ **overpopulation** [ˌəʊvə(r)ˌpɒpjʊˌleɪʃ(ə)n]	n. 인구과잉
17 ☐ **patriarchy** [ˈpeɪtriˌɑː(r)ki]	n. 부계제
18 ☐ **peasant** [ˈpez(ə)nt]	n. 농민, 소작농
19 ☐ **prehistoric** [ˌpriːhɪˈstɒrɪk]	a. 역사 이전의, 선사 시대의
20 ☐ **ruin** [ˈruːɪn]	n. 폐허, 유적지
21 ☐ **spark** [spɑː(r)k]	v. 유발하다
22 ☐ **topsoil** [ˈtɒpˌsɔɪl]	n. 표토
23 ☐ **tree ring**	n. 나이테
24 ☐ **vanish** [ˈvænɪʃ]	v. 사라지다
25 ☐ **vulnerable** [ˈvʌln(ə)rəb(ə)l]	a. 영향 받기 쉬운, 약한

History | Arts | Social Science

03 Archaeology I (고고학 I)

01	**artifact** [ˈɑrtəˌfækt]	n. (인간이 만든) 유물
02	**civilization** [ˌsɪvələˈzeɪʃən]	n. 문명
03	**date** [deɪt]	v. 연대를 추정하다
04	**digging** [ˈdɪgɪŋ]	n. 발굴
05	**dwelling** [ˈdwɛlɪŋ]	n. 거주(지)
06	**era** [ˈɪərə]	n. 시대, 연대 [syn] epoch
07	**excavate** [ˈɛkskəˌveɪt]	v. 발굴하다 [syn] unearth
08	**extinct** [ɪkˈstɪŋkt]	a. 멸종된 [syn] vanished
09	**flourish** [ˈflɜrɪʃ]	v. 번창하다 [syn] boom, thrive
10	**fossil** [ˈfɒsəl]	n. 화석
11	**hierarchy** [ˈhaɪəˌrɑrki]	n. 계급제도
12	**hieroglyph** [ˌhaɪərəˈglɪf]	n. 상형문자
13	**hominoid** [ˈhɒməˌnɔɪd]	n. 유인원
14	**Ice Age**	n. 빙하기 *cf.* Prehistoric times 선사 시대, Stone Age 석기 시대, Bronze Age 청동기 시대
15	**implement** [ˈɪmpləmənt]	n. 도구
16	**Neolithic** [ˌniəˈlɪθɪk]	a. 신석기 시대의
17	**Paleolithic** [ˌpeɪliəˈlɪθɪk]	a. 구석기 시대의
18	**pottery** [ˈpɒtəri]	n. 도자기
19	**primeval** [praɪˈmivəl]	a. 원시의, 태고의
20	**regime** [rəˈʒim]	n. 제도
21	**relics** [ˈrɛlɪk]	n. 유물 [syn] remains, ruins
22	**specimen** [ˈspɛsəmən]	n. 견본
23	**stratum** [ˈstreɪtəm]	n. 유적층 [syn] layer
24	**turmoil** [ˈtɜrmɔɪl]	n. 폭동 [syn] uprising, upheaval
25	**ups and downs**	흥망성쇠

04 Archaeology II (고고학 II)

01	anomaly [əˈnɒməli]	n. 차이, 변칙
02	boulder [ˈbəʊldə(r)]	n. 큰 바위
03	Bronze Age	n. 청동기 시대
04	compile [kəmˈpaɪl]	v. 모으다, 쌓다
05	deform [dɪˈfɔː(r)m]	v. 변형시키다
06	investigate [ɪnˈvestɪgeɪt]	v. 조사하다
07	Iron Age	n. 철기 시대
08	mammoth-tusk [ˈmæməθ tʌsk]	n. 맘모스 어금니
09	monument [ˈmɒnjʊmənt]	n. 기념 건축물
10	mound [maʊnd]	n. 고분
11	mount [maʊnt]	v. 올려놓다, 두다
12	polish [ˈpɒlɪʃ]	v. 광을 내다
13	prehistory [ˌpriːˈhɪst(ə)ri]	n. 선사시대
14	preserve [prɪˈzɜː(r)v]	v. 보존하다
15	prevalent [ˈprevələnt]	a. 널리 퍼져 있는
16	remains [rɪˈmeɪnz]	n. 유물
17	ruins [ˈruːɪn]	n. 유적
18	scraper [ˈskreɪpə(r)]	n. 긁어 내는 도구
19	site [saɪt]	n. 유적지
20	skeletal [ˈskelɪt(ə)l]	a. 해골의
21	Stone Age	n. 석기 시대
22	stratigraphy [strəˈtɪgrəfi]	n. 지층학
23	tribe [traɪb]	n. 부족
24	unearth [ʌnˈɜː(r)θ]	v. 발굴하다
25	warfare [ˈwɔː(r)feə(r)]	n. 전투, 전쟁

History

Arts   Social Science

05 US History I (미국역사 I)

01	annex [əˈneks]	v. (영토 등을) 병합하다
02	benefactor [ˈbenɪˌfæktə(r)]	n. 후원자
03	bonanza [bəˈnænzə]	n. 일확천금, 노다지
04	bootleg [ˈbuːtˌleg]	v. (주류 등을) 밀매하다
05	carpetbagger [ˈkɑː(r)pɪtˌbægə(r)]	n. 남북전쟁 후 이익을 노리고 남부로 건너온 북부 출신자
06	cavalry [ˈkævəlri]	n. 기병대
07	confederacy [kənˈfed(ə)rəsi]	n. 남부연방
08	crusade [kruːˈseɪd]	n. 십자가운동 v. (개혁, 박멸 등의) 운동에 참가하다, 운동을 추진하다
09	Declaration of Independence	n. 독립선언서
10	dismember [dɪsˈmembə(r)]	v. (국토 등을) 분할하다
11	doctrine [ˈdɒktrɪn]	n. 교리, 신조, 원칙
12	(the) Dust Bowl	n. 미국 중남부의 건조한 대초원 지대
13	electoral college	n. 선거인단
14	Emancipation Proclamation	n. 노예 해방 선언(1963)
15	framer [freɪmə(r)]	n. 입안자, 고안자
16	Great Depression	n. 대공항
17	Indian reservation	n. 인디언 보호 거주지
18	indiscriminate [ˌɪndɪˈskrɪmɪnət]	a. 무차별의, 닥치는 대로의
19	integration [ˌɪntɪˈɡreɪʃ(ə)n]	n. 통합, 인종 차별 폐지
20	Jim Crow laws	n. (특히 흑인에 대한) 인종 차별 정책
21	Lewis and Clark	n. 최초로 서부를 개척한 두 명의 탐험가
22	Louisiana Purchase	n. 루이지애나 구입 → 미국이 1803년 프랑스로부터 매입한 루이지애나 지역
23	Mexican War	n. 멕시코 전쟁 → 1846~48: 미국의 텍사스 병합이 전쟁의 발단
24	migrate [maɪˈɡreɪt]	v. 이주하다
25	minority [maɪˈnɒrəti]	n. 소수민족

06 US History II (미국 역사 II)

01	muckraking [ˈmʌkˌreɪkɪŋ]	n. 추문을 들추어냄, 사생활을 폭로함
02	pasture [ˈpɑːstʃə(r)]	n. 목초지
03	patent [ˈpeɪt(ə)nt]	n. 특허(권)
04	philanthropist [fɪˈlænθrəpɪst]	n. 박애주의자, 자선가
05	Pilgrim Fathers	n. 1620년 미국에 이주한 일단의 청교도들
06	plantation [plɑːnˈteɪʃ(ə)n]	n. 대농장
07	Prohibition [ˌprəʊɪˈbɪʃ(ə)n]	n. 금주법(1820~33)
08	provision [prəˈvɪʒ(ə)n]	n. 조항, 규정
09	Pulitzer Prize	n. 퓰리처상 → 헝가리 태생 미국 신문업자 Joseph Pulitzer의 유언으로 제정
10	Puritan [ˈpjʊərɪtən]	n. 청교도
11	racial discrimination	n. 인종차별
12	ranch [rɑːntʃ]	n. 목장
13	ratify [ˈrætɪfaɪ]	v. 비준하다
14	renewal [rɪˈnjuːəl]	n. (도시 등의) 재개발, 일신
15	Revolution [ˌrevəˈluːʃ(ə)n]	n. 미국 독립전쟁
16	Roaring Twenties	n. 격동의 20년대
17	segregation [ˌsegrɪˈgeɪʃ(ə)n]	n. 격리, 인종 차별
18	settlement [ˈset(ə)lmənt]	n. 정착지
19	Spanish-American War	n. 미서전쟁(1899)
20	steel magnate	n. 철강왕
21	Supreme Court	n. 대법원
22	Sutter's Mill	n. 서터즈밀 → 서터즈밀 부근에서 금이 발견되어 1849년 골드 러시가 생김
23	thirteen original colonies	n. 영국에서 최초로 독립한 미국의 13개 주
24	unconstitutional [ˌʌnkɒnstɪˈtjuːʃ(ə)nəl]	a. 위헌의
25	women's suffrage	n. 여성 참정권

| History | **Arts** | Social Science |

01 Art History Ⅰ (미술사 Ⅰ)

01 ☐	aesthetic [es-'the-tik]	a. 미적인, 미학의
02 ☐	brush stroke	n. 붓질
03 ☐	brushwork ['brəshwərk]	n. 화풍, 화법
04 ☐	bust ['bəst]	n. 반신상
05 ☐	caricature ['ker-i-kə-ˌchúr]	n. 풍자화
06 ☐	chromatic [krō-'ma-tik]	a. 유채색의
07 ☐	composition [ˌkäm-pə-'zi-shən]	n. (미술) 구도
08 ☐	connoisseur [ˌkä-nə-'sər]	n. (예술품의 감식) 전문가, 감정가
09 ☐	deformation [ˌdi:fo:(r)'meɪʃ(ə)n]	n. 변형
10 ☐	emboss [im-'bäs]	v. 도드라지게 새기다
11 ☐	engraving [ɪn'greɪvɪŋ]	n. 조각술, 조판술, 판화
12 ☐	environmental art	n. 환경 예술 → 관객과 빛, 소리, 색채 등 모든 소재로 공간 전체를 채우는 예술 형태
13 ☐	etching ['etʃɪŋ]	n. 부식 동판술, 에칭(화)
14 ☐	fauvism ['fō-ˌvi-zəm]	n. 야수파, 포비즘 → 20세기 초의 프랑스 회화의 한 유파로, 강렬한 색채의 대비와 거친 필치가 특징
15 ☐	fine arts	n. 미술
16 ☐	formative arts	n. 조형미술
17 ☐	fresco ['fres-kō]	n. 프레스코 화법
18 ☐	hue ['hyü]	n. 색조
19 ☐	illustrate ['ɪləstreɪt]	v. 삽화를 넣다, 구체적으로 설명하다
20 ☐	luminous ['lu:mɪnəs]	a. 밝은
21 ☐	luster ['lʌstə(r)]	n. 광택
22 ☐	opaque [əʊ'peɪk]	a. 불투명한
23 ☐	performance art	n. 육체의 행위를 음악, 영상 등으로 표현하려는 1970년대 예술 사조
24 ☐	pigment ['pɪgmənt]	n. 안료, 그림 물감
25 ☐	pop art	n. 팝아트 → 1960년대 미국에서 발전한 전위적 미술 운동, 대표화가는 Andy Warhol

02 Art History II (미술사 II)

01 ☐	abstractionism [æbˈstrækʃəˌnɪzəm]	n. 추상주의
02 ☐	adaptation [ˌædəpˈteɪʃən]	n. 각색, 개작
03 ☐	Art Deco	n. 아르 데코 → 1920-30년대 화려한 색채 및 기하학적 무늬
04 ☐	Art Nouveau	n. 아르 누보 → 19세기와 20세기에 유행한 건축 및 장식 예술의 새로운 양식으로 꽃이나 식물 등을 사용하여 복잡한 곡선의 형태로 표현
05 ☐	avant-garde [əˌvɑntˈgɑrd]	n. 아방가르드 → 20세기 초반 전위적 예술 사상
06 ☐	commentary [ˈkɒmənˌtɛri]	n. 해설, 논평
07 ☐	convention [kənˈvɛnʃən]	n. 관습
08 ☐	cubism [ˈkyuˌbɪzəm]	n. 입체파, 기하학적 표현
09 ☐	dadaism [ˈdɑdaɪzəm]	n. 다다이즘 → 기존 예술 양식을 부정한 비심미주의
10 ☐	exhibition [ˌɛksəˈbɪʃən]	n. 전시
11 ☐	expressionism [ɪkˈsprɛʃəˌnɪzəm]	n. 표현주의 → 개인의 주관 강조
12 ☐	formalism [ˈfɔrməˌlɪzəm]	n. 형식주의
13 ☐	futurism [ˈfyutʃəˌrɪzəm]	n. 미래파 → 1910년경 이탈리아에서 비롯된 예술의 새로운 양식
14 ☐	geometric [ˌdʒiəˈmɛtrɪk]	a. 기하학의
15 ☐	gothic [ˈgɒθɪk]	n. 고딕 → 12세기~15세기 유럽 미술, 건축, 음악의 양식; 스테인드 글라스, 뾰족한 지붕, 둥근 천장이 특징
16 ☐	impressionism [ɪmˈprɛʃəˌnɪzəm]	n. 인상주의 → 19세기 후반 미술사조로 빛과 함께 자연을 묘사
17 ☐	marvel [ˈmɑrvəl]	n. 경이
18 ☐	mimic [ˈmɪmɪk]	v. 모방하다
19 ☐	ornamentation [ˌɔrnəmɛnˈteɪʃən]	n. 장식, 꾸밈
20 ☐	post impressionism	n. 후기인상주의 → 세잔, 고흐, 고갱 등이 속함
21 ☐	post modernism [poʊstˈmɒdərˌnɪzəm]	n. 포스트모더니즘 → 모더니즘을 거부한 사조, 추상대신 재현추구
22 ☐	reproduction [ˌriprəˈdʌkʃən]	n. 복제
23 ☐	Rococo [rəˈkoʊkoʊ]	n. 로코코 양식 → 18세기 전반에 프랑스에서 발달된 화려하고 섬세한 건축양식
24 ☐	surrealism [səˈriəˌlɪzəm]	n. 초현실주의 → 다다이즘을 수정한 예술운동
25 ☐	symbolism [ˈsɪmbəˌlɪzəm]	n. 상징주의

| | History | **Arts** | Social Science |

03 Film (영화)

01 ☐	**appreciate** [əˈpriːʃiˌeɪt]	v. 평가하다
02 ☐	**audience** [ˈɔːdiəns]	n. 관객
03 ☐	**box office**	n. 매표소, 흥행성적
04 ☐	**cartoon** [kɑː(r)ˈtuːn]	n. 만화
05 ☐	**cinematic** [ˌsɪnəˈmætɪk]	a. 영화의
06 ☐	**commentary** [ˈkɒmənt(ə)ri]	n. 논쟁, 논평
07 ☐	**continuity** [ˌkɒntɪˈnjuːəti]	n. 촬영 대본, 콘티
08 ☐	**convert** [kənˈvɜː(r)t]	v. 개조하다
09 ☐	**critic** [ˈkrɪtɪk]	n. 비평가
10 ☐	**dramatize** [ˈdræmətaɪz]	v. 드라마로 만들다
11 ☐	**flick** [flɪk]	n. 영화제작사
12 ☐	**innovative** [ˈɪnəveɪtɪv]	a. 혁신적인
13 ☐	**intriguing** [ɪnˈtriːgɪŋ]	a. 매혹적인
14 ☐	**masterpiece** [ˈmɑːstə(r)ˌpiːs]	n. 걸작
15 ☐	**montage** [mɒnˈtɑːʒ]	n. 몽타주 → 합성 사진
16 ☐	**narrative** [ˈnærətɪv]	a. 서술형의, 이야기 식의
17 ☐	**nickelodeon** [ˌnɪkəˈloʊdiən]	n. 니켈로디언 → 5센트짜리 영화극장
18 ☐	**plot** [plɒt]	n. 줄거리
19 ☐	**short film**	n. 단편 영화
20 ☐	**sophisticated** [səˈfɪstɪˌkeɪtɪd]	a. 세련된
21 ☐	**studio** [ˈstjuːdiəʊ]	n. 방송실
22 ☐	**synopsis** [sɪˈnɒpsɪs]	n. 개요
23 ☐	**twist** [twɪst]	n. 반전
24 ☐	**venue** [ˈvenjuː]	n. 회합 장소
25 ☐	**western movie**	n. 서부영화

Life Science   Physical Science   Environmental Science

04 Literature I (문학 I)

01	bibliography [ˌbɪbliˈɒɡrəfi]	n. 참고문헌 목록
02	censorship [ˈsensə(r)ʃɪp]	n. 검열
03	civilized [ˈsɪvəˌlaɪzd]	a. 문명화된, 세련된
04	cliché [ˈkliːʃeɪ]	n. 판에 박은 문구, 진부한 표현
05	colloquial [kəˈləʊkwiəl]	a. 구어체의, 일상 회화의
06	commentator [ˈkɒmənˌteɪtə(r)]	n. 주석자
07	cynicism [ˈsɪnɪˌsɪz(ə)m]	n. 냉소주의
08	decadence [ˈdekəd(ə)ns]	n. 타락, 퇴폐
09	draft [drɑːft]	n. 초안
10	empiricism [ɪmˈpɪrɪˌsɪz(ə)m]	n. 경험주의
11	epic [ˈepɪk]	n. 서사시
12	excerpt [ˈeksɜː(r)pt]	n. 인용구, 발췌
13	existentialism [ˌeɡzɪˈstenʃ(ə)lɪz(ə)m]	n. 실존주의
14	flowery [ˈflaʊəri]	a. 미사여구를 쓴
15	lyric [ˈlɪrɪk]	a. 서정시의, 서정적인
16	materialism [məˈtɪəriəˌlɪz(ə)m]	n. 유물론
17	metaphor [ˈmetəfə(r)]	n. 은유
18	metaphysical [ˌmetəˈfɪzɪk(ə)l]	a. 형이상학의
19	paraphrase [ˈpærəˌfreɪz]	v. 바꾸어 말하다 n. 바꾸어 말하기
20	parody [ˈpærədi]	n. 패러디 (풍자적으로 모방한 글, 음악, 연극 등)
21	piracy [ˈpaɪrəsi]	n. 저작권 침해
22	plagiarize [ˈpleɪdʒəraɪz]	v. 표절하다
23	protagonist [prəʊˈtæɡənɪst]	n. (소설) 주인공
24	punctuate [ˈpʌŋktʃueɪt]	v. 돋보이게 하다, 구두점을 찍다
25	subscribe [səbˈskraɪb]	v. 정기 구독하다

History | **Arts** | **Social Science**

05 Literature II (문학 II)

01 ☐	**anonymous** [əˈnɒn əməs]	a. 저자 미상의
02 ☐	**archaic** [ɑrˈkeɪ ɪk]	a. 고어체인 *cf.* colloquial 구어체인
03 ☐	**archetype** [ˈɑrkɪˌtaɪp]	n. 전형
04 ☐	**autobiography** [ˌɔtəbaɪˈɒgrəfi]	n. 자서전 *cf.* biography 전기
05 ☐	**base** [beɪs]	n. 기반
06 ☐	**chronicle** [ˈkrɒnɪ kəl]	n. 연대기
07 ☐	**dialect** [ˈdaɪəˌlɛkt]	n. 방언, 사투리
08 ☐	**epitome** [ɪˈpɪtəmi]	n. 개요, 개략, 완전한 전형
09 ☐	**exterior** [ɪkˈstɪəriər]	n. 외부 ant. interior 내부
10 ☐	**fiction** [ˈfɪkʃən]	n. 소설
11 ☐	**folklore** [ˈfoʊkˌlɔr]	n. 민간 설화
12 ☐	**genre** [ˈʒɑnrə]	n. 장르
13 ☐	**irony** [ˈaɪrəni]	n. 반어법
14 ☐	**ornate** [ɔrˈneɪt]	a. 화려한, 장식적인
15 ☐	**paradox** [ˈpærəˌdɒks]	n. 역설
16 ☐	**prose** [proʊz]	n. 산문
17 ☐	**pseudonym** [ˈsudnɪm]	n. 익명
18 ☐	**ratio** [ˈreɪʃoʊ]	n. 비율
19 ☐	**rhetoric** [ˈrɛtərɪk]	n. 수사법, 수사학
20 ☐	**rhyme** [raɪm]	n. 각운
21 ☐	**satire** [ˈsætaɪər]	n. 풍자
22 ☐	**setting** [ˈsɛtɪŋ]	n. (작품의) 배경
23 ☐	**scroll** [skroʊl]	n. 두루마리 장식
24 ☐	**sonnet** [ˈsɒnɪt]	n. 소네트 (14행시)
25 ☐	**stereotype** [ˈstɛriəˌtaɪp]	n. 고정관념

06 Music I (음악 I)

01	☐	national anthem	n. 국가 cf. anthem 성가, 송가
02	☐	accompaniment [əˈkʌmp(ə)nɪmənt]	n. 반주
03	☐	arrangement [əˈreɪndʒmənt]	n. 편곡
04	☐	bow [baʊ]	v. (현악기를) 연주하다
05	☐	chamber music [ˈtʃeɪmbə(r) mjuːzɪk]	n. 실내악
06	☐	conservatory [kənˈsɜː(r)vət(ə)ri]	n. 음악학교, 예술학교
07	☐	fiddle [ˈfɪd(ə)l]	n. 바이올린
08	☐	fingering [ˈfɪŋɡərɪŋ]	n. 운지
09	☐	folk tune [foʊk tjuːn]	n. 민요음악
10	☐	harpsichord [ˈhɑː(r)psɪˌkɔː(r)d]	n. 하프시코드 → 쳄벨로라고도 불리는 16~18세기에 쓰인 건반
11	☐	major [ˈmeɪdʒə(r)]	a. 장음계의 cf. minor 단음계의
12	☐	march [mɑː(r)tʃ]	n. 행진곡
13	☐	movement [ˈmuːvmənt]	n. 악장
14	☐	musical notation	n. 기보법
15	☐	piece [piːs]	n. 작품
16	☐	pluck [plʌk]	v. (현악기를) 타다, 뜯다
17	☐	scale [skeɪl]	n. 음계
18	☐	score [skɔː(r)]	n. 악보
19	☐	solemn [ˈsɒləm]	a. 장엄한 cf. solemnity 엄숙, 장엄
20	☐	strike [straɪk]	v. (음, 악기 등을) 때려서 울리다
21	☐	string [strɪŋ]	n. (오케스트라의) 현악기 cf. string quartet 현악 4중주
22	☐	symphonic [sɪmˈfɒnɪk]	n. 교향악의
23	☐	tone [toʊn]	n. 음색 cf. tune 음조
24	☐	upbeat [ˈʌpbiːt]	n. 여린박 a. 경쾌한, 빠른
25	☐	variation [ˌveərɪˈeɪʃ(ə)n]	n. 편곡, 변주

07 Music II (음악 II)

01 ☐	**amplitude** [ˈæmplɪˌtud]	n. 진폭
02 ☐	**angle** [ˈæŋɡəl]	n. 각도
03 ☐	**beat** [bit]	n. 박자
04 ☐	**chord** [kɔrd]	n. 화음
05 ☐	**concerto** [kənˈtʃɛrtoʊ]	n. 협주곡
06 ☐	**conductor** [kənˈdʌktər]	n. 지휘자
07 ☐	**compose** [kəmˈpoʊz]	v. 작곡하다 n. composition 작곡
08 ☐	**chromatic** [kroʊˈmætɪk]	a. 반음계의
09 ☐	**harmonious** [hɑrˈmoʊniəs]	a. 화성의
10 ☐	**improvisation** [ɪmˌprɒvəˈzeɪʃən]	n. 즉흥 연주
11 ☐	**inventiveness** [ɪnˈvɛntɪvnɪs]	n. 독창성
12 ☐	**masterpiece** [ˈmæstərˌpis]	n. 명작
13 ☐	**note** [noʊt]	n. 악보
14 ☐	**overture** [ˈoʊvərtʃər]	n. 서곡 → 오페라나 연극이 공연되기 전에 막이 내려진 채 오케스트라가 연주하는 곡
15 ☐	**percussion instrument**	n. 타악기
16 ☐	**perform** [pərˈfɔrm]	v. 연주하다
17 ☐	**pitch** [pɪtʃ]	n. 음의 높낮이
18 ☐	**polyphony** [pəˈlɪfəni]	n. 다성음악
19 ☐	**rhythm and blues**	n. 리듬 앤 블루스 (R&B)
20 ☐	**string instrument**	n. 현악기
21 ☐	**tune** [tun]	n. 선율, 곡조
22 ☐	**undertone** [ʌndərtoʊn]	n. 반주음, 저음
23 ☐	**wavelength** [ˈweɪvˌlɛŋkθ]	n. 파장
24 ☐	**wind instrument**	n. 관악기
25 ☐	**word** [word]	n. 가사

Life Science | Physical Science | Environmental Science

08 Painting (회화)

01	appreciation [əˌpriʃiˈeɪʃən]	n. 예술품의 이해, 감상
02	engraving [ɛnˈgreɪvɪŋ]	n. 조판, 판화
03	etching [ˈɛtʃɪŋ]	n. 에칭 → 부식작용을 통해 제작한 판화 기법
04	figure painting [ˈfɪg yər ˈpeɪntɪŋ]	n. 인물화
05	formative art [ˈfɔr mə tɪv ɑrt]	n. 조형예술 → 공간의 형태적인 아름다움을 이루어 내는 예술
06	fresco [ˈfrɛskoʊ]	n. 프레스코화법 → 회반죽 벽토에 수채로 그리는 벽화 기법(13C-16C)
07	hue [hyu]	n. 색조, 색
08	illustrate [ˈɪləˌstreɪt]	v. 구체적으로 설명하다
09	landscape painting	n. 풍경화
10	lithograph [ˈlɪθəˌgræf]	n. 석판
11	marble [ˈmɑr bəl]	n. 대리석
12	mason [ˈmeɪ sən]	n. 석공
13	mural painting [ˈmyʊərəl ˈpeɪntɪŋ]	n. 벽화
14	pigment [ˈpɪgmənt]	n. 안료, 색소
15	plaster cast [ˈplæstər kæst]	n. 석고상
16	portrait [ˈpɔrtrɪt]	n. 초상화, 인물화
17	rendering [ˈrɛndərɪŋ]	n. 표현
18	tempera [ˈtɛm pərə]	n. 템페라화 → 프레스코화법에서 발달한 것으로 아교나 달걀노른자로 안료를 녹여 만든 불투명한 물감으로 그린 그림
19	translucent [trænsˈlusənt]	n. 반투명한 cf. opaque 불투명한
20	statue [ˈstætʃu]	n. 조각상
21	symbolize [ˈsɪmbəˌlaɪz]	v. 상징하다
22	symmetry [ˈsɪmɪtri]	n. 대칭, 균형 ant. asymmetry 비대칭
23	vandal [ˈvændl]	n. 예술품 파괴자
24	watercolor painting	n. 수채화
25	woodprint [ˈwʊdˌprɪnt]	n. 목각술

01 Communication (소통)

01 ☐	circulation [ˌsɜː(r)kjʊˈleɪʃ(ə)n]	n. 발행, 판매부수
02 ☐	contemporary [kənˈtemp(ə)r(ə)ri]	a. 현대적인
03 ☐	content [ˈkɒntent]	n. 내용
04 ☐	court [kɔː(r)t]	v. (남을) 꾀다
05 ☐	cover to cover	처음부터 끝까지
06 ☐	deciding factor	n. 결정적인 요인
07 ☐	deliver [dɪˈlɪvə(r)]	n. 보도하다
08 ☐	effectively [ɪˈfektɪv(ə)li]	ad. 효과적으로
09 ☐	fundamental [ˌfʌndəˈment(ə)l]	a. 근본적인
10 ☐	newsstand [ˈnjuːzˌstænd]	n. 신문 가판대
11 ☐	on time	정각에
12 ☐	overcome [ˌəʊvə(r)ˈkʌm]	v. 극복하다
13 ☐	peak [piːk]	v. 정점에 이르다
14 ☐	quote [kwəʊt]	n. 인용
15 ☐	readership [ˈriːdə(r)ʃɪp]	n. 독자
16 ☐	relevant [ˈreləv(ə)nt]	a. 연관된
17 ☐	reverse [rɪˈvɜː(r)s]	v. 반등시키다
18 ☐	scheme [skiːm]	n. 기획
19 ☐	section [ˈsekʃ(ə)n]	n. 섹션
20 ☐	significantly [sɪɡˈnɪfɪkəntli]	ad. 상당히
21 ☐	skim [skɪm]	v. 대충 훑어보다
22 ☐	spice [spaɪs]	v. 장식하다, 흥취를 더하다
23 ☐	subscribe [səbˈskraɪb]	v. 구독하다
24 ☐	target audience	n. 대상 독자
25 ☐	temporary [ˈtemp(ə)rəri]	a. 일시적인

Life Science | Physical Science | Environmental Science

 Economics (경제)

01 ☐	**bankruptcy** [ˈbæŋkrʌptsi]	n. 도산
02 ☐	**barter** [ˈbɑrtər]	n. 물물교환
03 ☐	**bond** [bɒnd]	n. 채권
04 ☐	**boom** [bum]	n. 급격한 증가
05 ☐	**budget** [ˈbʌdʒɪt]	n. 예산
06 ☐	**commodity** [kəˈmɒdɪti]	n. 생필품, 상품
07 ☐	**counterfeit** [ˈkaʊntərˌfɪt]	v. 위조하다
08 ☐	**current price**	n. 시가
09 ☐	**depression** [dɪˈprɛʃən]	n. 불경기, 침체 [syn] recession
10 ☐	**financial crisis**	n. 재정 위기, 금융 위기
11 ☐	**fiscal** [ˈfɪskəl]	a. 국고의, 재정상의
12 ☐	**inflation** [ɪnˈfleɪʃən]	n. 인플레이션
13 ☐	**levy** [ˈlɛvi]	v. 세금을 징수하다
14 ☐	**monetary system**	n. 통화제도
15 ☐	**monopoly** [məˈnɒpəli]	n. 독과점
16 ☐	**population density**	n. 인구밀도
17 ☐	**price fluctuation**	n. 물가 변동
18 ☐	**reimbursement** [ˌriɪmˈbɜrsmənt]	n. 상환, 변제
19 ☐	**retail** [ˈriteɪl]	n. 소매
20 ☐	**revenue** [ˈrɛvənˌyu]	n. 세입
21 ☐	**stock** [stɒk]	n. 주식
22 ☐	**subsidy** [ˈsʌbsɪdi]	n. 국가의 보조금
23 ☐	**tariff** [ˈtærɪf]	n. 관세
24 ☐	**transaction** [trænˈsækʃən]	n. 거래, 상거래
25 ☐	**wholesale** [ˈhoʊlˌseɪl]	n. 도매

History   Arts   **Social Science**

03 Law (법률)

01	accusation [ˌækyʊˈzeɪʃən]	n. 고소 syn complaint
02	accuse [əˈkyuz]	v. 고소하다, 고발하다
03	appeal [əˈpil]	v. 항소하다 → 판결에 대하여 불복하여 상소하다
04	code [koʊd]	n. 법전 → 국가가 제정한 법규집
05	conspiracy [kənˈspɪrəsi]	n. 불법 공모, 음모
06	constitution [ˌkɒnstɪˈtuʃən]	n. 헌법 → 국가최고 법률로, 국가 통치의 기초에 관한 모든 근본 법규
07	commit [kəˈmɪt]	v. 저지르다
08	enact [ɛnˈækt]	v. 실시하다, 시행하다
09	enforce [ɛnˈfɔrs]	v. 실시하다 syn force
10	executive [ɪgˈzɛkyətɪv]	n. 행정부 → 행정을 맡아 보는 국가 기관
11	fine [faɪn]	n. 벌금
12	imprisonment [ɪmˈprɪzənmənt]	n. 강제 구속
13	judiciary [dʒuˈdɪʃiˌɛri]	n. 사법부 → 대법원과 대법원의 관할 기관
14	lawsuit [ˈlɔˌsut]	n. 소송
15	legislature [ˈlɛdʒɪsˌleɪtʃər]	n. 입법부 → 입법 기관을 담당하는 국가 기관
16	lose a suit	소송에서 지다
17	petition [pəˈtɪʃən]	n. 항소 → 판결에 불복하여, 상급 법원에 법률적 처리를 다시 요구하는 신청 syn appeal, plea
18	precedent [ˈprɛsɪdənt]	n. 판례 → 법원에서 해당 사건과 동일하거나 비슷하게 행한 재판의 이전 사례
19	sentence [ˈsɛntns]	n. (형을) 판결, 선고(하다)
20	summon [ˈsʌmən]	n. 소환(장) → 법원이 증인, 피고인, 변호인 등의 사건과 관련된 사람들을 법원에 일정 시일에 부르는 행위
21	suspect [ˈsʌspɛkt]	n. 용의자
22	testimony [ˈtɛstəˌmoʊni]	n. 증언
23	the jury [ˈdʒʊəri]	n. 배심원 → 일반 국민들로 이루어진 재판에 참여하는 사람
24	trial [ˈtraɪəl]	n. 재판
25	violate [ˈvaɪəˌleɪt]	v. 위반하다

 Politics (정치학)

01	abolition [ˌæbəˈlɪʃən]	n. 폐지
02	address [əˈdrɛs]	v. 연설하다
03	appointment [əˈpɔɪntmənt]	n. 임명
04	authorities [əˈθɔrɪtis]	n. 당국
05	bureaucracy [byʊˈrɒkrəsi]	n. 관료주의
06	cabinet [ˈkæbənɪt]	n. 내각 → 국가의 행정권을 담당하는 최고 합의 기관
07	candidate [ˈkændɪˌdeɪt]	n. 후보자
08	congress [ˈkɒŋgrɪs]	n. (미국)의회 cf. parliament (영국)의회
09	communism [ˈkɒmyəˌnɪzəm]	n. 공산주의 [syn] socialism 사회주의
10	debate [dɪˈbeɪt]	n. 논쟁(하다)
11	delegate [ˈdɛlɪgɪt]	n. 대표자; 대의원
12	democracy [dɪˈmɒkrəsi]	n. 민주주의
13	hegemony [hɪˈdʒɛməni]	n. 패권 → 최고의 자리를 차지하여 누리는 공인된 힘과 권리
14	minority [maɪˈnɔrɪti]	n. 소수파
15	petition [pəˈtɪʃən]	n. 청원, 탄원
16	racialism [ˈreɪʃəˌlɪzəm]	n. 인종차별주의
17	ratify [ˈrætəˌfaɪ]	v. 비준하다 → 조약을 동의하다
18	representative [ˌrɛprɪˈzɛntətɪv]	n. 대표자
19	sovereignty [ˈsɒvrɪnti]	n. 주권
20	suffrage [ˈsʌfrɪdʒ]	n. 투표권
21	the House of representatives	n. 하원 cf. a member of the House of representatives 하원의원
22	the Senate	n. 상원 cf. the Senator 상원의원
23	totalitarianism [toʊˌtælɪˈtɛəriəˌnɪzəm]	n. 전체주의
24	unanimous [yuˈnænəməs]	a. 만장일치의
25	vote [voʊt]	n. 투표(하다)

05 Psychology I (심리학 I)

01	acute [əˈkjuːt]	n. 심한, 강한
02	anxiety [æŋˈzaɪəti]	n. 불안
03	cognitive [ˈkɒgnətɪv]	a. 인식의
04	confront [kənˈfrʌnt]	v. 직면하다
05	diarrhea [ˌdaɪəˈriːə]	n. 설사
06	disorder [dɪsˈɔː(r)də(r)]	n. 장애
07	dissect [dɪˈsekt]	v. 해부하다, 분석하다
08	effective [ɪˈfektɪv]	a. 효과적인
09	in conjunction with	~와 병행하여
10	medicament [məˈdɪkəmənt]	n. 약물
11	nausea [ˈnɔːziə]	n. 구역질
12	occurrence [əˈkʌrəns]	n. 발생
13	panic [ˈpænɪk]	n. 공포
14	physical [ˈfɪzɪk(ə)l]	a. 육체적
15	rational [ˈræʃ(ə)nəl]	a. 이성적인
16	reassure [ˌriːəˈʃʊə(r)]	v. 안심시키다
17	relaxation [ˌriːlækˈseɪʃ(ə)n]	n. 완화
18	relieve [rɪˈliːv]	v. 누그러뜨리다
19	routine [ruːˈtiːn]	n. 일상
20	side effect	n. 부작용
21	toddler [ˈtɒdlə(r)]	n. 유아
22	traumatize [ˈtrɔːmətaɪz]	v. 정신적으로 충격을 주다
23	unwilling [ʌnˈwɪlɪŋ]	a. 꺼리는, 마지못해
24	vary [ˈveəri]	v. 차이가 있다, 가지각색이다
25	vomit [ˈvɒmɪt]	v. 구토하다

06 Psychology II (심리학 II)

01 ☐	arousal [əˈraʊzəl]	n. 각성
02 ☐	awareness [əˈwɛərnɪs]	n. 자각
03 ☐	cognitive [ˈkɒgnɪtɪv]	a. 인지의 n. cognition 인지
04 ☐	concept [ˈkɒnsɛpt]	n. 개념
05 ☐	conscious [ˈkɒnʃəs]	a. 의식하는
06 ☐	depression [dɪˈprɛʃən]	n. 우울
07 ☐	disposition [ˌdɪspəˈzɪʃən]	n. 성향, 경향
08 ☐	ego [ˈigoʊ, ˈɛgoʊ]	n. 자아
09 ☐	emotion [ɪˈmoʊʃən]	n. 감정
10 ☐	envision [ɛnˈvɪʒən]	v. 상상하다
11 ☐	extrovert [ˈɛkstrəˌvɜrt]	a. 외향적인 ant. introvert 내성적인
12 ☐	feedback [ˈfidˌbæk]	n. 반응
13 ☐	identity [aɪˈdɛntɪti, ɪˈdɛn-]	n. 자아, 동질성
14 ☐	inconsistency [ˌɪnkənˈsɪstənsi]	n. 모순
15 ☐	motivation [ˌmoʊtəˈveɪʃən]	n. 동기, 주기
16 ☐	norm [nɔrm]	n. (행동의) 기준
17 ☐	perception [pərˈsɛpʃən]	n. 인지, 지각
18 ☐	predisposition [priˌdɪspəˈzɪʃən]	n. 성향
19 ☐	repression [rɪˈprɛʃən]	n. 억압, 억압된 욕망
20 ☐	resistance [rɪˈzɪstəns]	n. 반감, 저항
21 ☐	self-fulfillment [ˈsɛlf fʊlˈfɪlmənt]	n. 자기충족 cf. self-awareness 자각
22 ☐	stereotype [ˈstɛriəˌtaɪp]	n. 고정관념
23 ☐	stimulus [ˈstɪmyələs]	n. 자극
24 ☐	subconscious [sʌbˈkɒnʃəs]	a. 잠재의
25 ☐	trauma [ˈtraʊmə]	n. 정신적 외상

History | Arts | Social Science

07 Sociology (사회학)

01 ☐	acquaintance [əˈkweɪntəns]	n. 아는 사람, 지인
02 ☐	active [ˈæktɪv]	a. 활동적인
03 ☐	capacity [kəˈpæsəti]	n. 용량
04 ☐	co-worker	n. 동료
05 ☐	cortex [ˈkɔː(r)teks]	n. 대뇌피질
06 ☐	duration [djʊˈreɪʃ(ə)n]	n. 지속 기간
07 ☐	expose [ɪkˈspəʊz]	v. 노출하다
08 ☐	field of study	n. 연구 분야
09 ☐	hippocampus [hɪpəˈkæm pəs]	n. 해마
10 ☐	intimate [ˈɪntɪmət]	a. 친밀한
11 ☐	long-term	a. 장기적인
12 ☐	nature [ˈneɪtʃə(r)]	n. 천성, 본성
13 ☐	predict [prɪˈdɪkt]	v. 예상하다
14 ☐	process [ˈprəʊses]	n. 과정
15 ☐	purview [ˈpɜː(r)vjuː]	n. 이해의 범위
16 ☐	recall [rɪˈkɔːl]	v. 기억해내다
17 ☐	reclassify [riːˈklæsɪfaɪ]	v. 재분류하다
18 ☐	regression [rɪˈgreʃ(ə)n]	n. 회귀
19 ☐	settlement [ˈset(ə)lmənt]	n. 정착
20 ☐	shared behavior	n. 공통적인 태도
21 ☐	short-term	a. 단기적인
22 ☐	sociological [ˌsəʊsiəˈlɒdʒɪkəl]	a. 사회학적인
23 ☐	stable [ˈsteɪb(ə)l]	a. 안정적인
24 ☐	third world	n. 제3세계
25 ☐	tribal [ˈtraɪb(ə)l]	a. 부족의

Life Science

01 Biology I (생물학 I)

#	Word	Definition
01	aerobic [ɛəˈroʊbɪk]	a. 유산소의 ant. anaerobic 무산소의
02	beak [bik]	n. 부리 [syn] bill
03	chromosome [ˈkroʊməˌsoʊm]	n. 염색체
04	communicable [kəˈmyunɪkəbəl]	a. 전염성이 있는
05	dominant [ˈdɒmənənt]	a. 우성의 ant. recessive 열성의
06	exterminate [ɪkˈstɜrməˌneɪt]	v. 제거하다, 끝내다 [syn] terminate
07	ferment [ˈfɜrmɛnt]	n. 효모
08	fin [fɪn]	n. 지느러미
09	genus [ˈdʒinəs]	n. 속 cf. family 과, order 목, class 강, phylum 문, kingdom 계
10	gland [glænd]	n. 분비기관
11	heredity [həˈrɛdɪti]	n. 유전, 유전 형질 cf. genetic 유전자의
12	homeostasis [ˌhoʊmiəˈsteɪsɪs]	n. 항상성
13	host [hoʊst]	n. 숙주 ant. parasite 기생생물
14	hybrid [ˈhaɪbrɪd]	n. 잡종의
15	metabolism [məˈtæbəˌlɪzəm]	n. 물질대사
16	microbe [ˈmaɪkroʊb]	n. 미생물체
17	mutation [myuˈteɪʃən]	n. 돌연변이
18	nucleus [ˈnukliəs]	n. 핵 cf. nucleic acid 핵산
19	offspring [ˈɔfˌsprɪŋ]	n. 자손
20	parasitic [ˌpærəˈsɪtɪk]	n. 기생하는 ant. symbiotic 공생하는
21	respiration [ˌrɛspəˈreɪʃən]	n. 호흡
22	secretion [sɪˈkriʃən]	n. 분비
23	survival of the fittest	적자생존
24	taxonomy [tækˈsɒnəmi]	n. 분류학
25	tissue [ˈtɪʃu]	n. 조직 cf. membrane 세포막

02 Biology II (생물학 II)

01	amino acid	n. 아미노산
02	amphibian [æmˈfɪbiən]	n. 양서류
03	animal kingdom	n. 동물계
04	arthropod [ˈɑː(r)θrəpɒd]	n. 절지동물
05	asexual reproduction	n. 무성생식
06	biological clock	n. 생체시계
07	chlorophyll [ˈklɒrəfɪl]	n. 엽록소
08	circulation [ˌsɜː(r)kjʊˈleɪʃ(ə)n]	n. 순환
09	crustacean [krʌˈsteɪʃ(ə)n]	n. 갑각류
10	embryo [ˈembriˌəʊ]	n. 배아, 태아 [syn] fetus
11	enzyme [ˈenzaɪm]	n. 효소
12	evolution [ˌiːvəˈluːʃ(ə)n]	n. 진화
13	extinction [ɪkˈstɪŋkʃ(ə)n]	n. 멸종
14	feature [ˈfiːtʃə(r)]	n. 특징, 자질
15	fern [fɜː(r)n]	n. 양치류
16	fertilization [ˌfɜː(r)təlaɪˈzeɪʃ(ə)n]	n. 수정
17	genetic [dʒəˈnetɪk]	a. 유전의
18	glucose [ˈɡluːkəʊz]	n. 포도당
19	hermaphrodite [hɜː(r)ˈmæfrədaɪt]	n. 자웅 동체, 양성 동물
20	husk [hʌsk]	n. 과일이나 땅콩의 마른 껍질
21	incubation [ˌɪŋkjʊˈbeɪʃ(ə)n]	n. 배양, 부화
22	infest [ɪnˈfest]	v. (해충이나 병이) 만연하다
23	intake [ˈɪnteɪk]	n. 섭취
24	invertebrate [ɪnˈvɜː(r)tɪbrət]	n. 무척추동물
25	kernel [ˈkɜː(r)n(ə)l]	n. (견과류, 씨앗의) 알맹이

Life Science | Physical Science | Environmental Science

03 Biology III (생물학 III)

01	larva [ˈlɑː(r)və]	n. 유충
02	limb [lɪm]	n. 큰 가지, 마디, 사지
03	mammal [ˈmæm(ə)l]	n. 포유류
04	membrane [ˈmemˌbreɪn]	n. 막, 막 조직
05	mineral [ˈmɪn(ə)rəl]	n. 무기질
06	mutation [mjuːˈteɪʃ(ə)n]	n. 변이, 돌연변이
07	natural selection	n. 자연선택
08	nervous system	n. 신경계
09	niche [niːʃ]	n. 적소, 서식지
10	nocturnal [nɒkˈtɜː(r)n(ə)l]	a. 야행성의
11	organism [ˈɔː(r)gəˌnɪz(ə)m]	n. 유기체
12	pollination [ˌpɒləˈneɪʃ(ə)n]	n. 수분
13	primate [ˈpraɪmeɪt]	n. 영장류
14	protein [ˈproʊtiːn]	n. 단백질
15	reproduction [ˌriːprəˈdʌkʃ(ə)n]	n. 생식, 번식
16	reptile [ˈreptaɪl]	n. 파충류
17	scavenger [ˈskæv ɪn dʒər]	n. 썩은 고기를 먹는 동물
18	spore [spɔː(r)]	n. 포자
19	starch [stɑː(r)tʃ]	n. 전분
20	symbiotic [ˌsɪmbaɪˈɒtɪk]	a. 공생하는
21	tentacle [ˈtentək(ə)l]	n. 촉수, 촉모
22	trait [treɪt]	n. 특질
23	trunk [trʌŋk]	n. 줄기
24	vertebrate [ˈvɜː(r)tɪbrət]	n. 척추동물
25	yeast [jiːst]	n. 효모

Botany (식물학)

01 ☐	airborne [ˈɛərˌbɔrn]	a. 공기로 운반되는
02 ☐	bark [bɑrk]	n. 나무 껍질 *cf.* n. stem 줄기, n. thorn 가시
03 ☐	burgeon [ˈbɜrdʒən]	v. 싹트다 *cf.* n. sprout 식물의 싹, v. germinate 발아하다
04 ☐	cellulose [ˈsɛljəˌloʊs]	n. 섬유소 *cf.* n. chlorophyll 엽록소
05 ☐	conifer [ˈkoʊnəfər]	n. 침엽수 *cf.* deciduous trees 낙엽수
06 ☐	dense [dɛns]	a. 빽빽한 *cf.* a. lush 무성한
07 ☐	fertilization [ˌfɜrtləˈzeɪʃən]	n. 수정
08 ☐	foliage [ˈfoʊliɪdʒ]	n. 잎 *cf.* v. shed (잎을) 떨어뜨리다
09 ☐	glucose [ˈglukoʊs]	n. 포도당
10 ☐	indigenous [ɪnˈdɪdʒənəs]	a. 토종의, 토착의
11 ☐	kernel [ˈkɜrnl]	n. 씨
12 ☐	lichen [ˈlaɪkən]	n. 지의류 → fungus (곰팡이) + alga (조류, 바다말)가 공생하는 식물군
13 ☐	maize [meɪz]	n. 옥수수
14 ☐	meadow [ˈmɛdoʊ]	n. 목초지 [syn] grazing land
15 ☐	nectar [ˈnɛktər]	n. 과즙
16 ☐	perennial [pəˈrɛniəl]	a. 다년생의
17 ☐	petal [ˈpɛtl]	n. 꽃잎
18 ☐	pigment [ˈpɪgmənt]	n. 세포의 색소
19 ☐	pollination [ˌpɒləˈneɪʃən]	n. 수분 *cf.* pollen 꽃가루
20 ☐	resin [ˈrɛzɪn]	n. 송진 *cf.* n. sap 수액
21 ☐	starch [stɑrtʃ]	n. 녹말
22 ☐	taproot [ˈtæpˌrut]	n. 곧은 뿌리 *cf.* fibrous root 수염 뿌리
23 ☐	transpiration [ˌtrænspəˈreɪʃən]	n. 증산작용 → 식물이 뿌리를 통해 흡수한 물을 식물 잎의 구멍을 통해 내보내는 과정
24 ☐	vegetation [ˌvɛdʒɪˈteɪʃən]	n. 식물 n. weed 잡초
25 ☐	wilt [wɪlt]	v. 시들다

05 Entomology I (곤충학 I)

01	antenna [ænˈtenə]	n. 더듬이
02	beetle [ˈbiːt(ə)l]	n. 투구풍뎅이, 딱정벌레
03	bristle [ˈbrɪs(ə)l]	n. 강모 (센털)
04	caterpillar [ˈkætə(r)ˌpɪlə(r)]	n. 애벌레
05	cicada [sɪˈkɑːdə]	n. 매미
06	cocoon [kəˈkuːn]	n. 누에고치
07	compound eye	n. 쌍 눈
08	cricket [ˈkrɪkɪt]	n. 귀뚜라미
09	endoskeleton [ˈendəʊˌskelɪt(ə)n]	n. 내골격 *cf.* exoskeleton 외골격
10	fang [fæŋ]	n. 독니, 송곳니
11	firefly [ˈfaɪə(r)ˌflaɪ]	n. 반딧불
12	flap [flæp]	v. 날개를 퍼덕이다
13	flea [fliː]	n. 벼룩
14	foreleg [ˈfɔː(r)ˌleg]	n. 앞다리 *cf.* forewing 앞날개
15	grasshopper [ˈgrɑːsˌhɒpə(r)]	n. 여치, 메뚜기
16	hatch [hætʃ]	v. 알에서 깨어나다, 부화하다
17	locust [ˈləʊkəst]	n. 메뚜기
18	mayfly [ˈmeɪˌflaɪ]	n. 하루살이
19	molt [məʊlt]	v. 탈피하다, 허물을 벗다
20	pollen [ˈpɒlən]	n. 꽃가루, 화분
21	pupa [ˈpjuːpə]	n. 번데기
22	venom [ˈvenəm]	n. 독
23	wasp [wɒsp]	n. 장수말벌
24	wing beat	n. 날갯짓
25	wingspan [ˈwɪŋˌspæn]	n. 날개폭

06 Entomology II (곤충학 II)

01	abdomen [ˈæbdəmən]	n. 복부
02	anchor [ˈæŋkər]	v. 자리 잡다 syn hold in a place
03	bumblebee [ˈbʌmbəlˌbi]	n. 장수 말벌
04	butterfly [ˈbʌtərˌflaɪ]	n. 나비
05	centipede [ˈsɛntəˌpid]	n. 지네
06	dragonfly [ˈdrægənˌflaɪ]	n. 잠자리
07	eradicate [ɪˈrædɪˌkeɪt]	v. 없애다
08	excrete [ɪkˈskrit]	v. 분비하다
09	exoskeleton [ˌɛksoʊˈskɛlɪtn]	n. 외골격
10	feed on	v. 주식으로 먹다
11	gland [glænd]	n. 분비기관
12	infestation [ˌɪnfɛˈsteɪʃən]	n. 기생충의 체내 침입
13	insecticide [ɪnˈsɛktəˌsaɪd]	n. 살충제
14	larva [ˈlɑrvə]	n. 유충
15	mandible [ˈmændəbəl]	n. 절지 동물의 큰 턱
16	metamorphosis [ˌmɛtəˈmɔrfəsɪs]	n. 변형, 탈피
17	moth [mɔθ]	n. 나방
18	proboscis [proʊˈbɒsɪs]	n. 곤충의 긴 주둥이
19	resilient [rɪˈzɪlyənt]	a. 탄력적인
20	sac [sæk]	n. 주머니, 낭
21	termite [ˈtɜrmaɪt]	n. 흰개미
22	toxic [ˈtɒksɪk]	n. 독성의
23	viscosity [vɪˈskɒsɪti]	n. 점성
24	warning coloration	n. 경계색 cf. protective coloration 보호색
25	worm [wɜrm]	n. 벌레

07 Zoology I (동물학 I)

01	adapt to	v. ~에 적응하다
02	bear [beə(r)]	v. (여성, 암컷이 아이를) 낳다
03	capture [ˈkæptʃə(r)]	v. 포획하다
04	carnivorous [kɑː(r)ˈnɪv(ə)rəs]	a. 육식의
05	cold-blooded [ˌkəʊld ˈblʌdɪd]	a. 냉혈의
06	courtship [ˈkɔː(r)tʃɪp]	n. 구애, 짝짓기
07	den [den]	n. 굴, 우리
08	descend [dɪˈsend]	v. ~의 계통을 잇다
09	fend [fend]	v. 방어하다, ~을 부양하다
10	hatch [hætʃ]	v. (알, 병아리를) 까다, 부화하다
11	herd [hɜː(r)d]	n. 무리, 떼 syn grouping
12	hibernation [ˌhaɪbə(r)ˈneɪʃ(ə)n]	n. 동면, 겨울잠
13	lay [leɪ]	v. (알을) 낳다
14	leathery [ˈleðəri]	a. 가죽 같은
15	live off	v. ~에 기생하다
16	mate [meɪt]	v. 짝, 짝을 짓다
17	mollusk [ˈmɒləsk]	n. 연체동물 syn shellfish
18	omnivore [ˈɒmnɪˌvɔː(r)]	n. 잡식동물
19	plumage [ˈpluːmɪdʒ]	n. 깃털
20	rodent [ˈrəʊd(ə)nt]	n. 설치류
21	shell [ʃel]	n. (알 등의) 껍데기, (동식물의) 단단한 외피
22	spider [ˈspaɪdə(r)]	n. 거미류
23	spine [spaɪn]	n. 등뼈, 척추
24	strut [strʌt]	v. 뽐내다, 과시하다
25	swoop [swuːp]	v. 급습하다 syn grab

08 Zoology II (동물학 II)

01	**breed** [brid]	v. 번식하다 *cf.* mate 짝을 짓다, bear 새끼를 낳다, lay 알을 낳다, descend 계통을 잇다
02	**burrow** [ˈbɜroʊ]	v. 파다, 발굴하다
03	**camouflage** [ˈkæməˌflɑʒ]	v. 위장하다
04	**den** [dɛn]	n. 굴, 우리
05	**dinosaur** [ˈdaɪnəˌsɔr]	n. 공룡
06	**dormant** [ˈdɔrmənt]	a. 잠자는
07	**egg** [ɛg]	n. 난자 *cf.* sperm 정자
08	**flock** [flɒk]	n. 집단, 무리 [syn] herd
09	**game** [geɪm]	n. 사냥감
10	**habitat** [ˈhæbɪˌtæt]	n. 서식지
11	**herbivore** [ˈhɜrbəˌvɔr]	n. 초식동물 *cf.* carnivore 육식동물, omnivore 잡식동물
12	**hibernate** [ˈhɪbərˌneɪt]	v. 겨울 잠을 자다
13	**invertebrate** [ɪnˈvɜrtəbrɪt]	n. 무척추동물 *cf.* mollusk 연체동물, arthropod 절지동물, crustacean 갑각류, bug 곤충
14	**livestock** [laɪvˌstɒk]	n. 가축
15	**migrate** [ˈmaɪgreɪt]	v. 이동하다
16	**nocturnal** [nɒkˈtɜrnl]	a. 야행성의 *ant.* diurnal 주행성의
17	**predator** [ˈprɛdətər]	n. 약탈자
18	**prey** [preɪ]	n. 먹이
19	**proboscis** [proʊˈbɒsɪs]	n. 코끼리의 코, 곤충의 긴 주둥이
20	**ruminant** [ˈrumənənt]	n. 반추동물 *ant.* nonruminant 비반추동물
21	**scavenger** [ˈskævɪndʒər]	n. 죽은 고기를 먹는 동물
22	**sexual reproduction**	n. 유성생식 *ant.* asexual reproduction 무성생식
23	**spine** [spaɪn]	n. 등뼈
24	**tentacle** [ˈtɛntəkəl]	n. 촉수, 더듬이
25	**vertebrate** [ˈvɜrtəbrɪt]	n. 척추동물 *e.g.* amphibian 양서류, reptile 파충류, bird 새, mammal 포유류, primate 영장류, rodent 설치류

Life Science | **Physical Science** | Environmental Science

01 Astronomy I (천문학 I)

01	celestial sphere	n. 천구
02	cluster [ˈklʌstə(r)]	n. 성단
03	comet [ˈkɒmɪt]	n. 혜성
04	detect [dɪˈtekt]	v. 탐지하다
05	diameter [daɪˈæmɪtə(r)]	n. 지름
06	distant [ˈdɪstənt]	n. 먼
07	falling star [ˌfɔːlɪŋ ˈstɑː(r)]	n. 별똥별
08	field of vision	n. 시야
09	friction [ˈfrɪkʃ(ə)n]	n. 마찰
10	galaxy [ˈɡæləksi]	n. 성운, 은하, 은하수, 은하계
11	gravity [ˈɡrævəti]	n. 중력
12	in reverse	반대로
13	magnetic storm	n. 자기 폭풍
14	neutron star	n. 중성자 별
15	observatory [əbˈzɜː(r)vətri]	n. 관측소
16	observe [əbˈzɜː(r)v]	v. 관찰하다, 관측하다
17	planet [ˈplænɪt]	n. 행성
18	proton [ˈprəʊtɒn]	n. 양성자
19	pulsar [ˈpʌlsɑː(r)]	n. 펄서 ⇒ 강한 자기장을 가지고 고속 회전을 하는 천체
20	solar system	n. 태양계
21	stationary [ˈsteɪʃ(ə)n(ə)ri]	a. 정지된
22	stellar [ˈstelə(r)]	a. 별의
23	supernova [ˈsuːpə(r)ˌnəʊvə]	n. 초신성
24	telescope [ˈtelɪˌskəʊp]	n. 망원경
25	variable star	n. 변광성

02 Astronomy II (천문학 II)

01 ☐	**asteroid** [ˈæstəˌrɔɪd]	n. 소행성 *cf.* comet 혜성, planet 행성
02 ☐	**astronaut** [ˈæstrəˌnɔt]	n. 우주 비행사
03 ☐	**axis** [ˈæksɪs]	n. 축
04 ☐	**celestial body**	n. 천체 [syn] heavenly body
05 ☐	**concentration** [ˌkɒnsənˈtreɪʃən]	n. 농도
06 ☐	**constellation** [ˌkɒnstəˈleɪʃən]	n. 성좌, 성단
07 ☐	**crater** [ˈkreɪtər]	n. 분화구
08 ☐	**explosion** [ɪkˈsploʊʒən]	n. 폭발
09 ☐	**extraterrestrial** [ˌɛkstrətəˈrɛstrɪəl]	a. 외계의
10 ☐	**gravitational** [ˌgrævɪˈteɪʃən]	a. 중력의
11 ☐	**interstellar matter**	n. 성간 물질
12 ☐	**luminous** [ˈlumənəs]	a. 빛을 내는
13 ☐	**lunar eclipse**	n. 월식 *cf.* solar eclipse 일식, partial eclipse 부분식, total eclipse 개기식
14 ☐	**Mercury** [ˈmɜrkyəri]	n. 수성 *cf.* Venus 금성, Mars 화성, Jupiter 목성, Saturn 토성, Uranus 천왕성, Neptune 해왕성, Pluto 명왕성
15 ☐	**meteor (meteorite)** [ˈmitiər]	n. 유성, 운석
16 ☐	**naked eye** [ˈneɪkɪd aɪ]	n. 육안
17 ☐	**nebula** [ˈnɛbyələ]	n. 성운(星雲) : 구름 모양으로 퍼져 보이는 천체
18 ☐	**orbit** [ˈɔrbɪt]	n. 궤도 [syn] track
19 ☐	**red giant star**	n. 적색거성
20 ☐	**rotation** [roʊˈteɪʃən]	n. 자전 *cf.* revolution 공전
21 ☐	**satellite** [ˈsætlˌaɪt]	n. 위성
22 ☐	**supergiant star**	n. 초거성
23 ☐	**the Milky Way (= Galaxy)**	n. 은하, 은하수
24 ☐	**weightlessness** [ˈweɪt lɪsnɛs]	n. 무중력
25 ☐	**white dwarf star**	n. 백색왜성

Life Science | **Physical Science** | Environmental Science

03 Chemistry I (화학 I)

01 ☐	alkalinity [ˌælkəˈlɪnɪti]	n. 알칼리성 *cf.* acidity 산성
02 ☐	boiling point	n. 끓는점
03 ☐	composition [ˌkɒmpəˈzɪʃ(ə)n]	n. 합성
04 ☐	condense [kənˈdens]	v. 농축하다
05 ☐	crystal [ˈkrɪst(ə)l]	n. 결정
06 ☐	element [ˈelɪmənt]	n. 원소
07 ☐	evaporation [ɪˌvæpəreɪt]	n. 증발
08 ☐	filter [ˈfɪltə(r)]	v. 여과하다
09 ☐	freezing point	n. 어는점, 빙점
10 ☐	hydrochloric acid [ˌhaɪdrəˌklɒrɪk ˈæsɪd]	n. 염산
11 ☐	hydrogen [ˈhaɪdrədʒən]	n. 수소
12 ☐	matter [ˈmætə(r)]	n. 물질
13 ☐	melting point	n. 융(해)점, 녹는점
14 ☐	nitrogen [ˈnaɪtrədʒ(ə)n]	n. 질소
15 ☐	oxidize [ˈɒksɪdaɪz]	v. 산화하다
16 ☐	oxygen [ˈɒksɪdʒ(ə)n]	n. 산소
17 ☐	periodic table	n. 주기율표
18 ☐	property [ˈprɒpə(r)ti]	n. (어떤 물건 고유의) 특성, 특질
19 ☐	purify [ˈpjʊərɪfaɪ]	v. 정제하다
20 ☐	solution [səˈluːʃ(ə)n]	n. 용액
21 ☐	sulfuric acid [sʌlˌfjʊərɪk ˈæsɪd]	n. 황산
22 ☐	thermometer [θə(r)ˈmɒmɪtə(r)]	n. 온도계
23 ☐	variable [ˈveəriəb(ə)l]	n. 변수
24 ☐	volume [ˈvɒljuːm]	n. 부피, 양
25 ☐	zinc [zɪŋk]	n. 아연

04 Chemistry II (화학 II)

01	acid [ˈæsɪd]	n. 산 *cf.* alkalinity 알칼리성
02	alloy [ˈælɔɪ]	n. 합금
03	aluminum [əˈlumənəm]	n. 알루미늄
04	carbon [ˈkɑrbən]	n. 탄소
05	carbohydrate [ˌkɑrbouˈhaɪdreɪt]	n. 탄수화물 *cf.* oxygen 산소, hydrogen 수소, nitrogen 질소, helium 헬륨
06	catalyst [ˈkætlɪst]	n. 촉매 v. catalyze 촉매작용을 하다
07	concentration [ˌkɑnsənˈtreɪʃən]	n. 농축, 농도
08	condensation [ˌkɑndɛnˈseɪʃən]	n. 액화 → 기체가 냉각·압축되어 액체로 변하는 현상
09	content [ˈkɑntɛnt]	n. 함유량
10	compound [ˈkɑmpaʊnd]	n. 화합물 *cf.* oxide 산화물, oxidize 산화하다
11	corrode [kəˈroʊd]	n. 부식되다
12	decomposition [ˌdikɑmpəˈzɪʃən]	n. 분해
13	diffusion [dɪˈfyuʒən]	n. 확산
14	dilution [dɪˈluʃən]	n. 희석
15	enzyme [ˈɛnzaɪm]	n. 효소
16	isotope [ˈaɪsəˌtoʊp]	n. 동위 원소
17	lead [lid]	n. 납
18	molecule [ˈmɑləˌkyul]	n. 분자
19	neutralize [ˈnutrəˌlaɪz]	v. 중화하다
20	osmosis [ɑzˈmoʊsɪs]	n. 삼투현상 → 반투막을 사이에 두고 양쪽 용액에 농도 차가 있을 경우, 농도가 높은 쪽으로 용매가 옮겨 가는 현상 *cf.* osmoregulation 삼투 조절 작용
21	saturation [ˌsætʃəˈreɪʃən]	n. 포화
22	silicon [ˈsɪlɪkən]	n. 규소
23	soluble [ˈsɑlyəbəl]	a. 용해되는 ant. insoluble 용해되지 않는
24	solution [səˈluʃən]	n. 용매 → 용질(solute)을 녹여 용액을 만드는 물질
25	volatile [ˈvɑlətl]	n. 휘발성의

Life Science | **Physical Science** | Environmental Science

05 Physics I (물리학 I)

01	charge [tʃɑːr(r)dʒ]	n. 충전, 전하
02	diameter [daɪˈæmɪtə(r)]	n. 직경, 지름
03	discharge [dɪsˈtʃɑː(r)dʒ]	n. 방전
04	dynamic [daɪˈnæmɪk]	n. 원동력, 역학
05	electrode [ɪˈlektroʊd]	n. 전극
06	flexibility [ˌfleksəˈbɪləti]	n. 신축성
07	fluctuation [ˌflʌktʃuˈeɪʃ(ə)n]	n. 변동, 파동, 동요
08	fluorescent light	n. 형광등
09	incandescent light	n. 백열등
10	inertia [ɪˈnɜː(r)ʃə]	n. 관성
11	neutralize [ˈnjuːtrəlaɪz]	v. 중화하다
12	optics [ˈɒptɪks]	n. 광학
13	pendulum [ˈpendjʊləm]	n. 진자, 추
14	quantum [ˈkwɒntəm]	n. 양자
15	radiation [ˌreɪdiˈeɪʃ(ə)n]	n. 방사, 복사선
16	radius [ˈreɪdiəs]	n. 반지름
17	reflection [rɪˈflekʃ(ə)n]	n. 반사
18	resonance [ˈrezənəns]	n. 공명, 공진
19	semiconductor [ˌsemikənˈdʌktə(r)]	n. 반도체
20	specific gravity	n. 비중 → 어떤 물질의 질량과 그것과 동일한 체적의 표준물질의 질량과의 비율
21	static [ˈstætɪk]	a. 정적인
22	surface tension	n. 표면 장력
23	torsion [ˈtɔː(r)ʃ(ə)n]	n. 염력, 비트는 힘
24	velocity [vəˈlɒsəti]	n. 속도
25	wavelength [ˈweɪvˌleŋθ]	n. 파장

06 Physics II (물리학 II)

01	boiling point	n. 끓는점
02	buoyancy [ˈbɔɪənsi]	n. 부력
03	centrifugal force	n. 원심력
04	conduct [kənˈdʌkt]	v. 전도하다
05	deviation [ˌdiviˈeɪʃən]	n. (광선의) 굴곡 cf. radiation (광선의) 복사선, reflection (광선의) 반사
06	disperse [dɪˈspɜrs]	v. 빛을 분산시키다
07	elasticity [ɪlæˈstɪsɪti]	n. 탄성
08	electromagnetic wave	n. 전자파
09	flexibility [ˌflɛksəˈbɪləti]	n. 신축성
10	freezing point	n. 빙점
11	friction [ˈfrɪkʃən]	n. 마찰
12	kinetic energy	n. 운동에너지 cf. potential energy 위치 에너지, radiant energy 복사 에너지, mechanical energy 역학 에너지
13	malleability [ˌmæliəˈbɪlɪti]	n. 금속의 가단성 → 고체가 외부의 충격에 깨지지 않고 늘어나는 성질
14	melting point	n. 융(해)점
15	neutron [ˈnutrɒn]	n. 중성자 cf. proton 양성자, electron 전자
16	refraction [rɪˈfrækʃən]	n. 굴절
17	sound wave	n. 음파
18	steam [stim]	n. 수증기 syn vapor
19	strain [streɪn]	n. 당김, 찌그러짐, 변형
20	surface tension	n. 표면 장력
21	theory of relativity	상대성 이론
22	vacuum [ˈvækyum]	n. 진공
23	vibration [vaɪˈbreɪʃən]	n. 진동
24	visible rays	가시 광선 cf. ultraviolet rays 자외선, infrared rays 적외선
25	wave length	n. 파장

Environmental Science

01 Ecology I (생태학 I)

01	acid rain	n. 산성비
02	biosphere [ˈbaɪəʊˌsfɪə(r)]	n. 생물권
03	catastrophe [kəˈtæstrəfi]	n. 대재해, 파멸
04	conservationist [ˌkɒnsə(r)ˈveɪʃ(ə)nɪst]	n. (자연환경 등의) 보호론자
05	consumer [kənˈsjuːmə(r)]	n. (생태계의) 소비자 ↔ producer 생산자 *cf.* decomposer 분해자
06	ecological efficiency	n. 생태적 효율성
07	ecosystem [ˈiːkəʊˌsɪstəm]	n. 생태계
08	emission [ɪˈmɪʃ(ə)n]	n. 방출, 배출
09	energy flow	n. (생태계의) 에너지 흐름
10	exhaust [ɪɡˈzɔːst]	v. 고갈시키다
11	food chain	n. 먹이 사슬 *cf.* food web 먹이 그물
12	global warming	n. 지구 온난화
13	greenhouse effect	n. 온실효과
14	industrial waste	n. 산업 폐기물
15	landfill [ˈlæn(d)ˌfɪl]	n. 쓰레기 매립지
16	noxious [ˈnɒkʃəs]	a. 유해한, 유독한
17	oil spill	n. (해상의) 석유 유출
18	pest [pest]	n. 해충, 유해 생물
19	pollutant [pəˈluːt(ə)nt]	n. 오염 물질
20	purification [ˌpjʊərɪfɪˈkeɪʃ(ə)n]	n. 정화
21	salvage [ˈsælvɪdʒ]	n. 구조, 인양
22	sewage [ˈsuːɪdʒ]	n. 하수
23	soil contamination	n. 토양 오염
24	tract [trækt]	n. 토지의 넓이, 지역
25	untreated [ʌnˈtriːtɪd]	a. 처리되지 않은, 정화되지 않은

02 Ecology II (생태학 II)

01	aboriginal [ˌæbəˈrɪdʒənl]	a. 토착의
02	aquatic [əˈkwætɪk]	a. 물속의 *cf.* terrestrial 지상의
03	biodiversity [ˌbaɪoʊdɪˈvɜrsɪti]	n. 생물 다양성
04	biomass [ˈbaɪoʊˌmæs]	n. 생물량, 생물 자원
05	chemosynthesis [ˌkiomoʊˈsɪnθəsɪs]	n. 화학 합성
06	community [kəˈmyunɪti]	n. 군집
07	deforestation [diˈfɔrɪsteɪʃən]	n. 산림 벌채
08	desertification [dɪˌzɜrtəfɪˈkeɪʃən]	n. 사막화
09	domestic [dəˈmɛstɪk]	a. 길들여진
10	endangered [ɛnˈdeɪndʒərd]	a. 멸종 위기에 처한 [syn] extinct
11	evolutionary [ˌɛvəˈluʃəˌnɛri]	a. 진화의
12	fauna [ˈfɔnə]	n. 동물군 *cf.* flora 식물군
13	food chain	n. 먹이 연쇄 [syn] food web 먹이 그물
14	habitat [ˈhæbɪˌtæt]	n. 서식지 [syn] dwelling
15	intrude [ɪnˈtrud]	v. 침입하다
16	natural enemy	n. 천적
17	omnivore [ˈɒmnəˌvɔr]	n. 잡식 동물 *cf.* carnivore 육식 동물, herbivore 초식 동물
18	perish [ˈpɛrɪʃ]	v. 갑자기 죽다, 소멸하다
19	producer [prəˈdusər]	n. 생산자 *cf.* consumer 소비자, decomposer 분해자
20	rain forest	n. 열대 우림
21	recede [rɪˈsid]	v. 물러가다, 후퇴하다 [syn] retreat
22	reservoir [ˈrɛzərˌvwɑr]	n. 저수지
23	timber [ˈtɪmbər]	n. 목재
24	vegetation [ˌvɛdʒɪˈteɪʃən]	n. 식물, 초목
25	wetland [ˈwɛtˌlænd]	n. 습지

Energy (에너지)

01	alternative energy	n. 대체 에너지 *cf.* renewable energy 재생에너지, solar energy 태양 에너지, geothermal energy 지열 에너지
02	byproduct [ˈbaɪˌprɒdəkt]	n. 부산물
03	combustion [kəmˈbʌstʃən]	n. 연소
04	compress [kəmˈprɛs]	v. 압축하다
05	deplete [dɪˈplit]	v. 고갈시키다
06	drive [draɪv]	v. 추진하다
07	energy-efficient	a. 에너지 효율이 높은
08	exploit [ˈɛksplɔɪt]	v. 이용하다, 착취하다
09	extract [ɪkˈstrækt]	v. 추출하다 [syn] mine
10	eutrophication [yuˌtrɒfɪkeɪʃən]	n. 부영양화
11	fossil fuel	n. 화석 연료
12	gaseous [ˈgæsiəs]	a. 가스의
13	generator [ˈdʒɛnəˌreɪtər]	n. 발전기
14	global warming	n. 지구 온난화
15	harness [ˈhɑrnɪs]	v. 이용하다
16	oil drilling	n. 석유 시추
17	oil field	n. 유전
18	oil refinery	n. 정유 공장
19	petroleum [pəˈtroʊliəm]	n. 석유 *cf.* kerosene 등유, crude oil 원유
20	power plant	n. 전력 발전소
21	reservoir [ˈrɛzərˌvwɑr]	n. 매장 지역, 저수지
22	renewable	a. 재생 가능한
23	submerge [səbˈmɜrdʒ]	v. 가라앉히다
24	tidal power	n. 조력 *cf.* hydroelectric power 수력, thermal power 화력, nuclear power 원자력
25	wave energy	n. 파동에너지

| History | Arts | Social Science |

04 Geology I (지질학 I)

01	arctic [ˈɑː(r)ktɪk]	a. 북극의 cf. the Arctic 북극
02	bulge [bʌldʒ]	v. 툭 튀어나오다, 융기하다
03	cavern [ˈkævə(r)n]	n. 큰 동굴
04	corrosion [kəˈroʊʒ(ə)n]	n. 부식, 침식
05	delta [ˈdeltə]	n. 삼각주
06	epicenter [ˈepɪˌsentə(r)]	n. 진앙, 진원지
07	erosion [ɪˈroʊʒ(ə)n]	n. 침식
08	granite [ˈɡrænɪt]	n. 화강암
09	hot spring	n. 온천
10	lava [ˈlɑːvə]	n. 용암
11	levee [ˈlevi]	n. 제방
12	limestone [ˈlaɪmˌstoʊn]	n. 석회암
13	mantle [ˈmænt(ə)l]	n. 맨틀
14	mass [mæs]	n. (흙, 얼음, 구름의) 밀집체
15	molten [ˈmoʊltən]	a. 용해한
16	Pangaea [pænˈdʒi ə]	n. 판게아 ⇨ 판구조론에서 트라이아스기 이전에 존재했다고 보는 대륙
17	plate tectonics	n. 판구조론 ⇨ 대륙이 하나의 판으로 이어져 있다가 분리되었다고 보는 이론
18	river basin	n. (강의) 유역
19	submarine ridge	n. 해저산맥
20	tectonic plate	n. 지각의 플레이트
21	tremor [ˈtremə(r)]	n. 진동
22	trench [trentʃ]	n. 해구
23	upwarp [ˈʌpˌwɔrp]	n. 곡융
24	volcanic ashes	n. 화산재
25	weather [ˈweðə(r)]	v. 풍화시키다

Life Science | Physical Science | **Environmental Science**

05 Geology II (지질학 II)

01	**Antarctic** [ænt'ɑrktɪk]	n. 남극 cf. Arctic 북극
02	**canyon** ['kænyən]	n. 협곡
03	**cross-section**	n. 횡단면
04	**crust** [krʌst]	n. 지각, 지구의 표층
05	**debris** [də'bri]	n. 암석 파편
06	**delta** ['dɛltə]	n. 삼각주 → 강이 바다로 들어가는 어귀에 강물이 운반하여 온 모래나 흙이 쌓이 이루어진 편평한 지형
07	**deposit** [dɪ'pɒzɪt]	n. 퇴적물 v. 퇴적시키다
08	**Earth's axis**	n. 지축
09	**glacier** ['gleɪʃər]	n. 빙하 cf. iceberg 빙산
10	**igneous rock**	n. 화성암 cf. metamorphic rock 변성암, sedimentary rock 퇴적암, limestone 석회암, granite 화강암
11	**inlet** ['ɪnlɛt]	n. 후미, 입구 ant. outlet 배출구
12	**latitude** ['lætɪˌtud]	n. 위도 → 지구 위의 위치를 나타내는 좌표축 중에서 가로로 된 것 cf. longitude 경도
13	**law of superposition**	지층 누중의 법칙 → 퇴적암에서 아래 놓여 있는 것이 먼저 쌓인 지층이고 위에 놓여 있는 것이 그 후에 쌓인 지층이라는 법칙
14	**lithification** [ˌlɪθəfɪ'keɪʃən]	n. 석화작용 → 퇴적물이 쌓여 단단한 암석으로 변하는 것
15	**rugged** ['rʌgɪd]	a. (지형이) 울퉁불퉁한
16	**sand dune**	n. 모래언덕, 사구
17	**sediment** ['sɛdəmənt]	n. 퇴적물
18	**seismic** ['saɪzmɪk]	a. 지진의 cf. seismic intensity 지진의 강도, seismic wave 지진파
19	**stalactite** [stə'læktaɪt]	n. 종유석 → 동굴의 천장에 고드름처럼 매달린 광물질 cf. stalagmite 석순: 동굴 천장에서 떨어지는 물방울에 들어 있던 석회질 물질이 동굴 바닥에 쌓여 위로 자란 돌출물
20	**stratum** ['streɪtəm]	n. 지층
21	**subterranean** [ˌsʌbtə'reɪniən]	a. 지하의
22	**swamp** [swɒmp]	n. 늪지대 syn bog, fen, marsh
23	**tributary** ['trɪbyəˌtɛri]	n. 강의 (지류)
24	**upheaval** [ʌp'hivəl]	n. 융기 v. bulge 융기하다
25	**wear away**	v. 마멸시키다 syn weather 풍화시키다, erode 부식하다

06 Meteorology I (기상학 I)

01 ☐	air mass	n. 기단
02 ☐	below freezing	a. 어는점 아래의 (영하의)
03 ☐	climate [ˈklaɪmət]	n. 기후
04 ☐	cloudburst [ˈklaʊdˌbɜː(r)st]	n. 갑작스런 호우
05 ☐	dense [dens]	a. 밀도가 높은
06 ☐	dew [djuː]	n. 이슬
07 ☐	downpour [ˈdaʊnˌpɔː(r)]	n. 큰 소나기, 호우
08 ☐	drizzle [ˈdrɪz(ə)l]	n. 이슬비
09 ☐	fog [fɒg]	n. 안개
10 ☐	forecast [ˈfɔː(r)kɑːst]	n. 예상, 예보
11 ☐	hail [heɪl]	n. 우박
12 ☐	hailstorm [ˈheɪlˌstɔː(r)m]	n. 우박을 동반한 폭풍
13 ☐	mist [mɪst]	n. 연무, 옅은 안개
14 ☐	moisture [ˈmɔɪstʃə(r)]	n. 습기, 수분
15 ☐	pressure [ˈpreʃə(r)]	n. 압력, 기압
16 ☐	shower [ˈʃaʊə(r)]	n. 소나기
17 ☐	spin [spɪn]	v. 회전하다
18 ☐	squall [skwɔːl]	n. 돌풍, 스콜
19 ☐	temperate [ˈtemp(ə)rət]	a. 온대의
20 ☐	tornado [tɔː(r)ˈneɪdəʊ]	n. 토네이도
21 ☐	torrential rain	n. 호우
22 ☐	typhoon [taɪˈfuːn]	n. 태풍
23 ☐	water particle	n. 물의 미립자
24 ☐	weather bureau	n. 기상청
25 ☐	whirlwind [ˈwɜː(r)lˌwɪnd]	n. 회오리바람

Life Science | Physical Science | **Environmental Science**

07 Meteorology II (기상학 II)

01	air current	n. 기류
02	arid [ˈærɪd]	a. 건조한 [syn] parched
03	atmosphere [ˈætməsˌfɪər]	n. 대기
04	atmospheric pressure	기압
05	avalanche [ˈævəˌlæntʃ]	n. 눈사태
06	blast [blæst]	n. 돌풍
07	blizzard [ˈblɪzərd]	n. 눈보라
08	Celsius [ˈsɛlsiəs]	n. 섭씨
09	cold front	한랭 전선
10	continental climate	n. 대륙성 기후 cf. oceanic climate 해양성 기후, desert climate 사막 기후, subtropical climate 아열대 기후, monsoon climate 계절풍 기후, subarctic climate 아한대 기후, polar climate 한대 기후
11	deluge [ˈdɛlyudʒ]	n. 대홍수 [syn] inundation
12	droplet [ˈdrɒplɪt]	n. 작은 물방울
13	drought [draʊt]	n. 가뭄
14	Fahrenheit [ˈfærənˌhaɪt]	n. 화씨
15	frigid [ˈfrɪdʒɪd]	n. 추운 [syn] inclement, chilly
16	frost [frɔst]	n. 서리
17	humidity [hyuˈmɪdɪti]	n. 습기
18	monsoon [mɒnˈsun]	n. 계절풍
19	precipitation [prɪˌsɪpɪˈteɪʃən]	n. 강수량
20	scorching [ˈskɔrtʃɪŋ]	a. 몹시 뜨거운
21	sleet [slit]	n. 진눈깨비
22	sprinkle [ˈsprɪŋkəl]	n. 가랑비; 가늘게 내리는 비 cf. drizzle 이슬비; 아주 가늘게 내리는 비, torrential rain 폭우, thunderstorm 천둥 번개 치는 폭우
23	tropical [ˈtrɒpɪkəl]	a. 열대성의
24	warm front	n. 온난 전선
25	wind direction	n. 풍향

08 Oceanography (해양학)

01	Antarctic ocean	n. 남극해
02	Atlantic ocean	n. 대서양 n. Pacific ocean 태평양
03	circulation [ˌsɜrkyəˈleɪʃən]	n. 순환
04	continental shelf	n. 대륙붕 → 육지 가까운 곳에 육지의 연장으로 깊이 200m까지의 바다
05	coral reef	n. 산호초
06	drift [drɪft]	v. 표류하다
07	high tide (flood tide)	n. 밀물 cf. low tide (ebb tide) 썰물
08	Indian ocean	n. 인도양
09	ocean current	n. 조류, 흐름
10	ocean floor	n. 대양저, 해저
11	OTEC (Ocean Thermal Energy Conversion)	해양 온도 차 발전
12	overfishing	n. 물고기 남획
13	plankton [ˈplæŋktən]	n. 플랑크톤
14	salinity [səlínəti]	n. 염분, 염도
15	strait [streɪt]	n. 해협 → 육지 사이에 끼어 있는 좁고 긴 바다
16	submarine valley	n. 해저 협곡
17	submerge [səbˈmɜrdʒ]	v. 물에 잠기다
18	submersible [səbˈmɜrsəbəl]	a. 잠수할 수 있는
19	tidal wave	n. 해일, 쓰나미
20	topography [təˈpɒgrəfi]	n. 지형학, 지형도
21	trench [trɛntʃ]	n. 해구 → 깊은 바다에 움푹 들어간 곳
22	tsunami [tsʊˈnɑmi]	n. 쓰나미, 지진 해일
23	upwelling [ʌpˈwɛlɪŋ]	n. 용승 → 해양에서 찬 바닷물이 아래에서 위로 표면 바닷물을 제치고 올라오는 현상을
24	wave [weɪv]	n. 파도
25	whirlpool [ʰwɜrlˌpul]	n. 소용돌이

TOEFL
Answer Keys

Chapter 1
History

Chapter 2
Arts

Chapter 3
Social Science

**Chapter 4
Life Science**

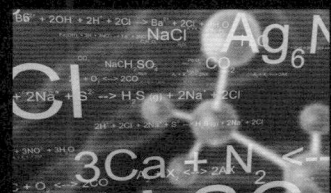
**Chapter 5
Physical Science**

**Chapter 6
Environmental Science**

Chapter 1. History

001	1. C	2. A, D	011	1. A	2. C
002	1. B	2. B	012	1. D	2. D
003	1. A	2. B	013	1. B	2. D
004	1. B	2. D	014	1. B, D	2. B
005	1. B	2. B	015	1. D	2. A
006	1. B	2. B	016	1. A, D	2. C
007	1. C	2. B	017	1. B	2. A
008	1. B	2. A	018	1. C	2. C
009	1. B	2. B	019	1. B	2. B
010	1. C	2. C	020	1. C	2. A

Chapter 2. Arts

021	1. T: A, C / F: B, D	2. A	031	1. B, D	2. A
022	1. B	2. C	032	1. D	2. A
023	1. B	2. C	033	1. D	2. C
024	1. A	2. C	034	1. A	2. A
025	1. A	2. B, C	035	1. B	2. D
026	1. C	2. A	036	1. D	2. D
027	1. A, B	2. A	037	1. D	2. B
028	1. A	2. A	038	1. A	2. A
029	1. B	2. A	039	1. A	2. A
030	1. A	2. B	040	1. B	2. D

Chapter 3. Social Science

041	1. C	2. C	051	1. A	2. C
042	1. D	2. A	052	1. C	2. B
043	1. D	2. C	053	1. B	2. A
044	1. A	2. C	054	1. B	2. D
045	1. B	2. B, D	055	1. D	2. A
046	1. A	2. A	056	1. A	2. A
047	1. A	2. D	057	1. B	2. D
048	1. A	2. D	058	1. B	2. C
049	1. D	2. D	059	1. A	2. B
050	1. C	2. C	060	1. A, B	2. A

Chapter 4. Life Science

061	1. C	2. A		071	1. B	2. C
062	1. B	2. B		072	1. A, B	2. A
063	1. B	2. D		073	1. A	2. A, B
064	1. B	2. C		074	1. C	2. B, C
065	1. D	2. D		075	1. A	2. B
066	1. A, D, E	2. B, C		076	1. B	2. C
067	1. A	2. C		077	1. A, D	2. D
068	1. B	2. D		078	1. A	2. C
069	1. A	2. D		079	1. A	2. A, D
070	1. D	2. A		080	1. B	2. D

Chapter 5. Physical Science

081	1. B	2. A, B		091	1. B	2. D
082	1. B	2. B		092	1. B	2. A
083	1. D	2. D		093	1. A	2. A, B, C
084	1. B, C	2. A		094	1. C	2. B
085	1. B	2. A		095	1. C	2. D
086	1. B	2. C		096	1. B	2. D
087	1. A	2. A		097	1. C	2. B
088	1. D	2. B		098	1. B, D	2. D
089	1. B	2. B, C		099	1. B	2. C
090	1. C	2. A		100	1. A	2. A

Chapter 6. Environmental Science

101	1. B, D	2. B		111	1. C	2. A
102	1. A	2. Yes: A, B / No: C, D		112	1. A	2. D
103	1. C	2. B		113	1. A	2. A
104	1. B	2. B		114	1. C	2. C
105	1. D	2. C		115	1. B	2. C
106	1. D	2. B		116	1. A, D	2. B
107	1. B	2. C		117	1. C	2. B
108	1. A	2. A		118	1. A, C	2. C
109	1. B	2. A		119	1. B→C→A	2. A
110	1. D	2. B		120	1. C	2. B